APPROACHES TO MEASUREMENT IN INTERNATIONAL RELATIONS

APPROACHES TO MEASUREMENT IN INTERNATIONAL RELATIONS

A NON-EVANGELICAL SURVEY

EDITED BY

John E. Mueller

University of Rochester

 APPLETON-CENTURY-CROFTS

Educational Division

New York MEREDITH CORPORATION

Copyright © 1969 by
MEREDITH CORPORATION
All rights reserved

659-1

Library of Congress Catalog Card Number: 72-75034

PRINTED IN THE UNITED STATES OF AMERICA

390-65640-2

CONTENTS

ACKNOWLEDGMENTS

I would like to thank the participants in a couple of noisy seminars at the University of Rochester; they were a constant source of inspiration, clamor, caustic comment, and error. In approximate order of decreasing volume, they are David Meltz, Peter Ordeshook, Wallace Gagne, Richard Babin, Kenneth Shepsle, Masakatsu Kato, Nathaniel Beck, Dennis Paranzino, William Stratmann, Kul Rai, John Happy, Daniel Schesch, and Mollie Heath. Needed help also came from Arthur Goldberg, Peg Gross, Gerald Kramer, Judy Mueller, William Riker, and Richard Rosecrance.

1

Introduction, or
What's in a Number?

A large proportion of statements in the international relations field, including this one, are basically quantitative in nature. Phrases like these abound in the literature: "very little of significance," "virtually all," "vary enormously," "great discrepancies," "not to the same degree."[1] In this sense at least, the purpose of this book is not so much to argue that practitioners in the field make quantitative observations, but to suggest that there may be benefit in doing so consciously and as precisely as possible and in using numbers for something other than pagination and footnotes.

For, when appropriately used, there is a great deal in a number. To begin with, numbers scale. Because of this happy feature a whole array of statistical, logical and mathematical methods of manipulation, frequently capable of generating new and unexpected observations, become more readily available.

Furthermore, counters usually are forced to consider carefully and to define meaningfully the thing that is being counted. It is probably easier to talk about something one knows nothing about than it is to count it. Partly because of this, perhaps, numerical research seems to have been more readily replicated and more cumulative than traditional endeavors.

Third, numerical statements characteristically are richer in information than less precise observations. The following statement is true: "In the Mau Mau rebellion of 1952–56, certain tribes in Kenya revolted, killing European and African civilians." The following statement is also true, but

---

[1] The examples have been taken from Hedley Bull, "International Theory: The Case for a Classical Approach," *World Politics*, Vol. 18 (April, 1966), pp. 361–77.

incomparably more informative: "In the Mau Mau rebellion of 1952–56, certain tribes in Kenya revolted, killing 32 European and 1826 African civilians."

Fourth, counting tends to be a systematic exercise. One must attempt to get a perspective about the entire area of content one wishes to examine; in this way gross generalizations from opportunistically selected examples are less likely.

Finally, to dangle from the limb a bit, in a sense numerical research is more "objective" than traditional research. There are of course many elements of subjective judgment involved in any numerical undertaking— from selecting the basic unit to be counted, to determining which items fall within the counted class, to choosing which data manipulation technique to apply. Nevertheless, once initiated, such research tends to take on its own momentum; data are gathered, after the initial assumptions, without substantial bias, and—a final test perhaps—the researcher seems to be more likely to be surprised (appalled even) with what he has found than is a more traditional worker in the field.

It should be generously admitted, however, that the superimposition of numbers on a problem hardly eliminates all difficulties. Important data are frequently missing or inadequate; one can miss the point of the problem by becoming preoccupied with that part of it which is easily counted; the cost of obtaining valid data may surpass in value the knowledge gained; one may be led to neglect substance for method; to facilitate counting, the problem may be so simplified that only trivial conclusions emerge; and so forth. It is often maintained, in addition, that measurement in international relations is fundamentally a hopeless enterprise because nothing important in the field is countable. This popular and of course extraordinarily destructive proposition is denied here. In fact it is the message of chapter 8 that *any* adequately conceptualized variable can be measured.

There is a kind of debate that bubbles along in the international relations literature which concerns itself with the merits, demerits, conceptions, and misconceptions of the "scientific" as opposed to the "traditional" approach to the study of international political phenomena.[2] There is no great hope that this book will do much to resolve the issue. Instead, the intention here is simply to present and comment upon a number of approaches to the use of quantitative and mathematical techniques in

[2] See Bull, *op. cit.*; Morton A. Kaplan, "The New Great Debate: Traditionalism vs. Science in International Relations," *World Politics*, Vol. 19 (October, 1966), pp. 1–20; Hayward Alker, Jr., "The Long Road to International Relations Theory: Problems of Statistical Nonadditivity," *ibid.*, Vol. 18 (July, 1966), pp. 623–55; Stanley H. Hoffmann, "International Relations: The Long Road to Theory," *ibid.*, Vol. 11 (April, 1959), pp. 346–77 and *Contemporary Theory in International Relations* (Englewood Cliffs, N. J.: Prentice-Hall, 1960); R. N. Rosecrance and J. E. Mueller, "Decision-Making and the Quantitative Analysis of International Relations," *Year Book of World Affairs 1967* (London: Stevens, 1967), pp. 1–19.

international relations. Each chapter contains an analytic essay on a different approach together with a survey of the published literature in the area, and each reprints one or two examples of the approach in use. Some effort has been made in the chapter introductions and in the selection of studies for reproduction to demonstrate how different approaches, to their mutual benefit, can be applied to aspects of a single problem of interest in international relations. Technical commentary of an intuitive rather than a rigorous sort has been inserted in the form of notes and appendixes to introduce the less prepared reader to the statistical procedures employed in some of the reprinted articles.

Each approach discussed seems to have some merit and, judiciously and knowledgeably applied, can help to illuminate certain areas of interest. Nowhere are traditional techniques declared to be primitive, prescientific, obsolete, criminally misconceived, or even wrong. This book proclaims only that certain quantitative techniques exist, that they can be helpful, and that they are often a pleasure to use. That seems humble enough.

2

Systematic History

Instead of beginning this discussion of "systematic history" with a definition of the subject—a procedure which characteristically obscures and pedantifies more than it illuminates—it may be more valuable to offer some illustrations of the method more or less in action.

Take for example one element of Secretary of Defense McNamara's defense of himself, his department, and his conception of the universe before the Senate Foreign Relations Committee in May, 1966. There had been some grumbling in the Senate, it appears, about American military aid which served to strengthen the military establishments of recipient countries which in turn led, the grumblers maintained, to a harvest of military coups. Mr. McNamara seems to have had someone in his own military establishment check into this relationship and came to the hearing armed with the following statistics: between 1961 and 1966 there were 31 military coups in the world and of these, only 13 were in countries which had been granted some form of military assistance by the United States.[1]

Or again, at about the same time, Secretary McNamara made the following observation before a group of newspaper editors. "In the last eight years alone," he announced, "there have been no less than 164 internationally significant outbreaks of violence . . . and the trend of such conflicts is growing rather than diminishing. At the beginning of 1958, there were 23 prolonged insurgencies going on about the world. As of February 1, 1966, there were 40. Further, the total number of outbreaks of violence has increased each year: in 1958, there were 34; in 1965, there were 58." The generalization: "The planet is becoming a more dangerous place to live on."[2]

[1] Senate Foreign Relations Committee, *Foreign Assistance*, 1966, pp. 216–17.
[2] Address before the American Society of Newspaper Editors, Montreal, May 18, 1966.

A final example from a rather different field: about 50 years ago, the eminent musicologist, Ernest Newman, set out to test the proposition popular then, as now, among artistic radicals that composers recognized to be great by posterity frequently were ahead of their time and spent their lives without due recognition from their contemporaries. Newman essentially scanned the biography of every important musical genius and found that the proposition applies to none of them.[3]

In each of the examples generalizations were based on a systematic examination of *all* the relevant events which fall within certain definitional limits: all the known military coups in the world for a five-year period, all internationally significant outbreaks of violence for an eight-year period, and the life experiences of all the composers currently recognized to be great.

Users of this method tacitly assume that history repeats itself, that when we classify a number of events under such headings as "coups," "outbreaks of violence," "wars," "summit meetings," "arms races," or "crises" there is enough similarity among the events under each classification to warrant generalizations about the group as a class. If not, it could be argued, there must be something wrong with the classification system. It is true that there is a certain precious sense in which every event is different from every other. Nevertheless vast areas of tedious, but valuable, repetition exist in human affairs, frequently rendering them highly predictable. When we drive on a crowded street we not only make dozens of predictions about the behavior of other people, we also literally stake our lives on the accuracy of the predictions.

Clearly the matter of definition is central to this method of systematic history. What exactly *is* an "internationally significant outbreak of violence" for the purpose of Secretary McNamara's analysis and, most important, would the conclusions derived from an exercise of the method be altered if the definition of the event under study were modified slightly?[4] When is a war a war? Most people would agree that what happened in Europe between 1914 and 1918 was a war, but was the invasion of Cuba in 1961 at the Bay of Pigs a war? If one attempts to examine all the known wars of eternity, as in fact several scholars have, do one's conclusions about wars as a class change if events like the invasion of Cuba are included in the classification?

This problem can sometimes be reduced by taking relatively homogeneous subgroups of events. It may well be true, for example, that nothing very interesting can be said about "wars" as a class except tautologous truisms like "people tend to get killed in them." A more fruitful unit of analysis may be "big wars" or "little wars," or "internal wars" or "international wars." Of course, too much subdivision of this sort ruins the

[3] A *Musical Critic's Holiday* (New York: Knopf, 1925).
[4] The study on which Secretary McNamara's remarks were based is classified.

purpose of the exercise; that set of events, "large European wars in which the Germans and the Austrians oppose the British, Italians, French, and Russians," is nearly empty.

Another important consideration is the question of delimiting the time period. Why does Secretary McNamara begin his survey of "internationally significant outbreaks of violence" in 1958 rather than earlier? Would his conclusion that the planet is becoming an increasingly dangerous place be altered if the events in Suez and Hungary in 1956 were included in his calculations?[5] While no line of demarcation will ever be unobjectionable, some are better than others. If one wishes to contemplate trends in violence, there is probably no terribly good reason to begin with 1958; there is, however, reason to begin with September, 1945.

But if there are painful cutoff points to contemplate and difficult categoric systems to activate, there are also important advantages to this method. The procedure is quantitative and systematic: the practitioner, after thinking carefully about what he wants to investigate, seeks out *all* the examples he can find of the event under consideration before generalizing.[6] He does not simply pontificate from a single instance that comes to mind[7] or from an opportunistic selection of examples. No small number of people have pondered over the proposition, "arms races lead to war." In casually casting about for empirical cases of arms races to speculate about, it is easy to select only those arms races which affirm the proposition. This is because the most *visible* arms races are precisely those which have distinguished themselves by preceding wars. Serious arms races which were dissipated by agreement, by the acceptance of inferiority by one side, or by a general easing of tension are far less likely to leap to mind.

• • •

Some of the problems and virtues of the method can be illustrated by a systematic examination of guerrilla war. Table 1 attempts to list all those wars in the postwar period generally agreed upon in the literature to involve substantial amounts of guerrilla activity. The world conflagration that ended in 1945 defines a convenient starting point for this exercise, although it is true that several of the guerrilla wars which began in the late 1940's had their origins in earlier times. Only in the case of China,

[5] Raymond Tanter finds that some 51,123 people were killed in violent interchange between countries in the 1955–57 period and only 974 in the 1958–60 period. Trends in the number of guerrilla wars and revolutions, however, were the opposite. "Dimension of Conflict Behavior Within and Between States, 1958–60," *Journal of Conflict Resolution*, Vol. 10 (March, 1966), p. 58.
[6] Of course, if there is a sufficiently large number of events in the class, one could sample randomly from them—perhaps after stratifying—rather than taking them all into consideration.
[7] The single case is often useful to illustrate, to provide an exception to a rule, or to demonstrate that something is possible. It is fascinating to note, however, how often casual generalizations from a single case can be deflated simply by asking the author to give *two* examples.

Table 1

GUERRILLA WARS SINCE 1945

Location	Period	Winner	Outside Support	
			Incumbent	Guerrillas
China	46–49	G	Great	None
Indonesia	45–49	G	Considerable	None
Indochina	45–54	G	Great	Considerable
Philippines	46–54	I	Great	None
Malaya	48–60	I	Great	None
Tibet	59–	I	Great	Little
So. Vietnam	58–	?	Very great	Great
Greece	46–49	I	Great	Great
Cyprus	54–59	G?	Great	Considerable
Algeria	54–62	G	Great	Great
Israel	45–49	G	Great	Great
Iraq	61–66	G?	Great	Little
Yemen	62–	?	Great	Great
Kenya	52–56	I	Great	None
Congo	64–65	I	Great	Great
Angola	61–	I	Great	Great
Colombia	48–58	I	Great	Little
Cuba	56–59	G	Great	Considerable
Venezuela	59–66	I	Great	Great
Guatemala	63–	?	Great	Considerable
Burma	48–50	I	Considerable	None
No. Korea	50–53	?	Great	Great
So. Korea	50–53	I	Great	None
Laos	60–62	G	Great	Great
Hungary	56–	I	Great	None

however, does this pose much of a problem—the 1946–49 war there was really the final, largely conventional stage of a 20-year conflict. Since the war in China is supposedly prototypic, it was decided not to let the historical problem disqualify it. Guerrilla wars which seemed in 1968 only to be in embryonic stages have been excluded.

With the time boundaries arranged one can look over the list to see if the wars are similar enough in content to comprise a single set of events. Five of the wars, those listed at the end, appear to differ from the rest in important ways so that, while they are frequently designated in the literature as guerrilla wars, it is doubtful whether they should remain on the list. The tactics used in the wars in Burma and Laos were essentially conventional. The insurgents in the two wars in Korea definitely used guerrilla tactics, but the wars were not important on their own but were fought in relation to a larger war that was going on. In fact the guerrilla war carried out in North Korea by the Americans and the South Koreans had no real end—a settlement to the larger war was achieved in 1953 and the guerrillas were pulled out. Thus these wars really differ significantly in type from the others and should be excluded. Furthermore, to leave them in would do violence to the 1945 time boundary. Guerrilla wars were carried out in at least 17 different countries during World War II as part of the war effort so, if wars of that sort are included, the whole problem would have to be restructured. Finally, the Hungarian revolt of 1956 is excised from the list on the grounds that the event was more of a riot than a guerrilla war.

The remaining wars on the list, then, all involve guerrilla violence that reached a noticeable degree of intensity over a significant period of time. This means that uprisings which may contain elements of guerrilla activity (some observers have defined guerrilla war as "a high crime rate") are excluded from the list. For the most part the listing will make guerrilla warfare look more successful than it has proven to be: guerrilla wars which were quashed in early stages by the incumbent forces are excluded while guerrilla wars which succeeded in overthrowing the incumbent regime are, because of their duration and intensity, very likely to be included.

With this bias in mind, it is clear from scanning the "Winner" column in the table that guerrilla war is far from the surefire method that its Chinese enthusiasts have proclaimed it to be. Of the 17 major postwar guerrilla wars for which winners can be declared, the incumbents have clearly emerged victorious more than half the time, while two of the seeming guerrilla victories—Cyprus and Iraq—are somewhat questionable.

Each war in the table has also been crudely scored for the amount of outside aid given to the incumbents and to the guerrillas. It is immediately clear that major guerrilla wars invariably have taken on important international consequences: in all cases the incumbents and in most cases the guerrillas have received substantial amounts of aid from outside the country.

More interestingly perhaps, it would appear that the Chinese experience is quite unusual. For, despite the efforts of prominent Chinese politicians to demonstrate to the contrary,[8] guerrilla victories have characteristically depended in large measure on outside aid. The only cases of unaided guerrilla success besides that of the Chinese occurred in Indonesia where circumstances allowed the guerrillas rather easily to make the cost of continued colonial empire seem intolerable to the war-weary Dutch; and in Iraq where the Kurdish guerrillas seem to have attained their limited goal of cultural independence without significant aid from the

[8] See, for example, Lin Piao, "The People's War," *Survival*, Vol. 7 (November, 1965), pp. 288–89.

outside.[9] In the other cases, guerrillas without considerable outside aid have fared badly.

The Chinese case is also peculiar in that it is the only instance of the supposedly "classical" Maoist guerrilla victory progressing by stages to a final all-out conventional defeat of the incumbent force. In all other cases in which the guerrillas have won, the incumbents have more or less concluded at one point in the fighting that continued resistance was likely to prove intolerably costly in the long run and thus they withdrew early, cutting their losses and making it unnecessary for the insurgents to engage in extensive conventional combat.

It is this long range nature of calculations in guerrilla war—characteristic of a war of attrition—which may make outside aid for the incumbent a vital determinant of the result of the war. If outside aid is reduced or if supplementary aid seen by the incumbent to be essential is not forthcoming, the incumbent is likely to retire from the war even without undergoing important defeats in the field. It is noteworthy in this regard that in all cases where Communists have come out on top in a guerrilla war and in all cases in Asia where guerrillas have won, whether Communist or not (China, Indochina, Indonesia, Cuba, and—if acceptable as a case—Laos) the incumbent has had American aid cut off or further additional aid denied.

                              •   •   •

A number of studies produced over the last several decades have used, with varying degrees of rigor and success, the method called here systematic history. Quincy Wright and Pitirim A. Sorokin have been interested in the unit, "war," defined by Wright as "a violent contact of distinct but similar entities." They have ambitiously taken all of history into account and have attempted to assess trends, patterns, and characteristics of warfare over the centuries.[10]

Similar investigations have been conducted by Lewis F. Richardson who studied the period 1820–1949 and took as his unit the "deadly quarrel" —a quarrel between two or more people in which one or more people are killed.[11] While this definition includes everything from murders to bandit raids to world wars, most of Richardson's analysis deals with wars in which there were at least 1000 fatalities. Richardson's work is notable for its ingenious use of statistical models and its careful efforts to deal fairly with

[9] See Dana Adams Schmidt, "Recent Developments in the Kurdish War," *Royal Central Asian Journal,* Vol. 53 (February, 1966), pp. 23–31.
[10] Quincy Wright, *A Study of War* (Chicago: University of Chicago Press, 1942): Pitirim A. Sorokin, *Social and Cultural Dynamics,* Volume III: "Fluctuation of Social Relationships, War, and Revolution" (New York: American, 1937), parts two and three.
[11] Lewis F. Richardson, *Statistics of Deadly Quarrels* (Pittsburgh: Boxwood Press, 1960). See also Anatol Rapoport, "Lewis F. Richardson's Mathematical Theory of War," *Journal of Conflict Resolution,* Vol. 1 (September, 1957), pp. 249–99.

imperfections in the data. Further investigations using and elaborating on Richardson's data have been carried out by a number of people. Frank Denton has assessed historical patterns of peace and war,[12] Herbert Weiss and William Horvath have investigated the duration and magnitude of wars,[13] Rudolph Rummel has factor analyzed a set of variables associated with dyadic war,[14] and David Singer and Melvin Small have extended Richardson's discussion of the relationship between alliances and war involvement.[15]

Other systematic studies have been and are being conducted of internal wars. Among the investigators are Harry Eckstein [16] and George Modelski.[17]

Included below is Samuel Huntington's systematic examination of arms races which transpired in the nineteenth and twentieth centuries. The thirteen cases are given in Table 2 together with summary information garnered from Professor Huntington's essay. As can be readily seen from this presentation, arms races are not always followed by wars. Instead, the relationship is a complex one with Huntington suggesting (1) that war is less likely to follow arms races which are basically *qualitative* (usually naval) than those which are quantitative in nature; and (2) that, for various reasons, wars tend to occur in the early stages of arms races. There is some experimental work, assessed in chapter 4, which tends to support the second proposition and the reasoning behind it. Huntington's essay has been criticized on the grounds that a more careful analysis would show many more arms races in the period covered and admissible ones in the centuries before the period.[18] It could also be argued that the essay is almost too charitable to the arms-race–war hypothesis: even some of those arms races which preceded wars may have occurred more because the belligerents saw war coming and thus rushed to arm for it rather than the

[12] Frank H. Denton, "Some Regularities in International Conflict, 1820–1949," *Background*, Vol. 9 (February, 1966), pp. 283–96.
[13] Herbert K. Weiss, "Stochastic Models for the Duration and Magnitude of a Deadly Quarrel," *Operations Research*, Vol. 11 (January–February, 1963), pp. 101–21; William J. Horvath, "A Statistical Analysis of the Duration of Wars and Strikes," *Behavioral Science*, Vol. 13 (January, 1968), pp. 18–28.
[14] R. J. Rummel, "Dimensions of Dyadic War, 1820–1952," *Journal of Conflict Resolution*, Vol. II (June, 1967), pp. 176–83.
[15] J. David Singer and Melvin Small, "National Alliance Commitments and War Involvement, 1815–1945," *Peace Research Society (International) Papers*, Vol. 5 (1966), pp. 109–40; "Formal Alliances, 1815–1939," *Journal of Peace Research*, (1966), pp. 1–32; and "Alliance Aggregation and the Onset of War, 1815–1945," in J. David Singer (ed.), *Quantitative International Politics* (New York: Free Press, 1968), pp. 247–86.
[16] Harry Eckstein (ed.), *Internal War* (New York: Free Press, 1964) and "On the Etiology of Internal Wars," in George H. Nadel (ed.), *Studies in the Philosophy of History* (New York: Harper, 1965), pp. 117–47.
[17] George Modelski, "International Settlement of Internal War," in James N. Rosenau (ed.), *International Aspects of Civil Strife* (Princeton: Princeton University Press, 1964), pp. 122–53.
[18] C. B. Joynt, "Arms Races and the Problem of Equilibrium," *Year Book of World Affairs 1964* (London: Stevens, 1964), pp. 23–40.

Table 2

ARMS RACES IN THE 19TH AND 20TH CENTURIES

	Duration	(Years)	Type	Outcome
1. France vs. England	1840–1866	27	Naval	France accepts inferiority
2. France vs. Germany	1874–1894	21	Land	Tension eased
3. England vs. France & Russia	1884–1904	21	Naval	Tension eased
4. Argentina vs. Chile	1890–1902	13	Naval	Agreement
5. England vs. Germany	1898–1912	15	Naval	Germany accepts inferiority
6. France vs. Germany	1911–1914	4	Land	War
7. England vs. U.S.	1916–1930	15	Naval	Agreement
8. Japan vs. U.S.	1916–1922	7	Naval	Agreement
9. France vs. Germany	1934–1939	6	Land	War
10. U.S.S.R. vs. Germany	1934–1941	8	Land	War
11. Germany vs. England	1934–1939	6	Air	War
12. U.S. vs. Japan	1934–1941	8	Naval	War
13. U.S.S.R. vs. U.S.	1946–		Nuclear	

other way around. For purposes of the systematic analysis, the ending date of the fifth arms race on the list—and therefore footnote 27 in Huntington's essay which justifies it—are particularly important. If that arms race is seen to end, not in 1912 as Huntington argues, but rather in 1914, it would form a damaging example of a long, qualitative arms race which led to war. A survey of some of the mathematical approaches to arms races is included in chapter 9. Huntington's empirical analysis can be used to suggest areas in which the models discussed there are perhaps overly simple.

The unit of analysis in systematic history can be less tangible. In the study reprinted below Bruce Russett has made a systematic investigation of 17 cases of deterrence between 1935 and 1961 in which a major power overtly threatened a small power with military force while another major power "had given, prior to the crisis, some indication of an intent to protect the pawn or make a commitment in time to prevent the threatened attack." [19] Russett argues that successful deterrence does not depend simply on "solemn oaths" or merely on having the physical means to fight. He suggests rather that the amount of economic, military, and political interdependence between the small power and the defending major power is of great importance. The instances Russett finds of unsuccessful deterrence tend to be dominated by those involving Hitler and thus his calculations look somewhat different if one segregates pre- and post-war cases— a point developed at length by one critic.[20] A somewhat related study of 49 cases of "threatening action" in international politics between 1931 and 1965 is currently underway under the direction of Richard Rosecrance.[21] Preliminary investigation finds that the quality of public morale in the threatening nation is the best predictor of its success and that the nation's quantity of military forces is *negatively* correlated with success— though again the Hitler cases tend to be major influences on the results.

William Gamson and Andre Modigliani have systematically investigated 31 major Soviet bloc actions which occurred between 1946 and 1953. To determine which Soviet bloc actions were "major" and to measure certain features about each of them, the authors relied on the judgment of a single informed source: the editor of the *New York Times*—an ingenious use of expert opinion for purposes of quantification, a subject to be dealt with at length in chapter 8. The editor of the *Times* is constantly making assessments about what is and isn't important in the news and he communicates this judgment by the size of the headline, placement of the story, and the amount of space he gives to the event. It is true that the editor may be biased or shortsighted at times, but the authors' assumption that day-by-day truth—gray as it may be—resides most nearly perfectly in the pages of the *New York Times* has considerable appeal. Advocates exist, Gamson and Modigliani argue, for three different belief systems about Soviet behavior: (A) those who advocate a hard line toward the Soviets, (B) those favoring a "firm-but-flexible" posture, and (C) those in favor of a soft line. Each position predicts Soviet response to American behavior—if the United States is tough, the A people would expect the

[19] The mathematical analysis of the deterrence concept, suggested in passing by Russett, is developed somewhat more fully in chapter 9, especially in Ellsberg's essay.
[20] Clinton F. Fink, "More Calculations about Deterrence," *Journal of Conflict Resolution*, Vol. 9 (March, 1965), pp. 54–65.
[21] Peter G. de Leon, James MacQueen, and Richard N. Rosecrance, "Situational Analysis in International Politics," UCLA Political Science Department, 1967 (Ditto). See also Richard L. Harris, "An Exploratory Analysis of Inter-Nation Influence," Security Studies Project, UCLA, January, 1964 (Mimeo).

Soviets to be conciliatory while those in the C position would expect such behavior to generate belligerent—"refractory"—responses from the Russians.[22] The study is still in progress, but when completed it will endeavor to compare predictions of Soviet behavior generated by each of the belief systems to the actual patterns of behavior.[23]

Other studies which might be mentioned include Johan Galtung's investigation of 147 summit meetings between 1941 and 1961 [24] and K. J. Holsti's examination of the outcomes of 77 international conflicts between 1919 and 1965.[25]

There are many comparative history studies which might be included loosely under the "systematic history" rubric; for example: Crane Brinton on revolution, Theodore Abel on the decision to go to war, and Paul Kecskemeti on strategic surrender.[26] Although frequently most capably executed, such studies have been excluded from consideration here because their selection of cases tends to be opportunistic and because the number of cases examined tends to be too small to make the ardent quantifier comfortable.

[22] A further study by Gamson and Modigliani of these belief systems, this time using public opinion data, is included in chapter 3.

[23] For a preliminary report, see William A. Gamson and Andre Modigliani, "Soviet Responses to Western Foreign Policy, 1946–53," *Peace Research Society (International) Papers*, Vol. 3 (1965), pp. 47–78.

[24] Johan Galtung, "Summit Meetings and International Relations," *Journal of Peace Research*, (1964), pp. 36–54. For a less systematic effort, see Keith Eubank, *The Summit Conferences 1919–1960* (Norman: University of Oklahoma Press, 1966).

[25] K. J. Holsti, "Resolving International Conflicts: A Taxonomy of Behavior and Some Figures on Procedures," *Journal of Conflict Resolution*, Vol. 10 (September, 1966), pp. 272–91.

[26] Crane Brinton, *The Anatomy of Revolution* (Englewood Cliffs, N. J.: Prentice-Hall, 1952); Theodore Abel, "The Element of Decision in the Pattern of War," *American Sociological Review*, Vol. 6 (December, 1941), pp. 853–59; Paul Kecskemeti, *Strategic Surrender* (Stanford, Cal.: Stanford Univer. Press, 1958). Other borderline studies might include Richard Rosecrance's comparison of historical systems: *Action and Reaction in World Politics* (Boston: Little, Brown, 1963); David C. Schwartz's exploratory study of a small, selected number of international crises: "Decision Theories and Crisis Behavior," *Orbis*, Vol. 11 (Summer, 1967), pp. 459–90; and Charles A. McClelland's analysis of the recurring crises in Berlin: "Access to Berlin: The Quantity and Variety of Events, 1948–1963," in Singer, *op. cit.*, pp. 159–86.

ARMS RACES: PREREQUISITES AND RESULTS

Samuel P. Huntington

INTRODUCTION

Si vis pacem, para bellum, is an ancient and authoritative adage of military policy. Of no less acceptance, however, is the other, more modern, proposition: "Armaments races inevitably lead to war." Juxtaposed, these two advices suggest that the maxims of social science, like the proverbs of folklore, reflect a many-sided truth. The social scientist, however, cannot escape with so easy an observation. He has the scholar's responsibility to determine as fully as possible to what extent and under what conditions his conflicting truths are true. The principal aim of this essay is to attempt some resolution of the issue: When are arms races a prelude to war and when are they a substitute for war?

Throughout history states have sought to maintain their peace and security by means of military strength. The arms race in which the military preparations of two states are intimately and directly interrelated is, however, a relatively modern phenomenon. The conflict between the apparent feasibility of preserving peace by arming for war and the apparent inevitability of competitive arms increases resulting in war is, therefore, a comparatively new one. The second purpose of this essay is to explore some of the circumstances which have brought about this uncertainty as to the relationship between war, peace, and arms increases. The problem here is: What were the prerequisites to the emergence of the arms race as a significant form of international rivalry in the nineteenth and twentieth centuries?

For the purposes of this essay, an arms race is defined as a progressive, competitive peacetime increase in armaments by two states or coalition of states resulting from conflicting purposes or mutual fears. An arms race is thus a form of reciprocal interaction between two states or coalitions. A race cannot exist without an increase in arms, quantitatively or qualitatively, but every peacetime increase in arms is not necessarily the result of an arms race. A nation may expand its armaments for the domestic purposes of aiding industry or curbing unemployment, or because it believes an absolute need exists for such an increase regardless of the actions of other states. In the 1880s and 1890s, for instance, the expansion of the United States Navy was apparently unrelated to the actions of any other power,[1] and hence not part of an arms race. An arms race reflects disagreement between two states as to the proper balance of power between them. The concept of a "general" arms race[2] in which a number of powers increase their armaments simultaneously is, consequently, a fallacious one. Such general increases either are not the result of self-conscious reciprocal interaction or are simply the sum of a number of two-state antagonisms. In so far as the arms policy of any one state is related to the armaments of other states, it is a function of concrete, specific goals, needs, or threats arising out of the political relations among the states. Even Britain's vaunted two-power naval standard will be found, on close analysis, to be rooted in specific threats rather than in abstract considerations of general policy.

PREREQUISITES FOR AN ARMS RACE

Prior to 1789 certain antagonistic relationships among states did at times have some characteristics of the modern arms race. Such relationships, however, were exceptional, and they usually lacked many essential features of the modern type of race. Certain conditions peculiarly present in the nineteenth and twentieth centuries would appear to be responsible for the emergence of the arms race as a frequent and distinct form of international rivalry. Among the more significant of these conditions are: a state system which facilitates the balancing of power by internal rather than external means; the preëminence of military force-in-being over territory or other factors as an element of national power; the capacity within each state to increase its military strength through quantitative or qualitative means; and the conscious awareness by each state of the dependence of its own arms policy upon that of another state.[4]

• • •

[1] See George T. Davis, A Navy Second to None (New York, 1940), pp. 48, 96–97.
[2] See Quincy Wright, A Study of War (Chicago, 2 vols., 1942), II, 690.
[4] Since an arms race is necessarily a matter of degree, differences of opinion will exist as to whether any given relationship constitutes an arms race and as to what are the

ABORTIVE AND SUSTAINED ARMS RACES

An arms race may end in war, formal or informal agreement between the two states to call off the race, or victory for one state which achieves and maintains the distribution of power which it desires and ultimately causes its rival to give up the struggle. The likelihood of war arising from an arms race depends in the first instance upon the relation between the power and grievances of one state to the power and grievances of the other. War is least likely when grievances are low, or, if grievances are high, the sum of the grievances and power of one state approximates the sum of the grievances and power of the other. An equality of power and an equality of grievances will thus reduce the chances of war, as will a situation in which one state has a marked superiority in power and the other in grievances. Assuming a fairly equal distribution of grievances, the likelihood of an arms race ending in war tends to vary inversely with the length of the arms race and directly with the extent to which it is quantitative rather than qualitative in character. This section deals with the first of these relationships and the next section with the second.

An arms race is a series of interrelated increases in armaments which if continued over a period of time produces a dynamic equilibrium of power between two states. A race in which this dynamic equilibrium fails to develop may be termed an abortive arms race. In these instances, the previously existing static equilibrium between the two states is disrupted without being replaced by a new equilibrium reflecting their relative competitive efforts in the race. Instead, rapid shifts take place or appear about to take place in the distribution of power which enhance the willingness of one state or the other to precipitate a conflict. At least one and sometimes two danger points occur at the beginning of every arms race. The first point arises with the response of the challenged state to the initial

---

precise opening and closing dates of any given arms race. At the risk of seeming arbitrary, the following relationships are assumed to be arms races for the purpose of this essay:

1.	France v. England	naval	1840–1866
2.	France v. Germany	land	1874–1894
3.	England v. France & Russia	naval	1884–1904
4.	Argentina v. Chile	naval	1890–1902
5.	England v. Germany	naval	1898–1912
6.	France v. Germany	land	1911–1914
7.	England v. United States	naval	1916–1930
8.	Japan v. United States	naval	1916–1922
9.	France v. Germany	land	1934–1939
10.	Soviet Union v. Germany	land	1934–1941
11.	Germany v. England	air	1934–1939
12.	United States v. Japan	naval	1934–1941
13.	Soviet Union v. United States	nuclear	1946–

increases in armaments by the challenging state. The second danger point is the reaction of the challenger who has been successful in initially achieving his goal to the frantic belated efforts of the challenged state to retrieve its former position.

The formal beginning of an arms race is the first increase in armaments by one state—the challenger—caused by a desire to alter the existing balance of power between it and another state. Prior to this initial action, a pre-arms race static equilibrium may be said to exist. This equilibrium does not necessarily mean an equality of power. It simply reflects the satisfaction of each state with the existing distribution of power in the light of its grievances and antagonisms with the other state. Some of the most stable equilibriums in history have also been ones which embodied an unbalance of power. From the middle of the eighteenth century down to the 1840s, a static equilibrium existed between the French and British navies in which the former was kept roughly two-thirds as strong as the latter. After the naval race of 1841–1865 when this ratio was challenged, the two powers returned to it for another twenty year period. From 1865 to 1884 both British and French naval expenditures were amazingly constant, England's expenditures varying between 9.5 and 10.5 million pounds (with the exception of the crisis years of 1876–77 when they reached 11 and 12 million pounds) and France's expenditures varying from 6.5 to 7.5 million pounds.[19] In some instances the equilibrium may receive the formal sanction of a treaty such as the Washington arms agreement of 1922 or the treaty of Versailles. In each of these cases, the equilibrium lasted until 1934 when the two powers—Germany and Japan—who had been relegated to a lower level of armaments decided that continued inferiority was incompatible with their national goals and ambitions. In both cases, however, it was not the disparity of power in itself which caused the destruction of the equilibrium, but rather the fact that this disparity was unacceptable to the particular groups which assumed control of those countries in the early 1930s. In other instances, the static equilibrium may last for only a passing moment, as when France began reconstructing its army almost immediately after its defeat by Germany in 1871.

For the purposes of analysis it is necessary to specify a particular increase in armaments by one state as marking the formal beginning of the arms race. This is done not to pass judgment on the desirability or wisdom of the increase, but simply to identify the start of the action and reaction which constitute the race. In most instances, this initial challenge is not hard to locate. It normally involves a major change in the policy of the challenging state, and more likely than not it is formally announced to the world. The reasons for the challenging state's discontent with the status quo may stem from a variety of causes. It may feel that the growth

[19] See [Richard] Cobden, "Three Panics" [*Political Writings* (London, 1867) II], p. 308; Cobden Club, *Burden of Armaments* [London, 1905], pp. 66–68.

of its economy, commerce, and population should be reflected in changes in the military balance of power (Germany, 1898; United States, 1916; Soviet Union, 1946). Nationalistic, bellicose, or militaristic individuals or parties may come to power who are unwilling to accept an equilibrium which other groups in their society had been willing to live with or negotiate about (Germany and Japan, 1934). New political issues may arise which cause a deterioration in the relationships of the state with another power and which consequently lead it to change its estimate of the arms balance necessary for its security (France, 1841, 1875; England, 1884).

Normally the challenging state sets a goal for itself which derives from the relation between the military strengths of the two countries prior to the race. If the relation was one of disparity, the initial challenge usually comes from the weaker power which aspires to parity or better. Conceivably a stronger power could initiate an arms race by deciding that it required an even higher ratio of superiority over the weaker power. But in actual practice this is seldom the case: the gain in security achieved in upping a 2:1 ratio to 3:1, for instance, rarely is worth the increased economic costs and political tensions. If parity of military power existed between the two countries, the arms race begins when one state determines that it requires military force superior to that of the other country.

In nine out of ten races the slogan of the challenging state is either "parity" or "superiority." Only in rare cases does the challenger aim for less than this, for unless equality or superiority is achieved, the arms race is hardly likely to be worthwhile. The most prominent exception to the "parity or superiority" rule is the Anglo-German naval race of 1898–1912. In its initial phase, German policy was directed not to the construction of a navy equal to England's but rather to something between that and the very minor navy which she possessed prior to the race. The rationale for building such a force was provided by Tirpitz's "risk theory": Germany should have a navy large enough so that Britain could not fight her without risking damage to the British navy to such an extent that it would fall prey to the naval forces of third powers (i.e., France and Russia). The fallacies in this policy became obvious in the following decade. On the one hand, for technical reasons it was unlikely that an inferior German navy could do serious damage to a superior British fleet, and, on the other hand, instead of making Britain wary of France and Russia the expansion of the German navy tended to drive her into their arms and consequently to remove the hostile third powers who were supposed to pounce upon a Britain weakened by Germany.[20] One can only conclude that it is seldom worthwhile either for a superior power to attempt significantly to increase its superiority or for a weaker power to

[20] For the risk theory, see Alfred von Tirpitz, *My Memoirs* (New York, 2 vols., 1919), I, pp. 79, 84, 121, 159–160, and for a trenchant criticism, Woodward, *Great Britain and the German Navy* [Oxford, 1935], pp. 31–39.

attempt only to reduce its degree of inferiority. The rational goals in an arms race are parity or superiority.

In many respects the most critical aspect of a race is the initial response which the challenged state makes to the new goals posited by the challenger. In general, these responses can be divided into four categories, two of which preserve the possibility of peace, two of which make war virtually inevitable. The challenged state may, first, attempt to counterbalance the increased armaments of its rival through diplomatic means or it may, secondly, immediately increase its own armaments in an effort to maintain or directly to restore the previously existing balance of military power. While neither of these responses guarantees the maintenance of peace, they at least do not precipitate war. The diplomatic avenue of action, if it exists, is generally the preferred one. It may be necessary, however, for the state to enhance its own armaments as well as attempting to secure reliable allies. Or, if alliances are impossible or undesirable for reasons of state policy, the challenged state must rely upon its own increases in armaments as the way of achieving its goal. In this case a sustained arms race is likely to result. During her period of splendid isolation, for instance, England met the French naval challenge of the 1840s by increasing the size and effectiveness of her own navy. At the end of the century when confronted by the Russo-French challenge, she both increased her navy and made tentative unsuccessful efforts to form an alliance with Germany. In response to the German challenge a decade later, she again increased her navy and also arrived at a rapprochement with France and Russia.

If new alliances or increased armaments appear impossible or undesirable, a state which sees its superiority or equality in military power menaced by the actions of another state may initiate preventive action while still strong enough to forestall the change in the balance of power. The factors which enter into the decision to wage preventive war are complex and intangible, but, conceivably, if the state had no diplomatic opportunities and if it was dubious of its ability to hold its own in an arms race, this might well be a rational course of behavior.[21] Tirpitz explicitly recognized this in his concept of a "danger zone" through which the German navy would pass and during which a strong likelihood would exist that the British would take preventive action to destroy the German fleet. Such an attack might be avoided, he felt, by a German diplomatic "peace offensive" designed to calm British fears and to assure them of the harmless character of German intentions. Throughout the decade after 1898 the Germans suffered periodic scares of an imminent British attack. Although preventive action was never seriously considered by the British government, enough talk went on in high British circles of "Copenhagen-

---

[21] On the considerations going into the waging of preventive war, see my "To Choose Peace or War," *United States Naval Institute Proceedings*, LXXXIII (April, 1957), pp. 360–62.

ing" the German flcct to give the Germans some cause for alarm.[22] In the "war in sight" crisis of 1875, the initial success of French rearmament efforts aimed at restoring an equality of military power with Germany stimulated German statesmen and military leaders carefully to consider the desirability of preventive war. Similarly, the actions of the Nazis in overthrowing the restrictions of the Treaty of Versailles in the early 1930s and starting the European arms build-up produced arguments in Poland and France favoring preventive war.[23] After World War II at the beginning of the arms race between the United States and the Soviet Union a small but articulate segment of opinion urged the United States to take preventive action before the Soviet Union developed nuclear weapons.[24] To a certain extent, the Japanese attack on the United States in 1941 can be considered a preventive action designed to forestall the inevitable loss of Japanese naval superiority in the western Pacific which would have resulted from the two-ocean navy program begun by the United States in 1939. In 1956 the Egyptians began to rebuild their armaments from Soviet sources and thus to disturb the equilibrium which had existed with Israel since 1949. This development was undoubtedly one factor leading Israel to attack Egypt and thereby attempt to resolve at least some of the outstanding issues between them before the increase in Egyptian military power.

At the other extreme from preventive action, a challenged state simply may not make any immediate response to the upset of the existing balance of power. The challenger may then actually achieve or come close to achieving the new balance of military force which it considers necessary. In this event, roles are reversed, the challenged suddenly awakens to its weakened position and becomes the challenger, engaging in frantic and strenuous last-ditch efforts to restore the previously existing military ratio. In general, the likelihood of war increases just prior to a change in military superiority from one side to the other. If the challenged state averts this change by alliances or increased armaments, war is avoidable. On the other hand, the challenged state may precipitate war in order to prevent the change, or it may provoke war by allowing the change to take place and then attempting to undo it. In the latter case, the original challenger, having achieved parity or superiority, is in no mood or position to back down; the anxious efforts of its opponent to regain its military strength appear to be obvious war preparation; and consequently the original challenger normally will not hesitate to risk or provoke a war while it may still benefit from its recent gains.

Belated responses resulting in last-gasp arms races are most clearly

---

[22] See Marder, *British Sea Power*, pp. 496ff.; Woodward, *Great Britain and the German Navy*, pp. 85–86; Alfred Vagts, *Defense and Diplomacy* (New York, 1956), pp. 295–96, 298–300.
[23] See Vagts, *Defence and Diplomacy*, pp. 310–11.
[24] See Huntington, *United States Naval Institute Proceedings*, LXXXIII, 363–66.

seen in the French and British reactions to German rearmament in the
1930s. The coming-to-power of the Nazis and their subsequent rearmament efforts initially provoked little military response in France. In part,
this reflected confidence in the qualitative superiority of the French army
and the defensive strength of the Maginot Line. In part, too, it reflected
the French political situation in which those groups most fearful of Nazi
Germany were generally those most opposed to large armies and militarism,
while the usual right-wing supporters of the French army were those to
whom Hitler appeared least dangerous. As a result, the French army and
the War Ministry budget remained fairly constant between 1933 and
1936. Significant increases in French armaments were not made until
1937 and 1938, and the real French rearmament effort got under way in
1939. France proposed to spend more on armaments in that single year
than the total of her expenditures during the preceding five years. By
then, however, the five-to-one superiority in military effectives which she
had possessed over Germany in 1933 had turned into a four-to-three
inferiority.[25]

Roughly the same process was going on with respect to the ratio
between the British and German air forces. . . .

A slightly different example of a belated, last minute arms race is
found in the German–French and German–Russian competitions of 1911–
1914. In this instance, deteriorating relations between the two countries
led both to make strenuous efforts to increase their forces in a short time
and enhance the willingness of each to go to war. For a decade or more
prior to 1911, German and French armaments had been relatively stable,
and during the years 1908–1911 relations between the two countries had
generally improved. The Agadir crisis of 1911 and the Balkan War of the
following year stimulated the Germans to reconsider their armaments
position. Fear of a Franco-Russian surprise attack and concern over the
quantitative superiority of the French army led the Germans to make a
moderate increase in their forces in 1912. In the spring of 1913 a much
larger increase of 117,000 men was voted. Simultaneously, the French
extended their term of military service from two to three years, thereby
increasing their peacetime army by some 200,000 men. The Russians also
had an extensive program of military reorganization under way. During
the three-year period 1911–14 the French army increased from 638,500
men to 846,000, and the German army from 626,732 to 806,026 men. If
war had not broken out in 1914, the French would have been faced with
an acute problem in maintaining a military balance with Germany. The
population of France was about 39,000,000, that of Germany 65,000,000.

[25] N. M. Sloutzki, World Armaments Race, 1919–1939 (Geneva Studies, Vol. XII, No.
1, July, 1941), pp. 45–46, 99–101. In 1933 the French army numbered approximately
508,000 men, the German army roughly 100,000. In 1939 the French army numbered
629,000 men, the German army 800–900,000.

During the twenty years prior to 1914 the French trained 82 per cent of their men liable for military service, the Germans 55 per cent of theirs. As a result, the two armies were approximately equal in size. If the Germans had continued to expand their army, the French inevitably would have fallen behind in the race: the extension of service in 1913 was a sign that they were reaching the limit of their manpower resources. Their alternatives would have been either to have provoked a war before Germany gained a decisive superiority, to have surrendered their goal of parity with Germany and with it any hope of retrieving Alsace-Lorraine, or to have stimulated further improvement of the military forces of their Russian ally and further expansion of the military forces of their British ally —perhaps putting pressure on Great Britain to institute universal military service. The Germans, on the other hand, felt themselves menaced by the reorganization of the Russian army. Already significantly outnumbered by the combined Franco-Russian armies, the Germans could hardly view with equanimity a significant increase in the efficiency of the Tsarist forces. Thus each side tended to see itself losing out in the arms race in the future and hence each side was more willing to risk a test of arms when the opportunity presented itself in 1914.

The danger of war is highest in the opening phases of an arms race, at which time the greatest elements of instability and uncertainty are present. If the challenged state neither resorts to preventive war nor fails to make an immediate response to the challenger's activities, a sustained arms race is likely to result with the probability of war decreasing as the initial action and counteraction fade into the past. Once the initial disturbances to the pre-arms race static equilibrium are surmounted, the reciprocal increases of the two states tend to produce a new, dynamic equilibrium reflecting their relative strength and participation in the race. In all probability, the relative military power of the two states in this dynamic equilibrium will fall somewhere between the previous status quo and the ratio-goal of the challenger. The sustained regularity of the increases in itself becomes an accepted and anticipated stabilizing factor in the relations between the two countries. A sustained quantitative race still may produce a war, but a greater likelihood exists that either the two states will arrive at a mutual accommodation reducing the political tensions which started the race or that one state over the long haul will gradually but substantially achieve its objective while the other will accept defeat in the race if this does not damage its vital interests. Thus, a twenty-five year sporadic naval race between France and England ended in the middle 1860s when France gave up any serious effort to challenge the 3:2 ratio which England had demonstrated the will and the capacity to maintain. Similarly, the Anglo-German naval race slackened after 1912 when, despite failure to reach formal agreement, relations improved between the two countries and even Tirpitz acquiesced in the British 16:10

ratio in capital ships.[27] Britain also successfully maintained her two-power standard against France and Russia for twenty years until changes in the international scene ended her arms competition with those two powers. Germany and France successively increased their armies from the middle 1870s to the middle 1890s when tensions eased and the arms build-up in each country slackened. The incipient naval races among the United States, Britain, and Japan growing out of World War I were restricted by the Washington naval agreement; the ten-year cruiser competition between the United States and England ended in the London Treaty of 1930; and eventually the rise of more dangerous threats in the mid-1930s removed any remaining vestiges of Anglo-American naval rivalry. The twelve-year arms race between Chile and Argentina ended in 1902 with a comprehensive agreement between the two countries settling their boundary disputes and restricting their armaments. While generalizations are both difficult and dangerous, it would appear that a sustained arms race is much more likely to have a peaceful ending than a bloody one.

QUANTITATIVE AND QUALITATIVE ARMS RACES

A state may increase its military power quantitatively, by expanding the numerical strength of its existing military forces, or qualitatively, by replacing its existing forms of military force (normally weapons systems) with new and more effective forms of force. Expansion and innovation are thus possible characteristics of any arms race, and to some extent both are present in most races. Initially and fundamentally every arms race is quantitative in nature. The race begins when two states develop conflicting

[27] Some question might be raised as to whether the Anglo-German naval race ended before World War I or in World War I. It would appear, however, that the race was substantially over before the war began. The race went through two phases. During the first phase, 1898–1905, German policy was directed toward the construction of a "risk" navy. During the second phase, 1906–1912, the Anglo-French entente had removed the basis for a risk navy, and the introduction of the Dreadnought opened to the Germans the possibility of naval parity with Britain. By 1912, however, it was apparent to all that Britain had the will and the determination to maintain the 60 per cent superiority which she desired over Germany, and to lay "two keels for one" if this should be necessary. In addition, increased tension with France and Russia over Morocco and the Balkans turned German attention to her army. In 1912 Bethmann-Hollweg accepted as the basis for negotiation a British memorandum the first point of which was: "Fundamental. Naval superiority recognized as essential to Great Britain." Relations between the two countries generally improved between 1912 and 1914: they cooperated in their efforts to limit the Balkan wars of 1912–13 and in the spring of 1914 arrived at an agreement concerning the Baghdad railway and the Portuguese colonies. By June 1914 rivalry had abated to such an extent that the visit of a squadron of British battleships to Kiel became the occasion for warm expressions of friendship. "In a sense," as Bernadotte Schmitt says, "potential foes had become potential friends." The Coming of the War: 1914, I, pp. 72–73. Sidney B. Fay, The Origins of the World War (New York, 2 vols., 1928), I, pp. 299ff., Tirpitz, Memoirs, I, pp. 271–72.

goals as to what should be the distribution of military power between them and give these goals explicit statement in quantitative ratios of the relative strengths which each hopes to achieve in the decisive form of military force. The formal start of the race is the decision of the challenger to upset the existing balance and to expand its forces quantitatively. If at some point in the race a qualitative change produces a new decisive form of military force, the quantitative goals of the two states still remain roughly the same. The relative balance of power which each state desires to achieve is independent of the specific weapons and forces which enter into the balance. Despite the underlying adherence of both states to their original ratio-goals, however, a complex qualitative race produced by rapid technological innovation is a very different phenomenon from a race which remains simply quantitative.

Probably the best examples of races which were primarily quantitative in nature are those between Germany and France between 1871 and 1914. The decisive element was the number of effectives each power maintained in its peacetime army and the number of reserves it could call to the colors in an emergency. Quantitative increases by one state invariably produced comparable increases by the other. . . .

A qualitative arms race is more complex than a quantitative one because at some point it involves the decision by one side to introduce a new weapons system or form of military force. Where the capacity for technological innovation exists, the natural tendency is for the arms race to become qualitative. The introduction of a new weapons system obviously is normally desirable from the viewpoint of the state which is behind in the quantitative race. The English–French naval rivalry of 1841–1865 grew out of the deteriorating relations between the two countries over Syria, Tahiti and Spain. Its first manifestation was quantitative: in 1841 the number of seamen in the French navy which for nearly a century had been about two-thirds the number in the British navy was suddenly increased so as to almost equal the British strength. Subsequently the large expansions which the French proposed to make in their dockyards, especially at Toulon, caused even Cobden to observe that "a serious effort seemed really to be made to rival us at sea." [29] The Anglo-French quantitative rivalry subsided with the departure of Louis Philippe in 1848, but shortly thereafter it resumed on a new qualitative level with the determination of Napoleon III to push the construction of steam warships. The *Napoléon*, a screw propelled ship of the line of 92 guns, launched by the French in 1850 was significantly superior to anything the British could bring against it, until the *Agamemnon* was launched two years later. The alliance of the two countries in the Crimean War only temporarily suspended the naval race, and by 1858 the French had achieved parity with

[29] "Three Panics," p. 224.

the British in fast screw ships of the line.[30] In that year the French had 114 fewer sailing vessels in their navy than they had in 1852, while the number of British sailing ships had declined only from 299 to 296. On the other hand, the British in 1852 had a superiority of 73 sailing ships of the line to 45 for the French. By 1858, however, both England and France had 29 steam ships of the line while England had an enhanced superiority of 35 to 10 in sailing ships. A head start in steam construction and conversion plus the concentration of effort on this program had enabled the French, who had been hopelessly outnumbered in the previously decisive form of naval power, to establish a rough parity in the new form. In view of the British determination to restore their quantitative superiority and the superior industrial resources at their disposal, however, parity could only be temporary. In 1861 the British had 53 screw battleships afloat and 14 building while the French had only 35 afloat and two building.[31]

By the time that the British had reëstablished their superiority in steam warships, their opponents had brought forward another innovation which again threatened British control of the seas. The French laid down four ironclads in 1858 and two in 1859. The first was launched in November 1859 and the next in March 1860. The British launched their first ironclad in December 1860. The British program, however, was hampered by the Admiralty's insistence upon continuing to build wooden warships. The French stopped laying down wooden line of battle ships in 1856, yet the British, despite warnings that wooden walls were obsolete, continued building wooden ships down through 1860, and in 1861 the Admiralty brought in the largest request in its history for the purchase of timber.[32] Meanwhile, in the fall of 1860 the French started a new construction program for ten more ironclads to supplement the six they already had underway. The British learned of these projects in February 1861 and responded with a program to add nine new ironclads to their fleet. In May 1861, the French had a total of fifteen ironclads built or building, the British only seven. From 1860 until 1865 the French possessed superiority or parity with the British in ironclad warships. In February 1863, for instance, the French had four ironclads mounting 146 guns ready for action, the British four ironclads mounting 116 guns. Thanks to the genius and initiative of the director of French naval construction, Depuy de Lôme, and the support of Napoleon III, there had occurred, as one British military historian put it,

> an astonishing change in the balance of power which might have been epoch-making had it not been so brief, or if France and Britain had

[30] Baxter, *Introduction of the Ironclad Warship* [Cambridge, 1933], p. 120.
[31] Cobden, "Three Panics," pp. 304–08, 392–93.
[32] *Ibid.*, pp. 343, 403; Robert G. Albion, *Forests and Sea Power* (Cambridge, 1926), p. 408.

gone to war, a reversal which finds no place in any but technical histories and which is almost entirely unknown in either country to-day. In a word, supremacy at sea passed from Britain to France.[33]

This was not a supremacy, however, which France could long maintain. By 1866, Britannia had retrieved the trident. In that year England possessed nineteen ironclads, France thirteen, and the English superiority was enhanced by heavier guns. Thereafter the naval strengths of the two powers resumed the 3:2 ratio which had existed prior to 1841.

•   •   •

Whether an arms race is primarily quantitative or primarily qualitative in nature has a determining influence upon its outcome. This influence is manifested in the different impacts which the two types of races have on the balance of military power between the two states and on the relative demands which they make on state resources.

Qualitative and Quantitative Races and the Balance of Power. In a simple quantitative race one state is very likely to develop a definite superiority in the long run. The issue is simply who has the greater determination and the greater resources. Once a state falls significantly behind, it is most unlikely that it will ever be able to overcome the lead of its rival. A qualitative race, on the other hand, in which there is a series of major technological innovations in reality consists of a number of distinct races. Each time a new weapons system is introduced a new race takes place in the development and accumulation of that weapon. As the rate of technological innovation increases each separate component race decreases in time and extent. The simple quantitative race is like a marathon of undetermined distance which can only end with the exhaustion of one state or both, or with the state which is about to fall behind in the race pulling out its firearms and attempting to despatch its rival. The qualitative race, on the other hand, resembles a series of hundred yard dashes, each beginning from a fresh starting line. Consequently, in a qualitative race hope springs anew with each phase. Quantitative superiority is the product of effort, energy, resources, and time. Once achieved it is rarely lost. Qualitative superiority is the product of discovery, luck, and circumstance. Once achieved it is always lost. Safety exists only in numbers. While a quantitative race tends to produce inequality between the two competing powers, a qualitative race tends toward equality irrespective of what may be the ratio-goals of the two rival states. Each new weapon instead of increasing the distance between the two states reduces it. The more rapid the rate of innovation the more pronounced is the tendency toward equality. Prior to 1905, for instance, Great Britain possessed a superiority in pre-Dreadnought battleships. By 1912 she had also established a clear and unassailable

[33] Cyril Falls, *A Hundred Years of War* (London, 1953), p. 102.

superiority in Dreadnoughts over Germany. But if Germany had introduced a super-Dreadnought in 1909, Great Britain could never have
established its clear superiority in Dreadnoughts. She would have had to
start over again in the new race. A rapid rate of innovation means that
arms races are always beginning, never ending. In so far as the likelihood
of war is decreased by the existence of an equality of power between rival
states, a qualitative arms race tends to have this result. A quantitative
arms race, on the other hand, tends to have the opposite effect. If in a
qualitative race one power stopped technological innovation and instead
shifted its resources to the multiplication of existing weapons systems, this
would be a fairly clear sign that it was intending to go to war in the
immediate future.

Undoubtedly many will question the proposition that rapid technological innovation tends to produce an equality of power. In an arms race
each state lives in constant fear that its opponent will score a "technological breakthrough" and achieve a decisive qualitative superiority. This
anxiety is a continuing feature of arms races but it is one which has
virtually no basis in recent experience. The tendency toward simultaneity
of innovation is overwhelming. Prior to World War I simultaneity was
primarily the result of the common pool of knowledge among the advanced
nations with respect to weapons technology. The development of weapons
was largely the province of private firms who made their wares available
to any state which was interested. As a result at any given time the armaments of the major powers all strikingly resembled one another.[39] During
and after World War I military research and development became more
and more a governmental activity, and, as a result, more and more en-
shrouded in secrecy. Nonetheless relative equality in technological innovation continued among the major powers. The reason for this was now
not so much access to common knowledge as an equal ability and opportunity to develop that knowledge. The logic of scientific development is
such that separate groups of men working in separate laboratories on the
same problem are likely to arrive at the same answer to the problem at
about the same time. Even if this were not the case, the greatly increased
ratio of production time to use time in recent years has tended to diminish
the opportunity of the power which has pioneered an innovation to produce it in sufficient quantity in sufficient time to be militarily decisive.

---

[39] See Victor Lefebure, "The Decisive Aggressive Value of the New Agencies of War,"
in the Inter-Parliamentary Union, *What Would Be the Character of a New War?* (New
York, 1933), pp. 97–101. See also Marion W. Boggs, *Attempts to Define and Limit
'Aggressive' Armament in Diplomacy and Strategy* (Columbia, Mo., 1941), p. 76:
". . . the history of war inventions tends to emphasize the slowness and distinctively
international character of peacetime improvements; no weapon has been perfected with
secrecy and rapidity as the exclusive national property of any one state. At an early stage
all nations secure access to the information, and develop not only the armament, but
measures against it."

When it takes several years to move a weapons system from original design to quantity operation, knowledge of it is bound to leak out, and the second power in the arms race will be able to get its own program under way before the first state can capitalize on its lead. The *Merrimac* reigned supreme for a day, but it was only for a day and it could be only for a day.

The fact that for four years from 1945 to 1949 the United States possessed a marked qualitative superiority over the Soviet Union has tended to obscure how rare this event normally is. American superiority, however, was fundamentally the result of carrying over into a new competitive rivalry a weapons system which had been developed in a previous conflict. In the latter rivalry the tendency toward simultaneity of development soon manifested itself. The Soviet Union developed an atomic bomb four years after the United States had done so. Soviet explosion of a hydrogen weapon lagged only ten months behind that of the United States. At a still later date in the arms race, both powers in 1957 were neck and neck in their efforts to develop long-range ballistic missiles.

The ending of an arms race in a distinct quantitative victory for one side is perhaps best exemplified in the success of the British in maintaining their supremacy on the seas. Three times within the course of a hundred years the British were challenged by continental rivals, and three times the British outbuilt their competitors. In each case, also, implicitly or explicitly, the bested rivals recognized their defeat and abandoned their efforts to challenge the resources, skill and determination of the British. At this point in a quantitative race when it appears that one power is establishing its superiority over the other, proposals are frequently brought forward for some sort of "disarmament" agreement. These are as likely to come from the superior side as from the inferior one. The stronger power desires to clothe its *de facto* supremacy in *de jure* acceptance and legitimacy so that it may slacken its own arms efforts. From 1905 to 1912, for instance, virtually all the initiatives for Anglo-German naval agreement came from the British. Quite properly, the Germans regarded those advances as British efforts to compel "naval competition to cease at the moment of its own greatest preponderance." Such proposals only heightened German suspicion and bitterness.[40] Similarly, after World War II the Soviet Union naturally described the American nuclear disarmament proposal as a device to prevent the Soviet Union from developing its own nuclear capability. A decade later a greater common interest existed between the Soviet Union and the United States in reaching an arms agreement which would permanently exclude "fourth powers" from the exclusive nuclear club. In disarmament discussions the superior power commonly attempts to persuade the inferior one to accept as permanent

[40] These reached a peak at the Hague Conference of 1907, the Germans viewing the British proposals at the time as "a scheme to arrest naval development." Fay, *Origins of the World War*, I, p. 233f., pp. 238–39.

the existing ratio of strength, or, failing in this effort, the superior power proposes a temporary suspension of the race, a "holiday" during which period neither power will increase its armaments. In 1899 the Russians, with the largest army in Europe, proposed that for five years no increases be made in military budgets. In 1912–14 Churchill repeatedly suggested the desirability of a naval building holiday to the Germans who were quite unable to perceive its advantages. In 1936 the United States could easily agree to a six year holiday in 10,000 ton cruisers since it had already under way all the cruisers it was permitted by the London Treaty of 1930. Similarly, in its 1957 negotiations with the Soviet Union the United States could also safely propose an end to the production of nuclear weapons. The inferior participant in disarmament negotiations, on the other hand, inevitably supports measures based not upon the existing situation but either upon the abstract principle of "parity" or upon the inherent evil of large armaments as such and the desirability of reducing all arms down to a common low level. Thus, in most instances, a disarmament proposal is simply a maneuver in the arms race: the attempt by a state to achieve the ratio-goal it desires by means other than an increase in its armaments.

   The Domestic Burden of Quantitative and Qualitative Races. Quantitative and qualitative arms races have markedly different effects upon the countries participating in them. In a quantitative race the decisive ratio is between the resources which a nation devotes to military purposes and those which it devotes to civilian ones. A quantitative race of any intensity requires a steady shift of resources from the latter to the former. As the forms of military force are multiplied a larger and larger proportion of the national product is devoted to the purposes of the race, and, if it is a race in military manpower, an increasing proportion of the population serves a longer and longer time in the armed forces. A quantitative race of any duration thus imposes ever increasing burdens upon the countries involved in it. As a result, it becomes necessary for governments to resort to various means of stimulating popular support and eliciting a willingness to sacrifice other goods and values. Enthusiasm is mobilized, hostility aroused and directed against the potential enemy. Suspicion and fear multiply with the armaments. Such was the result of the quantitative races between the Triple Alliance and the Triple Entente between 1907 and 1914:

> In both groups of powers there was a rapid increase of military and naval armaments. This caused increasing suspicions, fears, and newspaper recriminations in the opposite camp. This in turn led to more armaments; and so to the vicious circle of ever growing war preparations and mutual fears and suspicions.[41]

[41] Fay, *Origins of the World War*, I, p. 226.

Eventually a time is reached when the increasing costs and tensions of a continued arms race seem worse than the costs and the risks of war. Public opinion once aroused cannot be quieted. The economic, military and psychological pressures previously generated permit only further expansion or conflict. The extent to which an arms race is likely to lead to war thus varies with the burdens it imposes on the peoples and the extent to which it involves them psychologically and emotionally in the race. Prolonged sufficiently, a quantitative race must necessarily reach a point where opinion in one country or the other will demand that it be ended, if not by negotiation, then by war. The logical result of a quantitative arms race is a "nation in arms," and a nation in arms for any length of time must be a nation at war.

A qualitative arms race, however, does not have this effect. In such a race the essential relationship is not between the military and the civilian, but rather between the old and the new forms of military force. In a quantitative race the principal policy issue is the extent to which resources and manpower should be diverted from civilian to military use. In a qualitative race, the principal issue is the extent to which the new weapons systems should replace the old "conventional" ones. In a quantitative race the key question is "How much?" In a qualitative race, it is "How soon?" A quantitative race requires continuous expansion of military resources, a qualitative race continuous redeployment of them. A qualitative race does not normally increase arms budgets, even when, as usually happens, the new forms of military force are more expensive than the old ones. The costs of a qualitative race only increase significantly when an effort is made to maintain both old and new forms of military force: steam and sail; ironclads and wooden walls; nuclear and nonnuclear weapons. Transitions from old to new weapons systems have not normally been accompanied by marked increases in military expenditures. During the decade in which the ironclad replaced the wooden ship of the line British naval expenditures declined from £12,779,000 in 1859 to less than eleven million pounds in 1867.[42] Similarly, the five years after the introduction of the Dreadnought saw British naval expenditures drop from £35,476,000 in 1903–04 to £32,188,000 in 1908–09. During the same period estimates for shipbuilding and repairs dropped from £17,350,000 to £14,313,900. The years 1953–1956 saw the progressive adoption of nuclear weapons in the American armed forces, yet military budgets during this period at first dropped considerably and then recovered only slightly, as the increased expenditures for the new weapons were more than compensated for by reductions in expenditures for nonnuclear forces.

Quantitative and qualitative arms races differ also in the interests they mobilize and the leadership they stimulate. In the long run, a quan-

---

[42] See Baxter, *Introduction of the Ironclad Warship*, p. 321.

titative race makes extensive demands on a broad segment of the population. A qualitative race, however, tends to be a competition of elites rather than masses. No need exists for the bulk of the population to become directly involved. In a quantitative arms race, the users of the weapons—the military leaders—assume the key role. In a qualitative race, the creators of the weapons—the scientists—rival them for preëminence. Similarly, the most important private interests in a quantitative race are the large mass production industrial corporations, while in a qualitative race they tend to be the smaller firms specializing in the innovation and development of weapons systems rather than in their mass output.

While the rising costs of a quantitative race may increase the likelihood of war, they may also enhance efforts to end the race by means of an arms agreement. Undoubtedly the most powerful motive (prior to the feasibility of utter annihilation) leading states to arms limitations has been the economic one. The desire for economy was an important factor leading Louis Philippe to propose a general reduction in European armaments in 1831. In the 1860s similar motives stimulated Napoleon III to push disarmament plans. They also prompted various British governments to be receptive to arms limitation proposals, provided, of course, that they did not endanger Britain's supremacy on the seas: the advent of the Liberal government in 1905, for instance, resulted in renewed efforts to reach accommodation with the Germans. In 1898 the troubled state of Russian finances was largely responsible for the Tsar's surprise move in sponsoring the first Hague Conference. Eight years later it was the British who, for economic reasons, wished to include the question of arms limitation on the agenda of the second Hague Conference.

The success of rising economic costs in bringing about the negotiated end of an arms race depends upon their incidence being relatively equal on each participant. A state which is well able to bear the economic burden normally spurns the efforts of weaker powers to call off the race. Thus, the Kaiser was scornful of the Russian economic debility which led to the proposal for the first Hague Conference, and a German delegate to that conference, in explaining German opposition to limitation, took pains to assure the participants that:

> The German people are not crushed beneath the weight of expenditures and taxes; they are not hanging on the edge of the precipice; they are not hastening towards exhaustion and ruin. Quite the contrary; public and private wealth is increasing, the general welfare, and standard of life, are rising from year to year.[43]

On the other hand, the relatively equal burdens of their arms race in the last decade of the nineteenth century eventually forced Argentina and

[43] Quoted in Tate, *Disarmament Illusion* [New York, 1942], p. 281. See also pp. 193–94, 251–52.

Chile to call the race off in 1902. The victory of Chile in the War of the Pacific had brought her into conflict with an "expanding and prosperous Argentina" in the 1880s, and a whole series of boundary disputes exacerbated the rivalry which developed between the two powers for hegemony on the South American continent.[44] As a result, after 1892 both countries consistently expanded their military and naval forces, and relations between them staggered from one war crisis to another. Despite efforts made to arbitrate the boundary disputes,

> an uneasy feeling still prevailed that hostilities might break out, and neither State made any pretence of stopping military and naval preparations. Orders for arms, ammunition, and warships were not countermanded, and men on both sides of the Andes began to declaim strongly against the heavy expenditure thus entailed. The reply to such remonstrances invariably was that until the question of the boundary was settled, it was necessary to maintain both powers on a war footing. Thus the resources of Argentina and Chile were strained to the utmost, and public works neglected in order that funds might be forthcoming to pay for guns and ships bought in Europe.[45]

These economic burdens led the presidents of the two countries to arrive at an agreement in 1899 restricting additional expenditures on armaments. Two years later, however, the boundary issue again flared up, and both sides recommenced preparations for war. But again the resources of the countries were taxed beyond their limit. In August 1901 the Chilean president declared to the United States minister "that the burden which Chile is carrying . . . is abnormal and beyond her capacity and that the hour has come to either make use of her armaments or reduce them to the lowest level compatible with the dignity and safety of the country." [46] Argentina was also suffering from severe economic strain, and as a result, the two countries concluded their famous *Pactos de Mayo* in 1902 which limited their naval armaments and provided for the arbitration of the remaining boundary issues.

In summary, two general conclusions emerge as to the relations between arms races and war:

(1) War is more likely to develop in the early phases of an arms race than in its later phases.

(2) A quantitative race is more likely than a qualitative one to come to a definite end in war, arms agreement, or victory for one side.

● ● ●

[44] [Robert N.] Burr ["The Balance of Power in Nineteenth-Century South America], *Hispanic American Historical Review*, XXXV, p. 56.
[45] Charles E. Akers, *A History of South America* (New York, new ed., 1930), p. 112.
[46] Quoted in Burr, *Hispanic American Historical Review*, XXXV, 58n.

THE CALCULUS OF DETERRENCE [1]

Bruce M. Russett

A COMPARATIVE STUDY OF DETERRENCE

A persistent problem for American political and military planners has been the question of how to defend "third areas." How can a major power make credible an intent to defend a smaller ally from attack by another major power? Simply making an explicit promise to defend an ally, whether that promise is embodied in a formal treaty or merely in a unilateral declaration, is not sufficient. There have been too many instances when "solemn oaths" were forgotten in the moment of crisis. On the other hand, more than once a major power has taken up arms to defend a nation with whom it had ties appreciably less binding than a formal commitment.

Some analysts like Herman Kahn maintain that the determining factor is the nature of the over-all strategic balance. To make credible a promise to defend third areas the defender must have over-all strategic superiority; that is, he must be able to strike the homeland of the attacker without sustaining unacceptable damage to himself in return (Kahn, 1960). This analysis implies, of course, a strategy which threatens to retaliate, even for a local attack, directly on the home territory of the major power antagonist. Advocates of a strategy of limited warfare retort that, in the absence of clear strategic superiority, the capacity to wage local war effectively may deter attack.

Other writers, notably Thomas C. Schelling, have suggested that the credibility of one's threat can be considerably enhanced by unilateral actions which would increase the defender's loss if he failed to keep his promise (Schelling, 1960). One of the best examples is Chiang Kai-shek's decision in 1958 to station nearly half his troops on Quemoy and Matsu. While the islands were of questionable intrinsic importance, the presence of so much of his army there made it virtually impossible for Chiang, or his American ally, to abandon the islands under fire.

Reprinted by permission from *The Journal of Conflict Resolution*, Vol. 7 (June, 1963), pp. 97–109, copyright 1963 by The University of Michigan.
[1] This article is part of the research of the Yale Political Data Program. I am grateful to Paul Y. Hammond for comments on an earlier draft.

All of these explanations tend to stress principally the military elements in what is a highly complex political situation. There are, however, numerous nonmilitary ways in which one can strengthen one's commitment to a particular area. A government can make it a matter of prestige with its electorate. A nation might even deliberately increase its economic dependence upon supplies from a certain area, the better to enhance the credibility of a promise to defend it. W. W. Kaufmann's classic piece identified the elements of credibility as a power's capabilities, the costs it could inflict in using those capabilities, and its intentions as perceived by the enemy. In evaluating the defender's intentions a prospective attacker will look at his past actions, his current pronouncements, and the state of his public opinion (Kaufmann, 1956, pp. 12–38).

Kaufmann's formulation is better than simpler ones that stress military factors almost exclusively, but it needs to be expanded and made more detailed. One must particularly examine the potential costs to the defending power if he does not honor his commitments. In addition, propositions about factors which determine the credibility of a given threat need to be tested systematically on a comparative basis. On a number of occasions, for example, an aggressor has ignored the threats of a major power "defender" to go to war to protect a small nation "pawn" even though the defender held both strategic superiority and the ability to fight a local war successfully. Hitler's annexation of Austria in 1938 is just this kind of case, and one where the aggressor was correct, moreover.

In this paper we shall examine all the cases during the last three decades where a major power "attacker" overtly threatened a pawn with military force, and where the defender either had given, prior to the crisis, some indication of an intent to protect the pawn or made a commitment in time to prevent the threatened attack.[2] A threat may be believed or disbelieved; it may be a bluff, or it may be sincere. Often the defender himself may not be sure of his reaction until the crisis actually occurs. We shall explore the question of what makes a threat credible by asking which threats in the past have been believed and which disregarded. Successful deterrence is defined as an instance, when an attack on the pawn is prevented or repulsed without conflict between the attacking forces and regular combat units of the major power "defender." ("Regular combat units" are defined so as not to include the strictly limited participation of a few military advisers.) With this formulation we must ignore what are perhaps the most successful instances of all—where the attacker is dissuaded from making any overt threat whatever against the pawn. But these cases must be left aside both because they are too numerous to be treated in detail and because it would be too difficult to distinguish the elements

---

[2] These definitions are employed purely in an analytical sense with no intention of conveying moral content. The British-French "attack" in 1956, for instance, was certainly provoked to a large extent by the Egyptians themselves.

in most cases. Who, for example, really was the "attacker"? Was he dissuaded because of any action by the defender, or simply by indifference? Such questions would lead to too much speculation at the expense of the careful analysis of each case in detail.

Deterrence fails when the attacker decides that the defender's threat is not likely to be fulfilled. In this sense it is equally a failure whether the defender really does intend to fight but is unable to communicate that intention to the attacker, or whether he is merely bluffing. Later we shall ask, from the viewpoint of the attacker, which threats ought to be taken seriously. At this stage we shall simply examine past cases of attempted deterrence to discover what elements are usually associated with a threat that is believed (or at least not disbelieved with enough confidence for the attacker to act on his disbelief) and therefore what steps a defender might take to make his threats more credible to his opponent. Table 1 lists the cases for consideration.[3]

These cases are not, of course, comparable in every respect. Particularly in the instances of successful deterrence the causes are complex and not easily ascertainable. Nevertheless, a systematic comparison, undertaken cautiously, can provide certain insights that would escape an emphasis on the historical uniqueness of each case.

DETERRENCE IN RECENT DECADES

First, we may dismiss as erroneous some frequent contentions about the credibility of deterrence. It is often said that a major power will fight only to protect an "important" position, and not to defend some area of relatively insignificant size or population. As we shall see below, this is in

---

[3] Note that we have excluded instances of protracted guerrilla warfare. While preventing and defeating guerrilla war is a major problem, the differences from the matters considered here require that it be treated separately. (See a forthcoming paper by Morton H. Halperin of Harvard University for a comparative examination of these cases.) The current Berlin crisis was not included because, at the time of writing, it was still unresolved. Also excluded are those cases of aggression in the 1930's and 1940's where no particular power had given a previous indication of a readiness to defend the pawn. By "previous indication" we mean either at least an ambiguous official statement suggesting the use of military force, or the provision of military assistance in the form of arms or advisers. The League of Nations Covenant is not considered such an indication because, barring further commitments by a particular nation, it is impossible to identify any one defender or group of defenders.

Data on a number of factors are presented, for all of the cases, in the appendix.

[4] Despite its efforts to restrain the attackers, the United States was not a "defender" in the Suez affair. It neither supplied arms to the Egyptians before the crisis nor gave any United States government explicitly ruled out the use of military coercion. See *New York Times*, November 7, 1956.

[5] Possibly the Polish case is not really a failure at all, for Hitler may have expected Britain and France to fight but was nevertheless prepared to take the consequences. A. J. P. Taylor presents an extreme version of the argument that Hitler expected Poland and/or Britain and France to give in (Taylor, 1961).

Table 1

SEVENTEEN CASES—1935–1961

Pawn	Year	Attacker(s)	Defender(s)
		Success	
Iran	1946	Soviet Union	United States
			Great Britain—Secondary
Turkey	1947	Soviet Union	United States
Berlin	1948	Soviet Union	United States
			Great Britain ⎤
			France ⎦ Secondary
Egypt	1956	Great Britain	Soviet Union[4]
		France	
Quemoy–	1954–55	Communist	United States
Matsu	1958	China	
Cuba	1961	United States	Soviet Union
		(support of	
		rebels)	
		Failure—Pawn Lost	
Ethiopia	1935	Italy	Great Britain
			France
Austria	1938	Germany	Great Britain
			France
			Italy
Czechoslo-	1938	Germany	Great Britain
vakia			France
Albania	1939	Italy	Great Britain
Czechoslo-	1939	Germany	Great Britain
vakia			France
Rumania	1940	Soviet Union	Great Britain
Guatemala	1954	United States	Soviet Union
		(support of	
		rebels)	
Hungary	1956	Soviet Union	United States
		Failure—War Not Avoided	
Poland[5]	1939	Germany	Great Britain
			France
South Korea	1950	North Korea	United States
		(supported by	
		China &	
		Soviet Union)	
North Korea	1950	United States	Communist China

a nearly tautological sense true—if, by "important," we include the en-meshment of the defender's prestige with the fate of the pawn, the symbolic importance the pawn may take on in the eyes of other allies, and particular strategic or political values attached to the pawn. But if one means important in terms of any objectively measurable factor like relative population or Gross National Product, it is not true.

As Table 2 shows, in all of our cases of successful deterrence—Iran, Turkey, Berlin, Egypt, Quemoy–Matsu, and Cuba—the pawn's population was well under 15 per cent, and his G.N.P. less than 5 per cent of that of the principal defender.[6] (Britain was not Iran's chief protector.) Yet in five of the eleven cases where the attacker was not dissuaded the territory in question represented over 20 per cent of the defender's population (Ethiopia, Czechoslovakia in the Sudeten crisis and again in 1939, Po-land, and Rumania). Poland in 1939 constituted the largest prize of all, yet Hitler may not have been convinced that Britain and France would go to war to save it. Nor can one discover any special strategic or industrial importance of the pawn only in cases of success. Austria and both Czecho-slovakian cases met these criteria but were nevertheless overrun, and the United States did not expect Communist China to fight for North Korea, despite its obvious strategic significance.

Clearly too, it is not enough simply for the defender to make a formal promise to protect the pawn. Only in one case of success was there what could be described as a clear and unambiguous commitment prior to the actual crisis (Berlin). In the others the commitment was either ambiguous (Iran, Cuba, Quemoy–Matsu) or not made until the crisis was well under way (Turkey, Egypt). The United States' principal pre-crisis commitment to Iran was the Big Three communique from Teheran in 1943 (written chiefly by the American delegation) guaranteeing Iranian "independence, sovereignty, and territorial integrity."[7] Britain was allied with Iran, but the Russians recognized that any effective resistance to their plans would have to come from the United States rather than from an exhausted Britain. In July 1960 Khrushchev warned that the Soviet Union would retaliate with missiles if the United States attacked Cuba, but this was later qualified as being "merely symbolic" and the precise content of Soviet retaliation was left undefined. Neither Congress nor the President has ever stated the exact circumstances under which our formal guarantees of Taiwan would apply to the offshore islands.

Yet in at least six cases an attacker has chosen to ignore an explicit

---

[6] On the other hand one might argue that they were not of sufficient potential value to the attacker for him to run even a relatively slight risk that the defender might actually fight. A complete formulation involving these factors would have to include both the value of the pawn to the attacker and his estimate of the probability that the defender would fight. See below.

[7] See George Kirk on the Iranian case (Kirk, 1952, p. 473).

indication that it would employ military force against Britain and France. In fact, the

Table 2

SIZE (POPULATION AND GROSS NATIONAL PRODUCT) OF PAWN IN
RELATION TO DEFENDER(S)

Pawn	Defender(s)	Pawn's Population as Per Cent of Defender's Population	Pawn's G.N.P. as Per Cent of Defender's G.N.P.
Success			
Iran	United States	12	*
	Great Britain	34	4
Turkey	United States	13	1.7
Berlin	United States	1.5	*
	Great Britain	4	3
	France	5	3
Egypt	Soviet Union	12	2
Quemoy– Matsu	United States	*	*
Cuba	Soviet Union	3	1.5
Failure—Pawn Lost			
Ethiopia	Great Britain	28	1.8
	France	31	2
Austria	Great Britain	14	7
	France	16	8
	Italy	16	17
Czechoslo- vakia (1938)	Great Britain	30	14
	France	34	16
Albania	Great Britain	2	*
Czechoslo- vakia (1939)	Great Britain	23	11
	France	26	12
Rumania	United Kingdom	33	11
Guatemala	Soviet Union	1.6	*
Hungary	United States	6	1.0
Failure—War Not Avoided			
Poland	Great Britain	73	25
	France	82	29
South Korea	United States	14	*
North Korea	Communist China	2	3

*Less than one per cent.
Sources: Population—United Nations (United Nations, 1949, pp. 98–105; United
Nations, 1962, pp. 126–37).
G.N.P.—Norton Ginsburg (Ginsburg, 1962, p. 16). G.N.P. data are ap-
proximate and sometimes estimated.

and publicly acknowledged commitment binding the defender to protect the pawn. Britain, France, and Italy were committed by treaty to Austria, France by treaty to Czechoslovakia in 1938, France by treaty and Britain by executive agreement to Czechoslovakia in 1939, Britain by executive agreement to Rumania, Britain, and France by treaty with Poland, and China by public declaration to North Korea. In three others there was at least an ambiguous commitment on the "defender's" part that might have been more rigorously interpreted. By a treaty of 1906 Britain, France, and Italy pledged themselves to "cooperate in maintaining the integrity of Ethiopia," Britain and Italy agreed in 1938 to "preserve the status quo in the Mediterranean" (including Albania), and in the 1950's American officials made references to "liberating" the satellites that were tragically overrated in Hungary. Of the failures, in fact, only Guatemala and possibly South Korea lacked any verbal indication of their "protectors'" willingness to fight. (In these instances, the defenders showed their concern principally by sending arms to the pawns before the attack.) The analyst who limited his examination to the present cases would be forced to conclude that a small nation was as safe without an explicit guarantee as with one. At least such guarantees existed in fewer instances of success (one in six) than in cases of failure (six of eleven).

We must also examine the proposition that deterrence is not credible unless the defender possesses over-all strategic superiority; unless he can inflict far more damage on an aggressor than he would suffer in return. It is true that the successful deterrence of attack is frequently associated with strategic superiority, but the Soviet Union had, at best, strategic equality with the United States at the time of the Bay of Pigs affair. While Russia was clearly superior to Britain and France when it threatened to attack them with rockets in 1956, it just as clearly did not have a credible first strike force for use against their American ally.[8]

Furthermore, in at least five cases where the attacker was not dissuaded, it nevertheless appears that the defender definitely had the ability to win any major conflict that might have developed (in the cases of Ethiopia, Austria, Czechoslovakia in 1938, Albania, and South Korea) and in two others (Czechoslovakia in 1939 and Hungary) the defender had at least a marginal advantage. (*Post hoc* analysis of the relevant documents indicates this superiority was more often perceived by the attacker, who went ahead and took the chance it would not be used, than by the defender. Hitler consistently recognized his opponents' strength and discounted their will to use it.)

Even less is it necessary for the defender to be able to win a limited local war. Of all the cases of success, only in Egypt could the defender

[8] In both of these instances we must recognize that the "attacker's" failure to persevere to defeat of the pawn was probably due less to Soviet threats than to pressures from the "attacker's" own allies and world opinion.

plausibly claim even the ability to fight to a draw on the local level. In the other instances the defender could not hope to achieve equality without a long, sustained effort, and local superiority appeared out of reach. Yet in at least two failures the defenders, perhaps individually and certainly in coalition, had local superiority (Ethiopia and Austria) and in four others (Czechoslovakia in 1938, Albania, and the Korean cases) the defenders seemed to have been more or less on a par with their prospective antagonists.[9]

Yet if these two kinds of capabilities—local and strategic—are analyzed together, it would seem that a defender may not be clearly inferior in both and yet hope to restrain an attacker. Although the Soviet Union could not dream of meeting the United States in a limited war in the Caribbean, at least in 1961 its strategic nuclear capabilities seemed roughly on a par with America's.[10] And although Russia was inferior to Britain–France–United States on the strategic level, Soviet chances of at least matching their efforts in a local war over Egypt seemed a little brighter. Success requires at least apparent equality on one level or the other—this is hardly surprising—but when we remember that even superiority on both levels has often been associated with failure we have something more significant. *Superiority*, on either level, is not a condition of success. *Equality* on at least one level is a *necessary*, but by no means *sufficient*, condition. The traditionally conceived purely military factors do not alone make threats credible.

Nor, as has sometimes been suggested, does the kind of political system in question seem very important, though it does make some difference. Often, it is said, a dictatorial power can threaten much more convincingly than a democracy because the dictatorship can control its own mass media and present an apparently united front. Democracies, on the other hand, cannot easily suppress dissenting voices declaring that the pawn is "not worth the bones of a single grenadier." This argument must not be overstated—four of our successful cases of deterrence involved a democracy defending against a dictatorship. Yet in all of these cases the democracy possessed strategic superiority, whereas the other two successes, by a dictatorship, were at best under conditions of strategic equality for the defender. And in all but two (North Korea and Guatemala) of the eleven failures the defender was a democracy. Thus a totalitarian power's control over its citizens' expression of opinion may give it some advantage, if not a decisive one—particularly under conditions when the defender's strategic position is relatively weak.

[9] On the military situation prevailing in various crises before World War II see Winston Churchill (1948, pp. 177, 270–1, 287, 336–7).
[10] American intelligence reports were, however, far from unanimous. By the end of 1961 it was clear to those with good information that the Soviets' strategic forces were distinctly inferior to America's.

INTERDEPENDENCE AND CREDIBILITY

With some of these hypotheses discarded we may now examine another line of argument: the credibility of deterrence depends upon the economic, political, and military interdependence of pawn and defender. Where visible ties of commerce, past or present political integration, or military cooperation exist, an attacker will be much more likely to bow before the defender's threats—or if he does not bow, he will very probably find himself at war with the defender.

Military Cooperation. In every instance of success the defender supported the pawn with military assistance in the form of arms and advisers. In one of these cases, of course (Berlin) the defenders actually had troops stationed on the pawn's territory. The military link with Iran was somewhat tenuous, for Teheran received no shipments of American military equipment until after the 1946 crisis was past. Yet an American military mission was stationed in the country at the time, and 30,000 American troops had been on Iranian soil until the end of 1945 (Kirk, 1952, p. 150). America had given a tangible, though modest, indication of her interest in Iran. But in only five of the eleven failures were there significant shipments of arms to the pawn. France extended large military credits to Poland, and the British gave a small credit ($20 million) to Rumania. The Americans and the Chinese sent both arms and advisers to their Korean protégés. The Soviets sent small arms to Guatemala but no advisers, and they did not give any explicit indication of an intent to intervene in any American move against the Guatemalan government. A French military mission was stationed in Prague before and during the two Czechoslovakian crises, but no substantial amount of French equipment was sent (in part because of the high quality of the Czechoslovakian armament industry). In none of the other failures was there any tangible military interdependence. Some degree of military cooperation may not always be sufficient for successful deterrence, but it is virtually essential.

Political Interdependence. This is a helpful if not essential condition. Four of the instances of successful deterrence include some kind of current or recent political tie in addition to any current alliance. Western troops were stationed in Berlin and the three Western powers participated in the government of the city by international agreement. America and Nationalist China had been allies in a recent war. Turkey became allied with the Big Three toward the end of World War II. Iran had been occupied by British troops until early 1946 and American troops until the end of 1945.

In the case of failures only four of eleven pawns had any significant former tie with a defender. Britain and Rumania were allies in World War I, as were the U.S.S.R. and Guatemala in World War II. Obviously, neither of these ties was at all close. The other two, however, were marked by rather close ties. United States forces occupied South Korea after World War II, and the R.O.K. government was an American protégé. The Communist Chinese had close party and ideological ties with the North Korean regime, and not too many decades previously Korea had been under Chinese sovereignty.

Economic Interdependence. We shall work with a crude but simple and objective measure of economic interdependence. In 1954 all countries of the world, other than the United States, imported a total of $65 billion of goods, of which 16 per cent came from the United States. South Korea, however, took 35 per cent of its total imports from the United States, a figure well above the world average. This will be our measure: does the pawn take a larger than average proportion of its imports from the defender or, vice versa, does the defender take a larger than average proportion of its imports from the pawn? To repeat, this is a crude measure. It does not tell, for example, whether the defender is dependent upon the pawn for a supply of a crucial raw material. But there are few areas of vital economic significance in this sense—almost every commodity can be obtained from more than one country, though not always at the same price—and attention to over-all commercial ties gives a broad measure of a country's general economic stake in another.[11] In none of the cases where this test does not show general economic interdependence is there evidence that the defender relied heavily on the pawn for a particular product.

In five of the six cases of successful deterrence either the pawn took an abnormally high proportion of its imports from the defender or vice versa. In the remaining case, the Iranian economy was closely tied to Britain if not to the United States, but in only three of the eleven failures was there interdependence between pawn and defender. A higher than average proportion of Austria's trade was with Italy, though not with France and Britain, the other two parties bound by treaty to preserve her integrity. Both Korean regimes also traded heavily with their defenders. Economic interdependence may be virtually essential to successful deterrence.

[11] In the cases of Berlin and Quemoy–Matsu we must rely on trade figures for a larger unit (West Germany and Taiwan). West Germany conducted an above-average proportion of her trade with the United States and France in this period, but her trade with Britain was below average. Yet as Allied resolve in the Berlin crisis clearly depended upon American initiative it seems correct to include Berlin in the class of economically interdependent pawns.

DIVINING INTENTIONS

Briefly we may also examine the question from the viewpoint of the attacker. If the defender's threat is not challenged, one may never know whether it truly expresses an intention to fight or whether it is merely a bluff. Perhaps the defender himself would not know until the circumstances actually arose. But we can examine the eleven cases where deterrence was not sufficiently credible to prevent attack. Previously we asked what differentiated the instances when the attacker pressed on from those in which he restrained his ambitions. Now, what distinguishes the cases where the defender actually went to war from those where he did not? [12]

"Size," as defined earlier, again is not crucial. Poland, for which Britain and France went to war, was a very large prize but neither North nor South Korea represented a significant proportion of its defender's population or G.N.P. Of the eight instances where the defender's bluff was successfully called, four of the pawns (Ethiopia, Czechoslovakia on both occasions, and Rumania) represented over 20 per cent of the defender's population and four (Austria, Czechoslovakia both times, and Rumania) over 5 per cent of its G.N.P. Proportionately "large" pawns were more often the subject of "bluffs" than of serious intentions. Nor is there necessarily a formal, explicit commitment in cases which result in war. There were such commitments over Poland and North Korea, but South Korea is an obvious exception. And there was such a commitment in the case of half the "bluffs" (Austria, Czechoslovakia twice, and Rumania), and a vague, ambiguous one in three other cases (Ethiopia, Albania, Hungary).

The state of the military balance does not seem to have much effect either. In at least four "bluffs" (Ethiopia, Austria, Czechoslovakia in 1938, and Albania) the defenders were clearly superior *over-all* and in two other cases (Czechoslovakia in 1939 and Hungary) they were at least marginally so. Yet despite their bad military position Britain and France fought for Poland in 1939. And although the Chinese made some bold "paper tiger" talk they really could have had few illusions about their position should the United States counter their move into North Korea with its full conventional and nuclear might. In no instance where a defender fought did he have the ability to win a quick and relatively costless *local* victory.

---

[12] Remember that we have been dealing only with those cases in which deterrence was visibly in danger of failing, and not with instances where it was fully successful; i.e., where the attacker was dissuaded from ever making a serious explicit threat. As noted earlier the latter cases are extremely difficult to identify; nevertheless it seems likely that analysis would show similar results to those above. American protection of Western Europe is an excellent example. The political, economic, and military interdependence of Europe and the United States is great enough to make America's threat highly credible (though perhaps not as credible as we might sometimes wish).

But in the two cases where the defender probably did have this ability (Ethiopia and Austria) he did not employ it. Neither does the defender's political system appear to matter much. The Chinese fought to defend North Korea, but dictatorships did nothing to protect Austria and Guatemala.

Yet bonds of interdependence—economic, political, and military—do turn out to be highly relevant. In every case where the defender went to war he had previously sent military advisers and arms to the pawn. Only four of the eight "bluffs" were marked by either of these activities, and none by a significant level of both. The two Koreas both had important prior political ties to their eventual defenders, but only two of the instances of "bluff" (Rumania and Guatemala) were marked by even very weak ties of previous alliance. The two Korean states also were closely tied economically to their defenders, but of all the seven instances of bluff, only Italy–Austria show a bond of similar strength. Again it is the nature of the defender–pawn relationship, rather than the attributes of either party separately, that seem most telling in the event.

We must be perfectly clear about the nature of these ties. Certainly no one but the most inveterate Marxist would assert that the United States entered the Korean War to protect its investments and economic interests. The United States went to war to protect a state with which it had become closely identified. It was rather heavily involved economically in Korea, and its prestige as a government was deeply involved. It had occupied the territory and restored order after the Japanese collapse; it had installed and supported an at least quasi-democratic government; and it had trained, organized, and equipped the army. Not to defend this country in the face of overt attack would have been highly detrimental to American prestige and to the confidence governments elsewhere had in American support. Even though it had made no promises to defend Korea (and even had said it would not defend it in a general East-West war) the American government could not disengage itself from the fate of the Korean peninsula. Despite the lack of American promises, the American "presence" virtually guaranteed American protection.

MAKING DETERRENCE CREDIBLE

It is now apparent why deterrence does not depend in any simple way merely upon the public declaration of a "solemn oath," nor merely on the physical means to fight a war, either limited or general. A defender's decision whether to pursue a "firm" policy that risks war will depend upon his calculation of the value and probability of various outcomes. If he is to be firm the prospective gains from a successful policy of firmness must be greater, when weighted by the probability of success and discounted by the cost and probability of war, than the losses from retreat.[13] The attacker in turn will determine whether to press his attack in large part on his estimate of the defender's calculation. If he thinks the chances that the defender will fight are substantial he will attack only if the prospective gains from doing so are great.[14]

The physical means of combat available to both sides are far from irrelevant, for upon them depend the positions of each side should war occur. A defender's commitment is unlikely to be believed if his military situation is markedly inferior to his enemy's. Yet even clear superiority provides no guarantee that his antagonist will be dissuaded if the defender appears to have relatively little to lose from "appeasement." At the time of the Austrian crisis Neville Chamberlain could tell himself not only that appeasement was likely to succeed, but that prospective losses even from its possible failure were not overwhelming. In particular, he failed to consider the effects appeasement would have on Britain's other promises to defend small nations. By autumn 1939, however, it was clear that further appeasement would only encourage Hitler to continue to disregard British threats to fight, as British inaction over Austria in fact had done.

Under these circumstances the effectiveness of the defender's threat is heavily dependent on the tangible and intangible bonds between him and the pawn. If other factors are equal, an attacker will regard a military response by the defender as more probable the greater the number of military, political, and economic ties between pawn and defender. No aggressor is likely to measure these bonds, as commercial ties, in just the way we have sketched them here, but he is most unlikely to be insensitive to their existence.

Strengthening these bonds is, in effect, a strategy of raising the credibility of deterrence by increasing the loss one would suffer by not fulfilling a pledge. It illustrates in part why the American promise to defend Western Europe, with nuclear weapons if necessary, is so credible even in the absence of overwhelming American strategic superiority. Western Europe is certainly extremely important because of its large, skilled population

---

[13] Formally, the defender will pursue a firm policy only if, in his calculation:
$$V_f \cdot s + V_w \cdot (1 - s) > V_r$$
where
V_f = the value of successful firmness (deterrence without war)
V_w = the value (usually negative) of the failure of firmness (war)
V_r = the value (usually negative) of retreat
s = the probability that firmness will be successful.
Daniel Ellsberg presents a related formulation (Ellsberg, 1960).

[14] Precisely, he will press the attack only if:
$$V_a \cdot s + V_w \cdot (1 - s) > V_o$$
where
V_a = the value of a successful attack (no war)
V_w = the value (usually negative) of an attack which is countered (war)
V_o = the value of doing nothing in this instance (no attack, no war)
s = the probability of a successful attack.

and industrial capacity. Yet it is particularly important to the United States because of the high degree of political and military integration that has taken place in the North Atlantic Area. The United States, in losing Western Europe to the Communists, would lose population and industry, and the credibility of its pledges elsewhere. To put the case another way, America has vowed to defend both Japan and France from external attack, and there is much that is convincing about both promises. But the latter promise is somewhat more credible than the former, even were one to assume that in terms of industrial capacity, resources, strategic significance, etc., both countries were of equal importance. The real, if not wholly tangible, ties of the United States with France make it so.[15]

Interdependence, of course, provides no guarantee that the defender's threat will be believed. There have been a few cases where an attacker chose to ignore a threat even when relatively close interdependence existed. But if one really does want to protect an area it is very hard to make that intention credible *without* bonds between defender and pawn. If the United States wishes to shield a country it will be wise to "show," and even to increase, its stake in that country's independence. Because the strength of international ties is to some degree controllable, certain policy choices, not immediately relevant to this problem, in fact take on special urgency. Implementation of the Trade Expansion Act, allowing the American government to eliminate tariffs on much of United States trade with Western Europe, will have more than an economic significance. By increasing America's apparent, and actual, economic dependence on Europe it will make more credible America's promise to defend it from attack.

The particular indices of economic, military, and political integration employed here are less important in themselves than as indicators of a broader kind of political and cultural integration, of what K. W. Deutsch refers to as mutual sympathy and loyalties, "we-feeling," trust, and mutual consideration (Deutsch, 1954, pp. 33–64). These bonds of mutual identification both encourage and are encouraged by bonds of communication and attention. Mutual attention in the mass media, exchanges of persons (migrants, tourists, students, etc.), and commercial activities all make a contribution. Mutual contact in some of these areas, such as exchange of persons, tends to promote contacts of other sorts, and often produces mutual sympathies and concern for each other's welfare.[16] This

[15] This point is further illustrated by the 1962 Cuban crisis. The American government took great pains to indicate that it was reacting to the threat of Soviet missiles on the island, and only demanded their removal, not the overthrow of the Castro regime. To have directly threatened the existence of a Communist government in which the Soviets had such a heavy military and economic investment would have carried a much greater risk of Soviet military retaliation.

[16] The theoretical and empirical literature on this point is voluminous and cannot be discussed in more detail here. I have presented elsewhere a general theoretical examination of these problems and their application to Anglo–American relations (Russett, 1963).

process does not work unerringly, but it does work frequently nevertheless. And these mutual sympathies often are essential for the growth of a high level of commercial exchange, especially between economically developed nations rather than nations in an essentially colonial relationship with each other.[17]

In addition to the loss of prestige and of tangible assets, there is yet another way in which a defender may lose if he fails to honor his pledge. New Yorkers would sacrifice their own self-esteem if they failed to defend Californians from external attack; some of the same feeling applies, in lesser degree, to New Yorkers' attitudes toward Britishers. Though broad and intangible, this kind of relationship is nonetheless very real, and knowledge of it sometimes restrains an attacker.

Communication and attention both produce and are produced by, in a mutually reinforcing process, political and cultural integration. The appendix to this paper demonstrates the degree to which economic, military, and political interdependence are correlated. All this raises the "chicken and egg" kind of question as to which comes first. In such a "feedback" situation there is no simple answer; sometimes trade follows the flag, sometimes the flag follows trade (Russett, 1963, ch. 4). Yet these are also to some extent independent, and the correlation is hardly perfect. From the data available one cannot identify any single factor as essential to deterrence. But as more are present the stronger mutual interdependence becomes, and the greater is the attacker's risk in pressing onward.

[17] Few markets are perfectly analogous to the model of perfect competition, as the products of two sellers are seldom identical, at least in the mind of the buyer. Customs, habits, traditions, and "myths" about the goods or the seller differentiate two seemingly identical products. A seller who speaks the language and understands the mores of his customers has a great advantage over one who does not. Past habits can affect current prices through credit terms. Goods coming across a previously established trade route can be shipped more cheaply than those across one which has not yet developed much traffic.

APPENDIX: PRESENCE OR ABSENCE OF VARIOUS FACTORS ALLEGED TO MAKE DETERRENT THREATS CREDIBLE

	Attacker Holds Back						Attacker Presses On — Defender Does Not Fight								Defender Fights		
	Iran	Turkey	Berlin	Egypt	Quemoy–Matsu	Cuba	Ethiopia	Austria	Czechoslovakia (1938)	Albania	Czechoslovakia (1939)	Rumania	Guatemala	Hungary	Polard	South Korea	North Korea
Pawn 20% + of Defender's Population	*						×	×		×	×				×		
Pawn 5% + of Defender's G.N.P.								×	×	×	×				×		
Formal Commitment Prior to Crisis	?	×	?	?			?	×	×	?	×	×			?	×	×
Defender Has Strategic Superiority	×	×	×	×			×	×	×	×	?		?		×		
Defender Has Local Superiority							×	×	?	?						?	?
Defender is Dictatorship				×	×		*							×			×
Pawn–Defender Military Cooperation	×	×	×	×	×	×		×				×	×		×	×	×
Pawn–Defender Political Interdependence	×	×	×	×								×	×			×	×
Pawn–Defender Economic Interdependence	*	×	×	×	×	×	*									×	×

Key: × Factor present
    ? Ambiguous or doubtful
    * Factor present for one defender

REFERENCES

CHURCHILL, WINSTON S.   The Second World War, I, The Gathering Storm. Boston, Mass.: Houghton Mifflin, 1948.
DEUTSCH, KARL W.   Political Community at the International Level. Garden City, N.Y.: Doubleday, 1954.
ELLSBERG, DANIEL.   The Crude Analysis of Strategic Choice, RAND Monograph P-2183. Santa Monica, Calif.: RAND Corporation, 1960.
GINSBURG, NORTON.   Atlas of Economic Development. Chicago: University of Chicago Press, 1962.
KAHN, HERMAN.   On Thermonuclear War. Princeton, N.J.: Princeton University Press, 1960.
KAUFMANN, W. W., (ed.).   Military Policy and National Security. Princeton, N.J.: Princeton University Press, 1956.
KIRK, GEORGE.   The Middle East in the War: Royal Institute of International Affairs Survey of International Affairs, 1939–46. New York: Oxford University Press, 1952.
RUSSETT, BRUCE M.   Community and Contention: Britain and America in the Twentieth Century. Cambridge, Mass.: Massachusetts Institute of Technology Press, 1963.
SCHELLING, THOMAS C.   The Strategy of Conflict. Cambridge, Mass.: Harvard University Press, 1960.
TAYLOR, A. J. P.   The Origins of the Second World War. New York: Atheneum, 1962.
UNITED NATIONS.   Demographic Yearbook, 1948. New York, United Nations, 1949.
———.   Demographic Yearbook, 1961. New York, United Nations, 1962.

3

The Use of Public
Opinion Data

That much needs to be said about the use of public opinion data in international relations research seems doubtful. The value of such materials—as well as their patent limitations—has been widely accepted and the number of users is gradually rising. Furthermore, with the establishment of large data banks maintained by such institutions as the Roper Public Opinion Research Center at Williams College (otherwise known as "Roper") and the Inter-University Consortium for Political Research at the University of Michigan (otherwise known as "the Michigan thing"), massive quantities of public opinion data have been made accessible.[1]

This does not mean of course that all problems in the use of such data have been solved. After formulating a research project, one might find that the polling agencies never really asked the right questions or set of questions at the right time in the right way. Furthermore, the sheer bulkiness of the materials—each survey from Roper characteristically is represented on one to three thousand punch cards—often makes them awkward to use. And computer programs to deal with some of the peculiarities of poll data are yet inadequately dispersed.

Despite the availability of poll data, too often impressionistic specu-

---

[1] See Ralph L. Bisco, "Social Science Data Archives: A Review of Developments," *American Political Science Review*, Vol. 60 (March, 1966), pp. 93–109; Philip E. Converse, "The Availability and Quality of Sample Survey Data in Archives within the United States," in Richard L. Merritt and Stein Rokkan (eds.), *Comparing Nations: The Use of Quantitative Data in Cross-National Research* (New Haven: Yale, 1966), pp. 419–40; Philip K. Hastings, "The Roper Public Opinion Research Center: An International Archive of Social Science Data," *International Social Science Journal*, Vol. 16 (1964), pp. 90–97; and Warren E. Miller and Philip E. Converse, "The Inter-University Consortium for Political Research," *ibid.*, pp. 70–76.

lation is relied upon when poll data could be used to illuminate, if not solve, the problem. For example, much of the urgings for a multilateral force within NATO a few years ago were based on the assumption that there existed in Germany a growing desire for nuclear weapons; polls conducted both among elites and among masses showed that no such desire exists.[2] General de Gaulle, as "everyone knows," has caused an upsurge of anti-Americanism in France; yet poll data from France clearly show increasing favorableness toward the United States from the time de Gaulle took control until 1963 at least.[3] To change attitudes on segregation in the South, we have been told, would take decades; survey data show that a major shift of attitude toward increased toleration of desegregation in the South took place within two or three years.[4] If Hitler were alive today, would the Germans vote for him? Polling agencies have asked them and find, encouragingly, that few declare that they would vote for a man like Hitler, but, discouragingly, that the 80 per cent who assert that they would vote *against* him has not increased over the decade during which the question has been asked.[5]

Public opinion data can be of value in several overlapping areas of interest to students of international relations. One concerns the relationships between basic attitudes about international phenomena and numerous psychological, sociological, ideological, and political variables.[6] The article by Gamson and Modigliani, reprinted below, fits in this general area and is concerned with the interrelationships between belief system, knowledge of international affairs, and policy preference. Their conception of belief systems is applied in a different manner in a study reported in chapter 2.

The bearing of international events on general attitudes is another area in which public opinion data are of relevance. The short Sino-Indian war of 1962 was seen by many at the time to be the death knell of the Communist Party in India; polls conducted at the time gave evidence,

[2] Karl W. Deutsch et. al., *France, Germany and the Western Alliance*, (New York: Scribner's, 1967); USIA, Research and Reference Report, R-100-63, July, 1963, pp. 6 and 9.
[3] Donald J. Puchala (ed.), "Western European Attitudes on International Relations 1952–1961," Yale University, Political Science Research Library, January 1964; USIA, Research and Reference Report, R-98-63, July 1963, p. 11.
[4] *Gallup Political Index* (May, 1966), p. 16; Paul B. Sheatsley, "White Attitudes Toward the Negro," *Daedalus*, Vol. 95 (Winter, 1966), pp. 217–38; Hazel Gaudet Erskine, "The Polls: Race Relations," *Public Opinion Quarterly*, Vol. 26 (Spring, 1962), pp. 137–48.
[5] *Polls*, Vol. 1 (Summer, 1966), p. 27.
[6] For recent analysis and bibliography, see William A. Scott, "Psychological and Social Correlates of International Images," in Herbert C. Kelman (ed.), *International Behavior: A Social–Psychological Analysis* (New York: Holt, 1965), pp. 70–103; Herbert McClosky, "Personality and Attitude Correlates of Foreign Policy Orientation," in James N. Rosenau (ed.), *Domestic Sources of Foreign Policy* (New York: Free Press, 1967), pp. 51–109; and Johan Galtung, "Social Position, Party Identification and Foreign Policy Orientation: A Norwegian Case Study," *ibid.*, pp. 161–93.

however, now seemingly confirmed by election results, that Indian voters saw the invasion essentially as Chinese, not as Communist.[7] While excellent beginnings toward the investigation of the event–opinion linkage have been made,[8] the field remains wide open. The Korean War was one of the most important events of the postwar era; yet, except for tangential references in works basically concerned with other topics, there seems to exist no study on the impact of the war on public attitudes. Events like Suez, Hungary, the Berlin Blockade, and the Cuban missile crisis are often declared to be traumatic, but systematic investigation with the wealth of available public opinion data has been notably rare.

A final area of interest in international relations which might be mentioned concerns investigations of public opinion as an element in the process of foreign policy making.[9] The opinions of the general public are of course only part of the equation, and many attempts have been made to assess, in addition, the views of relevant elites. Divergences found between elite and mass opinion have often been pronounced, the classic example doubtless being Samuel Stouffer's finding in the area of civil liberties that community leaders—including even regents of the Daughters of the American Revolution—are far more tolerant than the general public of dissent within the community.[10] James Rosenau, in the study reprinted here, took advantage of a unique opportunity to survey an elite: in 1958 the Eisenhower administration held a conference in Washington attended by a number of notables who, as a group, approximated as nearly as possible the Power Elite. Rosenau surveyed the elite group, compared it with mass opinion, and is able to generate some notions about consensus and opinion leadership—and to explode others.[11]

Methodological problems with survey data exist, of course, as they do with any data, and there is no dearth of handbooks which examine the virtues and the limitations of the method at considerable length.[12] Only one problem will be discussed here, one basic to the method yet so easily overlooked that it seems continually to be rediscovered even by seasoned practitioners.

[7] Albert H. Cantril, Jr., "The Indian Perception of the Sino-Indian Border Clash," *Public Opinion Quarterly*, Vol. 28 (Summer, 1964), pp. 233–42.
[8] See especially Karl W. Deutsch and Richard L. Merritt, "Effects of Events on National and International Images," in Kelman, *op. cit.*, pp. 130–87.
[9] See Milton J. Rosenberg, "Images in Relation to the Policy Process: American Public Opinion on Cold-War Issues," *ibid.*, pp. 277–334.
[10] *Communism, Conformity, and Civil Liberties* (Garden City, New York: Doubleday, 1955), Chapter 2.
[11] A fuller development of the data is given in Rosenau's *National Leadership and Foreign Policy* (Princeton, N. J.: Princeton University Press, 1963).
[12] Recommended are Claus A. Moser, *Survey Methods in Social Investigation* (New York: Macmillan, 1958); Charles H. Backstrom and Gerald D. Hursh, *Survey Research* (Evanston, Ill.: Northwestern, 1963); and Claire Selltiz et al., *Research Methods in Social Relations* (New York: Holt, 1962).

This is the observation that many people simply don't *have* opinions, that, when they are asked in an interview how they feel about, say, the Peace Corps, it is the first time they have ever thought about the subject. Thus when the questions get too complicated, too remote, or too vague, the response is likely to be capricious. The most hair-raising statistic in this area has been generated by Philip Converse's superb analysis of public reactions to the statement: "The government should leave things like electric power and housing for private businessmen to handle." According to his calculations, fully 81 per cent of the American population either admits it has no opinion on this matter or else responds to it in a manner which can only be described as random.[13]

This matter is especially relevant to the analysis of public opinion data about foreign affairs, for it is perhaps in this area that the analyst may most easily assume his own intense interest in the subject to be shared by the respondent. One sobering statistic bears mentioning. In 1964 a cross-section of the American public was asked "Do you happen to know what kind of government most of China has right now—whether it's democratic, or Communist, or what?" and, if his answer was unclear, the respondent was further asked, "Do you happen to know if there is any Communist government in China now?" Fully 28 per cent admitted that they did not know.[14]

[13] "New Dimensions of Meaning for Cross-Section Sample Surveys in Politics," *International Social Science Journal*, Vol. 16 (1964), p. 26.
[14] A. T. Steele, *The American People and China* (New York: McGraw-Hill, 1966), p. 257. See also John P. Robinson, *Public Information About World Affairs* (Ann Arbor, Mich.: Survey Research Center, 1967).

KNOWLEDGE AND FOREIGN
POLICY OPINIONS: SOME
MODELS FOR CONSIDERATION

William A. Gamson and Andre Modigliani

There is a seldom cited but widely shared and appealing law of public opinion, which can be stated very simply: The more knowledgeable people are, the more likely they are to agree with me. This law would appear to be particularly applicable when one is concerned with public opinion on foreign policy, since these matters of state are far from most people's daily lives and highly complex. Unenlightened thinking will surely be more prevalent among those who have little information and understanding; those who are sophisticated and aware will tend to share the opinions of the prototype of these characteristics, oneself.

THE ENLIGHTENMENT MODEL

Many social scientists are strongly convinced of the inadequacy of military force or the threat of force as a means of influence in international relations. For such people, this "enlightenment" model leads to the expectation that, with increasing knowledge and sophistication, people are more likely to reject belligerent policies. An examination of public opinion data does not immediately disabuse one of this view. In one study, for example, the better-informed people were, the less likely they were to support the statement, "We should never compromise with Russia but just continue to demand what we think is right."[1] In a 1953 poll, 70 per cent of the college-educated favored United Nations atomic energy control, while 61 per cent of the high school–educated and only 52 per cent of the grade school–educated favored such an alternative.[2] Or, in a 1954 poll,

Reprinted by permission from *Public Opinion Quarterly*, Vol. 30 (Summer, 1966), pp. 187–99.
[1] Previously unreported data from Andre Modigliani, "The Public and the Cold War," Cambridge, Harvard University, 1962, unpublished undergraduate honors thesis.
[2] AIPO, May 24, 1953, reported in *Public Opinion Quarterly*, Vol. 27, 1963, p. 167.

only 9 per cent of the college-educated, against 16 per cent of the grade school–educated, felt we should give up trying to reach agreements with Russia on outlawing atomic weapons.[3]

On the other hand, certain results which show that more knowledgeable people are more likely to support a militaristic policy tend to come as a surprise to those who believe in the enlightenment model. Back and Gergen report some examples of such greater willingness to engage in war on the part of the more knowledgeable.[4] Of those who had opinions, 29 per cent who scored low on a measure of political knowledge, and only 9 per cent who scored high, favored decreasing the war effort in Korea. In a 1958 poll, 42 per cent of those who were poorly informed and only 18 per cent of those who were highly informed felt Berlin was not worth fighting over.[5]

THE MAINSTREAM MODEL

Such results give rise to a second explanation, more defensible than the enlightenment model. In this second explanation, education brings with it, not so much better understanding of the world as greater participation in it and attachment to the mainstream. The politically educated are not better analysts of complex situations but are simply more aware of what official U.S. policy is. Being more integrated into their society, and more susceptible to the influence of its institutions, their opinions are more likely to fall within the narrow boundaries of open official discussion. This occurs at the expense of either more conservative *or* more liberal alternatives that are not legitimized by the support of major political officials. The two models are summarized in Chart 1.

CHART 1

SUMMARY OF ENLIGHTENMENT AND MAINSTREAM MODELS

Enlightenment Model

Independent variable: The degree of enlightened understanding of the true and complex nature of foreign affairs. Such enlightenment tends to be a product of education and is reflected in sophisticated knowledge of foreign affairs.

Dependent variable: Willingness to use military force to influence international affairs.

Central hypothesis: The greater the understanding and knowledge of foreign affairs, the less belligerence in one's foreign policy opinions.

[3] AIPO, Apr. 28, 1954, reported in *ibid.*, p. 168.
[4] Kurt W. Back and Kenneth Gergen, "Public Opinion and International Relations," *Social Problems*, Vol. 11, Summer 1963, pp. 77–87, report on Gallup Survey 474, April 1951.
[5] Previously unreported data from Modigliani, *op. cit.* The exact wording of the Berlin item was; "We should try talking to Russia (about Berlin) but avoid fighting no matter what since it's not worth it to get into a war over Berlin."

Mainstream Model

Independent variable: The boundaries and clarity of official government foreign policy.

Intervening variable: One's attachment to the mainstream and the resultant exposure to influences such as the mass media. Such attachment and exposure are highly related to education and are reflected in factual information about foreign affairs and knowledge of the nature of, and rationale for, official policies.

Dependent variable: The degree of conformity of one's foreign policy opinions to official government policy.

Central hypothesis: The greater the attachment to the mainstream, the greater the degree of conformity of one's foreign policy opinions to official policy.

Note that both of the above explanations of the effect of knowledge are *consensus* theories, i.e. they predict that increasing knowledge will move all groups toward the same point. Either because they gain better understanding (the enlightenment model) or because they are more subject to social influence (the mainstream model), people are similarly affected by increased knowledge. In these theories, there is a single pole toward which knowledge impels people regardless of their starting point.

The above issue is vital, because we intend to present some data that appear to support the mainstream argument. However, on closer analysis they reveal a contradictory result—a polarization of opinion with increased knowledge. The data are drawn from a probability sample of 558 residents of the Detroit Metropolitan Area and are part of the Detroit Area Study data for 1963–64.[6] The questionnaire included a sixteen-item measure of knowledge of foreign relations. The questions were straightforward and factual but required considerable knowledge. Respondents were asked to state which among the following countries are located in Africa: Ecuador, Ghana, Afghanistan, Mongolia, and Morocco; which among West Germany, Algeria, France, Japan, England, and Russia have developed and tested their own atomic weapons; and which among Egypt, Poland, Spain, Mainland China, and India have Communist governments. They were scored for number right minus number wrong on the sixteen items and are here divided into high, medium, and low knowledge groups.

Respondents were also asked a number of items on particular policies toward the United Nations, trade with Communist countries, disarmament, and so forth. We have singled out for consideration here those with particular relevance for the mainstream theory. They are items in which respondents are asked to choose one among three alternative policies, one

[6] We are indebted to John C. Scott, Director of the Detroit Area Study, and Robert Hefner and Sheldon Levy, principal investigators for the 1963–1964 study, for allowing us to include several of our items in the questionnaire and making the data freely available to us.

of which had official government sanction at the time the survey was conducted.

According to the mainstream argument, we should expect that, with increasing knowledge, individuals will tend to reject both of the alternatives that are not officially endorsed and accept the one that is. With this in mind, we can examine the data in Table 1. On all three policy items, there is a pronounced increase in the percentage picking the official "mainstream," or middle, alternative as knowledge increases. This is at the expense of *both* more liberal and more conservative alternatives on China and on trade. However, on the question of military strength there seems to be some shift from right to left, as one might expect from the enlightenment theory.

The most striking feature of Table 1, though, is still the dramatic and consistent increase in support for government policy with increased knowledge. One might argue that, where there has been no policy shift, as in our policy toward China, increased knowledge will bring equal defections from both poles; where policy has recently shifted (as it did with trade with the Soviet Union and to some degree with the arms race), increased knowledge will exert its *dominant* pull on those who advocate the old official policy. By this reasoning, those low in knowledge are, because of their diminished contact with mainstream influences, more likely to lag behind in policy shifts. In this instance, the shift represents a liberalization. This would suggest that, where administration policy shifts to the right, the move to the official alternative that accompanies increased knowledge will be greatest among those who favor the more liberal rather than the more conservative alternative. While we cannot test this hypothesis here, Table 1 does seem to offer some encouragement.

THE COGNITIVE CONSISTENCY MODEL

However, we must consider still another theory relating knowledge of foreign affairs to policy opinions, the cognitive consistency model. This final model contrasts with earlier consensus models in its implication that increasing knowledge will change people in *different* directions leading to a greater polarization of opinion among the more knowledgeable. This model argues that endorsement of a specific policy position stems from more general attitudes and assumptions that are being applied to a specific case. Knowledge of foreign affairs is important not because it reflects enlightenment or exposure to mainstream influences but because it reflects conceptual sophistication. Such sophistication reflects the ability to integrate specific policies with more general attitudes and assumptions one holds.

Clearly, the cognitive consistency model implies a polarization of

Table 1

RELATION OF FOREIGN AFFAIRS KNOWLEDGE TO SELECTED POLICIES (*in per cent*)

Policy	Knowledge		
	Low	Medium	High
China:[a]			
The United States should withdraw some of its support of the UN if other nations admit Communist China	24	16	12
The United States should oppose letting Communist China into the UN but should continue to support the UN if other nations admit Communist China	46	60	66
The United States should not oppose letting Communist China into the UN	30	24	22
	100	100	100
(N)	(152)	(202)	(159)
$\chi^2 = 13.9, p < .05$			
Trade:[b]			
The United States should not sell anything to Russia	29	16	14
The United States should only sell surplus food to Russia	33	45	50
The United States should be willing to sell anything except military weapons to Russia	38	39	35
	100	100	100
(N)	(159)	(203)	(161)
$\chi^2 = 19.9, p < .05$			
Military strength:[c]			
Should be built up	40	28	17
About right	55	65	70
Should be cut back	5	7	13
	100	100	100
(N)	(153)	(198)	(151)
$\chi^2 = 22.8, p < .05$			

[a]The question read: "Which do you think would be the best United States policy toward admitting Red China to the UN?"

[b]The question read: "Some discussion concerning trade with Russia has been in the news recently. Which of these positions is closest to what you think about the matter?"

[c]The question read: "There are a number of different opinions about how much military strength the U.S. should have. How do you feel? Do you think that the present military strength of the U.S. should be cut back, built up, or is it about right?"

opinion among the more knowledgeable. Poorly informed individuals, even with different ideological orientations, will have difficulty relating their orientation to specific policies. The result is a good deal of randomness and inconsistency in the choices of such individuals and no clear differentiation among those members with different predispositions. However, among the sophisticated, those with different predispositions will rally around different specific policies, creating sharper differentiation among those with different ideological orientations. This model is summarized in Chart 2.

CHART 2

SUMMARY OF THE COGNITIVE CONSISTENCY MODEL

Independent variable: One's general political orientation, ideology, and beliefs. For example, assumptions about the nature of the Soviet Union and the nature of the Cold War.

Intervening variable: One's conceptual sophistication and the ability to integrate general attitudes and assumptions with specific policy opinions. Such sophistication is likely to be a product of education and will be reflected in knowledge of foreign affairs.

Dependent variable: The degree of relationship between one's specific foreign policy opinions and one's general attitudes and assumptions.

Central hypothesis: The greater the conceptual sophistication, the greater the relationship between general assumptions and specific policy opinions.

To explore the cognitive consistency model, we need some measure of general attitudes and assumptions; since we are considering policies relevant to the Cold War, attitudes and assumptions about the Soviet Union seem appropriate. In a separate study, the authors have been attempting to evaluate three coherent sets of assumptions or "belief systems" about the Soviet Union by examining, through an analysis of historical data, the predictions they imply about Soviet–Western interaction. The assumptions these belief systems make about long-range Soviet goals, Soviet risk-taking behavior, and the Soviet view of the West have been outlined elsewhere.[7] Using this earlier formulation as a guideline, we wrote three items to assess each respondent's assumptions about these aspects of the Soviet Union.

[7] See William A. Gamson, "Evaluating Beliefs about International Conflict," in Roger Fisher, ed., *International Conflict and Behavioral Science*, New York, Basic Books, 1964, pp. 27–40; William A. Gamson and Andre Modigliani, "Tensions and Concessions: The Empirical Confirmation of Beliefs about Soviet Behavior," *Social Problems*, Vol. 11, 1963, pp. 34–48 and William A. Gamson and Andre Modigliani, "The Carrot and/or the Stick: Soviet Responses to Western Foreign Policy, 1946–1953." Center for Research on Conflict Resolution, Carnegie Project No. 4, Working Document 10, paper presented at meetings of International Peace Research Society, Chicago, November 1964, mimeographed.

Each respondent was classified into one of three belief systems, which we shall refer to as Positions A, B, and C. Briefly, Position A states that the Soviet Union is actively pursuing the goal of world domination and is willing to incur high risks to achieve this goal. It views Western resistance as so sporadic that the Soviet Union can achieve its goals through continual pressure short of war. Position B states that the Soviet Union is actively interested in achieving a *limited* expansion of influence and is willing to incur only moderate risks in the achievement of its goals. It views the West as both susceptible to limited encroachments and as attempting such encroachments on the Soviet Union—much like an opponent in a game. Position C states that the Soviet Union is actively interested only in holding on to what it has and is unwilling to incur risks except in self-defense. The West is viewed as actively seeking to undermine Soviet influence and control in the world.

Each respondent was asked to make a first and second choice among the following sets of statements:

I. *On Soviet goals:* Many people are concerned about what the Russian government is really trying to do. Which of these do you think is closest to what their aims really are?

    a. When all is said and done, Russia is determined to conquer the United States. (Position A)

    b. Russia is trying to get the most it can from the United States but it isn't really trying to conquer us. (Position B)

    c. Russia is more interested in increasing its own security and standard of living than it is in getting the most it can from the United States. (Position C)

II. *On Soviet risk-taking behavior:* How willing do you think the Russians are to take chances to get what they want?

    a. Russia is cautious and will try to avoid starting any trouble which could lead to a serious crisis. (Position C)

    b. Russia is even willing to risk starting a serious crisis in order to get what it wants. (Position A)

    c. Russia is willing to stir up quite a bit of trouble to get what it wants, but it will try to avoid causing any really serious crisis. (Position B)

III. *On Soviet view of the West:* Which of these best describes what the Russians believe about the United States—even if they are wrong in what they believe:

    a. Russia almost always seems to believe that they can take advantage of us and get away with it. (Position A)

    b. Russia almost always seems to be afraid that we are trying to take advantage of them. (Position C)

    c. Russia seems to believe both that they can take advantage of us and that we try to take advantage of them. (Position B)

Table 2

BELIEF SYSTEMS BY SELECTED POLICIES
(*in per cent*)

Policy	Belief System		
	A	B	C
China:[a]			
Withdraw from the UN if China enters	24	16	16
Oppose entry but don't withdraw from the UN	56	62	48
Do not oppose Chinese entry to the UN	20	22	36
	100	100	100
(N)	(114)	(293)	(107)
$\chi^2 = 13.1, p < .05, C = .19$			
Trade:[a]			
Trade nothing with Russia	32	17	11
Trade surplus food only	39	47	36
Trade anything but weapons	29	36	54
	100	100	100
(N)	(117)	(297)	(109)
$\chi^2 = 20.5, p < .05, C = .24$			
Military strength:[a]			
Should be built up more	38	29	17
About right	57	64	70
Should be cut back	5	7	13
	100	100	100
(N)	(111)	(287)	(105)
$\chi^2 = 14.5, p < .05, C = .21$			

[a]See Table 1 for the exact wording of the items and alternative answers.

We neither expected nor found a consistency across items that matched our ideal or a priori statement of the three belief systems. However, there was sufficient relationship among answers to the three items to identify each respondent with the belief system he most nearly approximated.

It is a central premise of the cognitive consistency model that specific policy opinions flow from more general attitudes and assumptions. If this is correct, then we should expect some relation between assumptions about the Soviet Union and the sort of policy items included in Table 1. Table 2 indicates that the expected relationship exists.

On policy toward China, Position A people are the most likely of the three groups to be for withdrawing from the UN; Position B people to oppose Chinese entry but not withdraw; and Position C people not to oppose Chinese entry into the UN. The other two items show a similar pattern. However, the degree of relationship is quite small. Using as a measure of degree the contingency coefficient, corrected so that it has an upper limit of 1, the three items show C's of only .19, .24, and .21 respectively.

The slimness of the relation between belief system and specific policy opinion is easily accounted for by the cognitive consistency model. Such a relationship, it suggests, will be pronounced only among respondents high in conceptual sophistication and knowledge. Those low in knowledge will be unable to relate their general assumptions to the specific situation in a consistent manner. By controlling for knowledge of foreign affairs in Table 3, we see that the predicted pattern emerges. The relationship between belief system and policy for those high in knowledge has coefficients of .46, .51, and .31 as against coefficients of .14, .19, and .14 for those low in knowledge. Clearly, belief systems are connected with policy opinions primarily for the knowledgeable.

One of the striking implications of the cognitive consistency model is that increases in knowledge should have a polarizing effect on the opinions of a set of persons. Knowledge has the effect of allowing one to understand more clearly the policy most consistent with his predispositions. This means that subsets of persons who share different belief systems will tend to deviate from one another with increases in knowledge, each moving toward the policy most consistent with its underlying assumptions. Thus, Position A advocates, with more knowledge, will be more sharply in favor of withdrawing from the UN, trading nothing with Russia, and building up arms. Position C people will move in exactly the opposite direction, becoming *less* favorable on all these alternatives, while Position B people will show larger percentages for the official government policy on all these items.

Note how such an interpretation is possible in the results of Table 1. If Position A and Position C people are moving [8] in opposite and offsetting directions and Position B people are moving toward the center from the more extreme alternatives, then the over-all effect will be an increase in the support for the official policy. Combining advocates of all three positions may conceal the fact that knowledge has a different relationship for those with different images of the Soviet Union.

[8] We ask the reader's indulgence in the use of such process language to describe differences among individuals with different knowledge. Our data, of course, show nothing about process, but since the models we are contrasting are talking about the effects of knowledge on opinion formation, it is stultifying to make use of elaborate circumlocutions whenever we discuss interpretations of this data. We hope that this general reminder will be sufficient to allow us the convenience of such language in interpreting static results.

Table 3

BELIEF SYSTEMS BY SELECTED POLICIES, CONTROLLING FOR KNOWLEDGE

(*in per cent*)

| | Knowledge/Belief System | | | | | | | | |
| | Low | | | Medium | | | High | | |
Policy	A	B	C	A	B	C	A	B	C
China:[a]									
Withdraw	25	22	32	16	17	15	28	8	3
Oppose	45	50	35	58	63	51	67	71	54
Do not oppose	30	28	32	26	20	33	5	21	43
	100	100	100	100	100	100	100	100	100
(N)	(44)	(78)	(31)	(31)	(132)	(39)	(39)	(83)	(37)
		C = .14			C = .15			C = .46	
Trade:[a]									
Nothing	34	29	18	28	14	13	31	12	3
Surplus food	33	34	30	34	46	46	51	60	30
Anything	33	37	52	38	39	41	18	28	67
	100	100	100	100	100	100	100	100	100
(N)	(46)	(80)	(33)	(32)	(132)	(39)	(39)	(85)	(37)
		C = .19			C = .18			C = .51	
Military strength:[a]									
Build up	48	38	36	36	31	10	27	16	8
About right	48	57	61	61	61	80	65	75	66
Cut back	4	5	3	4	8	10	8	9	26
	100	100	100	100	100	100	100	100	100
(N)	(46)	(77)	(31)	(28)	(131)	(39)	(37)	(79)	(35)
		C = .14			C = .24			C = .31	

[a]See Table 1 for the exact wording of the items and alternative answers.

Table 4 (which is simply a rearrangement of Table 3, controlling for belief systems) shows the polarizing effect we have been discussing.[9] While the pattern is least clear with Position A people, by and large increases in knowledge tend to increase agreement with the policy that Table 2 showed to be associated with the belief system in question. Thus, Position A people are less likely to favor admitting China to the United Nations as knowledge increases, while Position C people are more likely to favor this alternative as knowledge increases. Similarly, on the question of trade with Russia, increasing knowledge moves Position A people away from freer trade, Position C people toward more liberal trade, and Position B people away from the extremes of trading nothing or anything.

CONCLUSION

The over-all pattern of results in Table 4 is not without its aberrations. We are inclined to feel that they are best illuminated by a combination of the mainstream and cognitive consistency models. We would suggest that two primary forces are operating, both of which tend to correlate with education and knowledge. On the one hand, *there is a strain toward attitudinal consistency that increases with knowledge;* this produces a higher relationship between belief system and policy among the more knowledgeable and an increasing polarization around different policy alternatives for those who start with different premises. At the same time, *there is greater attachment to society and susceptibility to social influences*—a force that produces support for official government policies.

If we can interpret our measure of knowledge as reflecting both these forces, then some of the aberrations in Table 4 make sense. Let us consider the question concerning policy toward UN admittance of China. Among advocates of Position A, the strain toward consistency would impel them toward the extreme right,[10] or "withdrawal from the UN," position with increased knowledge, while the strain toward conformity would impel them

---

[9] Our belief systems show only the slightest relationship to our measure of knowledge of foreign relations. Advocates of Position C are equally represented in all three knowledge groups; however, Position A people are slightly overrepresented at the expense of Position B people in the highest and in the lowest knowledge groups. The over-all relationship, however, is so slight and irregular that we will treat the two measures as independent.

[10] Our use of the terms "extreme right" and "extreme left" does not represent any judgment on our part about the true place of such alternatives in the political spectrum. We do not wish to imply, for example, that agreement with the proposition, "The United States should not oppose letting Communist China into the UN," reflects any kind of extremist position as that term is sometimes used; this opinion clearly may be held by moderates. We use the term "extreme left" *only* to refer to its position in the set of three alternatives offered. In fact, we attempted to word the items so that none of the policy alternatives would appear extreme in the absolute sense—that is, we wished to ensure some variance in our respondents' choices.

Table 4

KNOWLEDGE BY SELECTED POLICIES, CONTROLLING FOR BELIEF SYSTEMS
(*in per cent*)

Belief System/Knowledge

Policy	A			B			C		
	Low	Med.	High	Low	Med.	High	Low	Med.	High
China:[a]									
Withdraw	25	16	28	22	17	8	32	15	3
Oppose	45	58	67	50	63	71	35	51	54
Do not oppose	30	26	5	28	20	21	32	33	43
	100	100	100	100	100	100	100	100	100
(N)	(44)	(31)	(39)	(78)	(132)	(83)	(31)	(39)	(37)
		C = .34			C = .22			C = .38	
Trade:[a]									
Nothing	34	28	31	29	14	12	18	13	3
Surplus food	33	34	51	34	46	60	30	46	30
Anything	33	38	18	37	39	28	52	41	67
	100	100	100	100	100	100	100	100	100
(N)	(46)	(32)	(39)	(80)	(132)	(85)	(33)	(39)	(37)
		C = .25			C = .28			C = .33	
Military strength:[a]									
Build up	48	36	27	38	31	16	36	10	9
About right	48	61	65	57	61	75	61	80	66
Cut back	4	4	8	5	8	9	3	10	26
	100	100	100	100	100	100	100	100	100
(N)	(46)	(28)	(37)	(77)	(131)	(79)	(31)	(39)	(35)
		C = .24			C = .22			C = .45	

[a]See Table 1 for the exact wording of the items and alternative answers.

toward the middle, or "opposition without withdrawal," position. Hence, with increasing knowledge there are two forces pushing Position A advocates away from the left, or "acceptance of China," position, but only one force pushing them into the extreme right position. The data, in fact, show that defection from the left position is much more pronounced than increased endorsement of the right position (see Table 4, China question, under Position A: endorsement of the "withdrawal" position increases only from 25 to 28 per cent, while endorsement of the "do not oppose" position drops from 30 to 5 per cent).

Conversely, for advocates of Position C we have two forces pushing them away from the extreme right position and only one pushing them into the extreme left position. Again the data show that increased knowledge brings greater defection from the right position than increased endorsement of the left position (see Table 4, China question, under Position C: endorsement of the "do not oppose" position increases only from 32 to 43 per cent, while endorsement of the "withdrawal" position drops from 32 to 3 per cent).

For Position B advocates *both* forces act to push them out of the extreme right *and* left positions and into the middle, and the data show defections from both extremes with increasing knowledge (see Table 4, China question, under Position B: endorsement of the "do not oppose" position decreases from 28 to 21 per cent, and endorsement of the "withdrawal" position also decreases from 22 to 8 per cent).

As a final complication, we would suggest that in cases where government policy has recently shifted, the pure direction of such a shift may be an important variable. Specifically, a shift to the left in government policy (as had recently occurred on trade with the Soviet Union and perhaps on arms build-up) may act as added reinforcement for leftward shifts, and deterrent to rightward shifts. And, indeed, on these two policy questions the data show that increased knowledge brings a much greater increase for the left alternative among Position C advocates than increase for the right alternative among Position A advocates.

We cannot disentagle the contribution of these hypothesized forces in our own results. But with a careful selection of policy questions and with independent measures of conceptual sophistication and conformity to official doctrine, it should be possible to parcel out the effects of each.

CONSENSUS-BUILDING IN THE AMERICAN
NATIONAL COMMUNITY: SOME HYPOTHESES
AND SOME SUPPORTING DATA *

James N. Rosenau

A large "if," followed by an even larger "of course," pervades discussion of the problems which confront the United States. Whatever the problem, whether it be one of expanding foreign assistance programs or of contracting tariff and trade barriers, the feasibility of various solutions invariably turns on the question of the readiness of the public to make the necessary sacrifices. *If* the American people are willing, and *if* their support can be mobilized—these are the great qualifiers which dominate discussions of the American future. And, whenever they are introduced, it is standard procedure to assert that *of course* the people are willing and *of course* they can be mobilized.

One can hardly deny the importance of the qualifiers. The public's potential for sacrifice is relevant in a number of ways, ranging from group actions supporting national policy to personal acts implementing it, from organized pressure endorsing higher taxes to individual integrity in paying them. On the other hand, there is something plaintive and unreal about the confident assertion that the public is responsive. For the fact is that the foreign aid program has never enjoyed wide support, that tariff reduction efforts have foundered on the rocks of self-interested publics,† and that a similar fate has befallen most proposals designed to extend our cold war involvement. Only in military and defense matters have enlarged responsibilities been shouldered, and even here new commitments have not been accepted with alacrity or celerity. In short, ever since the early months of

Reprinted by permission from *The Journal of Politics*, Vol. 24 (November, 1962), pp. 639–61.
* This essay is a revised version of a paper presented at the Annual Meeting of the American Political Science Association, St. Louis, Missouri, September 1961.
† Obviously this comment cannot be applied to the 1962 Trade Expansion Act, which was approved by Congress 15 months after this paper was written. However, while the new tariff legislation undermines this interpretation of the past, it is consistent with the prediction that concludes this paper.

the Korean war a substantial gap has existed between the policies which have emerged from the policy-making process and those which seem necessary to contest an aggressive and skillful enemy.[1]

Efforts to account for this gap have followed along several lines of inquiry. One, what might be called the "societal decay" hypothesis, denies the premise that the public is capable of sacrifice. Instead a parallel is discerned between the United States of today and the Roman Empire of fifteen centuries ago: both societies are posited as having selfishly succumbed to the temptations of wealth, unaware of external dangers and unconcerned about internal decay.[2]

But castigating the public is deceptively easy. It focuses attention on the results rather than the sources of social change. To posit national deterioration is to overlook the complexity of the processes whereby the values and aspirations of the society are translated into public policy. To see the nation's potential for sacrifice dwindling down to zero is either to ignore the function of leadership or to assume that the nation's leaders have acquiesced to the process of decay—and there is no evidence that the voices criticizing American values and practices have been silent. If the role of leaders is fully recognized, it becomes readily apparent that the attitudes and capacities of the citizenry are largely shaped by elite opinion. Presumably, then, a united and vigorous leadership could foster a readiness to sacrifice and a diminution of complacency. Conceivably, to be sure, the sacrifice potential of the nation is so low that even an active and dedicated leadership could not overcome the inertia and the preference for, as Barbara Ward puts it, "easy choices, surface excitements, and the temporary stimulus of pleasure." [3] However, given present knowledge about the dynamics of social change (and being not unmindful of the American response to World War II), it is more plausible to assume that a potential for sacrifice does exist and that therefore the main problem is one of mobilization—of first nourishing and then tapping and channeling the energies and aspirations of a contented but not obdurate people.

Recognition of the leadership function underlies a second explanation of the gap between the external threat and the internal response. This

[1] A spate of books and articles have recently called attention to the existence of this gap. See, for example, the Hearings before the Subcommittee of National Policy Machinery of the Committee on Government Operations, U.S. Senate, 86th Congress, *Organizing for National Security* (Washington: Government Printing Office, 1960), Parts I and VII; Meg Greenfield, "The Great American Morality Play," *The Reporter*, June 8, 1961, pp. 13–18; Robert L. Heilbroner, *The Future as History* (New York: Harper & Brothers, 1960); Emmett John Hughes, *America the Vincible* (Garden City: Doubleday & Company, 1959); Karl E. Meyer, *The New America: Politics and Society in the Age of the Smooth Deal* (New York: Basic Books, 1961).
[2] An eloquent presentation of the Roman Empire analogy will be found in J. William Fulbright, "Challenge to Our Complacency," *New York Times Magazine*, September 14, 1958.
[3] Barbara Ward, "The Challenge of the Sixties," *New York Times Magazine*, December 27, 1959, p. 5.

might be designated the "presidential leadership" hypothesis, and it is one which has enjoyed great vogue in recent years. Stated briefly, this school of thought accepts the premise that the public is capable of sacrifice, but asserts that only strenuous efforts by a strong occupant of the White House can unleash and harness the energies of the people. A concise assertion of this hypothesis has been provided by Walter Lippmann, who recently observed that

> This is a most peculiarly Presidential country. The tone and example set by the President have a tremendous effect on the quality of life in America. The President is like the conductor of a big symphony orchestra—and a new conductor can often get different results with the same score and the same musicians.[4]

But reliance on the President is also deceptively easy. If the societal decay hypothesis ignores the leadership function, then the presidential leadership hypothesis oversimplifies it. Such reasoning tends to posit social change as stemming from a single cause and, in so doing, it also fails to account for the complex processes whereby public policies come to reflect public aspirations. Surely this must be why, for example, the foreign aid program has foundered despite emphatic support by post-war presidents.[5] Presidential leadership is not, in other words, the only independent variable. It may be, and doubtless is, necessary to the mobilization of the nation's sacrifice potential, but it is not a sufficient condition of social change along these lines. Obviously the public cannot be mobilized if, say, members of Congress or leaders of the business community and the labor movement resist presidential blandishments. The various segments of the public can be as responsive to their respective leaders as to the occupant of the White House, so that presidential leadership requires a followership which is both more complex and more structured than the amorphous entity called the "American people." To extend Lippmann's analogy, orchestras are not automatically melodious in response to waves of a conductor's baton. Their members must be willing to play together and must interpret movements of the baton in the same way if harmonious music rather than incoherent noise is to fill the concert hall.

A more sophisticated conception of the role of leadership, one which might be called the "consensus-building" hypothesis,[6] constitutes still a third approach to the problem of mobilizing the public. This posits a

---

[4] William Attwood, "A Visit With Walter Lippmann," *Look*, April, 25, 1961, p. 105.
[5] While Eisenhower had a more passive view of the presidency than either his predecessor or his successor, he was consistently energetic on behalf of the foreign aid program.
[6] The relevance of consensus-building as a variable in national policy-making processes is cogently analyzed in Roger Hilsman, "The Foreign-Policy Consensus: An Interim Research Report," *The Journal of Conflict Resolution*, Vol. III (December 1959), pp. 361–82.

structure of national leadership which can serve as a link between public policies and public opinion. Just as leaders from all walks of a local community's life initiate and sustain its policies, so are diverse groups of national leaders—those whose opinions are regularly transmitted across state boundaries to unknown persons [7]—assumed to perform similar functions for the continental community. The policies of the federal government are viewed as resulting mainly from the actions which national leaders take on the basis of assessments of what is needed both to cope with the course of events and to satisfy the aspirations of the public segment from which they derive their leadership. In making these assessments national leaders, or national opinion-makers as they shall henceforth be designated,[8] can be oriented to serve their particular segment of the public or they can take a larger view of their roles and conceive of themselves as also having continental responsibilities. The content of any policy adopted at the national level is thus significantly shaped by the extent to which continental or segmental orientations prevail within the leadership structure.

By the *structure* of leadership is meant a differentiation between opinion-makers who are active at the national and local levels. Even though dissension and disunity may characterize national opinion-makers, their ranks are regarded as structured in the sense that their activities overlap and do so apart from those whose scope of leadership is limited to a city or a state. Thus, for example, the structure of national leadership encompasses top officials of the executive branch, members of Congress, prominent corporation executives, officers of large labor unions, education and religious leaders, publishers and commentators, high-ranking military officers, and leaders of the many voluntary associations which are organized on a national scale. Stated differently, national opinion-makers are the members of Mr. Lippmann's orchestra, while the rest of the citizenry is the audience hearing the concert.

The consensus-building hypothesis derives directly from this conception of a national leadership structure. For it follows that mobilization of the nation's sacrifice potential is a function of the extent to which a consensus on the need for sacrifice can be fashioned among the diverse groups which comprise the national opinion-making public. If these various types of leaders possess, presently or potentially, a common evaluative and perceptual framework, and if they are therefore capable of similar responses to external threats (as magnified and dramatized through presidential leadership), then presumably the energies of the entire citizenry can be tapped and channeled in a manner commensurate with the requirements of a

[7] An elaborate breakdown and analysis of this definition, as well as distinctions between sixteen basic types of opinion-makers, will be found in my *Public Opinion and Foreign Policy: An Operational Formulation* (New York: Random House, 1961), Chap. 5.
[8] A full discussion of why this designation seems preferable to "elites," "opinion leaders," and other common terms in the leadership lexicon is provided in *ibid.*, pp. 42–5.

prolonged cold war. In short (and to paraphrase Gabriel Almond), "Who mobilizes the opinion-makers, mobilizes the public." [9]

I

Two versions of the consensus-building hypothesis have come to be held by students of the policy-making process. One version asserts that the structure of national leadership militates against the fashioning of meaningful consensuses within the opinion-making public. Functional autonomy and ideological heterogeneity are considered to be major structural characteristics of the opinion-making public which prohibit, or at least greatly restrict, the formation of nationwide consensuses. Even a vigorous occupant of the White House is hypothesized to be incapable of coordinating diverse leadership segments which ordinarily function independently of each other and which "differ significantly among themselves with regard to both the means and ends of policy." [10] Members of the opinion-making public, in other words, are regarded as constituting a community in only the loosest sense of the term. Their orientations are segmental and not continental. They lack common values and a common framework for perceiving and interpreting events and trends abroad. Hence they cannot be expected to respond similarly, much less uniformly, to the same stimuli.[11]

In contrast to this conception of a heterogeneous opinion-making public is a version of the consensus-building hypothesis which asserts that the national leadership structure is changing as the nation becomes increasingly complex and its parts increasingly interdependent. It is reasoned that leadership groups are therefore less and less able to function autonomously and that, indeed, they are compelled to interact frequently. This recurring interaction is hypothesized to foster understanding and the integration of perspectives, thereby dissipating the value differences which have divided the opinion-making public into so many diverse segments. In turn, these changes are presumed to encourage a sense of shared responsibility and a readiness to shoulder the burdens of cold war leadership. As a result of continuous contact and common experiences, in other words, the opinion-making public is regarded as acquiring an integrated structure and the dynamics of a thriving community. Thus it is assumed that leaders at the national level will respond similarly to external threats and, given an energetic and persuasive President, that they are capable of being coordinated and mobilized.[12]

[9] Gabriel A. Almond, *The American People and Foreign Policy* (New York: Harcourt, Brace and Co., 1950), p. 138.
[10] *Ibid.*, p. 144.
[11] For statements of this version of the consensus-building hypothesis see *ibid.*, pp. 143-44, and John W. Gardner, *Excellence* (New York: Harper & Brothers, 1961), pp. 123-26.
[12] Reasoning along this line is clearly presented in W. W. Rostow, *The United States in the World Arena* (New York: Harper & Brothers, 1960), pp. 513-14.

Obviously one of these versions of the consensus-building hypothesis must be incorrect. But which one? Do national opinion-makers have common values or do they not? Do they come from similar backgrounds and have similar sources of information, or do they lack the bases of a common frame of reference? Do they respond in similar way to shared experiences or do they not? Is it, in short, possible to fashion a consensus among diverse national leaders and, if it is, will widespread agreement at this level produce corresponding public policies? An attempt to shed empirical light on these questions occupies the remainder of this essay.[13]

II

Convinced that the foreign aid program would meet more Congressional resistance than ever in the recession year of 1958, the Eisenhower administration sought to build public support by exposing a gathering of national leaders to a series of bipartisan speeches extolling the merits of the program and explaining its operations. An enthusiastic and informed group of national leaders were expected to precipitate a flow of opinion favorable to foreign aid that would eventually reach the halls of Congress and diminish hostility to the program. This reasoning culminated in a gathering called the "Conference on Foreign Aspects of U.S. National Security." The proceedings included ten speeches and two panels, and they were held at the Hotel Statler in Washington, D.C., on February 25, 1958, from nine-thirty in the morning until ten o'clock in the evening. The conferees, about 1,400, were selected by a staff in the White House and the invitations to attend the Conference were issued on White House stationery in the name of the President of the United States. Included among the conferees were about 250 leading corporation executives, 100 college and university presidents, 20 high-ranking labor leaders, 25 distinguished entertainers, scientists, and sports stars, 400 officers of large voluntary associations, 10 admirals and generals, 100 publishers and journalists, 135 members of Congress, and 75 top officials of the executive branch—in short, a sample of national leaders drawn from all walks of life. Among the Conference speakers were President Dwight D. Eisenhower and his predecessor, Harry S. Truman, Vice President Richard M. Nixon and defeated presidential candidate Adlai E. Stevenson, Secretary of State John Foster Dulles and his predecessor, Dean G. Acheson, Secretary of Defense Neil H. McElroy, C.I.A. Director Allen W. Dulles, presidential science advisor James R. Killian, Jr., and several State Department specialists in the foreign

[13] The author is indebted to the Center of International Studies of Princeton University for its support of the project which yielded the data presented herein and which is scheduled for publication by the Princeton University Press in 1963 under the title of *National Leadership and Foreign Policy: A Case Study in the Mobilization of Public Support*.

aid program. Both the Republican and Democratic speakers endorsed the foreign aid program in urgent and unqualified terms.[14]

Exactly three months after the Conference, 1,067 of the conferees [15] were mailed an 8-page, 71-item questionnaire soliciting information about their social backgrounds, their reactions to the Conference, and their subsequent behavior with respect to foreign aid. Of these, 61 per cent responded,[16] and what follows is a summary of those aspects of the data yielded by the 647 returned questionnaires which pertain to the consensus-building hypothesis.[17]

III

While there is insufficient evidence to claim that the conferees were a representative sample of the opinion-making public,[18] it is clear from the data that they were drawn primarily from the ranks of leaders active on the national level. This conclusion is manifest in the responses to a series of multiple-choice questionnaire items that inquired into the extent of the conferees' access to various channels of communication: two-thirds of the conferees estimated that they could "reach" about ten thousand persons if they "wanted to disseminate a new idea" and one-fifth cited a potential audience of at least one million; two-thirds reported that they participated in "the deliberations of organizations which take stands on public issues;" three-fifths indicated they had "some voice in determining the contents of a publication;" three-fifths said that every month they received at least one request to give "a lecture or talk on any subject" and more than one-third said their requests averaged at least five a month; three-fifths said they appeared on at least one television or radio program a year and nearly two-fifths cited a frequency of at least four annual appearances; one-half said they were "responsible for the writing and distribution

---

[14] The speeches and proceedings of the Conference, as well as a listing of the names and affiliations of all the conferees and speakers, are reproduced in *Foreign Aspects of U.S. National Security: Conference Report and Proceedings* (Washington: Committee for International Economic Growth, 1958), pp. 1–120.

[15] That is, all those in attendance other than Congressmen and officials of the Eisenhower administration.

[16] Not only did a remarkably high proportion respond (a return rate of 20 per cent is generally considered a good return rate for a mailed 2-page questionnaire), but they did so diligently and discriminately. Four-fifths of the respondents, for example, appended written comments to questions calling for the checking off of provided alternatives. One-eighth even signed their names in spite of an explicit notation that this was not necessary in order to preserve anonymity and encourage unbiased responses. Equally impressive, three-fourths answered no fewer than 68 of the 71 questions, and two-fifths answered every question.

[17] It must be emphasized that the data are based on the conferees' self-reports and that therefore even the "factual" responses may have been exaggerated or otherwise distorted.

[18] But the 647 respondents do appear to have been a representative sample of the 1,067 nongovernmental conferees. Of the seventy-seven variables which were tested for representatives, in only one case (the residual category of "other occupations") was a statistically significant difference uncovered between the sample and the population.

of press releases;" one-half said that "quite often" they were asked to lend their name "to advance worthy causes;" nearly one-half estimated that they were "quite often" or "occasionally" quoted in newspapers; two-fifths reported having written at least one "article published in a magazine circulated nationally and sold at newsstands;" one-fourth reported having written at least one book; and one-fourth said they had been recipients of an honorary degree.

An even more impressive indication that the White House did succeed in convening a group of national opinion-makers is provided by this datum: an index of opinion-making potential was compiled out of the responses to ten of the foregoing items and, with possible scores ranging from 0 to 100, the conferees registered a mean score of 49.0, whereas the equivalent figure for parents or friends of students at Rutgers University who completed just this part of the questionnaire [19] was 15.9. Only 4 per cent of the conferees had an index score below this "ordinary citizen" mean and this figure is perhaps a good indication of the small proportion of conferees who cannot properly be designated as national leaders.

As for the social backgrounds of the conferees, a profile of their major characteristics is presented in Table 1. Here it can be seen that on the basis of this White House-selected sample [20] the structure of national leadership is composed primarily of middle-aged, white, Protestant, well-educated males who are located mainly on the Eastern seaboard and who have not had extensive governmental or political experience. On the other hand, the profile is much less clearcut with respect to the conferees' political allegiances and their occupations, albeit businessmen were clearly the predominant group. National opinion-makers, in sum, would appear to have affiliational and experiential bases for a common frame of reference even though in important respects diversity of background also characterizes their ranks.

The basis for a common frame of reference is further suggested by data pertaining to the foreign travels and the reading habits of the conferees. These point to the conclusion that opinion-makers tend to rely on the same or similar sources for information about world affairs. It would seem, for example, that first-hand contact with people and places outside of the United States is an experience widely shared by national leaders.

[19] This sample consisted of thirty-three males and two females who averaged 47 years of age.

[20] The selection of conferees was carried out under considerable pressure of time and accomplished in three weeks. Consequently, criteria of selection were simple and not fully explicit. Five members of the White House staff served as the core of a committee which went over long lists of "prominent persons" and voluntary associations, from which were culled individuals and associated officials who might be influential and who seemed likely to have at least a remote interest in the foreign aid program. Neither the party affiliations nor the foreign aid attitudes of potential conferees were used as criteria for selection nor, with few exceptions, were they even known when the invitations were issued.

Table 1

SOCIAL BACKGROUND OF THE CONFEREES
(in percentages)

(n = 647)

SEX
  Male   — 77
  Female   — 23

AGE
  Under 30   — 2
  30–39   — 9
  40–49   — 28
  50–59   — 28
  60–69   — 19
  Over 70   — 1
  Unknown   — 13

REGION
  Northeast   — 37
  Washington, D.C.   — 32
  Midwest   — 14
  South   — 11
  Far West   — 5
  Other   1

UNDERGRADUATE
EDUCATION
  Did not attend college   — 9
  Attended college but
    either did not gradu-
    ate (10) or did not
    specify graduation (14)   — 24
  Graduated from college   — 65
  Unknown   — 2

POST-GRADUATE
EDUCATION
  Did not attend graduate
    or professional school   — 31
  Attended but did not ob-
    tain a degree (16) or did
    not specify whether a
    degree was obtained (4)   — 20
  Attended and obtained a
    degree   — 43
  Unknown   — 6

RACE
  Negro   — 2
  White   — 85
  Unknown   — 13

RELIGION
  Protestant   — 74
  Jewish   — 11
  Catholic   — 9
  Other   — 4
  Unknown   — 2

PARTY
  Democrat   — 37
  Republican   — 34
  Independent   — 23
  Unknown   — 6

OCCUPATIONAL FIELD*
  Business   — 27
  Communications   — 13
  Educational Ad-
    ministration   — 11
  Religion   — 10
  Politics and Government   — 8
  Law   — 8
  Welfare   — 7
  Teaching–Research   — 6
  Housewives   — 5
  World Affairs
    Organizations   — 5
  Women's Groups   — 5
  Agriculture   — 3
  Veterans   — 3
  Labor   — 2
  Other   — 3
  Unknown   — 3

*Due to multiple coding the total of the subcategories exceeds 100 per cent.

Table 1

SOCIAL BACKGROUND OF THE CONFEREES (Continued)
(in percentages)

PRIOR GOVERNMENT EXPERIENCE* (Local, State, and National)		PRIOR POLITICAL EXPERIENCE	
Held elective office	— 16	Served as a delegate or alternate to a presiden- tial nominating conven- tion	— 9
Held appointive office	— 35		
Held consultative office	— 47		
Never held any office	— 38	Never served in this capacity	— 88
OCCUPANCY OF HIGH POST IN A VOLUNTARY ASSOCIATION		Unknown	— 3
Associational Conferees	— 41		
Nonassociational Conferees	— 56		
Unknown	— 3		

More than four-fifths of the conferees reported that they had travelled abroad at least once since 1945 and more than one-fourth said they had been out of the country on no less than six different occasions. All in all, the conferees registered a mean of 6.1 trips abroad since World War II, a frequency which no doubt greatly exceeds the foreign travel experience of most Americans.[21] No less striking are the findings concerning the second-ary sources through which world affairs are experienced by opinion-makers. Not only did almost all the respondents indicate that newpapers serve as their main source of information, but the same source was cited by three-fourths of those who listed specific media (Table 2). The *New York Times* would seem to be, so to speak, a bible for opinion-makers.[22] Indeed, no other source received even half as many citations as the *Times*. Nor does the finding merely reflect the large number of conferees who came from

[21] The finding that opinion-makers commonly share the experience of foreign travel is consistent with the results of other inquiries along this line. Indeed, two of these turned up even smaller proportions of leaders who had never been abroad at all: Harold R. Isaacs, *Scratches on Our Minds: American Images of China and India* (New York: John Day Co., 1958), p. 19, and Ithiel de Sola Pool, Suzanne Keller, and Raymond A. Bauer, "The Influence of Foreign Travel on Political Attitudes of American Businessmen," *Public Opinion Quarterly*, Vol. XX (Spring 1956), p. 161.
[22] Isaacs also found that "by far the largest single number" of his sample depended on this source; in the case of his data the *Times* was cited by 70 per cent of the respondents (*ibid.*, p. 21). The same newspaper was also "prominent" among the sources cited by the subjects of a survey of Midwestern opinion-makers: Kenneth P. Adler and Davis Bobrow, "Interest and Influence in Foreign Affairs," *Public Opinion Quarterly*, Vol. XX (Spring 1956), p. 93.

Table 2

RESPONSES TO AN ITEM WHICH ASKED, "ON WHAT SOURCES DO YOU RELY FOR INFORMATION ABOUT FOREIGN AFFAIRS?" (in percentages)

A. General Sources (n = 647)*

Newspapers	— 94
Magazines	— 90
Columnists or commentators	— 71
Word of mouth	— 40
Other sources	— 33
Question not answered	— 2

B. Specific Sources (n = 401)*

Top Five (of 57) Newspapers Cited

New York Times	— 77
Washington Post & Times Herald	— 32
New York Herald Tribune	— 13
Wall Street Journal	— 5
Christian Science Monitor	— 9

Top Five (of 64) Magazines Cited

Time	— 37
U.S. News & World Report	— 24
Newsweek	— 20
The Reporter	— 16
Foreign Affairs	— 15

Top Five (of 58) Columnists or Commentators Cited

Walter Lippmann	— 22
the Alsop Brothers	— 14
James Reston	— 11
Edward R. Murrow	— 9
Marquis Childs	— 8

*Due to multiple coding the total of the subcategories exceeds 100 per cent.

New York City and for whom the *Times* is a local newspaper. Only 43 per cent of those who cited it came from the Northeast and nearly half of these came from elsewhere in the region than New York. Stated even more impressively, reliance upon the *Times* was reported by 46 per cent of the Far Westerners, 55 per cent of the Southerners, 60 per cent of the Midwesterners, and 81 per cent of those from Washington, D.C., as well as by 90 per cent of the Northeasterners.

Turning now to the question of whether national leaders experience interaction with other members of the opinion-making public, substantial evidence was uncovered in support of the assertion that they do. It is clear, for example, that they are physically mobile and that consequently their paths are continuously crossing. One-third of the conferees who neither lived nor worked in Washington, D.C., estimated that they visit the capital at least six times a year and only 8 per cent cited a frequency of less than one annual visit. That this extensive domestic travel involves interaction with other opinion-makers, as well as professional or personal business, is indicated by the responses to an item which inquired into the frequency of attendance at "conferences, conventions, meetings, etc.:" three-fifths responded "frequently," one-third "occasionally," and only a fraction "very rarely."

An indication of what kinds of occasions serve as settings for interaction is provided by the pattern of responses to still another item, one which focused on the extent to which the conferees held university trusteeships, corporation directorships, charity board memberships, and similar "top posts in organizations for which you receive *no* financial remuneration." Three-fourths reported occupancy of positions of this sort and more than two-fifths listed at least three such posts. Indeed, five respondents specified more than twenty, and one conferee, a business executive from Ohio, reported that he held twenty-eight unremunerated positions. Furthermore, these positions were held in a wide variety of fields, with 34, 23, 21, 20 and 15 per cent citing, respectively, educational, charitable, religious, business, and foreign policy organizations (to note only the most frequently mentioned types.)

That an elaborate network of acquaintanceship among national leaders may be emerging from their frequent interaction and overlapping activities is suggested by the response to a question which asked, "Did you run into any old friends at the Conference?" Not only did 98 per cent of the conferees reply in the affirmative, but two-thirds said they encountered more than ten friends and one-third reported running into more than twenty-five friends. As many as one hundred friends were listed by a gregarious 4 per cent.

Since the communication of values from nongovernmental opinion-makers to legislative, executive, and party officials is central to the consensus-building process, it is important to note that the network of acquaintanceship and interaction also appears to embrace officialdom, albeit to a noticeably lesser extent in the case of Congressmen. More than two-thirds of the conferees said they were "personally acquainted with a national committeeman or woman of either political party" and one-third specified at least six such acquaintances. Asked if "you have ever conferred with a Secretary of State or a President of the United States," nearly one-half indicated prior contact with at least one of these top officials and one-fourth specified both of them. Presumably the number of affirmative responses would have been substantially higher if the question had also asked about prior contact with, say, assistant secretaries. As for legislative officials, one-third selected "quite often" as characteristic of the frequency with which they "correspond or confer with members of Congress," nearly one-half said "occasionally," and one-fifth responded "very rarely." In addition, one-third replied "yes" and two-thirds responded "no" to the question of whether they had "testified before a committee of Congress since 1953."

IV

Thus far the data have indicated that the backgrounds, experiences, informational sources, and interactions of national leaders provide the basis for welding them together into a community of interests. Yet, the question remains as to whether these variables are sufficiently potent to foster (or at least not inhibit) common assessments of the world scene and similar responses to the same stimuli. Attitudinal and behavioral consensus does not automatically follow from frequent interaction or shared experiences. Quite conceivably other variables, especially those tending to reflect heterogeneity, such as occupation and party allegiance, may intervene to prevent agreement on such an important matter as foreign aid. Or possibly personality factors may have differentially shaped reactions to the experience of listening passively to ten speeches and three panels for twelve consecutive hours. In short, the materials for building a consensus have been uncovered, but whether one was built is yet to be determined.

Two questionnaire items, one focusing on the monetary dimensions of the foreign aid program and the other on its administration, yielded data which clearly indicate wide agreement among the conferees on this issue. While it is difficult to determine whether consensus preceded the Conference or was fashioned by it, the finding is unmistakeable that most of those in attendance supported the President's 1958 request for long-term spending authority [23] and for $3.9 billion in funds. Two-thirds re-

[23] At the time of the Conference the Eisenhower Administration was advancing the idea that money appropriated to the Development Loan Fund could be spent more effectively if Congress made it available for periods longer than a year. A year later, however, the Administration altered its position and, in effect, abandoned the fight for long-term authorizations.

sponded "yes" to the proposal "that instead of legislating annually in this area, Congress should give the President long-term (say, five years) authority and funds for the foreign aid program." One-half of the conferees thought Congress should "approve as is" the entire "foreign aid request for 1958–59" and one-third felt that the appropriation should exceed the presidential request. More than four-fifths, in other words, endorsed the proposition that the United States should be extensively committed in the foreign aid field.

To be sure, the endorsement was given with varying degrees of enthusiasm. Significant party and regional differences,[24] for example, were uncovered by an index of foreign aid attitude compiled out of the relevant items. While the mean index score for all the conferees was 64.2, the equivalent figures for the Democrats, Republicans, and Independents in attendance were, respectively, 70.6, 57.4, and 67.0. Similarly, the Southerners were noticeably less enthusiastic than their colleagues, having registered a mean score of 49.8 in comparison to the scores of 57.6, 62.9, 67.8, and 69.8 tallied by the Far Westerners, Midwesterners, Washingtonians, and Northeasterners. It must be emphasized, however, that these scores represent differences in degree and not in kind. Only 10 per cent of the conferees registered scores in the lowest third of the index range and equivalent to an attitude of opposition to foreign aid.

This consensus among diverse national leaders is all the more remarkable because its content is in sharp contrast with the views of the man-in-the-street at about the same time. In March 1957 a national poll[25] revealed widespread discontent with the foreign aid program, especially its economic aspects. Indeed, as can be seen in Table 3, the fact that one-third of the conferees favored an expansion of the amount requested by the President, and that less than one-tenth thought it ought to be reduced, is almost exactly contrary to the equivalent datum for the general public. Among the latter, even the differentiation between economic and military aid did not raise the number who favored increased expenditures above 5 per cent. Thus it would appear that on this central issue of public policy a wide disparity exists between the mass and opinion-making publics. Since Congress's final disposition of the President's request was more in line with the public's attitudes than with those of its leaders, this disparity raises a number of questions about the structure of national leadership which the consensus-building hypothesis assumes. The relevance of the disparity becomes even more apparent when it is noted that foreign aid is not the only policy area toward which the mass public tends to take a more con-

[24] All measurements of statistical significance were based on a chi square test, with significance being attributed to differences that had no more than a 5 per cent probability of occurring by chance.

[25] Conducted by Elmo Roper and Associates, and cited in H. Field Haviland, Jr., "Foreign Aid and the Policy Process: 1957," *American Political Science Review,* Vol. LII (September 1958), p. 700.

Table 3

COMPARISON OF THE CONFEREES' AND THE PUBLIC'S ATTITUDE
TOWARD FOREIGN AID EXPENDITURES
(in percentages)

Changes in Foreign Aid Expenditures	Responses of the Conferees	Responses of the Public (as Polled by Elmo Roper and Associates*)	
		Economic Aid	Military Aid
Increased	33.6	4.0	5.0
Kept at current level	48.7	24.0	47.0
Decreased	7.1		
A little		31.0	20.0
Drastically		27.0	14.0
Reduced to zero		3.0	2.0
Don't know	3.4	11.0	11.0
Other views and question not answered	7.2		
	100.0	100.0	99.0
	(n = 647)		

*And as reported in and adapted from H. Field Haviland, Jr., "Foreign Aid and the Policy Process: 1957," *American Political Science Review*, Vol. LII, (September 1958), p. 700.

servative stance than do opinion-makers. Similar discrepancies between the leaders and citizens of American communities have also been found with respect to civil liberty questions [26] and the issue of desegregation.[27]

The data are no less clearcut with respect to the conferees' evaluation of their common experience. While it might have been anticipated that many opinion-makers, being old and wise insofar as conferences and famous speakers are concerned, would react to an event such as the Conference with skepticism, boredom, or cynicism, this was far from the case. Both the quantified responses and the qualitative comments reveal that the occasion was enormously stimulating for a large proportion of those in attendance. Seven-eighths characterized it as a "rewarding experience" and only one-sixteenth responded that it was "unstimulating" or a "waste of time." This evaluation is substantiated by the extent to which the conferees talked about the experience upon returning home and by their readiness to do it again if asked. More than three-fifths reported having described

[26] Samuel A. Stouffer, *Communism, Conformity, and Civil Liberties* (New York: Doubleday, 1955), Chapter 2.
[27] Melvin M. Tumin, *Desegregation: Resistance and Readiness* (Princeton: Princeton University Press, 1958), Chapter 10.

the Conference experience to family and friends "at length," one-third did so "somewhat," and a mere 3 per cent related the events "hardly at all." To the question of whether they would attend again "if the Conference were a recurring event," 61 per cent responded "yes" and 30 per cent "probably," whereas only 7 per cent said "probably not" or "no." Furthermore, and most important from the standpoint of mobilizing and directing the energies of opinion-makers, four-fifths said they had learned something "about foreign aid and the Mutual Security Program at the Conference" with which they were "not previously familiar" and three-fourths estimated that they had returned "home from the Conference more determined than ever to do something for or against foreign aid."

A concise picture of the extent to which the proceedings had an impact upon the conferees is provided by the distribution of their scores on an index of "nonbehavioral effect" that was compiled out of six items such as the foregoing. Arrayed on a scale ranging from 0 to 100, one-third registered a score above 75 and two-thirds scored above 50, whereas only one-sixth were located in each of the two lowest quartiles. The mean score for all the conferees was 58.9.

Innumerable comments appended throughout the questionnaire are perhaps even more indicative of the enthusiasm which the Conference engendered. "More people seemed to be having a good time about something they believed in than is usual at such conferences," wrote one conferee, adding that "people stayed at the sessions more than usual and there was a sense of expectancy among the participants." The validity of this assessment is amply demonstrated by a sample of typical comments:

> An executive of a women's association from Virginia: "A very thrilling day that will long be remembered."
>
> An attorney from Texas: "I was favorably impressed with the manner in which the Conference was organized and the program presented. The best and smartest I've ever seen."
>
> A state university president: "I enjoyed it thoroughly from beginning to end."
>
> A minister from Ohio: "It was one of the greatest days of my life."
>
> A director of an education association from Washington, D.C.: "One of the most stimulating days of my entire experience."
>
> A newspaper publisher from Georgia: "Let's have some more on other pressing questions."
>
> A professor from Pennsylvania: "It was the finest conference I have ever attended, and I would not have missed any of it. This was the comment of many people."
>
> A business executive from Louisiana: "One of the 'best spent' days of my life."

This is not to say, of course, that all of the conferees were impressed by the occasion. As indicated by the scores on the index of nonbehavioral effect, a small minority were either unaffected or disaffected by the experience. Interestingly, neither party affiliation nor foreign aid attitude were as closely related to negative reactions to the Conference as were assessments of its size.[28] A few of those in attendance were apparently frustrated by the lack of opportunity to participate actively in the proceedings. The following are typical of the comments appended by conferees who tallied scores in the lowest quartile of the nonbehavioral index:

> It wasn't a "conference." No one conferred with anyone. It was a bunch of speeches, generally repeating what has been said many times before to people who have heard it. No chance for more than a handful to ask even a question, much less state an opinion.

> Purpose was not truly represented in original invitation. It is a mistake to lead busy men to believe their opinion is desired and then throw them into a mass arena with one-way loud-speakers. I have no objection to being "sold" something, but this affair did not impress me favorably from an organizing standpoint. Speakers were good and subject important, but I was misled in getting me there.

It bears repeating, however, that reactions such as these were distinctly in the minority and that a large proportion of those in attendance were favorably impressed with what they saw and heard. Furthermore, many conferees subsequently engaged in activity on behalf of the foreign aid program. As can be seen in Table 4, almost all of them were active at the level of face-to-face communication and nearly half publicly committed themselves on the issue. A further measure of subsequent behavior is provided by the distribution of scores on an index of post-Conference activity that was constructed out of several relevant items. Again arrayed on a scale from 0 to 100, 22 per cent of the conferees registered a score above 75, 34 per cent scored between 50 and 75, and 22 per cent were classified in each of the lowest two quartiles. The mean score for all the conferees was 53.4.

While this is not to say that the Conference was the only—or even

---

[28] Not only were low and high scores on the nonbehavioral index closely associated with, respectively, the 24 per cent who characterized the Conference as "too large to accomplish very much" and the 66 per cent who said it was "just about the right size," but also this association invariably persisted when the party and attitude variables were held constant. Indeed, in cross-tabulating the data no variable proved to be as persistent as did the Conference-size responses. They were also not erased when the regional variable and the scores on a scale of involvement in foreign affairs were held constant. That is, regardless of whether a conferee was a Republican or a Democrat, a Northeasterner or a Far Westerner, a friend or an enemy of foreign aid, or an "involved" or "uninvolved" follower of world events, the less he was upset by the size of the conference the more was he likely to register a high score on the scale of nonbehavioral effect.

Table 4

POST-CONFERENCE ACTIVITY ENGAGED IN BY THE CONFEREES
(in percentages)

Since the Conference Have You	Proportion of the Conferees Who Checked "Yes" or Made an Equivalent Response*
discussed foreign aid with your colleagues or co-workers?	87
discussed foreign aid with business or professional acquaintances (other than colleagues or co-workers)?	80
publicly announced your own attitude toward foreign aid?	49
talked or written to Congressmen about foreign aid?	45
delivered a speech either for or against foreign aid?	42
tried to affect the position of an organization either for or against foreign aid?	27
written an article, item, report, etc., on foreign aid which has appeared in any publication?	25
written an editorial either for or against foreign aid?	13
	(n-647)
Proportion of the Conferees who responded "yes" to eight of the above activities	3
seven " " " "	5
six " " " "	8
five " " " "	15
four " " " "	18
three " " " "	22
two " " " "	21
one " " " "	7
none " " " "	1
	100
	(n-647)

*Due to multiple coding the total of the subcategories exceeds 100 per cent.

the primary—source of the activities that were undertaken,[29] there is evidence that the event did move some of the conferees into action. Asked to compare their "activities with respect to foreign aid in March–April of 1958 with that of the equivalent period in 1957," 50 per cent of the conferees "guessed" they had been "more active" in 1958 and 45 per cent estimated they were "just as active as in 1957." Although undoubtedly some of the "more active" group exaggerated their activity, its size suggests that at least a few of the conferees carefully compared the two years and then indicated greater activity in 1958 because they had been spurred into action by the Conference. Such a conclusion is impressively supported by a cross-tabulation of responses to this comparative item and the scores on the indices of nonbehavioral effect and post-Conference activity. In both cases, the linkages proved to be highly significant ($P<.001$) and, in fact, the questionnaire yielded few discrepancies so wide and striking as the difference between the mean nonbehavioral score of 71.3 recorded by the "more active" conferees and the equivalent figure of 48.2 registered by those who were equally active in both years. Translating this finding into the words of a Midwestern educator, "I would probably not have given *any* time to [circulating opinions about foreign aid] had I not felt inspired and *obligated* by the Conference."

VI

Returning to the questions posed at the outset, *on the basis of the data*[30] it does seem possible to fashion a consensus among diverse groups of national leaders and then to enlist their energies in support of it. Ap-

---

[29] A series of cross-tabulations between the activity scores on the one hand, and the other indices and the background variables on the other, yielded the finding that involvement in foreign affairs was the primary source of post-Conference activity. With opinion-making potential held constant, no other variable was so directly and unmistakeably linked to the conferees' subsequent behavior as were the scores on an index of foreign affairs involvement. Stated briefly, the more a conferee was involved in foreign affairs the more of his opinion-making potential was he likely to utilize in the ensuing months. Those located in the highest quartile on the involvement scale tallied a mean activity score of 63.1, and the equivalent figures for those in the second, third, and lowest quartile were, respectively, 52.1, 42.6, and 26.7.

[30] Italics have been added throughout this paragraph in order to emphasize the tentative and restricted nature of these conclusions. Clearly a number of limitations are inherent in the data examined. No single event such as the Conference is sufficient to "prove" the consensus-building hypothesis. Nor is a mailed questionnaire sufficiently precise as a measuring instrument to claim that data have been uncovered which "confirm" one version of the hypothesis rather than another. Proof and confirmation require the convergence of findings from many types of surveys undertaken at various times with respect to a variety of foreign policy issues. Yet, despite the substantive and methodological limitations of the findings presented here, it would be excessively cautious simply to ignore what they seem to indicate about the structure and functioning of national leadership. For, in the absence of other surveys of top opinion-makers, the Conference data do shed light on the consensus-building hypothesis even if they do not test it, and it is in this context that these general conclusions have been derived from the responses to the questionnaire.

parently national opinion-makers do interact frequently and *apparently* they are getting to know one another. Their perceptions of the world scene do *appear* to be derived from similar frames of reference and similar sources of information. Their assessments of how the United States should respond to trends abroad do *seem* to rest on a common core of values. Behaviorally they do *appear* to react similarly to shared experiences. In short, there *seems* to be some validity to the version of the consensus-building hypothesis that posits the emergence of a continental community based on an integrated structure of national leadership.[31]

Whether the processes of national leadership integration are sufficiently rapid to allow for the development of public policies that are commensurate with the requirements of a prolonged cold war cannot, of course, be inferred from the data. Nor does foreign aid legislation since the Conference shed light on this crucial question. In 1958, notwithstanding the opinion-making activity precipitated by the Conference, the foreign aid appropriation was some $644 million less than the President had requested. In 1961, notwithstanding a new President's vigorous efforts to enlarge the scope of the program, Congress lopped off $861 million from the presidential request and approved a long-term financing measure only after its key implementing provisions had been eliminated. Yet, Congressional acceptance of the principle of long-term financing does seem to have developed, thereby suggesting that possibly the members of the national legislature are slowly being integrated into the national leadership structure.[32] If so, and if both the consensus-buiding hypothesis and the data presented here are accurate, then the coming years should witness a gradual narrowing of the gap between what the nation does and what many believe is required to cope with revolutionary trends abroad.

[31] Regional affiliations were found to be the main obstacle to the building of a continental community. The differences which recurred most frequently during the inquiry were those which distinguished the Southerners, Midwesterners, and Far Westerners from leaders located in the Northeast and Washington, D.C. The former tend to be less involved in foreign affairs, less informed about them, and more conservative in their attitudes toward foreign aid than are opinion-makers from the Northeast and the Capital. Neither young and old leaders, nor men and women, nor Republicans and Democrats, nor the college educated and those with less formal training proved to be as differentiated along involvement, informational, and attitudinal lines as did these two main groupings. More often than not, in fact, differences introduced by age, sex, party, and education disappeared when examined within each region. Even some of the occupational differences were erased when each region was separately analyzed. But the regional obstacle to a nationwide consensus may not be insurmountable. If reactions to the Conference are any indication, opinion-makers from the South and West are capable of responding to new information. Large numbers of conferees from these regions reported having learned about foreign aid as a result of their presence at the Conference. Members of these groups also tended to be highly and favorably affected by the event. There is, in other words, good reason to believe that opinion-makers located in the South and West can, given the proper stimulus and authoritative information, be brought more fully into a national consensus about the larger aspects of the international scene.

[32] For a discussion of how the process of integrating members of Congress into the national leadership structure might be hastened, see James N. Rosenau, "Leadership, Consensus, and Foreign Policy," *SAIS Review*, Vol. 6 (Winter 1962), p. 10.

4

Experimentation

The value of experimental techniques has only recently impressed itself upon political scientists. Through the 1950's, political science literature was nearly barren of studies based upon experimental methods,[1] but since then interest has increased greatly. Part of the reason for this has been the growing awareness that some of the strange happenings in psychology in such areas as bargaining behavior, coalition formation, and behavior under stress have considerable relevance to traditional concerns in political science and international relations.

An illustration of this connection may prove helpful. Samuel Huntington, in the essay reprinted in chapter 2, argues that "The danger of war is highest in the opening phases of an arms race, at which time the greatest elements of instability and uncertainty are present." If this initial danger period is somehow traversed without war, "a sustained arms race is likely to result with the probability of war decreasing as the initial action and counteraction fade into the past." [2] In part, Huntington's proposition has been inadvertently tested in the laboratory and found to hold. In an experiment conducted by Richard Willis and Norma Jean Long, three

---

[1] Exceptions were Harold F. Gosnell, *Getting Out the Vote: An Experiment in the Stimulation of Voting* (Chicago: University of Chicago Press, 1927); S. J. Eldersveld and R. W. Dodge, "Personal Contact or Mail Propaganda? An Experiment in Voting Turnout and Attitude Change," in Daniel Katz et al. (eds.), *Public Opinion and Propaganda* (New York: Dryden, 1954), pp. 532–42; Samuel J. Eldersveld, "Experimental Propaganda Techniques and Voting Behavior," *American Political Science Review*, Vol. 50 (March, 1956), pp. 154–65; Herbert A. Simon and Frederick Stern, "Effect of Television Upon Voting Behavior in Iowa in the 1952 Election," *ibid.*, Vol. 49 (June, 1955), pp. 470–77; Albert Somit, Joseph Tanenhaus, Walter H. Wilke, and Rita W. Cooley, "The Effect of the Introductory Political Science Course on Student Attitudes Toward Personal Political Participation," *ibid.*, Vol. 52 (December, 1958), pp. 1129–32.
[2] See p. 23.

subjects, each with the ability to destroy the others (on paper), confronted each other in a series of trials. One of the most striking findings is that, when attacks occur, they are overwhelmingly likely to occur at the beginning of the experiment; "the probability of an act of aggression," the authors conclude, "decreases rapidly over time." [3] This finding also suggests that revisions may be due in some of the assumptions underlying the mathematical models of arms races as surveyed in Intriligator's essay in chapter 9.

The psychological literature relevant to the studies of international relations is far too vast to be surveyed here—in fact some psychologists might argue that *all* their literature is in some sense relevant. Quite expert surveys of the literature in the most closely related areas of psychology are available and can be consulted for further elaboration.[4]

The study reprinted below which has been selected to represent the general line of psychological experimentation falls in the area of bargaining behavior.[5] The authors, Gerald Shure, Robert Meeker, and Earle Hansford, are particularly interested in testing the efficacy of the pacifist strategy. Real pacifists proved to be a scarce commodity, so the experimenters, undaunted, programmed a computer to act like one. The unwitting subjects play against the machine while the experimenters carefully watch their reactions to its friendly and conciliatory moves.

Experimental evidence in this area has led psychologists to the conclusion lately (rather belatedly, one might complain) that sex and money are (almost) as important in bargaining games as in real life. Women prove to be distinctly bad bargainers: they are unwilling to get tough even in their own interest and frequently find techniques in the experiment for getting out of the bargaining dilemma—usually by following an unthinking noncooperative strategy.[6] To an extent this is disappointing, for it means that one's conclusions about bargaining only hold for the sex group being used as subjects. To be truly general, one cannot merely do a single experiment to test a proposition, in a sense one must do at least three: one with male

---

[3] "An Experimental Simulation of an International Truel," *Behavioral Science*, Vol. 12 (January, 1967), p. 31.
[4] See Herbert C. Kelman (ed.), *International Behavior: A Social–Psychological Analysis* (New York: Holt, 1965) and J. David Singer (ed.), *Human Behavior and International Politics* (Chicago: Rand McNally, 1965).
[5] Outstanding reviews of this area have been contributed by Dean G. Pruitt, "Definition of the Situation as a Determinant of International Action," James A. Robinson and Richard C. Snyder, "Decision-Making in International Politics," and Jack Sawyer and Harold Guetzkow, "Bargaining and Negotiation in International Relations," all in Kelman, *op. cit.*, pp. 391–520.
[6] See the discussion in Harold H. Kelley, "Experimental Studies of Threats in Interpersonal Negotiations," *Journal of Conflict Resolution*, Vol. 9 (March, 1965), pp. 79–105. In some experiments the sex differences emerge only after the bargaining game has been played a number of times. See Anatol Rapoport's editorial comments, *ibid.*, Vol. 11 (June, 1967), p. 197.

subjects, one with females, and one with men competing against women. Then, if the experiment involves *three* participants—well, the problems clearly multiply.

A similar problem exists with money.[7] Bargaining behavior depends, in part, on the stakes of the game. Penny-ante poker is a different game from poker played with high stakes: if it costs but a few cents to call a possible bluff, one is inclined to stay in; if the expense is much higher, one is likely to reconsider. Experimenters have often found the same thing. If each trial of a bargaining game gains the subject only a few cents—or if the gain is in "imaginary money"—the subjects are more likely to get bored earlier and play *with* the game rather than within it. If the stakes are high, boredom is costly and the participants are inclined to adopt a no-nonsense attitude. Moreover, not only does the size of the stakes make a difference, but the marginal utility for money varies from subject to subject. Experimenters at one wealthy upstate New York university claim that the stakes have to be quite high before undergraduates get serious, while graduate student subjects can be bought for a song.

These considerations mean that studies of bargaining, as they get more sophisticated, also get more micro. Where once one could make grand conclusions about a thing called "bargaining behavior," one now must talk of "bargaining behavior among men undergraduates with high stakes." It is this phenomenon that inspires the complaint that psychologists are coming to know more and more about less and less. The disease, however, is an inevitable one as sophistication increases. At the same time the *cumulative* and *replicative* nature of the science is something political scientists can view with envy.

For the record, the subjects in the Shure experiment were all male undergraduates and they stood to gain a maximum of 25¢ or 50¢ from each trial. The stakes presumably are high enough to generate seriousness in the subjects, but it is rather disturbing that the money was enough to impel them to give someone a supposed electric shock. Other experiments have found that it is appallingly easy to get ordinary people to administer supposedly *severe* shocks simply by having a mild-mannered psychologist tell them to—even if no money is involved at all.[8]

The Shure experiment uses, in part, randomization to test certain variations in the bargaining situation. This is quite a simple procedure, but one

[7] See Philip S. Gallo, Jr., and Charles G. McClintock, "Cooperative and Competitive Behavior in Mixed-Motive Games," *ibid.*, Vol. 9 (March, 1965), pp. 68–78; Charles G. McClintock and Steven P. McNeel, "Reward Level and Game Playing Behavior," *ibid.*, Vol. 10 (March, 1966), pp. 98–102; Kelley, *op. cit.*; and Philip S. Gallo, Jr., "Effects of Increased Incentives Upon the Use of Threat in Bargaining," *Journal of Personality and Social Psychology*, Vol. 4 (July, 1966), pp. 14–20.
[8] Stanley Milgram, "Behavioral Study of Obedience," *Journal of Abnormal and Social Psychology*, Vol. 67 (October, 1963), pp. 371–78.

which has proven to be profoundly powerful.[9] One example can be found on page 108 where the experimenters wish to determine whether cooperation is improved when the pacifist has an opportunity directly to communicate his motives and intentions to the subject. Accordingly, a group of subjects is *randomly* divided into two sub-groups: one to receive the communications, one not. It is then found that the group with the communication was more cooperative than the group without the communication. The question then is this: some people are naturally more cooperative than others; what is the probability that by sheer bad luck most of the natural cooperators were put in the communication group and thus that the difference between the two groups has nothing to do with communication, but is simply determined by luck? Statistical tests have been devised to test such propositions—in this case the chi square test is used. If the test pronounces that there is no better than one chance in twenty that such a difference between groups could occur by chance, then the result is conventionally accepted as "statistically significant." [10]

Randomization tends to take care of most problems of "internal validity": did the experimental intervention (in this case the imposition of the communication) really have an impact or not? Little except arm-waving and further experimentation, however, can answer the important question of "external validity": is the experimental result relevant to the real world or does the artificiality of the experimental situation render any generalization questionable?

In the case of the pacifist experiment, it could always be argued that the results hold at best for a peculiar set of undergraduates and, had real people been used instead, pacifism would do much better in engendering cooperation. Or it might be insisted that the subjects were only playing a game to please an experimenter and that they would behave differently in a real-life situation. Or it might be said that the problem is in part unrealistically structured: in the real world, pacifists are proposing that the United States, with its hard-nosed reputation, *now* adopt a pacifist strategy thus adding an element of threat to the pure pacifism.

---

[9] An excellent exposition is Donald L. Campbell and Julian C. Stanley, "Experimental and Quasi-Experimental Designs for Research in Teaching," in N. L. Gage (ed.), *Handbook of Research on Teaching* (Chicago: Rand McNally, 1963), pp. 171–246. Standard treatments of experimental statistics are given by Quinn McNemar, *Psychological Statistics* (New York: Wiley, 1962, 3rd ed.) and Allen L. Edwards, *Experimental Design in Psychological Research* (New York: Rinehart, 1960, rev. ed.).

[10] It might be gratuitously noted that many problems in the humanities, as well as in the social sciences, can be fruitfully investigated by experimental methodology. For example, arguments have raged for years about the most effective way to present *Hamlet*. The play is too long for most purposes and there are various notions about which parts should be cut and which left in. Helpful information about the effectiveness of various cuttings could be gained by giving the play in its various versions to randomly segregated audiences of, say, college students. Questionnaires administered after the performances could be used to determine what, if any, differences the cuttings have made in audience reaction.

Sometimes objections can be met with further experimentation: replication with different subjects or under somewhat altered circumstances. The last objection mentioned above has been, in fact, indirectly tested and found to have merit. In some bargaining experiments it has been discovered that a strategy that begins noncooperatively and then turns cooperative is more likely to induce cooperation from the opponent than one which is cooperative from the beginning.[11] In the end, however, the artificiality of laboratory experimentation cannot be entirely eliminated and the results, like those in any scientific enterprise, at most can be entirely convincing, never absolutely conclusive.

SIMULATION EXPERIMENTS

It is in an effort to reduce some of the problems of external validity that simulation experiments have been devised. They differ from the experiments so far discussed principally in their conscious effort to duplicate the real world more closely and in their willingness to relax some of the provisions of control characteristic of most psychological experimentation. A rather large number of subjects, arranged as nations in an explicit international "world," characteristically participate in a single simulation run— frequently, incidentally, making the analysis of group processes more feasible than in the typical psychological experiment.

To an extent, a comparison of the two types of experimentation is afforded by a study carried out in Norway by Malvern Lumsden.[12] Four games were played in this study. Two of them, the "prisoners' dilemma" and "chicken" games, were standard bargaining games about which there is a rapidly growing literature.[13] As in Shure's pacifist experiment, the subjects have a situation posed for them in which they can compete in an effort to gain the greatest individual profits—with the risk that *both* will lose— or they can cooperate to maximize joint profits. The other two games apparently were similar except that the subjects were asked to picture the stakes in real world terms: the "prisoners' dilemma" game was put in terms of resistance to German occupation during World War II and the "chicken" game was put in terms of a nuclear confrontation over Cuba. The amount of cooperation engendered, as can be seen in Table 1, is sub-

[11] Thomas Harford and Leonard Solomon, " 'Reformed Sinner' and 'Lapsed Saint' Strategies in the Prisoner's Dilemma Game," *Journal of Conflict Resolution*, Vol. 11 (March, 1967), pp. 104–09; A. Scodel, "Induced Collaboration in Some Non-Zero-Sum Games," *ibid.*, Vol. 6 (December, 1962), pp. 335–40.

[12] Malvern Lumsden, "Perception and Information in Strategic Thinking," *Journal of Peace Research*, (1966), pp. 257–77.

[13] See Anatol Rapoport and A. M. Chammah, *Prisoner's Dilemma* (Ann Arbor, Mich.: University of Michigan Press, 1965) and the gaming section of the *Journal of Conflict Resolution*.

Table 1

RESPONSE CHARACTERISTICS OF 30 SUBJECTS PLAYING
NON-ZERO-SUM GAMES FOR 100 TRIALS EACH

	Prisoners' Dilemma	Chicken	Resistance	Cuba
Mean per cent of cooperation on first trial:				
Men	58	74	100	82
Women	36	36	100	100
Total	50	60	100	93
Mean per cent of cooperation over 100 trials:				
Men	52.5	67.2	95.8	97.2
Women	41.6	58.9	100.0	95.3
Total	48.5	62.5	97.1	96.1

From: Malvern Lumsden, "Perception and Information in Strategic Thinking,"
Journal of Peace Research, (1966), p. 267.

stantially greater when the real world is "simulated" in this very rudimentary way. The stakes have been greatly increased, if only in the subjects' imagination, and they approach the game with a different, presumably more serious, outlook—one which, incidentally, eliminates in this case the often-found difference between the sexes.

The military establishments of a number of countries have played war games which are a form of simulation, although one in which the hoped-for results are usually practical rather than theoretical. In the 1930's the U.S. Navy carried out war games based on the assumption of a Japanese attack on Pearl Harbor, but apparently found neither practical nor theoretical value in it.

More directly relevant for present purposes are the gaming exercises carried out at such places as RAND and MIT.[14] These games are character-

[14] R. E. Barringer and B. Whaley, "The MIT Political–Military Gaming Experience," *Orbis*, Vol. 9 (Summer, 1965), pp. 437–58; Lincoln P. Bloomfield, "Political Gaming," *U.S. Naval Institute Proceedings*, Vol. 86 (September, 1960), pp. 57–64; Lincoln P. Bloomfield and Norman J. Padelford, "Three Experiments in Political Gaming," *American Political Science Review*, Vol. 53 (December, 1959), pp. 1105–15; Robert H. Davis, "Arms Control Simulation: The Search for an Acceptable Method," *Journal of Conflict Resolution*, Vol. 7 (September, 1963), pp. 590–602; Herbert Goldhamer and Hans Speier, "Some Observations on Political Gaming," *World Politics*, Vol. 12 (1959), pp. 71–83; M. T. Price, "Applying Wargaming to the Cold War," *PROD*, Vol. 3 (1959), pp. 3–6 and "Wargaming the Cold War," *U.S. Naval Institute Proceedings*, Vol. 85 (1958), pp. 44–47; RAND Corporation, Social Science Division, "Experimental Research on Political Gaming," P-7540-RC, Santa Monica, California, 1958. For comments, see Bernard Brodie, *Strategy in the Missile Age* (Princeton: Princeton University

istically loosely structured with the subjects—usually academic, diplomatic, and military professionals playing specific country roles—permitted to roam on their own, seeking new alternatives and generating new outcomes. The experimenter tends to play the game by ear, often intervening and manipulating as much by inspiration as by plan.

Rather more tightly structured are the simulation experiments developed at Northwestern University by Harold Guetzkow, a political scientist who was trained as a psychologist.[15] While the subjects in these experiments are more carefully hovered over than in most gaming exercises, they are considerably more on their own than they are in the typical psychological experiment.

There seems to exist a growing number of simulators whose work is more or less based on the Guetzkow procedures, but of course with individualistic additions or subtractions to suit specific purposes. Among the studies so far published or nearly published have been contributions in a number of areas. Richard Brody, in the study excerpted below, has investigated the problem of the dispersion of nuclear weapons while Michael Driver, a psychologist, has made use of the same simulation data to explore how the behavior of people who view the world in simple terms differs under varying situations of stress from that of people with more complex cognitions.[16] The difference, Driver finds, is considerable and the study strongly suggests that simulators can ignore psychological variables only at their peril.

In a somewhat related study, Dina Zinnes has attempted to compare crisis behavior in the Brody–Driver simulation runs with content data from the 1914 crisis; the results are limited, but promising.[17] One effort has been made to simulate the 1914 crisis directly, matching present-day subjects with their psychological counterparts among the decision-makers of the

---

Press, 1959), pp. 246–47, 385–89, and *Escalation and the Nuclear Option* (Princeton: Princeton University Press, 1966), pp. 37–39; and Richard A. Brody, "Some Systemic Effects of the Spread of Nuclear Weapons Technology: A Study through Simulation of a Multi-Nuclear Future," *Journal of Conflict Resolution*, Vol. 7 (December, 1963), Chapter 1. See also Bernard J. Cohen, "Political Gaming in the Classroom," *Journal of Politics*, Vol. 24 (1962), pp. 367–81.

[15] Harold Guetzkow, "A Use of Simulation in the Study of Inter-Nation Relations," *Behavorial Science*, Vol. 4 (July, 1959), pp. 183–91 and *Simulation in Social Science* (Englewood Cliffs, N.J.: Prentice-Hall, 1962); Harold Guetzkow, Chadwick F. Alger, Richard A. Brody, Robert C. Noel, and Richard C. Snyder, *Simulation in International Relations: Developments for Research and Teaching* (Englewood Cliffs, N.J.: Prentice-Hall, 1963).

[16] Michael J. Driver, "Conceptual Structure and Group Processes in an Inter-Nation Simulation. Part One: The Perception of Simulated Nations," *Educational Testing Service Research Bulletin*, RB 62-15 (April, 1962). See also Harold M. Schroder, Michael J. Driver, and Siegfried Streufert, *Human Information Processing* (New York: Holt, 1967).

[17] Dina A. Zinnes, "A Comparison of Hostile Behavior of Decision-Makers in Simulate and Historical Data," *World Politics*, Vol. 17 (April, 1966), pp. 474–502.

earlier period.[18] The subjects, unfortunately, were able to see the historic parallels through the experimenters' camouflage and thus the study is presented as exploratory only. Another attempt to simulate a historical situation, this time the Vietnam situation, is under way.[19] Other areas of investigation include alliance formation [20] and the feasibility of proposals for tension reduction in world affairs.[21] Inter-Nation Simulation has also been explored as a teaching aid.[22] Meanwhile, reviews and critiques of the procedure continually appear, reassessing and reformulating the problem.[23]

Also worthy of mention are developments in the area of all-computer simulation. In this method, a lengthy series of assumptions and best guesses about how the world operates are programmed and then different inputs are read in at one end of the machine to see what sorts of outputs are emitted at the other.[24]

[18] Charles F. Hermann and Margaret G. Hermann, "An Attempt to Simulate the Outbreak of World War I," *American Political Science Review*, Vol. 61 (June, 1967), pp. 400–16.
[19] John MacRae and Paul Smoker, "A Vietnam Simulation," *Journal of Peace Research*, (1967), pp. 1–25.
[20] Philip M. Burgess and James A. Robinson, *Nations in Alliance: A Simulation of Coalition Processes* (Columbus, Ohio: Ohio State University Press, 1968).
[21] Wayman J. Crow, "A Study of Strategic Doctrines Using the Inter-Nation Simulation," *Journal of Conflict Resolution*, Vol. 7 (September, 1963), pp. 580–89. See also Marc Pilisuk, "Timing and Integrity of Inspection in Arms Reduction Games," *Peace Research Society (International) Papers*, Vol. 5 (1966), pp. 99–108.
[22] James A. Robinson et al., "Teaching with Inter-Nation Simulation and Case Studies," *American Political Science Review*, Vol. 60 (March, 1966), pp. 53–65; Chadwick F. Alger, "Use of Inter-Nation Simulation in Undergraduate Teaching," in Guetzkow et al., *op. cit.*, pp. 150–89. Private industry is not far behind: Science Research Associates, a subsidiary of IBM, has put out an Inter-Nation Simulation kit for use in the classroom.
[23] J. David Singer, "Data-Making in International Relations," *Behavioral Science*, Vol. 9 (January, 1965), pp. 68–80; Charles F. Hermann, "Validation Problems in Games and Simulations with Special Reference to Models of International Politics," *ibid.*, Vol. 12 (May, 1967), pp. 216–31; William D. Coplin, "Inter-Nation Simulation and Contemporary Theories of International Relations," *American Political Science Review*, Vol. 60 (September, 1966), pp. 562–78; Richard Chadwick, "Theory Development through Simulation," American Political Science Association Paper, 1966 (mimeo); Harold Guetzkow and Lloyd Jensen, "Research Activities on Simulated International Processes," *Background*, Vol. 9 (February, 1966), pp. 761–74; Harold Guetzkow, "Some Uses of Mathematics in Simulation of International Relations," *Mathematical Applications in Political Science*, Vol. 1 (1965), pp. 21–40; R. N. Rosecrance and J. E. Mueller, "Decision-Making and the Quantitative Analysis of International Relations," *Year Book of World Affairs 1967* (London: Stevens, 1967), pp. 1–19; Sidney Verba, "Simulation, Reality, and Theory in International Relations," *World Politics*, Vol. 16 (1964), pp. 490–519.
[24] Clark C. Abt, "War Gaming," *International Science and Technology*, Vol. 32 (August, 1964), pp. 29–37. See also Oliver Benson, "A Simple Diplomatic Game," in James N. Rosenau (ed.) *International Relations and Foreign Policy* (New York: Free Press, 1961), pp. 504–11 and "Simulation of International Relations and Diplomacy," in H. Borko (ed.) *Computer Applications in the Behavioral Sciences* (Englewood Cliffs, N.J., Prentice-Hall, 1962).

Brody's simulation experiment was conducted at Northwestern using the Guetzkow approach. Brody was interested in ascertaining what happens to alliance patterns when nuclear weapons are diffused to minor members of the blocs. Accordingly, a simulation of a binuclear world is set up and midway through the experimental run, the bomb is dispersed. It should be said that the excerpt below contains, for the most part, only the grim mechanics devised to explore this notion—particularly the description of the Inter-Nation Simulation itself. For further analysis of the substantive issue—the nth country problem—as well as of Brody's broader model of the cold war system and of his use of Timothy Leary's (presumably pre-psychedelic) content analysis techniques, the reader is urged to consult the original article.

In comparison with Shure's pacifism experiment, the Brody undertaking is striking in its sheer size. To marshall 357 high school students around for a summer, analyze their every communication, prepare computer programs to monitor their activities, and ride herd on more than a dozen research assistants takes a truly impressive amount of time, patience, and effort. Ordinary psychological experiments frequently can be carried out with far less effort and at a far lower cost.

The gain in going to simulation is a greater richness of experience and a closer approximation to reality, at a cost in precision and control. But of course no simulation can duplicate the real world and thus one can always complain about the imperfection of the approximation. Do high school students act like trained diplomats? Some unpublished work suggests that they do. At any rate there appears to be no simulator extant who will not on query insist that the subjects take the experiment very seriously indeed —Brody's contribution is on page 121. Would the simulation have been more realistic if the alliances had had an element of ideological cohesion— simulated perhaps by choosing subjects for each alliance from the same fraternity or the same high school? Or if the diffusion of nuclear capacity had left some of the new nuclear powers with only minimal nuclear capabilities instead of the very sophisticated capabilities they were given? Might the weakening of alliance patterns have occurred even without the nuclear diffusion simply because the subjects became bored with existing patterns after several hours of experimentation? [25] How much unreality is introduced

[25] Like many specific criticisms of experiments, this particular caveat could be investigated, if it seemed worth the effort and cost, by further experimentation. In this case control runs would be needed—runs like the others except that no nuclear weapon dispersion took place. If alliances crumbled anyway, then clearly something other than the proliferation of weapons was to blame. This procedure checks for the "regression effect." The students were subtly led to arrange themselves in a rather extreme structure: a tightly bipolar world. If alliance patterns were to change at all—for whatever reason —it is to be expected that this change would be toward decreased cohesion since it would be difficult for the national actors to become even more tightly allied.

by the experimental demand on the subjects that they must always *do* something under a pressing time constraint and cannot, unlike their real life counterparts, take the evening off and go to the ballet?

Reality itself is unpleasantly complicated of course and it is for precisely this reason that experimentation—whether of the simulation sort or not—is resorted to. If the basic relationship under investigation has been adequately represented, then the omission from the experimental situation of extraneous conceptual and factual clutter is scientific gain. If, however, an essential variable has been tossed out with the clutter, the results of the experiment will be misleading at best.

THE EFFECTIVENESS OF PACIFIST
STRATEGIES IN BARGAINING GAMES [1]

Gerald H. Shure, Robert J. Meeker, and Earle A. Hansford [2]

> You begin with the relations between might and right, and this
> is assuredly the proper starting point for our inquiry. But, for the
> term "might," I would substitute a tougher and more telling word:
> "violence." In right and violence, we have today an obvious antinomy.

This quotation from Sigmund Freud's essay, "Why War?" points to
the heart of the puzzling contradiction between our assertion of ethical
principles, which repudiate violence, and the basis on which they too frequently rest—warfare, threats, and hostilities. To the pacifist, the inherent
conflict and moral bankruptcy that is involved in using these means to
promote justice lead not only to our current international deadlock but to a
profound ethical dilemma. He believes we cannot repudiate violence as
immoral and at the same time resort to it without violating our basic psychological integrity. To avoid such corruption he eschews the use of any
form of violence, harmful coercion, or threats of these.

We shall not argue with the social idealism or morality reflected in the
nonviolent approach, but rather shall direct ourselves to the task of identifying some of the essential features of these alternatives to violence and ex-
ploring the extent and conditions of their effectiveness. As Janis and Katz
(1959) have shown, these approaches, largely based upon ethical principles, contain a rich matrix of hypotheses about the constructive forces in
man and society, hypotheses that are worthy of investigation and that have
been relatively unexplored by the social scientist. There are, of course, sig-

Reprinted from *The Journal of Conflict Resolution*, Vol. 9, No. 1 (March, 1965), pp.
106–17, copyright 1965 by The University of Michigan, by permission of System Development Corporation and *The Journal of Conflict Resolution*.
[1] This paper, based on research sponsored by the Advanced Research Projects Agency,
contract SD-97, was presented at the American Psychological Association meetings, Los
Angeles, California, September 7, 1964. The authors wish to acknowledge the helpful
suggestions of Kathleen Archibald, Harold H. Kelley, and Melvin Seeman on problems
associated with a laboratory study of pacifist behavior.
[2] Mr. Hansford carried out the computer programming required for this study.

nificant differences among such movements as passive resistance, nonresistance, nonviolent direct action, satyagraha, and others, which are all generally classified as nonviolence movements. We shall not attempt to review or catalogue these differences. An excellent major step toward such an undertaking has already been made by Gene Sharp (1959). In our series of studies we shall ignore many of the qualifications and distinctions which characterize the real-life versions of these movements, and we shall not attempt to distinguish conceptually between the uses of force and resistance that constitute instances of violence or nonviolence. These are major issues that require study and analysis, but we shall sidestep them to pursue our more limited aims.

In an earlier series of experiments (Meeker, Shure, and Moore, 1964; Shure, Meeker, and Moore, 1963), we investigated the effects of providing bargainers with equivalent threat capabilities. A series of hypotheses was tested that concerned threat availability and psychological factors in conflict escalation. Among other results, we found that the pairing of a cautious, well-intentioned bargainer with an aggressive bargainer led to greater loss and disruption of negotiations than occurred between pairs of equally belligerent bargainers. The current series of studies was initiated in an attempt to identify those features of conciliatory bargaining that prove to be helpful or detrimental to the realization of cooperative bargaining outcomes, and to specify the range of circumstances that influence these features.

In an initial conceptual analysis three types of conciliatory bargainers were identified and selected for further study: the ethically motivated cooperator, the irresolute or timid cooperator, and the resolute or strategic cooperator. This paper reports on a pacifist version of the ethically motivated cooperator. We recognize that our use of the term pacifist does not coincide with common usage, but we retain it because it does have the advantage of familiarity and affords us a simple name for referring to the Ss (subjects) in our study who, among other beliefs, reject violence as a means for resolving issues. As will soon become apparent, the pacifist S lives up to his namesake rather better than many of his counterparts outside the laboratory.

This paper, then, will report on the measured effectiveness of pacifist bargaining strategies as studied under the controlled conditions of laboratory experimentation. On the face of it, this proposition has an untoward sound. Pacifism doesn't seem to belong in a laboratory and the mere prospect of its being there deserves some preliminary comment.

In one respect the whole enterprise seems profane. The emphasis on "measured effects" suggests that a basically moral concept is somehow being subjected to a test solely on the basis of its practical effectiveness. We recognize that practical effectiveness is not the sole criterion, and, for many, not even the essential criterion by which pacifism should be judged, but we point out that it is seldom, if ever, totally irrelevant as a consideration. Indeed, pacifists are as convinced of the ultimate efficacy of their approach as of its moral correctness.

Granting that we should study the problem, the restrictive atmosphere of a laboratory hardly seems like an appropriate or even an adequate setting for a demonstration of pacifism. The main advantage, as with any laboratory study, is control. In the case of pacifist behavior this assumes added importance. Outside the laboratory there is virtually no opportunity to gather systematic behavioral evidence on the effectiveness of pacifist strategies. This is not necessarily for want of pacifists. There are, to be sure, an increasing number of people who advocate nonviolent means of social and political action; there are even some who practice what they advocate. The difficulty is in measuring their effectiveness. Pacifist methods as practiced are seldom pure in form. It is seldom that an individual pacifist or a pacifist group is solely responsible for setting a given social or political policy. It is therefore difficult to say how much belongs to Martin Luther King and how much to Malcolm X; how much to the march on Washington and how much to the Cambridge riots. A mixture of nonviolence and threat may be effective, but it is not pacifism.

As with most experimental studies, there are also the obvious limitations. To transport the phenomenon from the street into the laboratory one must abstract, compress, and simplify until one reaches some satisfactory compromise between a fully representative situation and a manageable one. In the present case, the situation is completely wrested from the larger questions and rich complexities of international and national politics to the complex simplicities of an interpersonal bargaining situation. The lack of pressure from the larger social scene, frequently a critical factor in the pacifist's appeal, and the vagueness of the appropriate institutional norms are the two most general and obvious limitations of our laboratory situation. These are limitations of some importance and must be duly noted in qualifying our results.

Since pacifism has never, to our knowledge, been placed in the laboratory before, and since our particular representation of it is of considerable importance in interpreting the results, we should like to describe our study in some detail. Let's turn to the immediate problem of providing a conflict situation within which the pacifist's response may be distinguished. There can be conflict situations in which no singularly pacifist response can be made. In fact, of all the conflict situations generated by bargaining theories and studies of bargaining behavior, few, if any, afford an opportunity for a uniquely pacifist response. How, then, do we create a confrontation between a pacifist and an intractable adversary in our experimental situation?

PROCEDURE

In our experimental situation, Ss are told that they are going to perform as operators in a communication system (see Figure 1). Their task is to transmit messages. At the beginning of each work period, Ss are given a five-unit message to transmit. Transmission of a message can be accomplished only by inserting the message unit, letter by letter, into a communication channel. Only completely inserted messages are transmitted.

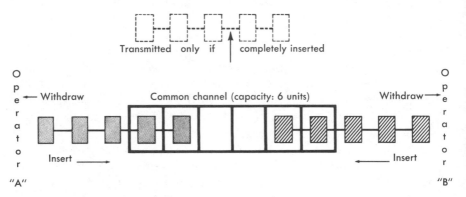

Fig. 1.   Schematic illustration of bargaining game.

Each S is informed that he is assigned to a communication channel that will also be used by one other S. This channel, common to a pair of Ss, has a total storage capacity of six units (message units are stored in the channel until all five units are inserted into the channel). Upon successful insertion of the fifth unit, the complete message is transmitted and the channel storage is emptied of the transmitted units. It then becomes available for the other operator to transmit his message. However, the six-unit channel storage limitation prevents concurrent transmission of messages by both Ss. Only one S can transmit first.

The Ss perform their task during work periods made up of 15 opportunities for joint action (called "turns"). During each turn, an S chooses from one of two action alternatives: inserting a letter unit into channel storage or withdrawing a letter unit from channel storage. This latter action also permits the S to pass or take no action if he has not already inserted. Thus an S can successfully insert a complete message into the channel in five turns if the spaces in the channel are not already occupied. To do so requires that the other S not try to transmit simultaneously but wait for the first S to complete his transmission.

If both attempt to do so—whenever their insertions exceed the channel capacity of six units—an "overload" results. This is a costly situation, since the S is charged operating costs for each of the turns that is expended until his message is transmitted. Thus it is to the S's advantage to transmit his message first and with as little overload trouble as possible. In this feature lies the source of potential conflict and cooperation. Since each S temporarily needs exclusive use of five of the six channel units to transmit his message, the Ss have to work out an arrangement for effective channel utilization. In the event that neither operator is willing to relinquish use of the channel temporarily to allow the other to go first, a deadlock will occur; under such a state of mutual interference, turns are wastefully expended and both operators suffer losses. Under these conditions, three relationship patterns may emerge: dominance–submission, in which one operator continually uses the channel first and the other transmits second; sharing, in which the operators adopt an alternating pattern of transmitting first and second from one period of operation to the next; or continued mutual interference.

THE ESSENTIAL FEATURES OF THE TACIT BARGAINING SITUATION

This basic situation is one which we have used in other bargaining research. It is interpersonal, repetitive, and capable of generating conflict and cooperation. It can also be a source of great involvement to the Ss because successful transmission is rewarded by actual monetary payment. For all that, this type of situation is not yet sufficient for a well-defined pacifist–adversary confrontation. In order to achieve this, we need to incorporate the following additional features: (1) the means of bargaining control must involve the availability of an ethically questionable means, preferably physical violence; (2) we need aggressive bargainers who will use this means to gain a bargaining advantage; (3) this advantage should be incompatible with the *prima facie* claims for a fair share by the pacifist; (4) the situation should be so contrived that, if the pacifist employs resistance, the aggressor can achieve his ends only by using means that cause physical harm; and finally, (5) we need a threatening or hostile action that is available to the pacifist but that he refuses to employ even though his adversary uses means that cause him physical pain.

We translated these requirements into the conditions of our laboratory situation by modifying its rules and moves as follows. In addition to earning more money, the operator who transmits his message first in the current operating period acquires an additional power move, which he may employ in the subsequent work period. This move, called a JOLT BACK action, enables him to override the other operator. In effect, the possessor who employs his JOLT BACK can push back the other operator's inserted units and thereby guarantee himself first transmission. Repeated use of this move enables one bargainer to perpetuate his domination as long as he is willing to do so. It is important to note that this power move is not initially available but is acquired by one bargainer or the other *within* the bargaining relationship, and that the initial acquisition of the move can only occur with the tacit consent of the other bargainer.

Introduction of this power move greatly increases the role that trust plays in initiating a cooperative resolution. To let the other S go first is essentially to hand over control of one's future fate to him with the adverse possibility that he may never hand it back. Great as this risk may be, the alternative is a mutually dysfunctional deadlock, since someone must go first on each work period or neither can earn anything.

While some of our Ss might identify the continued use of the JOLT BACK action as an unwarranted exercise of power, others might see it as a necessary act in the face of the unmeasurable risk associated with giving it up. In either case, we also wished the move to carry with it the onus of unfairness of means—both as a potential source of moral concern for the user and as a basis for rejection of its use as an immoral and violent act by our pacifist. We tried to achieve this by pairing the use of the JOLT BACK action with the administration of a painful electric shock to the other S. With this modification and the resistance of our pacifist, the self-perpetuating use of force by the JOLT BACK action requires the user to shock the other operator repeatedly if his domination is contested. A sample shock was administered to each S by the experimenter to demonstrate the effect of the JOLT BACK action.

Given this conflict situation, modified by the introduction of a move which affords a sustained power advantage to the S willing to inflict physical pain, we felt we had now provided for a meaningful pacifist response. Let us follow our players through a few hypothetical work periods. In the first period the pacifist makes a cooperative gesture by letting the other operator go first. By taking this initiative, he demonstrates he is acting not out of weakness but rather in a spirit of cooperation and trust. In the next work period the pacifist, in keeping with a claim to a "fair" division of earnings, will now wish to take his turn transmitting first. However, his adversary now has the means of controlling the next encounter. Assuming that he plans to exploit his power advantage, he will, if necessary, use his JOLT BACK action to perpetuate his domination. What does our pacifist do? He can avoid being shocked by waiting for the dominator to transmit first. Instead, the pacifist demonstrates his resistance by entering units into the channel, and standing in the way of the dominator. By presenting himself in this way, period after period if necessary, the pacifist forces the dominator to use his JOLT BACK action if he wishes to maintain his position. For the pacifist there is no difference in monetary costs between standing in the path and waiting on the sidelines; the difference is simply and solely in terms of forcing the adversary to employ violence and through this, presumably, to recognize the pacifist's claim to a fair share of the payoff.

Through this act of passive resistance, the pacifist obliges the other operator to do something unethical and dramatically symbolizes that domination is wrong. While a change of status cannot be wrested from the possessor of the JOLT BACK, through this behavior or any other available action, the pacifist is provided with one additional response which enhances the clarity of his commitment to nonviolence. The action simply provides an opportunity for each player to shock the other side. While this shock action does not effect the position of either bargainer in the channel, it does afford a means of threat or retaliation for the operator who otherwise has no direct way to influence the dominating operator. The pacifist, of course, does not shock or threaten to shock the other operator and thus further conveys his commitment to nonviolence.

THE SIMULATED PACIFIST AND THE SUBJECT UNDER PRESSURE

This then is our laboratory bargaining situation. Next, of course, we need to bring our pacifists and aggressors into our situation for a confrontation. As one might guess, even among the American college sophomore species, that self-replenishing reservoir of Ss for psychological experiments, pure forms of the subspecies *homo pacifist* are hard to come by. We have settled instead for a programmed pacifist, who behaves just as we have indicated. By simulating the performance of one member, we also avoid the obscuring effects of the unique patterns of interaction that evolve between two live players. As a result, the data obtained permit more adequate comparison and summarization at intermediate and critical stages of the experiment.

With each incoming S our simulated pacifist makes an initial demonstration of good faith by letting the other man go first; he always makes the claim that alternation is fair; if he meets an aggressor, he invariably stands in the way to force the use of violence until his claim is responded to; and finally, he himself never resorts to retaliation with electric shock. To face this simulated pacifist, we dip into the pool of college freshmen and sophomores for our real Ss. Now it is obvious that, even if the college student is not typically a pacifist, neither is he overwhelmingly an aggressive dominator. To encourage as many as possible to adopt this role, each S is placed on a three-man team; the other team members are programmed confederates who are presumably performing other essential team tasks and are to share equally in the money that the S earns as operator and representative of his team in confronting the other team operator. Before the first trial, and after the second and fourth trials, these "teammates" send messages to the S to persuade him to adopt a dominating strategy. The team is also given an opportunity to choose their payoff level for the game by a majority vote. The teammates invariably vote for a payoff favoring a dominating strategy in preference to one more favorable to cooperation. All of the incoming Ss receive these same sets of pressures encouraging the adoption of a dominating orientation. The S, of course, is still free to do whatever he decides during the task itself and the teammates cannot interfere with his decisions.

The experiments described are carried out in the System Development Corporation research laboratory, using the Philco 2000 computer and computer-tied TV consoles and associated switch-insertion facilities. Twenty-four Ss are concurrently paired against the simulated pacifist. Ss send messages (moves, bids, threats, offers) to their paired opponents by making switch insertions. These are processed by the computer and then the results are displayed on the receiver's TV console. Computer programs assist in umpiring moves, providing displays of game-relevant information, and recording all moves, messages, and times. We also have our computer perform as 24 standardized, yet flexible, interviewers. Between game messages and moves, computer-generated questions based on the Ss' particular responses interrogate the players to elicit amplifying subjective information on the bases of their actions, their current intentions and expectations, their perception of the opponent, etc. As already noted, the computer is also programmed to assume the roles of the S's two teammates as well as the pacifist's role. By simulating the pacifist's behavior, we achieve a rigorously controlled representation of this bargaining style in the context of flexibility of detailed behavior.

RESULTS

Let us turn now to some of our results. One of the first questions we asked was what our Ss planned to do before beginning their first encounter with their pacifist adversary or their own teammates—before having an opportunity to interact with anyone. Recall that a cooperative move involves serious risk of loss of bargaining power and that a domination attempt may initiate a stalemate of mutual losses and exchanges of electric shock. Of the 143 Ss, slightly more than half (75) indicated that they planned to dominate from the outset; two Ss planned to settle for less than half, and the remaining 66 Ss planned to try to share the profits equally. However, following the first four trials (including the period of pressure from other team members toward domination and the initial exposure to the pacifist's behavior), 54 of the 68 Ss who planned to cooperate had changed to a strategy of dominant behavior, and four who planned to dominate were now cooperating. Over this period, the shift away from cooperation was significantly greater than the shift toward it. Thus, urged on by their teammates, about four-fifths of the Ss who planned to cooperate had changed to dominating behavior in which they knowingly shocked our resisting pacifist at least twice each trial. As meager consolation to those who are about to despair over our students' basic humanity, 18 of our Ss (about one-eighth) refused to employ the shock in any of the work periods.

What happened to the remaining 125 dominators? How effective was the pacifist's appeal in converting them? By experiment's end, 40 additional Ss had adopted an alternating pattern; the other 85, approximately two-thirds, continued to dominate and shock. Considering that approximately 48 percent of our total number of Ss began with plans to cooperate and that we ended up with only 39 percent cooperating, the overall effectiveness of the pacifist's strategies cannot be considered impressive. Taken at face value, it would even appear that many potential recruits to cooperation may have been *lost* rather than *gained*.

WHY WAS THE PACIFIST'S STRATEGY RELATIVELY INEFFECTIVE?

While of considerable interest, these summary findings, by themselves, tell us little about the situational factors and psychological processes associated with player intractability or conversion to a cooperative stance. We should like to attempt to understand more completely why our pacifist did not persuade two-thirds of the Ss.

To help structure our search for answers, let us identify some of the tactics of persuasion employed by our pacifist and, by doing so, perhaps we can better isolate those failures of strategy that limited his success. The first thing the pacifist must establish is that the situation is not a simple contest of wills and that some outcomes are inherently unjust and/or rest upon immoral means. To make this point, the pacifist should force the recognition on the part of the adversary that by dominating he is maintaining an unfair advantage and is doing so by immoral means. The pacifist should also establish that his cooperative behavior is not due to personal submissiveness, weakness, or cowardice—without this, the adversary is again left free to define the situation as a simple contest of wills in which he is, flatteringly enough, superior. And finally, to assuage any fears of recrimination and suspicions of duplicity, the pacifist should give his adversary every reassurance and guarantee possible. In summary, the pacifist's tactics aim to induce in his adversary a recognition of the unfairness of his claims and the immorality of his means, to establish his own personal resolve, and to give reassurance that he has acted and will act in good faith.

While the pacifist's behavior in the task is intended to communicate these points, a number of experimental manipulations were employed to increase the clarity with which each of them would be represented. Let us see, then, to what extent the pacifist succeeds in satisfying these conditions for persuading his adversary through his actions and in the context of additional experimental manipulations.

A factor that might be expected to exert a considerable influence on the pacifist's appeal would be the opportunity for direct exchanges of messages above and beyond that afforded by information tacitly communicated in game moves. Thus, in one experimental manipulation, the opportunity for *operators* to exchange additional messages either is or is not available. When available, the communication period is interposed between some of the working periods. (In the first part of the experiment, operator communications were permitted following work periods 5, 6, and 7.) In his messages, the pacifist amplifies on the intentions behind his actions. He states his conciliatory intent, presents a statement of fair demands, and emphasizes his refusal to use the shock and his intention to force the other to shock him if he is going to remain unfair.

The comparisons of Ss in the two conditions were statistically significant on two counts. First, all Ss who switched from dominating to sharing during work period 6, 7, or 8 (the periods following operator-to-operator messages) were in the communication condition and received these messages. No Ss in the noncommunication condition were converted during this period. Second, dominating Ss in the communication condition (as evidenced by responses to computer interrogations) thought it more likely than those in the noncommunication condition that the pacifist was trying to make them feel guilty or embarrass them and that he was trying to trick or deceive them. These results suggested that the person-to-person communications made the moral issue more salient. However, this salience had two opposite effects. For a limited number of Ss, it produced the desired conversion, but for many others, their resolve to dominate was strengthened, or at least rationalized, by attributing trickery to the motives of the pacifist.

As a second feature of our experimental design, we manipulated the experimental conditions related to the matter of projecting the pacifist's character and motives to his adversary. Common sense and many studies have shown that prior knowledge of and acquaintance with an individual exercise an influence over the interpretation that is made of his behavior. In our laboratory situation, Ss did not know with whom they would be paired as adversaries, believing only that their opposite number would be selected from among the other 23 students receiving instruction. Furthermore, their interaction in the context of the task was limited to game moves communicated via television and switch buttons. Was the pacifist's behavior likely to be perceived less clearly under these conditions of minimal knowledge than if the S received additional personal information

about him? Furthermore, would such perceptions influence the S's interpretation of and responses to the pacifist? To answer this question, we
had all Ss fill out personal information questionnaires. These were presumably exchanged with the opposing operator either at the beginning of
or midway into the experiment. In fact, all Ss received personal information for the programmed pacifist which was designed to project an image
of a Quaker who is morally committed to principles of nonviolence. Before
the initiation of the work periods, and either with or without the benefit
of this material, Ss characterized their bargaining adversary on eight semantic differential rating scales. Chi-square comparisons of the initial
ratings made by Ss with and without this personal information showed
that the Ss who exchanged this information perceived the pacifist as significantly more moral, wiser, more peaceful, and more honest—and even
braver and stronger. Thus the initial exposure to this information clearly
succeeded in conveying and establishing a favorable image of the pacifist—
an image that should serve to reduce the ambiguity of intentions that his
game behavior communicated. Did this factor influence the overall frequency of a favorable response to the pacifist's appeal? Not in the slightest.
Chi-square tests showed that Ss receiving prior personal knowledge showed
no greater tendency toward cooperative behavior in the ensuing trials. On
the face of it this was a puzzling and unexpected result. To compound
our puzzlement, we found that the mid-game semantic differential ratings
of the pacifist were essentially identical for Ss in the communication and
noncommunication conditions, although a significantly greater shift toward
cooperation had already occurred in the condition where communications
were previously exchanged. Together these results suggest that more than
a clear picture and favorable image of the pacifist is necessary for an effective appeal, and that the significant shift to cooperation in the communication condition was not achieved by providing more information about
the pacifist.

Consider one additional variation of the pacifist bargaining strategy.
Supposing that an S had been shocking the pacifist, and even supposing
that he admitted this was wrong or at least morally questionable, he might
still have faced a problem. He may have wondered whether he could
afford to cooperate at this point; he may have hesitated for fear of recrimination. At this point, then, it should have been effective if the pacifist
could assuage his fears by giving him some guarantee or overt reassurance
against retaliation. To test this we provided one-half of the Ss with a
mid-game opportunity to "give up" or reject future acquisition of the
harmful actions (the JOLT BACK and electric shock) for the remainder of
the work periods. The pacifist always did so. Thus roughly half of the
dominators faced a "disarmed" pacifist while the other half faced a pacifist
who had had no opportunity to disarm. The manipulation had no effect.
Again we were puzzled.

Why did the intended reassurance of the act of "disarmament" fail to induce more dominators to convert? Strangely enough, because it apparently was irrelevant. On various occasions when dominators were queried by the computer on why they believed the pacifist did not employ his shock, only 5 to 13 percent cited fear as a reason, whereas about half believed he refrained from using his shock action out of principle. Reassurance, then, was apparently not a factor, since these are approximately the same percentages found in the converted group.

The results for these three experimental manipulations suggest that when the pacifist fails it is not primarily because he fails to project a clear image of his intentions. Naively we had assumed that the various manipulations would only serve to strengthen the pacifist's case—the personal profile information, the availability of communication, the opportunity to forgo harmful actions—all of these would ostensibly contribute to the effectiveness of the pacifist's bargaining strategy. Behind this lay the assumption that the pacifist would more than likely benefit from anything that served to bring his character, his claims, and his commitments into sharper focus. Our results suggest that this assumption needs to be questioned or at least seriously qualified. While the pacifist appeal can persuade some adversaries away from their initial positions, and it does influence a small proportion to do so, particularly under the condition of personal communications, it also fails to influence many Ss who plan to dominate. But beyond these obvious alternatives it may have another effect; it may encourage exploitation among Ss who otherwise do not entertain such plans prior to interacting with the pacifist.

Let us pursue this somewhat further by considering the following effects which knowledge of the adversary produced. In replying to a post-experimental question, 78 percent of all Ss indicated that the personal information about the pacifist had a significant influence on their strategy. Even among the unremitting dominators only about one-fourth indicated this information had negligible or no influence. While the influence among those who are converted to cooperation is readily understandable, what is the nature of this self-acknowledged influence among the intractable dominators?

Two possibilities suggest themselves. First, though the dominators refuse to give up their control, they may continue to dominate with greater reluctance and an increased sense of guilt, caused by the knowledge that they are shocking somebody who isn't likely to shock back. To check this possibility, an index of reluctance to shock (the use of the *insert* action on turns when the JOLT could have been employed) was calculated and used as a manifest expression of experienced guilt. Only 14.5 percent of the intractable dominators made a sustained effort (on more than two trials) to avoid shocking the operator facing them; about 45 percent made no effort to avoid shocking the other operator by first testing to see whether he would back out voluntarily. Thus, for the dominators, the influence of knowledge did not lead to increased manifest guilt in more than a small percentage of cases, if indeed it accounted for any of this guilt.

A second possibility is that the information on the pacifist may be used as a basis for adopting and maintaining an exploitive attitude. Before the initiation of the work periods, Ss were given an opportunity to vote for one of two payoffs that determine their potential earnings in each work period. Other things being equal, voting for the low payoff is less risky—Ss do not lose as much money if they go second or reach an impasse. With the high payoff they earn more if they successfully dominate, but they lose more if they get into trouble or go second. Before the start of bargaining and with no knowledge of the other operator, only 37 percent of the dominators voted for the payoff which favors a successful dominating strategy. At mid-game, half of our Ss were afforded the opportunity to vote to revise their payoff for the remainder of the game. What did our Ss do? On their second vote, in those conditions where a second vote took place, 94 percent of the dominators voted for this payoff. Reassured by their knowledge of the pacifist that they could dominate with impunity, they did not soften their demands but planned for continued exploitation. The pacifist's tactics apparently invite exploitation and aggression even among those who do not begin with such intentions.

The judgment that many bargainers—some initially cooperative—end up exploiting the pacifist is hard and unflattering, but it is supported by a configuration of indices based on both objective behavior and on amplifying subjective ratings made by the Ss themselves. Furthermore, the failure of conversion does not arise from misperception of the pacifist's intention or fear of reprisal. While suspicious to some extent, our Ss were not holding back because of the Orwellian dictum that "Saints should always be judged guilty until they are proven innocent." Clarification of pacifist intentions does not lead to a greater number of conversions.

These findings, of course, must be viewed from the perspective of the restrictive conditions of our experiment. The Ss were operating under considerable pressure from their "teammates" to dominate. Although the real-life counterpart of such pressure is a factor with which the pacifist appeal frequently must contend, it will be of considerable interest to see what happens when such pressure is absent. Furthermore, our pacifist is a pure type—absolute in his commitment to principles of nonviolence. Thus he does not avail himself of some of the adjunct coercive techniques used by many resistance groups. The situation also narrowly limits the bargainers' options and permits little or no opportunity for intermediate resolution; there are no available means of gradually expanding limited areas of mutual agreement or of cooperative initiatives where risk is less than all-or-none. Social norms, sanctions, and pressures are vague and ill-defined for the Ss. There are, then, some rather stringent qualifications within which our results must be phrased.

But for all this we have at least made a bench mark for additional experimentation in the area of cooperative strategies in bargaining. While the pacifist's limited success may be attributable to the recognized limitations of our situation—the purity of his bargaining style, the sparseness of the bargaining space, and especially the absence of societal pressures— we may duly note that this tells us something about the limitations of pacifist strategies as well as about our restrictive conditions. Thus, if we need to enrich our situation to find those conditions necessary for effectiveness, this also helps us to see more clearly the qualifications for nonviolent bargaining strategies. Through systematic modifications in both environment and cooperative strategies in our future research, we hope to map out some of the limits and bases for the effectiveness of strategies based on cooperative rather than dominating intent.

As for the findings themselves, no summary on our part could match a commentary on the use of force written in 1929 by theologian Reinhold Niebuhr:

> Where there is a great inequality of physical advantage and physical power, it is difficult to establish moral relations. Weakness invites aggression. Even the most intelligent and moral individuals are more inclined to unethical conduct with those who are unable to offer resistance to injustice than with those who can. . . .
>
> It is obviously possible to resist injustice without using physical force and certainly without using violence. . . . But it seems that the world in which we live is not so spiritual that it is always possible to prompt the wrong doer to contrition merely by appealing to his conscience. . . .

REFERENCES

Janis, I. L., and D. Katz. "The Reduction of Intergroup Hostility: Research Problems and Hypotheses," *Journal of Conflict Resolution,* 3, 1 (Mar. 1959), 85–100.

Meeker, R. J., G. H. Shure, and W. H. Moore, Jr. "Real-time Computer Studies of Bargaining Behavior: The Effects of Threat upon Bargaining," *AFIPS Conference Proceedings, 1964 Spring Joint Computer Conference,* Vol. 25, 115–23.

Sharp, G. "The Meanings of Non-Violence: A Typology (Revised)," *Journal of Conflict Resolution,* 3, 1 (Mar. 1959), 41–66.

Shure, G. H., R. J. Meeker, and W. H. Moore, Jr. "Human Bargaining and Negotiation Behavior: Computer-based Empirical Studies. I. The Effects of Threat upon Bargaining." System Development Corporation Document TM-1330/000/00, June 25, 1963.

SOME SYSTEMIC EFFECTS OF THE SPREAD
OF NUCLEAR WEAPONS TECHNOLOGY:
A STUDY THROUGH SIMULATION
OF A MULTI-NUCLEAR FUTURE

Richard A. Brody

• • •

The approach taken in this study stems from the assumption that to conceive of the "cold war" as a pattern of interaction is a useful heuristic. The "cold war" can be thought of as a system of action with certain describable regularities—interaction processes—which serve to define it as a steady state.

Proceeding from this heuristic, we may ask the following question: *If one characteristic of the "cold war" system—the number of nations with nuclear capability—is changed, will the system survive or will a new steady state emerge?*

Another way to ask the question is to query the cruciality of the nuclear capability differential within the blocs which comprise the "cold war" system. If the nuclear differential is crucial to the interaction pattern we call the "cold war," then we would expect that the spread of nuclear weapons (the nth-country situation) would alter the pattern of interaction.

The null hypothesis (H_0) is that this change will not materially change the state of the system. The experimental hypothesis (H_1) is that a marked change in the number of nuclear nations will be reflected in a marked (i.e., "step-level") change in the "cold war" system—a new steady state will result.

• • •

. . . the "cold war" system is composed of two hierarchically-organized bloc-alliances with the leading nations in the bloc possessing a virtual monopoly of nuclear strike and counter-strike capability. Moreover, there is tension-generating hostility between the blocs which reinforces cohesion within the blocs and which itself is reinforced by this cohesion. The relationship within the blocs is one of dependency, born of necessity. In part, the dependency relationship is due to the hostility of the nuclear armed leader of the opposing bloc and in part to the nuclear disparity within the alliance. It is in this context that the effects of the spread of nuclear weapons will be essayed and explored.

• • •

. . . the expected change in the "cold war" system is the fragmentation of the blocs which comprise it. This (step-level) change will be prompted by the increased independence of the formerly nonnuclear national actors after they achieve nuclear capability; the increased sense of independence and a lowering of the perceived threat from the opposing bloc will lessen the intra-bloc cohesion and eventuate in the predicted fragmentation.

• • •

Deprived, as we are, of on-going, crucial, "natural" experiments we are left with the choice between waiting for the nth-country situation to evolve in actuality or working with the two extant, approximate cases—i.e., the British and French developments—or trying to artificially reproduce the "cold war" system and then experimentally inducing the spread of nuclear capability.

In the final analysis, the confirmation or disconfirmation of the model will depend upon the effects of nuclear diffusion in the *real* world; in this sense we have no choice but to wait for the situation to evolve. But if our interest is in evaluating the plausibility of the model *prior* to the actual occurrence, substitutes for a full-blown, crucial, natural experiment must be sought.

The two alternative approaches which are available—case studies of extant developments and simulation—are by no means mutually exclusive enterprises. The paucity of case material augurs ill for the exploration of the nth-country situation with any statistical model in mind.[1] But these cases can be productive of hypotheses and offer potential reality checks for ideas and measuring tools developed in the simulation.

• • •

The particular gaming approach employed—the Northwestern Inter-Nation Simulation (hereafter, INS)—was chosen because of the author's experience with this operating model and because it was felt that the INS was flexible enough to offer a reasonable prospect of providing a model world in which the spread of nuclear weapons could be examined.

THE INTER-NATION SIMULATION: A BRIEF DESCRIPTION

Since detailed descriptions of the INS exist elsewhere, it would be redundant to present more than a synopsis here. For full-blown discussions

[1] On the problems and benefits of using case materials, see Paige (1959).

and descriptions of the INS, the reader should see: Guetzkow (1959);
Brody and Noel (1960); and Guetzkow, et al. (1963).

The INS is comprised of a group of groups, i.e., a system of interacting units, where the units are teams of individuals. The unit-actors are
styled "nations." The individuals who act for the nation are its "decision-
makers."

As a convenience, before entering a discussion of the interaction between nations, the "domestic" structure of a single nation will be
explicated.

The nation in the INS is a system of roles. Some of these roles (the
"decision-making" roles) are occupied by live individuals—the "participants" or "subjects"—the other roles (validation roles) exist only insofar
as they provide a source of constraints on the freedom of action of the live
decision-makers.

The internal organization of the nation is determined, in large measure, by the participants. The "Central Decision-Maker" (CDM) represents
the chief-of-state and performs the executive function of government. He
maintains his position by satisfying those who validate his office-holding.
The "Internal Decision-Maker" (IDM) represents the director of the
budget; he is economic advisor to the CDM and performs such other
tasks as are assigned to him by the CDM. The "External Decision-Makers"
(EDMx and EDMy) represent the foreign relations structure of the nation
and perform the corresponding function. They are, as are the IDM and
the "Decision-Maker with respect to Force" (DMF), dependent upon the
CDM for their continuance in office. The DMF is the military advisor to
the CDM; it is his responsibility to advise on matters of strategy, allocation
of resources to force capability and defense. The division of labor among
these decision-makers is a matter for the CDM to decide; the "cabinet"
holds office at the pleasure of the CDM. Outside of the "government" is
an aspiring Central Decision-Maker (CDMa) who represents the leadership of competing elites in the nation who aspire to become the group in
power.

The number of participants who fill these roles will vary with the
number of subjects available and the problem being studied. The six key
roles are always represented but one participant may be called upon to
perform more than one role, e.g., CDM and IDM. The CDMa role has
often been represented symbolically (rather than by a participant); on
these occasions the pressure exerted by the "opposition" becomes part of
the over-all pressure exerted by the "validators" on the decision-makers.
On only one occasion has the number of participants per nation been
less than three; in that instance, two decision-makers per nation were used
with a specific research purpose in mind (Hermann and Hermann, 1962).

The "validators" are conceptually the group or groups, within a nation, to whom decision-makers (especially the CDM) are responsive and
responsible. The office-holding of the CDM (and, consequently, the office-

holding of his "cabinet") is functionally related to the level of "satisfaction" of the validators. Since not all decision-makers (in real nations) are equally responsive and responsible to their validators, we have allowed the degree of relationship to vary in the simulation. This degree of relationship (termed "decision latitude") is expressed in terms of a ten-point scale —the higher the decision latitude, the less sensitive is the CDM's office-holding to the level of validator satisfaction.

Validator satisfaction stems from two basic sources: (1) from "consumption," i.e., from expenditure (by the CDM) for consumer goods and services *beyond* the minimum needed to sustain the population; and (2) from felt "national security," i.e., from the level of capability (military and economic) of the nation and its allies in comparison with its strongest nonally and that nation's allies.

Time, in the simulation, is expressed in terms of decision periods. A period (from 50–70 minutes of *real* time) is a unit of domestic, fiscal decision-making—other types of decisions are made more or less continuously and are unprogrammed with respect to game time.

At the beginning of a period, the CDM receives a "decision form." This form constitutes the CDM's primary source of information about his domestic, political–economic setting; on it are found the results of his previous period's decision-making. These "results" include data on validator satisfaction, the level of the nation's economy—expressed as "basic capability"—and the level of the nation's military strength—termed "force capability." The decision form also informs the CDM about the minimum amount of basic capability which must be allocated to generating consumer goods and services. Thus, the decision form gives the CDM basic information about the nature of his domestic environment at time "t_i"— information which is vital to his decision-making at time "t_{i+1}."

Emphasis, thus far in this synopsis, has been on the domestic setting of one (any one) nation in the INS; this emphasis is not inordinate. In the INS, in contradistinction to the other operating models presented in Chapter I [of the original article], an effort has been made to represent the *domestic* constraints on the *foreign* policy-making process. These constraints are presented to the decision-maker as parametric values for a set of (hopefully) prototypic variables—public opinion, economic level, military level, decision latitude, and consumer demands.

By manipulating these parametric values at the outset of the simulation (i.e., time "t_0"), parallels to real world nations can be drawn. In this manner, role-playing of one sort (i.e., where the participant is charged with the responsibility of reproducing a "predicted" strategy for a nation which is not his own, but about which he knows a great deal) can be avoided. The participants in the INS are not instructed to "react the way the Soviet Union would react to the strategy of the United States"; rather, they are instructed to "react to the situation in which you find yourself."

To further reduce pressure for this type of role-playing, nations in the INS are not given real world names. A set of imaginary nations (*viz.*, Algo, Erga, Ingo, Omne, and Utro) have been created, with characteristics which vary with the research problem under consideration.

Despite the emphasis on the domestic constraints on decision-making, the INS is an operating model of the international system; prototypic classes of international behavior exist in the model. Thus, a nation may remain at peace or engage in war; moreover, wars may be limited or total; a nation may trade with other nations and seek or give foreign aid; alliances may be formed for a variety of reasons and with differing degrees of cohesion; international organizations may be founded or foundered. Several media of international communication are available: written messages, face-to-face conferences, international organization, and a "world press."

In general, in the INS, international interaction is less highly programmed than the domestic setting—in this arena participants are dealing with each other rather than with a conceptual reference group. Since the pattern of interaction is the primary locus of analysis, we have endeavored to leave the participants as free as possible to respond to and shape the international situation in which they find themselves.

INS-8: STRUCTURING THE BASIC SIMULATION TO ADMIT THE
EXPLORATION OF THE *n*TH-COUNTRY SITUATION

In the "exploratory," "feasibility," and "classroom laboratory" runs of the simulation (runs INS-1 through INS-7) we adhered to our policy of nonintervention once the simulation was underway. These runs were invaluable in the development and 'shaking down' of the model (Guetzkow, *et al.*, 1963).

As a result of this experience, we felt that certain changes and restructuring of the basic system were required if the theoretical model of the "cold war" and the predicted effects of the spread of nuclear capability (presented in Chapter II [of the original article]) were to be given a fair test. The basic system so amended was dubbed "INS-8"—the eighth running of the INS. INS-8 was itself run seventeen times—i.e., seventeen iterations of the same starting situation with differing groups of decision-makers. These runs were designated INS-8-I through INS-8-XVII.

A detailed description of the emendation of the simulation, for this study, exists elsewhere (Guetzkow, *et al.*, 1960); a brief presentation here should be sufficient to give the reader a feel for INS-8.

For INS-8, it was decided that the theretofore usual number of nations (five) would not be sufficient; two new nations were added—Yora and Zena. We felt that the larger number of nations would give us a closer approximation to the real world system we were modeling and provide a more stable statistical base for the testing of hypotheses—for example, if we are testing a hypothesis about behavior in the dyad, in a five-nation system twenty such (nonsymmetric) dyads exist; by adding two nations we more than double ($N=42$) the number of nonsymmetric dyads.

In three ways we increased the kinds of goods and services that could be generated by the allocation of basic capability: (1) force capability, which had been of one type only, was now differentiated into "nuclear" and "conventional"; (2) the nations were permitted to allocate basic capability to the "hardening"—i.e., passive defense against attack—of both nuclear force capability and basic capability; and (3) a procedure for conducting "research and development" projects was introduced. Plainly, these changes were dictated by the problem being considered.

The differentiation of force capability, into two types, was accomplished by developing two sets of "destruction ratios"—nuclear weapons are more effective than conventional weapons against certain targets—and by making nuclear capability more expensive to produce; i.e., it takes more basic capability to produce one unit of nuclear force capability than it does to produce one unit of conventional force capability.

For the sake of realism, it was ruled that a nation's economy (i.e., absolute level of basic capability) would have to pass a size threshold before allocation to nuclear capability would be permitted; this threshold was set high enough to preclude attainment of this capability prior to the programmed experimental intervention.

The possibility of acquiring passive defense was introduced because of the emphasis it has received in the literature on deterrence strategy (e.g., Morgenstern, 1959; and Kahn, 1958). We made it possible for a CDM to achieve invulnerability for a portion of his nuclear force capability and to "dig in" or "harden" part of his basic capability (a feature analogous to civil defense). Both of these forms of passive defense are expensive—the defense of basic capability is decidedly more expensive than the defense of nuclear force capability.

The cost of defense notwithstanding, this provision made possible the adoption of strategies which reduce the pressures for preemption—we sought to provide decision-makers with a wide range of potential strategies.

The third change—the addition of research and development programs (R & D)—was prompted by two considerations: (1) the experimenters' desire to add a category of decision-making which had important domestic and international consequences (Rummel, 1961); and (2) the experimenters' need for a plausible "cover" for the experimental intervention. R & D was presented to the participants as follows:

> . . . . one of the decisions which aids economic growth is the decision to allocate basic resources to research and development. This decision is indicated on the Decision Form (BCrd decision, Decision

Form, line 59) at the beginning of each period. A nation must have accumulated 2,000 BC's [units of basic capability] allocated to research and development before it can expect to receive any return. Both the amount of return and the time of return are to some extent uncertain. A nation will have to wait from two to four periods before a research and development project will begin to pay off; once payoff begins it will last for three periods. There is one chance in six that a project will fail; i.e., never pay off. Once payoff begins, the nation receives 14,000 BC's in the first period of payoff, 10,000 BC's in the second period, and 6,000 BC's in the third period; however, there is one chance in six that in a given payoff period these amounts will be reduced by half or lost entirely for that one period. Once a nation has received all the return from one 2,000 BC 'project' it may begin another research and development project which would operate in the same manner as the first project. *There is also a small probability that research and development will yield return in the form of nuclear force capability rather than BC's* [Brody and Noel, 1960, p. 14, emphasis added].

The italicized sentence was our cover for the programmed spread of nuclear capability. All nations had an R & D project under way at time "t_0"; this project yielded nuclear capability to the nonnuclear nations according to a schedule which will be presented below.

We decided, for INS-8, to have an international organization established at time "t_0." This decision has been explained as follows:

> In earlier work, the simulation's tendency to generate international organizations was great enough to obviate any need to start the system-run with a structured organization already in existence among the nations. However, considerable effort often was devoted by the nations to the development of an international organization, be it a political, military, and/or economic institution. Therefore, in an attempt to allow concentration upon the n-countries problem *per se*, the seventeen system-runs were initiated with an international organization already in existence. The charter of this 'IO' provided for universal membership with regular sessions of permanent representatives . . . [Guetzkow, et al., 1960, p. 5].

The EDMy was the permanent delegate to the IO.

As was indicated above, roles for up to six participants are provided for in the simulation. To have filled all of these roles—one person per role—for multiple runs would have taken us far beyond our potential supply of subjects. Faced with a choice between more runs with fewer participants per nation and fewer runs with more participants per nation, we chose the former. Our experience has been that combining roles works—i.e., the functions embodied in these roles get performed.

We used three participants per nation—combining the CDM and

IDM, and EDMx and DMF, and giving the EDMy the twin responsibilities of aiding the EDMx with foreign affairs and attending the IO as permanent delegate. With seven nations per run and seventeen runs accomplished, 357 subjects participated in INS-8.

THE PARTICIPANTS AND THEIR SELECTION [3]

The participants in INS-8 were 357 North Shore and Northern Chicago high school students (172 males and 185 females). Those who participated were chosen from 709 students tested by Driver during June and July, 1960.

"The crucial variable in both selecting subjects and assigning them to nations in the INS," according to Driver, "was generalized abstractness. The degree of abstractness was measured by a form of the Situational Interpretation Test [SIT] developed by Schroder and Hunt" (Driver, 1962, p. 36). The SIT score was used to identify the subjects' locations on a "concrete–abstract" dimension. From these results, the subjects were classified into three groups, viz., "abstract" (Type IV), "concrete" (Type I), and "neutral" (Types II and III). The distribution of participants, so classified, was as follows: 122 "concrete," 122 "neutral," and 133 "abstract." Whenever possible, subjects from the same SIT category were grouped together in a nation. Care was taken to distribute nations, so composed, randomly over the seventeen runs (Guetzkow, et al., 1960, pp. 16–7).

In addition to the SIT, Form 40–45 of the California F Scale was used as a selection instrument. The F Scale correlates with the SIT and was used by Driver to increase the polarization of "Type I" and "Type IV" subjects. The distribution of participants' scores on the F Scale is "single-peaked," $\overline{X} = 53.8$, $X_{0.50} = 54.5$, $s = 8.62$—the distribution appears normal.

The subjects were almost all high school juniors and seniors; the exceptions were the few participants who had just completed their high school training five weeks prior to the beginning of the INS-8 runs.

Data (from the schools) on I.Q. (unfortunately, not complete and not always drawn from comparable measuring instruments) indicate that our participants were "average" or "above average" on this variable.

The ages of the subjects ranged from 15–18. The average age was 16. As far as possible, nations and runs were populated with participants, so as to reduce error variance from these subject psycho-social characteristics.

[3] Dr. Michael Driver, Educational Testing Service, assumed primary responsibility for the selection and assignment of participants—for this I am deeply grateful. For a detailed description of the selection and assignment process, see: Driver (1962), and Guetzkow, et al., (1960).

Despite the degree of simplification, operating a nation in the INS is still a complex task—it has been suggested that operating an INS nation is a task of about the same order of complexity for the high school or college student as operating a real nation is for the more experienced adult decision-maker (Driver, 1962). It is impossible to assess the merit of this suggestion but it is an interesting idea—this complexity is a potential source of bewilderment to the subjects. To reduce potential bewilderment of the participant (and, consequently, the error variance deriving therefrom) a two-phase program of training in the mechanics of the INS was instituted. In the first phase, the basic operating documents of the INS (the Participants Manual, a handbook covering the details of one of the roles, and information about the starting situation, i.e., time "t_0") were mailed to the subject in advance of his participation. In addition, a one-hour, on-the-job, training period (phase two) was used to further orient the subjects to the operation of the simulation.

In this training, the seriousness of the enterprise was emphasized. The subjects' mastery of the mechanics, involvement, and sober approach to the experiment was altogether remarkable. As evident of this involvement and sobriety, the fact is offered that out of over 9,000 inter-nation messages content coded, less than one per cent were coded "extra system," i.e., contained material not pertinent to the simulation.

TIME "t_0": THE STARTING SITUATION FOR INS-8

The starting situation was programmed to yield two bloc-alliances (one of three nations, the other of four) which were very nearly alike in their military and economic capacities. Only one nation in each bloc had nuclear force capability at the outset—these nations were also the major economic powers. Table 3.1 summarizes the starting parameters—all seventeen runs began in the same manner.

Table 3.2 presents the "generation rates" of the several nations for the production of goods and services. The generation rate is an expression of the ratio of units of a given commodity produced to a unit of basic capability allocated—it is thus a measure of the efficiency of production.

In the absence of a medium of exchange, the differential generation rates, between nations on the same commodity, permit barter-trade according to comparative advantages.

In addition to this information about the starting parameters, the participants were given information on the initial military–economic–diplomatic situation *via* the following "World Perspective" (this document was offered in lieu of a scenario):

Table 3.1

BLOC-ALLIANCE STRUCTURE WITH INITIAL BASIC AND FORCE
CAPABILITIES[a]

The Omne–Yora–Erga Bloc Capabilities				The Utro–Zena–Ingo–Algo Bloc Capabilities			
Nation	Basic	Force		Nation	Basic	Force	
		FCc	FCn			FCc	FCn
Omne	34,000	1,600	28	Utro	30,000	1,500	25
Yora	12,000	700	—	Zena	8,000	200	—
Erga	8,500	750	—	Ingo	9,000	800	—
				Algo	7,500	100	—
Total	54,000	3,050	28		54,500	2,600	25

[a]The "basic capability" of the nation (subsuming, as it does, resources, both physical and human) represents the nation's ability to produce all goods and services. The "conventional" (FCc) and "nuclear" (FCn) force capability of the nation represents its ability to mount military operations against other nations. All units in the simulation are arbitrary, reflecting only the relative position of one nation *vis-à-vis* another.

In the simulation world two nations are the dominant centers of power. Omne and Utro, in addition to being the only nuclear powers at this time, are also in possession of large amounts of BC's, that is, economic potential. The other five nations cluster about these power centers in two bloc-alliances; the two bloc-alliances are relatively equal in comparison with each other—neither enjoying a clear superiority in all areas of present position or growth potential. All nations have research and development projects underway which *if* they bear fruit will yield increased economic potential or, perhaps, nuclear force capability.

The present positions of the nations represent the project of both internal growth and international trade. The principal trading partners have been Omne, Yora, and Erga, on the one hand, and Utro, Algo, Ingo, and Zena on the other; trade has not been exclusively among these groups but it has tended to follow these lines.

The bloc-alliances—the nations of Omne, Yora, and Erga making up one bloc and Utro, Zena, Ingo, and Algo the other—are trade as well as military alliances; both are secured by formal treaty [Quoted in: Guetzkow, *et al.*, 1960, pp. 24–5].

In this manner, the participants learned of the situation in which they would begin to operate their nations—the situation which emerged from their decision-making beyond time "t_0" was of their own making. The "worlds" beyond time "t_0" were unstructured by the experimenters

Table 3.2

GENERATION RATES[a]

Nation	Rate			
	BC/BC	CS/BC	FCn/BC	FCc/BC
Algo	0.8	1.0	0.06	0.5
Erga	0.8	1.5	0.02	0.5
Ingo	0.9	1.0	0.02	1.5
Omne	1.0	1.5	0.08	2.0
Utro	1.0	1.5	0.08	2.0
Yora	0.9	1.0	0.06	1.5
Zena	0.8	1.5	0.02	0.5

[a] BC = basic capability unit.
    CS = consumption satisfaction unit.
    FCn = nuclear force capability unit.
    FCc = conventional force capability unit.

except for the experimental intervention (the effects of which the study was designed to determine).

DATA SOURCES

In order to determine the effects of the experimental intervention, measures (i.e., operational definitions of the variables) needed to be constructed. These measures were drawn from two classes of data from INS-8: (1) system endogenous data; and (2) system exogenous data.

"System endogenous data" are those data which result from the operation of the simulation by the participants: decision forms, force utilization plans, messages, conference and IO transcripts, press releases, trade and aid transactions, treaties—in short, the totality of materials, generated by the decision-makers, which lend themselves to the diagnosis of system process from time "t_0" to time "t_1." These data have been used to aid in the production of the "history" of each of the seventeen runs of INS-8 (Brody, et al., 1961). The use of endogenous data in the exploration of the model will be discussed at length below [in the original article].

The "system exogenous data" were generated from the administration of a battery of "pencil and paper" instruments. At three points during the simulation—just prior to the experimental intervention, just after the experimental intervention, and during the final period—the participants were asked to complete each of three "Policy Planning Aids."

"Planning Aid #1," a multi-dimensional scaling instrument, was developed and used by Driver in his work on INS-8 (Driver, 1962). This instrument will enter into this study only insofar as Driver's results are drawn upon for confirmatory or disconfirmatory data.

"Planning Aid #2," a form of the "Semantic–Differential" (Osgood, et al., 1957), was used to assess decision-makers' perceptions of the nations in the system. Data from the "Semantic–Differential" do not enter into the analyses which follow; subsequent analyses are planned.

"Planning Aid #3," a rating sheet consisting of five "Lickert Scales," was used to assess the attitudes of decision-makers toward the other nations in the system. The participants were asked to "rate the friendliness, trust-worthiness, helpfulness, and cooperativeness of the other nations" and to express their perception of the likelihood of the other nation "becoming involved in a war" with their nation. This rating form appears as Appendix I.

• • •

Event Flow in INS-8. Before turning to the actual experiment and the testing of hypotheses, it is felt that "feel" for INS-8 can be enhanced by the presentation of a model of the flow of events in the simulation.

Each of the seventeen system-runs covered four half-days of real time —twelve periods of simulation time. In each case, the first period was given over to the on-the-job training discussed above. The decision-makers, therefore, received and completed eleven Decision Forms (the Period 12 Decision Form was completed but not returned to the decision-maker after calculation). The international organization met once each period— eleven times in all. The "pencil and paper" instruments were administered during Periods 4, 7, and 12. The experimental intervention was phased-in during Periods 5 and 6—our feeling was that a two period "transition" from binuclear to n-nuclear would aim in maintaining our cover story, i.e., seem less unnatural to the participants.

Figure 3.2 summarizes the flow of experimenter controlled events in INS-8.

• • •

THE COLD WAR SYSTEM: CONDITIONS AND LINKAGES

Perception of Out-Group Hostility. The first "condition" to be established in our exploration of the "cold war system" is the perception of the external bloc (i.e., the nations with whom a nation is not allied) as being hostile. The tendency of groups to distinguish "ins" and "outs" is pervasive and serves to bind aggregates of actors into a group (Campbell and Levine, 1961). By extension, the presence of such distinctions should aid in binding aggregates of nations into bloc-alliances.

Null Hypothesis—H_o: perception of inter-bloc hostility is no greater

Fig. 3.2 — Event flow in INS-8

	Period 1	2	3	4	5	6	7	8	9	10	11	12
Algo DF		x	x	x	x	x	x	x	x	x	x	x
FCn's		no---	---	---→	yes-	---	---	---	---	---	---	↑
Erga DF		x	x	x	x	x	x	x	x	x	x	x
FCn's		no---	---	---	---	→yes-	x	x	x	x	x	↑
Ingo DF		x	x	x	x	x	x	x	x	x	x	x
FCn's		no---	---	---	---	→yes-	---	x	x	x	x	↑
Omne DF		x	x	x	x	x	x	x	x	x	x	x
FCn's		yes---	x	x	x	x	x	x	x	x	x	x
Utro DF		x	x	x	x	x	x	x	x	x	x	x
FCn's		yes---	---	x	x	x	x	x	x	x	x	↑
Yora DF		x	x	x	x	x	x	x	x	x	x	x
FCn's		no---	---	---	→yes	---	x	x	x	x	x	x
Zena DF		x	x	x	x	x	x	x	x	x	x	x
FCn's		no---	---	---	---	→yes-	---	x	x	x	x	↑
IO meeting		000	000	000	000	000	000	000	000	000	000	000
Planning Aid				xxx			xxx					xxx

Legend:

DF — Decision form

FCn's — Presence of nuclear force capability (Note: phase transition from bi-nuclear to n-nuclear)

X — Time of arrival of DF to CDM (Note: the delivery of DF's was staggered through the period but each CDM had his form in his possession the same length of time)

000 — Span of 30-minute IO meeting

xxx — Time of administration of exogenous measures — 30 minutes for each administration

Fig. 3.2. Event flow in INS-8.

than the perception of intra-block hostility. H_1: the inter-bloc dyads will rank higher on perceptions of hostility than will the intra-block dyads.

Statistical Test—Systems Questionnaire (Appendix I), Scale #1 is the measure of perceived hostility. On it, each of the seven nations rated the other six nations as to their "friendliness–unfriendliness"—high scores are toward the "unfriendly" end of the scale. The experimental hypothesis, in effect, predicts the relative rankings of perceptions across bloc lines in contrast with perceptions within the bloc. The "Mann–Whitney U Test" (Siegel, 1956, pp. 116 ff.) is appropriate for analyzing these data.

Significance Level—Let $\alpha = 0.05$ (α = probability of a Type I error). $n_1 = 18$ = the number of intra-bloc dyads; $n_2 = 24$ = the number of inter-bloc dyads.

Sampling Distribution—For $n_2 > 20$ the following formula yields values of z (*ibid.*, 1956, p. 123):

$$z = \frac{U - (n_1 n_2 / 2)}{\sqrt{(n_1)(n_2)(n_1 + n_2 + 1)/12}} \tag{4.1}$$

The probabilities associated with occurrence under H_0 of values as extreme as an observed z may be determined by reference to a table of probabilities under the normal curve with zero mean and unit variance.

Rejection Region—Since H_1 predicts the direction of the differences, the region of rejection is one-tailed. It consists of all values of z which are so extreme that their associated probability under H_0 is equal to or less than $\alpha = 0.05$.

Decision—The hostility perception scores of each of the 42 dyads are shown in Table 4.1, together with the rank of each dyad. For these data, $R_1 = 171$ and $R_2 = 732$. The value of U is found by substituting the observed values in the following formulae (*ibid.*, 1956, p. 120):

$$U = n_1 n_2 + \frac{n_2(n_2 + 1)}{2} - R_2 \tag{4.2a}$$

or equivalently,

$$U = n_1 n_2 + \frac{n_1(n_1 + 1)}{2} - R_1. \tag{4.2b}$$

From Formula 4.2a we find that:

$$U = 732 - R_2 = 0;$$

using Formula 4.1, we find:

$$z = U - 216/39.34 = 5.40.$$

Table 4.1

PERCEPTIONS OF INTER-BLOC AND INTRA-BLOC HOSTILITY

Inter-bloc Dyads			Intra-bloc Dyads		
Dyad	Score	Rank	Dyad	Score	Rank
1. AE	230	27.5	1. AI	162	11
2. AO	229	26	2. AU	169	13
3. AY	234	29	3. AZ	178	18
4. EA	225	25	4. EO	134	2
5. EI	224	23.5	5. EY	149	7
6. EU	252	37	6. IA	160	10
7. EZ	239	33	7. IU	171	15
8. IE	224	23.5	8. IZ	165	12
9. IO	268	40	9. OE	151	8
10. IY	238	31.5	10. OY	142	5
11. OA	186	19	11. UA	177	17
12. OI	238	31.5	12. UI	139	3
13. OU	285	42	13. UZ	141	4
14. OZ	251	36	14. YE	144	6
15. UE	237	30	15. YO	124	1
16. UO	277	41	16. ZA	170	14
17. UY	259	39	17. ZI	173	16
18. YA	195	20	18. ZU	152	9
19. YI	222	22			$\Sigma = 171 = R_1$
20. YU	246	35			
21. YZ	242	34			
22. ZE	218	21			
23. ZO	254	38			
24. ZY	230	27.5			
		$\Sigma = 732 = R_2$			

Reference to the "Table of Probabilities Associated with Values as Extreme as Observed Values of z in the Normal Distribution" (*ibid.*, p. 247) reveals that $z = 5.40$ has a one-tailed probability under H_0 of $p < 0.00003$. [*That is, if hostility were to distribute itself randomly, there is a probability of less than .00003 that it would find itself distributed in the manner displayed in Table 4.1—with much hostility between blocs and little among them. One is inclined, therefore, to suspect that hostility has not been doled out by chance.—Ed.*] Since the p is less than $\alpha = 0.05$, our decision is to reject H_0 in favor of H_1. *Nations in the external bloc are perceived as being more hostile than nations within the bloc.*

[*In a related manner, the following conclusions are arrived at:*]

More hostility is transmitted external to the bloc than internal to it.

There is a greater perception of threat from nations outside of the bloc than from nations within the bloc.

There is a positive relationship between perceptions of hostility and perceptions of threat.

There is a positive relationship between the receipt of expressed hostility and perceptions of threat.

There is greater tendency for dependency themes to appear in messages directed to nuclear bloc members than to nonnuclear bloc members.

Dependent themes appear to increase with perceptions of threat (the correlation is in the right direction) but the relationship may very well be random.

Dependent themes appear to increase with increases in the receipt of hostile themes from the external nuclear power but the relationship may be random.

There is more interaction within the blocs than between the blocs— the blocs are highly cohesive units.

There is a negative relationship between perceptions of threat and level of interaction.

Dependent themes appear to be related to affiliation themes (the correlation is in the right direction) but the relationship may be random.

The nuclear members act as distributors in their communication nets; the nets exhibit the properties of the wheel structure—a two-level hierarchy.

There is a tendency for nonnuclear bloc members to communicate with the leaders of their bloc rather than with the external nuclear power —the system prior to the spread of nuclear capability is not only bipolar, it is tightly bipolar.

THE *n*TH-CENTURY SITUATION: CONDITIONS AND LINKAGES

The reader will, we believe, grant, on the evidence contained in the foregoing section, that the "cold war system" as we have defined it, emerged in the binuclear periods of INS-8. In this section we will attempt to assess the effects of the diffusion of nuclear weapons capability on this "cold war system."

Perceptions of Threat from Nations External to the Bloc in the Nth-Country Situation [We predict a] reduction in the level of perceived threat from the external bloc as a result of the spread of nuclear capability.

Null Hypothesis—H_0: there is no difference between the level of perceived threat, from the external bloc, before and after the spread of nuclear capability. H_1: the level of perceived threat will be lower after the spread of nuclear weapons.

Statistical Test—Our measure of threat perception is, as before, Scale #2 on the Systems Questionnaire (Appendix I). The comparison will be made on the 24 inter-bloc ratings before and after spread took place (i.e., Periods 4 and 12, see Figure 3.2, above). The U Test will be used in this comparison.

Significance Level—Let $\alpha = 0.05$. $n_1 = 24 =$ the number of inter-bloc dyads in the pre-spread periods; $n_2 = 24 =$ the number of inter-bloc dyads in the post-spread periods.

Sampling Distribution—Same as above.

Region of Rejection—Same as above.

Decision—The level of perceived threat for each of the 48 dyads is shown in Table 4.14, together with the rank of the dyad. For these data, $R_1 = 811.5$ and $R_2 = 364.5$. The value of U is determined by substitution of the observed value into Formula 4.2b:

$$U = 876 - R_1 = 64.5.$$

Using Formula 4.1, we find:

$$z = U - 288/47.94 = 4.66.$$

Reference to the table of normal probabilities (Siegel, 1956, p. 247) reveals that $z = 4.66$ has a one-tailed probability under H_0 of $p < 0.00003$. Since this p is less than $\alpha = 0.05$, our decision is to reject H_0 in favor of H_1. *After the spread of nuclear weapons, the perception of inter-bloc threat is markedly reduced.*

[In a related manner, the following conclusions are arrived at:]

After the spread of nuclear capability there is still a significant difference between the levels of inter- and intra-bloc threat.

After the spread of nuclear weapons, there is an increase in the perception of threat from members of the internal bloc.

There may be as much interaction (cohesion) between the blocs as within the blocs—the marked preference for communicating within the bloc, which existed prior to nuclear diffusion, is no longer evident.

The predicted link between threat and cohesion does not emerge.

Threat perception and level of interaction (in intra-bloc dyads) appear to be negatively related but the relationship may be random.

The hierarchical structure of the bloc does not break down under the impact of the spread of nuclear weapons.

After the spread of nuclear weapons, the former nonnuclear nations may be as likely to communicate with the external bloc leader as with their own bloc leader. The bipolarity appears to fragment; the hierarchies appear to be based on the economic differentials.

Table 4.14

PERCEPTIONS OF INTER-BLOC THREAT

Pre-spread			Post-spread		
Dyad	Score	Rank	Dyad	Score	Rank
1. AE	206	35	1. AE	161	9
2. AO	243	42	2. AO	148	2
3. AY	197	29.5	3. AY	156	5.5
4. EA	207	36.5	4. EA	187	25
5. EI	211	38	5. EI	176	19
6. EU	257	45	6. EU	164	10
7. EZ	207	36.5	7. EZ	157	7
8. IE	198	31	8. IE	201	33
9. IO	272	46	9. IO	192	28
10. IY	224	40	10. IY	165	11
11. OA	186	24	11. OA	130	1
12. OI	220	39	12. OI	154	4
13. OU	286	48	13. OU	175	18
14. OZ	197	29.5	14. OZ	172	15.5
15. UE	185	23	15. UE	182	22
16. UO	279	47	16. UO	200	32
17. UY	236	41	17. UY	179	21
18. YA	150	3	18. YA	169	13
19. YI	189	26.5	19. YI	169	13
20. YU	246	43	20. YU	172	15.5
21. YZ	169	13	21. YZ	178	20
22. ZE	174	17	22. ZE	159	8
23. ZO	252	44	23. ZO	189	26.5
24. ZY	203	34	24. ZY	156	5.5

$$\Sigma = 811.5 = R_1 \qquad \qquad \Sigma = 364.5 = R_2$$

We are now in possession of sufficient data to permit an answer to the "macro-question" posed above: Is the international system different before and after the spread of nuclear weapons?" The answer is an unqualified "Yes.". . .

The [binuclear] system was comprised of two heirarchical, cohesive bloc-alliances. The nations of the external bloc were perceived as more hostile and threatening than the nations of the internal bloc. The communication between the blocs was characterized by a greater level of expressed hostility than the communication within the blocs. The non-nuclear nations expressed dependency upon the nuclear bloc leader—a dependency which appears to be related to outgroup hostility and threat. (However, neither correlation coefficient was high enough to rule out random occurrence.) The dependency on the bloc leader and the hierarchical ordering of the blocs stem from both military and economic insufficiencies—the economic insufficiency continued into the post-spread situation. In sum, the binuclear system is tightly bipolar.

Four key elements of the pre-spread system are different after the spread of nuclear capability: (1) threat external to the bloc is reduced; (2) threat internal to the bloc is increased; (3) the cohesiveness of the blocs is reduced; and (4) the bipolarity is fragmented. All of these add up to a step-level change in the "cold war system."

• • •

INS-8 registered successes. A high level of prediction was accomplished; that is to say, changes in the simulated international system, after the spread of nuclear capability, conformed in most respects to the theoretical model posited in advance of the experiments. The pre-spread system was a plausible model of reality, i.e., the pattern of interaction, which developed prior to diffusion of nuclear capability, resembled real world patterns which have developed since the end of World War II.

This "pattern matching" is highly desirable. With respect to the validity of experimental findings, Zelditch and Evans caution, "before experimenting on a simulate the investigator ought to run a sufficiently long series of uniformity trials to show that, left to itself, the simulate behaves like the process simulated at least in those ways necessary to investigation" (1962, p. 60). The real world pattern matching in the pre-spread periods of INS-8 would seem to meet this requirement. . . .

But these "successes" by no means eliminate all problems and reservations concerning the meaning of the findings. To question the "meaning" of the findings is to make public the author's concern about the generality of knowledge derived from the laboratory. What is the relationship of knowledge about the behavior of the simulate to knowledge about the real system? Or, more directly, what is the relationship of the simulate to the real international system?

We do not argue that the inter-nation simulation is a complete representation (i.e., is totally isomorphic) of all aspects of the international system. However, we do not accept the argument that we have merely gained knowledge about the behavior of high school students in a defined laboratory situation. But where between these extremes, on this continuum of generalizability, do the findings from INS-8 fall?

Any answer to this question must derive initially from the assumptions of the simulation designers about the correspondence of "concrete" and "analytic" structures (Levy, 1958) in the simulation to the same structures in the real international system, and ultimately must derive from the pragmatic test—prediction of real world behavior.

Among the "concrete" structures (i.e., observable entities or types of behavior) represented in the simulation are "nation," "decision-maker," "alliance," "trade," "war," "message," and "international organization." Some of the "analytic" structures (i.e., non-observable relations and processes) represented in the INS are "public opinion," "communication," "communication net," "validation of decisions," and "cohesion of alliances."

From these two lists, it can be seen that the "concrete" structures appear most different after the transposition from the natural setting to the laboratory. The "analytic" structures are linguistic conventions used to describe actions found in both research settings and are, by definition, isomorphic in both loci.

In the context of these concepts the problem of generalizing from the artificial setting to the political world is the problem of determining whether the change in "concrete" structure also alters the nature of the performance of the unit in its relationships with other units. For example, the *process* by which a decision is reached in the simulate is more apt to be the same after transposition to the laboratory than is the content of decisions under the same transformation. This belief informed the decision to concentrate on interaction process in this study.

Snyder contends that, "the primary aim of laboratory representations is to set key variables and their interrelationships *in motion* and to create, explicitly, imitations of and substitutes for the hidden explanatory or conditioning factors assumed to operate in life. Moreover, the experimental situation is usually designed to achieve *not actual effects* observed outside of the laboratory but *equivalent kinds of effects* using the most economical representations of causal variables" (1962, p. 109).

The ability to set key variables and their interrelations in motion and to achieve equivalent kinds of effects or to achieve a degree of correspondence between laboratory and real world structures is a function of the adequacy of the theory which informs the construction of the operating model. Theory indicates which variables and interrelations are central to the reality being modeled; the correspondence of the model to reality after operation (i.e., its predictiveness) is a test of the salience of the variables chosen for inclusion in the simulate, and of the fidelity of the reproduction of the interrelations among these variables.

Failure to predict is a signal that adjustments in the theory need to be made—new variables need to be included and/or old interrelations need to be reset. This is the essence of the theory-building aspect of laboratory experimentation: a cycle of THEORY-BUILDING, EXPERIMENTATION, PREDICTION, OBSERVATION, THEORY-BUILDING . . . until the model is fine-tuned.

INS-8 is the culmination of three phases of this cycle: theory-building and model construction in INS's 1 through 7; experimentation and prediction in INS-8. Observation of the predicted phenomena, in the real world, must await the arrival of the *n*th-country situation.

POLICY PLANNING AID #3

This document is designed to aid you in your planning of future international decisions. The questions are a simplified form of the kinds of questions foreign policy decision-makers ask of the world situation. The fact that your answers may differ from time to time reflects the changeable nature of the world situation.

In addition to helping you clarify your thinking about the other nations in the world, this document will serve as a permanent record of your views of the world situation and, thereby, help us to understand your picture of the world for experimental purposes.

In the questions below you will be asked to rate the other nations on various qualities; two or more nations may be rated as equal but a rating must be given to each of the six nations.

Example: Indicate the *courteousness to your nation* of the other six nations.

: _____1_____ : _____ : ___2.3___ : ___4___ :
    extremely courteous   very   quite   slightly

: _____ : _____ : _5_ : _____ : _____6_____ :
          slightly   quite   very   extremely discourteous

(Note that in the example nations 2 and 3 are rated equally, while nations 1, 4, 5, and 6 are rated non-equally. In the example, numbers were used for the nations; in your answers, you will *use the first letter of the nation's name*: A, E, I, O, U, Y, and Z.

1. Indicate the *friendliness to your nation* of the other six nations.

: _____ : _____ : _____ : _____ :
    extremely friendly   very   quite   slightly

: _____ : _____ : _____ : _____ :
      slightly   quite   very   extremely unfriendly

2. Indicate the likelihood of each of the other six nations becoming involved in a war with your nation.

: _____ : _____ : _____ : _____ : _____ :
    extremely likely   very   quite   slightly

: _____ : _____ : _____ : _____ :
      slightly   quite   very   extremely unlikely

3. Indicate the *trustworthiness* of the other six nations in their dealings with your nation.

: _____ : _____ : _____ : _____ : _____ :
    extremely trustworthy   very   quite   slightly

: _____ : _____ : _____ : _____ :
      slightly   quite   very   extremely untrustworthy

Appendix I
(Continued)

4. Indicate the *helpfulness to your nation* of the other six nations.

: _____ : _____ : _____ : _____ : _____ :

   extremely helpful   very   quite   slightly

: _____ : _____ : _____ : _____ :

   slightly   quite   very   extremely harmful

5. Indicate the degree of cooperation or conflict which the other six nations show toward your nation.

: _____ : _____ : _____ : _____ : _____ :

   extremely cooperative   very   quite   slightly

: _____ : _____ : _____ : _____ :

   slightly   quite   very   extremely conflicting

REFERENCES

BRODY, R. A., BEACH, P., and SAMUELS, E.   *Chronologies of Runs in INS-8*. Evanston, Ill.: Program of Graduate Training and Research in International Relations, 1961.

BRODY, R. A. and NOEL, R.   *Inter-Nation Simulation Participants' Manual*. Evanston, Ill.: Program of Graduate Training and Research in International Relations, 1960.

CAMPBELL, D. T. and LEVINE, R.   "A Proposal for Cooperative Cross-Cultural Research on Ethnocentrism," *The Journal of Conflict Resolution*, 5 (1961), 82–108.

DRIVER, M. J.   *Conceptual Structure and Group Processes in an Inter-Nation Simulation*. Princeton, N.J.: Princeton University and Educational Testing Service, 1962.

GUETZKOW, H.   "The Use of Simulation in the Study of Inter-Nation Relations," *Behavorial Science*, 4 (1959), 183–91.

GUETZKOW, H., ALGER, C., BRODY, R., NOEL, R., and SNYDER, R. C. *Simulation in International Relations: Developments for Research and Teaching*. Englewood Cliffs, N.J.: Prentice-Hall, 1963.

GUETZKOW, H., BRODY, R., DRIVER, M., and BEACH, P.   *An Experiment of the N-Country Problem through Simulation*. St. Louis, Mo.: The Social Science Institute, Washington University, 1960.

HERMANN, C. F. and HERMANN, M. G.   *On the Possible Use of Historical Data for Validation Study of the Inter-Nation Simulation*. China Lake, Calif.: U. S. Naval Ordnance Test Station, 1962.

KAHN, H.   *Report on a Study of Non-Military Defense*. Santa Monica, Calif.: The RAND Corp. (#R-322-RC), 1958.

LEVY, M.   "Some Aspects of 'Structural-Functional' Analysis in Political Science." In R. Young (ed.), *Approaches to the Study of Politics*. Evanston, Ill.: Northwestern University Press, 1958.

Morgenstern, O. *The Question of National Defense*. New York: Random House, 1959.

Osgood, C., Suci, G., and Tannenbaum, P. *The Measurement of Meaning*. Urbana, Ill.: University of Illinois Press, 1957.

Paige, G. "Problems and Uses of the Single Case in Political Research." In G. Paige, *The Korean Decision (June 24–30, 1950): A Reconstruction of Decision-Making Events*, Doctoral Dissertation, Northwestern University, 1959, Chapter 10.

Rummel, R. J. *Technology and War: A Correlational Analysis*. M. A. Thesis, University of Hawaii, 1961.

Siegel, S. *Nonparametric Statistics*. New York: McGraw-Hill, 1956.

Snyder, R. C. "Experimental Techniques and Political Analysis: Some Reflections in the Context of Concern over Behavioral Approaches." In D. C. Charlesworth (ed.), *The Limits of Behavioralism in Political Science*. Philadelphia: American Academy of Political and Social Science, 1962.

Zelditch, M., Jr. and Evans, W. M. "Simulated Bureaucracies: A Methodological Analysis." In H. Guetzkow (ed.), *Simulation in Social Science: Readings*. Englewood Cliffs, N.J.: Prentice-Hall, 1962.

5

Voting in International Organizations

An extraordinarily rich source of readily quantifiable information about the foreign policy postures of governments is furnished by the voting records of international organizations. It is as if the nations of the world were continually being surveyed on a large number of specific issues to which they can react with a limited number of strictly structured response options. A growing body of techniques for analyzing legislative voting behavior has been developed in studies of state and national legislatures and much of this material is applicable to roll-call voting in international bodies.[1]

The United Nations General Assembly is the international legislature which so far has received the most attention. A battery of techniques has been applied by researchers, some principally trying to sort out and analyze voting blocs in the Assembly,[2] others concerned more with the

[1] A superb introductory handbook in this area is Lee A. Anderson, Meredith W. Watts, Jr., and Allen R. Wilcox, *Legislative Roll-Call Analysis* (Evanston, Ill.: Northwestern University Press, 1966). For some later developments, see Duncan MacRae, Jr., "A Method for Identifying Issues and Factions from Legislative Votes," *American Political Science Review*, Vol. 59 (December, 1965), pp. 909–26, and "Cluster Analysis of Congressional Votes with the BC TRY System," *Western Political Quarterly*, Vol. 19 (December, 1966) pp. 631–38. See also John Wahlke and Heinz Eulau (eds.), *Legislative Behavior* (Glencoe, Ill.: The Free Press, 1959).

[2] M. Margaret Ball, "Bloc Voting in the General Assembly," *International Organization*, Vol. 5 (February, 1951), pp. 3–31; William W. Ellis and John Salzberg, "Africa and the U.N.: A Statistical Note," *American Behavioral Scientist*, Vol. 8 (April, 1965), pp. 30–32; Thomas Hovet, Jr., *Bloc Politics in the United Nations* (Cambridge: Harvard, 1960) and *Africa in the United Nations* (Evanston, Ill.: Northwestern University Press,

relationships between issues.[3] Other international bodies, such as the Western European Union and the International Labor Organization, have also involuntarily undergone analysis.[4]

The investigation of international roll-call voting poses several layers of procedural problems which require thoughtful consideration by the practitioner. Most basically, what do roll-calls mean, anyway? While they surely must reflect in some way the nature of many of the important conflicts in the legislative arena, it hardly needs to be pointed out that much of the stuff of international politics never is conveniently codified in a formal vote on the floor of an international organization.[5] Additionally the social scientist is not able to formulate the issues that come to a vote and thus the votes are not always phrased in a way which is of great help to him. Even if the issue is a meaningful one, the vote options open to the legislative voter are quite limited and give him little opportunity to express the intensity of his feeling on the issue,[6] although scaling techniques sometimes can be helpful in this regard if a series of appropriately interlinked issues is voted on.

1963); Arend Lijphart, "The Analysis of Bloc Voting in the General Assembly: A Critique and a Proposal," *American Political Science Review*, Vol. 57 (December, 1963), pp. 902–17; Leroy N. Rieselbach, "Quantitative Techniques for Studying Voting Behavior in the UN General Assembly," *International Organization*, Vol. 14 (Spring, 1960), pp. 297–304; Bruce M. Russett, "Discovering Voting Groups in the United Nations," *American Political Science Review*, Vol. 60 (June, 1966), pp. 327–39, and *International Regions and the International System* (Chicago: Rand McNally, 1967), especially chapters 4 and 5.

[3] Hayward R. Alker, Jr., "Dimensions of Conflict in the General Assembly," *American Political Science Review*, Vol. 58 (September, 1964), pp. 642–57 and "Supranationalism in the United Nations," *Peace Research Society (International) Papers*, Vol. 3 (1955), pp. 197–212; Hayward R. Alker, Jr. and Bruce M. Russett, *World Politics in the General Assembly* (New Haven: Yale, 1965); Edward T. Rowe, 'The Emerging Anti-Colonial Consensus in the United Nations," *Journal of Conflict Resolution*, Vol. 8 (September, 1964), pp. 209–30; Bruce M. Russett, *Trends in World Politics* (New York: Macmillan, 1965), Chapters 4, 5, and 6; Marshall R. Singer and Barton Sensenig III, "Elections Within the United Nations: An Experimental Study Utilizing Statistical Analysis," *International Organization*, Vol. 17 (Autumn, 1963), pp. 901–25.

[4] Ernst B. Haas, "System and Process in the International Labor Organization, A Statistical Afterthought," *World Politics*, Vol. 14 (January, 1962), pp. 339–52 and *Consensus Formation in the Council of Europe* (Berkeley: University of California, 1960); Ernst B. Haas and Peter H. Merkl, "Parliamentarians Against Ministers: The Cast of Western European Union," *International Organization*, Vol. 14 (Winter, 1960), pp. 37–59; Peter H. Merkl, "European Assembly Parties and National Delegations," *Journal of Conflict Resolution*, Vol. 8 (March, 1964), pp. 50–64.

[5] See especially Chadwick F. Alger, "Personal Contact in Intergovernmental Organizations," in Herbert Kelman (ed.), *International Behavior: A Social–Psychological Analysis* (New York: Holt, 1965), pp. 521–47; "Non-Resolution Consequences of the United Nations and Their Effect on International Conflict," *Journal of Conflict Resolution*, Vol. 5 (June, 1961), pp. 128–45; and "Interaction in a Committee of the United Nations General Assembly," in J. David Singer (ed.), *Quantitative International Politics* (New York: Free Press, 1968), pp. 51–84.

[6] For an able effort to assess intensity of attitude in the U.N. by the analysis of speeches, see Alker and Russett, *op. cit.*, Chapter 10.

Substantive voting options in the U.N., incidentally, are a bit more varied than they are in most legislative bodies. In the United States Congress, for example, a voter may approve or disapprove the measure up for consideration; in the U.N. he has the additional middle range option of formally abstaining. Member states who are not present to vote on an issue are listed as "absent." The preference of an absent member can sometimes be inferred from other evidence, but usually he is simply not present for reasons which are best attributed to apathy or disinterest. Some analysts equate absences with abstentions while others persuasively argue that absences should be treated as what they are—missing data.[7]

Secondly, if roll calls are accepted to have some meaning, one still must decide which roll calls to use. The very frequent unanimous votes are usually excluded from consideration since they convey little helpful information.[8] Often, of course, these are about rather trivial matters, best left out of consideration, although at times they may represent vital issues the importance of which never gets reflected in a roll call because the issue has been so watered down for voting purposes that it no longer garners any objection. Near-unanimous votes, those with, say, 90 or 95 per cent agreement, are also characteristically excluded as are duplicated votes which occur when a resolution is voted on paragraph-by-paragraph.

Thirdly, after selecting the roll calls to be used, one must decide about their relative weight in the analysis. No legislator would deny that some votes are more important than others, but how does the analyst quantify these differences? Usually he doesn't: all included roll calls are given an equal weighting, or perhaps better, all included roll calls are given a weight of one, while all excluded roll calls are given a weight of zero. This method is sometimes contrasted with an approach which judgmentally assigns "arbitrary weights" to different issues. The equal weight procedure, however, is not really any less "arbitrary" than any other method, it is simply less courageous—or, if you prefer, more cautious.[9]

Finally, one must select summary measures and an analytic apparatus to deal with the data. Hayward Alker, in the study reprinted below, applies factor analysis and multiple regression analysis, techniques which are discussed in the appendix. Others have used Guttman scaling and various procedures of bloc and cluster analysis.[10]

Of course each measure and method has its own peculiarities and can

---

[7] See Lijphart, op. cit., p. 910.

[8] See Catherine Senf Manno, "Majority Decisions and Minority Responses in the UN General Assembly," Journal of Conflict Resolution, Vol. 10 (March, 1966), pp. 1–20 and Hovet, Bloc Politics, Chapter 1.

[9] For an ingenious method designed to measure the importance of a vote in a legislature, see William H. Riker, "A Method for Determining the Significance of Roll Calls in Voting Bodies," in Wahlke and Eulau, op. cit., pp. 377–83.

[10] See especially Rieselbach, op. cit.

illuminate and distort information in its own special way. There is no substitute for a thorough acquaintance with the limitations as well as the virtues of all measures used. To illustrate, some of the idiosyncrasies of some commonly used measures will be briefly assessed.

In studies of bloc voting in the U.N., it is common first to designate a number of groups by canvassing habits, geographic location, common interest, etc. To measure cohesion in a given group, the percentage of times all members of the group voted exactly the same way is sometimes taken as an indicator. The trouble with this measure, as Arend Lijphart has shown,[11] is that the amount of cohesion will depend in part on the size of the group: all other things equal it is much easier to get unanimity out of a three-nation group like Benelux than out of a twenty-nation group like Latin America. Alker and Russett use as a comparable measure the average deviation from the mean for each group on a series of votes, a measure which is not influenced by group size in this manner.[12]

The same problem appears, only in reverse, when one counts the number of times the majority of an individual group votes with the majority of the entire Assembly. The majority of a large group is very likely, all other things equal, to be on the side of the Assembly majority simply because the majority of a large group itself represents a substantial body of opinion in the Assembly; a small group, on the other hand, contributes little to the direction of the Assembly majority. It is hardly surprising, then, to see that Latin America did very well on this measure in the early years of the U.N. when it represented a massive proportion of the entire Assembly vote and then to see its influence seem to decline as more and more countries were admitted reducing the proportionate influence of the Latin American bloc.

Another index frequently used is the Pearson product–moment correlation coefficient—otherwise known as "r"—which is discussed in Appendix A of this book. The coefficient can be used to measure the similarity of voting patterns between two states or between two issues as illustrated in Tables 1, 2, and 3. A problem with the index is that, when applied to a 3 by 3 table, it does not treat the middle cell in a consistent manner.[13] It allows the figures in the outer cells to determine its general direction with wildly varying results in the extreme examples used here. Despite the fact that the two states were in utter agreement at least 80 per cent of the time in each of the three cases, the r asserts that there is perfect positive correlation on voting patterns between the two states in one case, perfect negative correlation in another, and no correlation at all in the third. Lijphart's index of agreement (IA), on the other hand, simply assesses the

[11] *Op. cit.*
[12] *Op. cit.*
[13] For the behavior of r in the 2 by 2 table, see Anderson et al., *op. cit.*, pp. 56–57. See also the discussion in chapter 6 below.

Table 1

		State A			
		Yes	Abst	No	
	Yes	10	0	0	r = +1.00
State B	Abst	0	80	0	IA = 100%
	No	0	0	10	

Table 2

		State A			
		Yes	Abst	No	
	Yes	0	0	10	r = —1.00
State B	Abst	0	80	0	IA = 80%
	No	10	0	0	

Table 3

		State A			
		Yes	Abst	No	
	Yes	5	0	5	r = 0.00
State B	Abst	0	80	0	IA = 90%
	No	5	0	5	

percentage of times the two states are in agreement and seems, in this extreme case at least, to be a more adequate measure.[14]

Reprinted below is Hayward Alker's factor analytic examination of roll-call voting behavior in the 1961–62 session of the General Assembly. The study contains a noteworthy attempt to quantify and systematize notions about dimensions of U.N. voting which can be found in abundant disarray in the qualitative literature. Alker's efforts at the end of the article to link U.N. voting data with aggregate data are an especially valuable beginning.

[14] *Op. cit.* See also John E. Mueller, "Some Comments on Russett's Discovering Voting Groups in the United Nations," *American Political Science Review*, Vol. 61 (March, 1967), pp. 146–48 and Professor Russett's reply, *ibid.*, pp. 149–50.

DIMENSIONS OF CONFLICT IN
THE GENERAL ASSEMBLY *

Hayward R. Alker, Jr.

Although there has been considerable work on voting patterns in the United Nations,[1] almost none of it has contributed cumulatively to existing theories of international relations. Methodological problems or a descriptive intent have often stood in the way of such advancement. For example, the main findings of Thomas Hovet, Jr.'s *Bloc Politics in the United Nations*, the most comprehensive work to date, are based on trends in the voting cohesion of regional and caucusing groups in the Assembly and time-series data on how often these groups vote with the majority.

Voting with the majority, as used by Hovet—and Riggs before him— is a poor measure of national power in the General Assembly because of the problems associated with discovering the extent to which nations are "satellites" or "chameleons."[2] Hovet himself has recognized the chameleon-like nature of the Soviet Union:

Reprinted by permission from *The American Political Science Review*, Vol. 58 (September, 1964), pp. 642–57.
* An earlier version of this paper was delivered at the Annual Meeting of the American Political Science Association, New York City, September 1963. In addition to the Computation Center, M.I.T., and the Yale Computer Center, where the calculations presented here were performed, the author is indebted to Karl W. Deutsch, Ernst B. Haas and Bruce M. Russett for helpful comments, and to Bruce Russett and the Yale Political Data Program for collecting most of the variables in Table IV. The Data Program's work is supported by the National Science Foundation.
[1] For example, M. Margaret Ball, "Bloc Voting in the General Assembly," *International Organization*, Vol. 5, No. 1 (February, 1951), pp. 3–31; Jan F. Triska and Howard E. Koch, Jr., "Asian–African Coalition and International Organization: Third Force or Collective Impotence?" *Review of Politics*, Vol. 21, No. 2 (April, 1959), pp. 417–55; Geoffrey Goodwin, "The Expanding UN; I-Voting Patterns," *International Affairs*, Vol. 36, No. 2 (April, 1960), pp. 174–87; Leroy N. Rieselbach, "Quantitative Techniques for Studying Voting Behavior in the UN General Assembly," *International Organization*, Vol. 14, No. 2 (Spring 1960), pp. 297–304; Arend Lijphart, "The Analysis of Bloc Voting in the General Assembly: A Critique and a Proposal," this REVIEW, Vol. 57, No. 4 (December, 1963), pp. 902–17; Robert E. Riggs, *Politics in the United Nations* (Urbana, University of Illinois Press, 1958); Thomas Hovet, Jr., *Bloc Politics in the United Nations*, (Cambridge, Harvard University Press, 1960), and *Africa in the United Nations* (Evanston, Northwestern University Press, 1963).
[2] These distinctions are made by Robert Dahl, "The Concept of Power," *Behavioral Science*, Vol. 2, No. 3 (July, 1957), pp. 201–15.

> It would be a serious misjudgment . . . to conclude that the high degree of cohesion of these African groups and factions with the Soviet Union means that the Soviet Union dominates their voting behavior. . . . The policy of the Soviet Union is to associate itself with the proposals and statements of the African states, especially when these issues are of vital interest to Africa, and at the same time to stress the fact that the United States is not a friend of Africa.[3]

If this is true, voting with the majority cannot be used as a measure of Soviet power. The trouble with an alternative inference, that the Africans have influenced the Russians, is that the Russians *want* to be persuaded. If exercising power means getting someone else to do something he otherwise would not do, neither the Soviets nor the Africans have appreciably influenced each other. Within the majority, then, it is not clear who is more powerful nor do voting percentages indicate very clearly the deprivations suffered by the minority.

This problem aside, Hovet and Riggs have made a significant contribution to the study of power and of group cohesion in distinguishing among the various kinds of issues before the Assembly. As Dahl has clearly shown,[4] groups have more power on some kinds of issues than on others. In terms of such Charter-based issue-categories as "collective measures, including regulations of armaments, etc.," "peaceful settlement," "economic questions," "human rights," "self-determination" or "administrative, procedural or structural" questions, comparative and trend studies of the functional areas of group cohesion and influence are possible.[5]

Conclusions from such analyses, however, are often controversial. One problem is that of making reproducible and widely acceptable assignments of roll calls to the "correct" issue category. Some observers, for instance, would like to consider Tibet a question involving self-determination and human rights.[6] Others might refer to it as a basically political controversy, related to the cold war. To take another example, is a resolution recommending negotiations on West Irian primarily one about "peaceful settlement," "self-determination" or a structural attempt to establish a certain kind of negotiating committee? Perhaps it is all of these. But *multiple* assignments on the basis of the language of the resolution raises another problem: the relative "importance" of the various parts and impli-

---

[3] *Africa in the United Nations*, pp. 181–85.
[4] Robert Dahl, *Who Governs?* (New Haven, Yale University Press, 1963).
[5] See Hovet, *Bloc Politics in the United Nations, op. cit.*, pp. 130–88. Ernst B. Haas has used to advantage a somewhat more specific set of issue-groupings in an analysis of the "coverage" of different conventions ratified by members of the International Labor Organization. See his "System and Process in the International Labor Organization, A Statistical Afterthought," *World Politics*, Vol. 14, No. 2 (January, 1962), pp. 339–52.
[6] Sydney Bailey has presented an interesting discussion of the different tactical approaches to this issue in "The Question of Tibet," *The General Assembly of the United Nations* (New York, 1961), ch. 10.

cations of a particular roll call. In fact most of the disagreement expressed in the General Assembly is about just this question: which Charter norms should be applied in what manner in a particular situation? "What kind of self-determination and for whom?" has been a basic controversy in both the Tibetan and the West Irian questions. Whether or not "self-determination" or "domestic jurisdiction" or the need for "peaceful settlement" is most appropriate to an African conflict situation is always a matter of debate.

If agreement on the relevant Charter *norms* is often difficult, perhaps one can be more objective in describing the political *conflicts* which a voting alignment contains. These conflict categories can be used in combination with objective verbal, structural or functional classifications to test various theories about the substance and causes of international conflict.

Thinking in terms of international conflicts brings up another question which is unanswered in most studies of group cohesion: in what voting context did these positions occur? Telling us that Latin Americans were divided on "self-determination" questions like West Irian or South Africa does not tell us about the positions of the other main participants such as the United States, Russia, Indonesia, the Netherlands or South Africa. We would need to know how these and other states voted before we can say that Cold War or anti-colonial perceptions dominated the voting. Simply measuring group cohesion on heterogeneous issue-categories, we cannot be very sure who disagreed with whom, to what extent, and about what kinds of issues.[7]

Another major omission in previous analyses of voting patterns in the General Assembly has been a comparative analysis of the various proposed influences on Assembly voting. One can argue with Hovet that group loyalties and pressures are important determinants of voting behavior, but unless one has a measure of the actual voting *positions* of different states on such major conflicts as the Cold War in the U.N., the relative impact of caucusing-group influences and domestic social, economic and political considerations cannot be compared. Many current theories of international politics suggest that racial, economic, geographic and military variables are also at work in influencing voting positions.

---

[7] Hovet, *Bloc. Politics, op. cit.*, p. 112, feels it "premature" to attempt any formal conclusions about the implications of the total phenomenon. He does suggest, however, that with its mixed blessings the "bloc" phenomenon is likely to increase and should be better understood. Fortunately in *Africa in the United Nations* considerably more attention is given to the specific issues on which group members disagree and how their votes are related to the American and Soviet positions. This methodology is much more useful than the *ad hoc* verbal descriptions of group differences that supplemented the bar graphs in *Bloc Politics*. Arend Lijphart, *op. cit.*, pp. 913–17, has also studied voting cohesion with the positions of other states in mind. His Figure 2 seems quite clearly two-dimensional. The proper dimensionality of UN voting patterns is discussed in detail below.

Ernst Haas, for example, has characterized the U.N. as a multi-phase system "whose characteristics and evolutionary potential must be specified in terms of the changing environment in which it operates." [8]

This paper will concentrate on two aspects of contemporary politics in the General Assembly. Factor analysis will be used in an attempt to uncover the principal dimensions of conflict underlying votes at the Sixteenth General Assembly and the location of states on these main issues. The relative importance of the various determinants of voting behavior suggested above will then be assessed, using correlation and regression techniques.[9] Findings from these analyses will serve both as a test of several hypotheses in international relations theory and as a basis for further studies of conflict and consensus, cohesion and power in the General Assembly.[10]

I. CONFLICTS IN THE GENERAL ASSEMBLY

The Sixteenth General Assembly met intermittently, from September 1961 through June 1962. Seventy important votes from this session were chosen for intensive analysis. They include all distinct, non-unanimous, non-procedural, plenary roll calls, as well as 26 of the most important committee votes. Grouped according to the main committee of the Assembly in which they were originally discussed, these votes are briefly described on the left-hand sides of Tables I and II.[11]

[8] Ernst B. Haas, "Dynamic Environment and Static System: Revolutionary Regimes in the United Nations," in Morton Kaplan (ed.), *The Revolution in World Politics* (New York, 1962), p. 278. Italics omitted.
[9] Neither of these techniques is new to political science. Glendon Schubert has factor-analyzed judicial votes in "The 1960 Term of the Supreme Court: A Psychological Analysis," this REVIEW, Vol. 56, No. 1 (March, 1962), pp. 90–107; see also Duncan MacRae, Jr., and James A. Meldrum, "Critical Electronics in Illinois: 1888–1958," this REVIEW, Vol. 54, No. 3 (September, 1960), pp. 669–83. Regression is a basic deductive technique in *The American Voter*. See Stokes, Campbell and Miller, "Components of Electoral Decision," this REVIEW, Vol. 52, No. 2 (June, 1958), pp. 367–87. A readable summary of both techniques may be found in Hubert Blalock, Jr., *Social Statistics* (New York, 1960), chs. 17–19 and 21. What is new about these techniques is the ease with which they may be applied. The seventy roll call factor analyses reported here took eleven minutes on the IBM 7090. The regressions took less than a minute each on the IBM 709.
[10] Hayward R. Alker, Jr. and Bruce M. Russett, *World Politics in the General Assembly* (forthcoming). Power measurements are facilitated by the use of both the conflict dimensions presented below and additional information on the sponsorship of resolutions and the intensity of involvement of different groups on these conflicts. Voting cohesion may satisfactorily be measured in terms of mean deviations on the factor scores presented below.
[11] Designating plenary meetings as the "Eighth Committee" and the Special Political Committee as the "Oth Committee," the first digit of the identification numbers for each roll call in the Tables corresponds to the Committee in which the vote occurred; the number after this digit refer to the order of occurrence of the roll call within the

Table I

DIMENSIONS OF CONFLICT AT THE 16th GENERAL ASSEMBLY: UNROTATED FACTOR MATRIX

Roll Call		I	II	III	IV	V	VI	VII	VIII	IX
						Factor				
8004.	Censure South Africa	.63	.33	−.36	.02	.09	−.03	−.11	−.11	−.00
8022.	Sanction South Africa	.84	.25	−.28	−.13	.01	−.01	.05	.06	−.03
8023.	Security Council & S. Africa	.88	.28	−.22	−.13	−.04	−.03	.00	.01	.07
8024.	No arms to South Africa	.83	.22	−.15	−.21	−.05	.04	.18	.07	−.02
8025.	No petroleum to S. Africa	.85	.21	−.20	−.16	−.03	.00	.20	.11	−.05
8027.	Oman self-determination	.84	.06	−.16	.26	−.11	−.05	−.02	−.01	.10
0018.	Reconstitute Pal. Con. Com.	.38	−.03	−.00	.04	−.11	−.57	.32	.49	−.14
8045.	Reconstitute Pal. Con. Com.	.72	−.01	.01	.39	−.07	−.24	.01	.14	−.20
8046.	Protect Arab refugees	.77	−.02	.07	.38	−.13	−.18	−.00	.03	−.17
8047.	U.N.R.W.A.	−.64	.20	−.03	−.32	.33	−.22	.11	.16	.17
8048.	U.S.Palestine Resolution	−.70	.22	−.02	−.28	.26	−.17	.11	.22	.08
0003.	Czech Res. on S.C.E.A.R.	.81	−.09	.01	−.12	−.12	−.02	−.07	−.04	−.06
8006.	Czech Res. important ?	−.87	.05	.02	.03	−.03	−.02	.16	.00	.00
8007.	Admit Mauritania	−.77	.17	−.14	−.28	.16	−.04	.05	−.16	−.00
8029.	China question important ?	−.74	.19	−.49	.04	−.21	−.10	.09	−.16	.00
8030.	China Declaration	.67	.15	.54	−.25	.05	.17	−.17	.16	.07
8031.	Seat Peoples' Rep. of China	.63	.16	.55	−.32	.02	.11	−.15	.14	−.00
8032.	Representation of China	.74	−.13	.45	−.27	.15	.12	−.12	.15	.02
8008.	Stop 50 megaton bomb	−.55	.64	.17	−.03	−.34	.04	−.14	.09	−.02
1010.	General & complete Disarm.	.88	.04	.03	−.11	−.08	.05	−.03	−.09	−.16
8009.	Regrets tests; need treaty	−.01	.86	.12	.15	.10	.18	−.04	−.06	.07
8010.	Regrets rejection of US–UK	−.70	.50	−.07	−.04	−.17	−.08	.11	−.07	.02
8012.	Denuclearize Africa	.70	.06	.43	.17	.06	.10	.24	−.14	.07

Factor

Roll Call		I	II	III	IV	V	VI	VII	VIII	IX
8016.	Nuclear vs. Humanity	.87	.31	−.11	−.11	.04	.05	.06	−.07	.04
1023.	Non-nuclear club	.67	.10	.41	.17	.19	.12	.22	−.19	.01
8044.	Question of Algeria	.68	.16	.43	.12	.14	.03	.27	−.20	.04
1026.	P.D.R. & UNCURK	−.75	.32	−.25	.02	−.22	−.05	.11	−.11	.13
8054.	Report of UNCURK	−.88	.25	−.18	−.01	−.08	−.00	.14	.08	−.01
8055.	Deplores Hungary	−.92	.07	.04	.20	−.04	−.04	.05	.04	.05
8064.	Non interference (Cuba)	.86	−.08	.23	.09	−.01	−.06	−.10	.09	−.06
8065.	Friendly relations with Cuba	.92	.05	.10	−.11	−.00	−.02	.00	.12	−.09
2002.	Trade Conference	.88	.23	−.06	−.17	−.09	−.03	.15	−.06	−.03
2005.	Primary commodities	.44	.41	−.10	.25	.41	.08	.14	.16	.37
8033.	Study trade conference	−.74	.37	−.03	−.17	−.14	.00	.07	−.06	.11
2010.	Special int. devel. agency	.57	.38	−.42	.34	.21	−.02	−.12	.12	−.04
2015.	Conference on patents	−.58	−.21	.36	−.37	−.16	.05	.28	.00	−.21
8039.	Capital & technical assist.	−.25	.74	.09	.01	−.14	−.03	−.28	.16	.05
8041.	Population & econ. devel.	.53	−.13	.38	−.23	.00	−.17	.27	.04	.25
8001.	Tibet on agenda	−.83	.31	−.03	.04	.10	.02	.15	−.04	−.01
8043.	Resolution on Tibet	−.79	.44	−.17	−.06	.06	−.03	.19	−.02	.00
3001.	Absentee marriage	−.02	−.38	−.33	−.17	.50	−.28	−.11	−.16	−.33
3007.	"Hatred and hostility"	.78	.17	−.31	−.15	.03	−.05	−.16	.04	−.02
3013.	Safeguard right of reply	.68	−.17	.10	−.07	−.29	−.07	.17	−.26	−.16
8011.	Algerian prisoners	.78	.30	.10	−.15	−.04	.08	.34	−.04	.06
8017.	1962 end of colonialism	.91	−.05	−.05	−.19	.07	−.01	.03	−.01	−.04
8019.	W. Iran self-determination	−.74	.11	−.25	−.34	.13	.17	−.04	−.03	−.08
8020.	Commission on W. Irian	−.78	.09	−.26	−.31	.09	.14	−.10	.01	−.07
8021.	Indian res. on W. Irian	.76	.01	.24	.40	.08	−.08	.05	−.10	.09
8035.	Regrets Port. non-compliance	−.83	−.29	.20	.09	.04	.02	−.07	.00	−.15

Table I

DIMENSIONS OF CONFLICT AT THE 16th GENERAL ASSEMBLY: UNROTATED FACTOR MATRIX (Continued)

Roll Call		I	II	III	IV	V	VI	VII	VIII	IX
						Factor				
8037.	Renew CINSGT	−.26	.84	.15	.08	−.04	.14	−.03	.07	−.07
4009.	Swedish res. on South Africa	−.80	−.12	.34	.18	−.05	.01	.17	.03	−.07
8066.	Ask SC 17: S. Rhodesia SGTP	.87	.32	−.27	−.05	−.03	−.00	.03	−.01	.04
8068.	S. Rhodesia on agenda	.84	.34	−.25	−.04	−.04	−.06	.05	−.07	.03
8073.	"1 man 1 vote", S. Rhodesia	.86	.24	−.16	−.14	−.10	.02	.09	−.07	−.01
8075.	Regret UK on S. Rhodesia	.73	.40	−.30	.10	.06	.03	.04	−.10	.02
8056.	Condemn Portugal	.92	.04	−.05	−.13	.02	−.07	.03	−.01	−.07
8058.	Report on Angola	.80	.03	−.03	−.08	.04	−.10	−.07	−.02	.11
8059.	Angola & SC 17	.89	.16	−.08	−.00	−.00	−.10	−.05	−.06	.02
4001.	Burundi Prime Minister	−.88	−.24	.18	.01	.04	.02	.06	.11	−.05
4021.	Rwanda & Burundi sovereign	−.82	.01	−.12	.09	−.05	.11	.12	.09	−.09
8069.	Evacuate R. & B. by 1 Jul. 62	.95	.02	−.01	−.11	.00	−.10	.00	−.04	−.03
8070.	Rwanda & Burundi Evacuation	.30	.40	−.05	.21	.46	.29	.16	.03	−.49
4023.	Rwanda & Burundi Evacuation	−.30	.73	.06	.20	.04	.19	.01	.31	−.18
8071.	$2 million to S.G. for R. & B.	−.24	.66	.26	−.16	−.22	−.00	.03	−.08	−.30
5004.	5 Secretariat members/country	.57	.56	.07	−.02	−.33	.01	−.13	.02	−.03
8049.	Congo expenses and I.C.J.	−.74	.39	.20	.14	.14	−.19	.05	−.08	.00
8051.	Congo cost	−.42	.55	.43	.07	.12	−.37	−.22	−.20	−.01
8052.	U.N.E.F. expenses	−.50	.45	.43	−.02	.13	−.33	−.24	−.19	.06
8053.	Budget for year 1962	−.39	.60	.29	−.21	.16	−.28	−.02	−.15	−.14
8033.	Conf. on consular relations	.91	−.06	.06	−.15	.01	−.04	−.18	.03	−.02

Each conflict underlying more than one of these votes could be described by *a set of correlations* between the conflict and each of the 70 selected rolls calls (r_{jk} for roll call j and voting component k). If two such sets of correlations were themselves uncorrelated, we could say these conflicts were distinct. Each roll call could then be analyzed in terms of a set of its own correlations with separate voting components. Tables I and II contain these kinds of correlations: the *vertical* sets of correlations describe distinct conflicts in the General Assembly; the *horizontal* rows give each roll call's correlations with the conflict alignments.

Table entries were calculated in the following manner. Voting positions on each roll call ("Yeses," "Abstains" and "Nos") were quantified as ranks with zero means and unit standard deviations. These positions (V_{ji} for roll call j and country i) were assumed to result from a summation of underlying conflict positions (C_{ik} for conflict k) after multiplication by a *set of coefficients* (a_{jk}) indicating the relevance of each conflict to each roll call. These coefficients, called "conflict loadings" or "factor loadings" can be presented in as many rows as there are roll calls and in as many columns as there are general conflicts in Assembly voting.[12] For the case of standardized voting scores and uncorrelated voting components, $r_{jk} = a_{jk}$; *thus Tables I and II can be interpreted both as correlations between roll calls and voting components, and as factor loadings.*

Factor analysts have traditionally sought to extract distinct sets of factor loadings, each explaining a maximum proportion of the correlations among variables (in our case, roll calls). A sequential procedure for determining uncorrelated columns of as many high factor loadings as possible can be derived using the calculus. In Table I the resulting columns of a_{jk}'s are presented in the same order as the amount of voting variance they explain. For any particular column, factor loadings will have the same signs when "Yeses" represent the same point of view.

In this kind of analysis some analysts who believe that a Cold War

---

Committee. "S.C.E.A.R." stands for the Scientific Committee on the Effects of Atomic Radiation; "P.D.R." symbolizes the People's Democratic Republic of Korea; and "S.C.17" refers to the Special Committee of 17 set up at the Fifteenth Session to implement the Declaration on the Granting of Independence to Colonial Countries and Peoples. "UNCURK" is the United Nations Commission for the Unification and Rehabilitation of Korea, while "CINSGT" is the author's label for the Committee on Information from Non-Self-Governing Territories.

[12] Symbolically the model of voting positions used in factor analysis is

$$V_{ji} = \sum_k a_{jk}C_{ik} + u_{ji},$$

where u_{ji} is the unexplained voting position of country i on roll call j. For more details on the roll calls and methods described above, see Hayward R. Alker, Jr., *Dimensions of Voting in the General Assembly* (Ph.D. Dissertation, Department of Political Science, Yale University, 1963). Harry H. Harmon, *Modern Factor Analysis* (Chicago, University of Chicago Press, 1960), ch. 9, derives the "principal component" method of factor analysis used in this article.

Table II

DIMENSIONS OF CONFLICT AT THE 16th GENERAL ASSEMBLY: ROTATED FACTOR MATRIX

Roll Call	I	II	III	IV	V	VI	VII	VIII	IX
8004. Censure South Africa	.77	.02	.00	.17	.16	.08	-.11	.03	-.09
8022. Sanction South Africa	.88	-.10	.19	.13	.05	-.11	.03	-.03	-.11
8023. Security Council & S. Africa	.91	-.06	.25	.16	.06	-.07	.06	-.06	-.00
8024. No arms to South Africa	.82	-.12	.28	.08	-.05	-.15	.14	-.15	-.11
8025. No petroleum to S. Africa	.84	-.14	.24	.11	-.02	-.20	.11	-.13	-.14
8027. Oman self-determination	.67	-.19	.15	.51	.17	-.06	.09	-.07	.02
0018. Reconstitute Pal. Con. Com.	.24	-.08	.09	.19	-.01	-.85	-.02	-.03	.03
8045. Reconstitute Pal. Con. Com.	.43	-.12	.19	.65	.08	-.33	-.06	-.02	-.13
8046. Protect Arab refugees	.45	-.12	.23	.71	.03	-.22	-.03	-.07	-.08
8047. U.N.R.W.A.	-.33	.28	-.18	-.67	.18	-.18	-.18	-.01	.09
8048. U.S.Palestine Resolution	-.38	.32	-.21	-.65	.13	-.21	-.10	.06	.01
0003. Czech Res. on S.C.E.A.R.	.60	-.25	.40	.30	-.14	-.03	-.01	-.04	.06
8006. Czech Res. important?	-.64	.25	-.44	-.33	-.05	-.02	.05	-.01	.00
8007. Admit Mauritania	-.37	.28	-.40	-.59	-.08	.13	-.18	.02	.03
8029. China question important?	-.22	.20	-.83	-.30	-.10	.05	.01	.15	.09
8030. China Declaration	.34	.13	.86	.12	.00	.03	.15	-.09	.00
8031. Seat People's Rep. of China	.33	.16	.84	.08	-.09	-.01	.11	-.09	.01
8032. Representation of China	.33	-.17	.87	.12	-.01	-.03	.01	-.11	-.01
8008. Stop 50 megaton bomb	-.22	.79	-.21	-.16	-.12	.04	.30	.20	.06
1010. General & Complete Disarm.	.69	-.16	.42	.33	-.18	.01	-.01	-.10	-.08
8009. Regrets tests; need treaty	.24	.76	-.04	-.02	.25	.20	.17	-.13	-.23
8010. Regrets rejection of US–UK	-.26	.59	-.51	-.32	-.09	.00	.12	.01	.05
8012. Denuclearize Africa	.31	-.03	.48	.42	.05	.01	.11	-.52	-.10

Roll Call		I	II	III	IV	V	VI	VII	VIII	IX
						Factor				
8016.	Nuclear vs. humanity	.85	−.02	.29	.17	.07	.01	.04	−.19	−.09
1023.	Non-nuclear club	.31	.00	.47	.38	.09	.06	.01	−.53	−.19
8044.	Question of Algeria	.35	.07	.46	.30	.05	−.00	.02	−.58	−.12
1026.	P.D.R. & UNCURK	−.29	.37	−.67	−.32	−.04	.07	.15	.05	.14
8054.	Report of UNCURK	−.47	.35	−.58	−.43	−.03	−.04	.11	.12	−.05
8055.	Deplores Hungary	−.72	.31	−.47	−.22	.07	−.00	.07	.08	.03
8064.	Non-interference (Cuba)	.48	−.17	.57	.49	.03	−.13	−.01	−.07	−.02
8065.	Friendly relations with Cuba	.67	−.15	.54	.29	−.04	−.17	.02	−.09	−.08
2002.	Trade conference	.83	−.06	.31	.19	−.11	−.11	.07	−.23	−.04
2005.	Primary commodities	.44	.11	.11	.03	.67	−.04	.11	−.25	−.19
8038.	Study trade conference	−.34	.48	−.41	−.45	−.09	.07	.14	.03	.12
2010.	Special int. devel. agency	.67	.06	−.09	.30	.43	−.05	−.08	.13	−.29
2015.	Conference on patents	−.60	.05	.03	−.38	−.51	−.10	.09	−.14	.01
8039.	Capital & technical assist.	.06	.78	−.07	−.10	.12	.02	.18	.26	.03
8041.	Population & econ. devel.	.23	−.16	.51	.05	−.02	−.26	.07	−.43	.25
8001.	Tibet on agenda	−.49	.43	−.47	−.39	.05	.05	.01	−.04	−.12
8043.	Resolution on Tibet	−.32	.48	−.56	−.49	.03	−.01	.03	−.02	−.10
3001.	Absentee marriage	.01	−.38	−.08	−.18	−.03	−.03	−.74	.12	−.14
3007.	"Hatred and hostility"	.82	−.13	.22	.13	.06	−.03	−.08	.13	−.02
3013.	Safeguard right of reply	.45	−.26	.23	.40	−.39	−.05	.01	−.27	.09
8011.	Algerian prisoners	.69	.01	.35	.09	−.01	−.11	.17	−.44	−.13
8017.	1962 end of colonialism	.72	−.30	.45	.19	−.04	−.08	−.07	−.13	−.05
8019.	W. Irian self-determination	−.32	.16	−.35	−.65	−.12	.20	−.07	.22	−.10
8020.	Commission on W. Irian	−.36	.16	−.38	−.63	−.10	.18	−.06	.29	−.06
8021.	Indian res. on W. Irian	.37	−.09	.35	.63	.23	−.05	−.02	−.33	−.03
8035.	Regrets Port non-compliance	−.85	.05	−.20	−.15	−.12	.06	−.11	.14	−.02

Table II

DIMENSIONS OF CONFLICT AT THE 16th GENERAL ASSEMBLY: ROTATED FACTOR MATRIX (Continued)

Roll Call	I	II	III	IV	V	VI	VII	VIII	IX
8037. Renew CINSGT	.04	.84	-.11	-.11	.08	.07	.23	.02	-.24
4009. Swedish res. on S. Africa	-.84	.19	-.21	-.10	-.10	-.05	.08	-.09	-.04
8066. Ask SC17:S Rhodesia SGT P	.91	-.04	.16	.21	.09	-.05	.06	-.07	-.06
8068. S. Rhodesia on agenda	.90	-.00	.13	.22	.06	-.06	.02	-.12	-.04
8073. "1 man 1 vote" S.Rhodesia	.86	-.07	.23	.20	-.07	-.04	.09	-.15	-.05
8075. Regret UK on S. Rhodesia	.82	.05	.02	.23	.18	.04	.01	-.12	-.16
8056. Condemn Portugal	.76	-.21	.40	.25	-.05	-.12	-.07	-.12	-.04
8058. Report on Angola	.65	-.17	.37	.24	.10	-.05	-.07	-.10	.10
8059. Angola & SC 17	.77	-.09	.31	.34	.06	-.05	-.06	-.11	.02
4001. Burundi Prime Minister	-.85	.06	-.22	-.30	-.07	-.04	.00	.09	-.01
4021. Rwanda & Burundi sovereign	-.58	.14	-.49	-.30	-.05	.00	.11	.14	-.14
8069. Evacuate R. & B. by 1 Jul. 62	.75	-.20	.42	.31	-.03	-.11	-.08	-.15	.02
8070. Rwanda & Burundi Evacuation	.30	.19	.09	.10	.12	.04	-.15	-.13	-.81
4023. Rwanda & Burundi Evacuation	-.05	.70	-.14	-.09	.16	-.08	.26	.15	-.44
8071. $2 million to S.G. for R. & B.	.01	.75	-.04	-.11	-.35	-.01	.10	-.03	-.14
5004. 5 Secretariat members/country	.64	.41	.21	.28	-.10	-.02	.24	.04	.03
8049. Congo expenses and I.C.J.	-.51	.61	-.32	-.20	.11	-.02	-.13	-.10	-.01
8051. Congo cost	-.28	.83	-.01	-.00	.07	.01	-.30	-.08	.17
8052. U.N.E.F. expenses	-.36	.76	.02	-.11	.07	.06	-.29	-.06	.23
8053. Budget for year 1962	-.12	.76	-.03	-.29	-.10	-.06	-.27	-.13	.01
8033. Conf. on consular relations	.65	-.23	.56	.29	-.02	-.04	-.08	.01	.06

alignment is paramount in all voting at the United Nations would expect correlations between all Assembly roll calls and this factor to be nearly unity. More sophisticated students of U.N. affairs suggest that at least two distinct voting conflicts underlie particular roll calls in differing degrees. Ernst Haas has interpreted Assembly politics in terms of a "balancing" process between Cold War demands and the political economic and anti-colonial demands of the underdeveloped countries.[13] John Stoessinger considers the two principal conflicts of our time to be the struggle between the Communist and the non-Communist worlds, and between the "new nationalism" of Asia, Africa and the Middle East and the waning empires of Europe.[14] In a similar way, Lincoln Bloomfield has described the General Assembly as

> . . . a prime political forum for the nations which remain outside the East–West camps and pursue their own goals of political independence, economic improvement and racial dignity. In this situation what might be called the North–South conflict cuts across the East–West issues and makes its own powerful demands on American diplomacy at the same time offering frequent opportunities for the Soviets to seize the political initiative.[15]

The most frequent conflicts in Assembly voting behavior. Looking at what is called the unrotated factor matrix in Table I, we see that a single conflict, which we shall call "East vs. West," did in fact dominate most issues before the United Nations, with the exception of budgetary concerns. By adding up squared correlations in the first column of Table I, we can say that this one factor accounts for the equivalent of 37 entire roll calls. This represents about 53 per cent of all votes cast on the seventy roll calls being analyzed or about 64 per cent of "explainable" voting alignments.[16] Prominent among the variety of issues loading above 0.60 on this "East-West" factor are South Africa, Palestine, Chinese membership, disarmament, Hungary, Korea, West Irian, Southern Rhodesia, Angola, and Rwanda and Burundi.

A second conflict, "explaining" about 13 per cent of the "interpretable" voting variation, was paramount on several resolutions dealing with nuclear testing, economic aid, the renewal of the Committee on Informa-

---

[13] Ernst Haas, "Regionalism, Functionalism, and Universal International Organization," *World Politics*, Vol. 8, No. 2 (January, 1956), pp. 238–63.
[14] John G. Stoessinger, *The Might of Nations* (New York, 1961).
[15] Lincoln Bloomfield, *The United Nations and United States Foreign Policy* (Boston, 1960), p. 10.
[16] All uncorrelated factors underlying or "explaining" more than the variance of a single roll call were extracted and are presented in Table I. For the rationale for stopping factoring at this point, see Harry H. Harmon, *op. cit.*, ch. 14. The variances "explained" by these nine dimensions of conflict are 37.0, 7.8, 4.2, 2.4, 1.8, 1.4, 1.1, 1.0, leaving only 17% of all voting "unexplained."

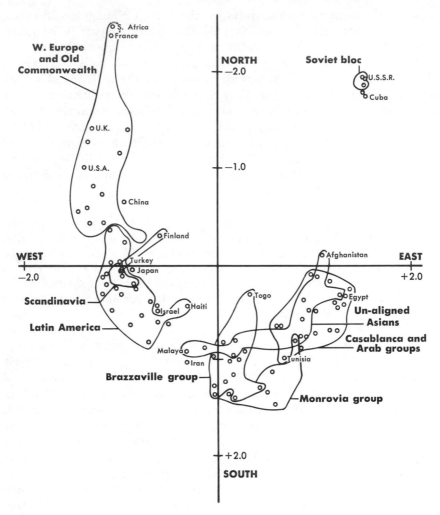

Fig. 1.   Unrotated factor scores on the East-West and North-South conflicts at the Sixteenth General Assembly.

tion from Non-Self-Governing Territories, other votes on Rwanda and Burundi, and most of the questions regarding the financing of the Congo Operation.

The inferred alignments of the main states and regional groupings in the Assembly on these two factors are plotted in Figure 1.[17] Looking at

[17] In matrix notation the equation(s) in footnote 12 can be written as $\hat{V} = AC$. When A is not a square matrix, component scores are given by the equation $C = (A^1A)^{-1}A'V$. See Henry Kaiser,"Formulas for Component Scores," Psychometrika, Vol. 27 (March, 1962), pp. 83–8. As calculated here, these sets of factor scores are very nearly uncorrelated with each other.

Figure 1 helps to suggest why Bloomfield's "North South" and "East-West" labels have been chosen from among various possibilities to identify the two most frequent conflicts in the Assembly. With only a few obvious exceptions, the similarity between inferred voting positions of states and regional groupings and their geographical locations in a two-dimensional map of the world are rather striking. West Europeans, Latin Americans, Afro-Asians and the Soviet Bloc are almost entirely in their correct quadrants. The most notable exceptions are that South Africa and France are farther "North" than the other "colonial" countries; non-colonial Scandinavians are farther "South"; and pro-West Asians are farther "West" because of their ties with the United States. Note how the Soviet Union was very "Northern" on the 50-megaton bomb issue; she joined a few extreme colonial powers on the renewal of the Committee on Information from Non-Self-Governing Territories, and agreed further with these states on economic aid, and financing U.N. operations in the Congo and Rwanda and Burundi.

Another significant finding, however, is that besides these two major voting alignments, the matrix in Table I suggests that other conflicts and disagreements underlay voting positions at the Sixteenth Assembly. In fact, seven other alignments were found in the factor analysis, accounting for about 23 per cent of the "interpretable" voting variation. Like those noticed above, they can perhaps be interpreted by looking at the votes loading heavily on them in the factor matrix and by looking at the inferred policy positions (factor scores) of states on them. The third principal conflict, for instance, contains aspects of the Cold War, including Chinese membership in the United Nations, uncaptured by the first two factors.

A *substantive interpretation of Assembly conflicts.* One way to get a "better look" at the specific content of the first two as well as the remaining factors would be somehow to adjust the factor matrix, keeping the factors uncorrelated, so that each roll call would load very highly on *just one* factor. Such a new factor would be purely and simply interpretable in terms of the common content of, and voting positions on, the roll calls correlating heavily with it. Keeping the same number of voting dimensions, it is possible to find new sets of factor loadings approximating such an ideal factor matrix containing only zeros or ones. This can be done objectively by the use of Kaiser's "normal varimax" rotation technique for obtaining a factor matrix with a "simple structure." [18]

Geometrically, this technique can be visualized in terms of a space of dimensionality sufficient to explain all the main components of Assembly voting. Keeping the same configuration of roll calls in this space, its per-

[18] See Harmon, *loc. cit.* A further step, not taken in this article, would be to find the simplest factor structure using correlated (oblique) factors.

pendicular axes can be rotated until the roll calls have the desired loadings (coordinates) on the factor axes. Although the rotated sets of coordinates would still be uncorrelated, they would no longer come in the order of maximum additional voting behavior "explained." Rather, the axes are rotated to a position where their substantive, as opposed to their behavioral, meaning should be most clear. Whether or not these newly perceived conflicts will have any relation to the functional committees where they occurred should also be more clearly discernible than was possible in the unrotated factor matrix.

Before turning to the rotated factor matrix, it may be helpful to recall several existing theoretical conceptions of the multi-dimensional conflict process in the General Assembly. George Liska has suggested that international organization may be treated as part of a "dynamic interplay of institutional military–political, and socio-economic factors and pressures," constituting to a greater or lesser degree, a "multiple equilibrium." [19] Writing in 1956, Ernst Haas suggested that the functional and security claims of the different regional systems have emerged as "the source of the actual functioning of universal international organizations" and that a "balancing" or equilibrium process in both regional groups and the international system connect the two together.[20] Something of the specifics of how a variety of controversies interact in U.N. votes is suggested by the following prescription of an experienced diplomat for predicting voting behavior:

> Apart from genuine satellites, . . . there are other cases where reasonably safe predictions may be made, but on the basis of a more complex calculus. Thus Pakistan . . . as a member of CENTO [likes] to vote with the West, but is also sensitive to Afro-Asian opinion, particularly sensitive to opinion in Moslem countries and strong on self-determination (Kashmir). A Western canvasser can therefore safely count on Pakistan's vote in a direct East-West controversy (Cuba, Hungary) but must make separate calculations if relevant racial, religious or colonial factors are involved. For example, in a "colonialist" issue where the "Moslem" factor tells on the "colonialist" side (Cyprus), or where the Kashmir issue comes into play (Goa), the West may reasonably expect Pakistan's support. On the other hand, on a straight racial issue (*apartheid*), or an issue where a Western power is, or has been, in conflict with Moslem populations (Suez, Algeria, Tunisia, Israel) Pakistan will be . . . the most anti-colonialist Afro-Asian. On such issues where both anti-colonialism and the Cold War are involved —for example the Soviet moves on the liquidation of colonialism— accurate prediction of a Pakistan vote becomes impossible.[21]

[19] George Liska, *International Equilibrium* (Cambridge, Harvard University Press, 1957).
[20] Ernst B. Haas, "Regionalism," *op. cit.*, esp. pp. 238–41, 260–63.
[21] Conor Cruise O'Brien, *To Katanga and Back* (London, Hutchinson, 1962), p. 18.

While not dealing explicitly with the different functional nature of these conflicts, this quotation, as we shall see, is very suggestive of a set of adequate political categories for describing substantive conflicts in the General Assembly.

Turning to the rotated factor matrix in Table II, we see that most factors are quite simply structured and also remarkably clear in their substantive content. The first four of them, all relatively frequent conflicts in the General Assembly, will receive more detailed consideration.[22] It should be made clear that these interpretations are based on the author's judgment, with which others may disagree; under the assumptions of the model being used, however, the factors themselves are objectively derived from actual voting behavior.

New factors need new names; we shall call the first *"self-determination"* because it consists of most of the anti-colonial demands of the Afro-Asian states regarding South Africa, Angola, Southern Rhodesia and Rwanda-Burundi. Boxing the factor loadings greater than 0.60 in magnitude helps substantiate this description. The economic component of Afro-Asian "self-determination" demands is also brought out clearly by the high loadings of votes 2002, 2010 and 2015 on trade, aid and patent inquiries. Their desire for more jobs and a greater voice in the Secretariat explains why vote 5004 also loads on this factor. Vote 3007 found a similar group of states opposing the advocacy of racial hatred, as an incitement to discrimination and hostility.

Although it is important to distinguish "self-determination" questions from "East-West" alignments, it is clear from comparing the first columns of Table I and Table II that our new perspective is not yet very different from the earlier one. Almost all of the votes loading highly on the "self-determination" conflict also were closely correlated with characteristic "East-West" voting positions as summarized in Figure 1. The main difference is that quite a few Cold War controversies—Tibet, Cuba, Korea and especially Chinese membership—load more heavily on the new third rotated factor which we shall now examine.

It is quite clear from the boxed entries in the third column of the rotated factor matrix that the proper representation of China forms the largest part of a second distinct conflict in the General Assembly. We shall therefore identify the third factor as *Cold war membership* controversies. The usual alignment on this question at the Sixteenth Assembly pitted the United States, Latin America (except Cuba), most of the Brazzaville group, pro-Western Asians and most Western Europeans against India, Scandinavians, the Soviet bloc and most other Afro-Asians. A slightly confounding feature of the voting was that it was not clear on

[22] These rotated factors "explain" the equivalent of 22.7, 8.7, 10.2, 7.6, 1.8, 1.4, 1.6, 2.4, and 1.6 roll calls respectively.

votes 8030 and 8031 that a declaration to remove Nationalist China was also binding. On these two votes the Soviet bloc, Cuba and several other states in favor of admission abstained; on vote 8032, however, they took their customary positions.

One of the most interesting results of this analysis is the degree to which such *bona fide* Cold War issues as Hungary, Cuba, disarmament and Korea overlapped the self-determination and Cold War membership conflicts. Granting "recognition" to the People's Democratic Republic of Korea at UNCURK meetings (vote 1026) was mostly a Cold War membership question; inviting everyone to a conference on consular relations (vote 8033), however, looks slightly more like a self-determination issue. As we have already noted, one reason for this phenomenon has to do with the similarity between East–West and self-determination controversies. Their relations to the Cold War membership controversy may be brought out more clearly by examining more closely the behavior of the Soviet Bloc, of the Latin Americans and of the Brazzaville group of Africans. It is clear that Soviet disarmament moves were designed to invoke an increasingly East–West or anti-European response: votes 8006 and 1010 called for a modest approval of the work of the U.N. Scientific Committee on the Effects of Atomic Radiation and for "general and complete disarmament;" vote 8016 summarizes the plenary voting on several paragraphs to the effect that the use of thermonuclear weapons is contrary to the laws of humanity and the Charter. Russia joined an almost solid Afro-Asian caucus in supporting the resolution. Most Afro-Asians also supported a preambular paragraph invoking the principles of non-intervention and self-determination regarding Cuba (vote 8064). On the other hand, almost solid Arab–African abstentions greeted a Western resolution (8055) deploring the disregard of Assembly resolutions regarding Hungary. The distinctive feature of the Chinese membership votes was that the Brazzaville group of states either abstained or backed the American position, while Scandinavians, the Casablanca group and non-aligned Asians did not.

Another reason why "self-determination" and some Cold War alignments have become similar is that Latin Americans, who in previous years have often voted in favor of "self-determination," were much less inclined to do so at the Sixteenth Assembly. They were probably reacting both to increased Soviet initiatives on "self-determination" questions and to the new, powerful and more radical African members of the Assembly. Thus they abstained on vote 8066 requesting the Committee of 17 to consider Southern Rhodesia and opposed a Soviet initiative (8069) on troop evacuations from Rwanda-Burundi.

Mongi Slim, the President of the Sixteenth General Assembly, has called the United Nations a "supranational framework within which conflicts of interest between nations could be at least attenuated, if not solved."[23] The main reasons for identifying the second rotated factor as "*U.N. supranationalism*" are the heavy loadings of crucial UNEF and Congo budgetary questions on it. The increasingly supranational role the United Nations has played in the Suez situation and the Congo crisis has been a major subject of controversy in the General Assembly, related to self-determination and the Cold War, but also distinct from them. Along with the enhancement of United Nations authority in these and related areas as a result of her activities there, some colonial states, such as France, Portugal, Belgium and South Africa have joined with the Soviet Bloc in obstructing the supranationalist strivings of the smaller U.N. members. Alone among the Great Powers, the United States has usually backed such initiatives. As such, these conflicts cut squarely across the East–West struggle. States normally close to the Soviet Union, such as Yugoslavia, Ghana, Guinea, India and Indonesia, voted against her on the apportionment of UNEF costs (vote 8052), the Congo authorization for 1962 (8051), a request for the Soviet Union to refrain from exploding her fifty megaton bomb (8008) and an expression of regret at the resumption of nuclear tests (8009). Belgium, France, South Africa, Portugal, and even the United States (on nuclear testing) opposed at least some of these resolutions. Votes 4023, 8071 and 8072 discussed above, also represent a successful "supranational" effort by the majority of U.N. members, despite Soviet objections and certain colonial hesitations, to ease the birth pains of Rwanda and Burundi in what might have become another Congo situation. Finally, votes 8039, requesting one percent of National Products in "capital" and technical assistance, and 8037, renewing the Committee of Information on Non-Self-Governing Territories, represent similar small-power aspirations and Great Power objections.

The fourth major component of U.N. voting, which we might call the "*Moslem factor*" after Conor Cruise O'Brien, is composed of Palestine and West Irian mediation attempts.[24] On these questions the Soviet Bloc supported Arab demands, Old Europeans and Latin Americans were somewhat divided, and most importantly, the Brazzaville states, objecting to Arab and Indonesian notions of "self-determination," refused to support the majority of Afro-Asians.[25]

---

[23] Cited in N. J. Padelford and R. Emerson, *Africa and World Order* (New York, 1963), p. 45.
[24] The West Irian roll calls were all in plenary meetings but are listed in Tables I and II with other colonial questions because they were discussed in terms of the Declaration on the Granting of Independence to Colonial Countries and Peoples.
[25] An important argument for both this fourfold substantive classification and the two-dimensional geopolitical interpretation offered earlier is that similar analyses seem appropriate for the Second, Seventh and Twelfth General Assemblies. *Cf.* Alker, *op. cit.*, or Alker and Russett, *op. cit.* (forthcoming).

We may describe the remaining five voting components in lesser detail. Factor VI reflects certain Latin, Benelux and Scandinavian misgivings about the composition of the Conciliation Commission (vote 0018, discussed above). The ninth rotated factor is limited to residual colonial misgivings about intervention in Rwanda and Burundi (vote 8070). These same European colonial states have usually been the ones refusing to support anti-colonial domestic intervention by the United Nations in condemning *apartheid* (perhaps what O'Brien would call a "race factor"). About half of the West European and Old Commonwealth states were isolated on vote 2005 concerning commodity regulations, probably because of the definite anti-Common Market flavor of Second Committee discussions (Factor V). A more peculiar coalition of the Soviet Bloc and several Latin Americans appeared in voting on marriage rules in the Third Committee (vote 3001, Factor VII). Finally, the coalition of conservative Westerners with conservative Afro-Asians (the Brazzaville group) on votes 8012, 1023 and 8044 is probably due to special "French concerns" on nuclear testing and Algerian problems (Factor VIII).

Some comparisons. This paper has empirically characterized the principal conflicts in the General Assembly. The results of the unrotated and the rotated factor analyses shed some light on current interpretations of international politics. Looking at frequent voting alignments, one-factor theories were found at best to describe 64 per cent of explainable Assembly voting. Again focusing on voting behavior more than substantive interpretations, a two-dimensional geopolitical picture was offered that corresponded quite closely to several previous descriptions of current international politics. East–West and North–South alignments (as shown in Figure 1) together underlie about 77 per cent of interpretable Assembly voting behavior. Because the unrotated factors were more easily identified by looking at voting alignments, the geopolitical interpretation was given a behavioral label.

In looking at the same spatial configuration of roll calls from a different perspective (the simply structured factor matrix in Table II), *four* different substantive issues were found: self-determination, Cold War and related membership questions, U.N. supranationalism, and Moslem questions (in the Near and Far East). Going beyond an increasingly popular two-dimensional view of world politics, this four-dimensional perspective helps to explain 85 per cent of generally interpretable Assembly voting. It also has the advantages of clearer substantive meaning than the unrotated factor matrix [26] and of labels corresponding quite closely to several

[26] Analyses of the East–West conflict in simple behavioral terms often run into the same confusion that Hovet notes regarding similar Soviet and Afro-Asian voting behavior: they do not distinguish Cold War from self-determination issues. Empirically, the "substantive" and "behavioral" viewpoints are complementary. Each roll call can be checked as to both its rotated and unrotated components. Correlating factor loadings or factor

interpretations of Assembly politics offered by diplomatic participants. O'Brien, for example, missed only supranationalism among these four factors, while he also distinguished one of the most important remaining conflicts.

Several of the rotated factors also turn out to be more functionally specific than the East–West and North–South divisions. From the rotated factor matrix (Table II) it is clear that self-determination issues pervade the General Assembly. Supranationalist votes are found in disarmament, economic, and especially Trusteeship and Fifth Committee contexts. The Special Political and Fourth Committees were the scene of Moslem demands evoking alignments unlike the usual anti-European or anti-West self-determination response; Cold War issues, including Chinese membership, have been largely "political" questions.

To some extent controversies in the Assembly with particular functional bases have produced "cross-cutting conflicts" as suggested by Chadwick Alger and others.[27] Problems of enlarging the scope of U.N. activities in these areas have divided both East and West. Negative agreements between colonial powers and the Soviet bloc on North–South or supranationalist issues have temporarily brought opponents in the East–West struggle closer together. But on major political conflicts issues such as ONUC and UNEF, increments to U.N. authority have come not so much from an indirect functional approach to world peace, as from American policy decisions to cooperate with the developing countries in opposition to other colonial powers and the Soviet bloc. Russian commitment to the symbols of self-determination has to some extent influenced the anti-colonial states; but this commitment has also restricted Soviet movements with supranationalist consequences. With anti-colonial Afro-Asians against Soviet or American intervention in the Congo, the Soviet Union had gradually and belatedly to withdraw from her support of the U.N. Congo operation.[28] Subsequent Russian financial vetoes have been only partly successful in preventing the U.N. from performing its peace-keeping role.

II. CORRELATES AND CONSEQUENCES OF ASSEMBLY CONFLICTS

The suggestion that *political* conflicts preoccupy members of the United Nations implies that the national interests of U.N. members,

---

scores makes this relationship explicit. The East–West and North–South correlations of self-determination factor scores are 0.74 and 0.43. The same numbers for the Cold War alignment are 0.50 and −0.20; for Moslem questions they are 0.39 and −0.12; and for supranationalism factor scores −0.25 and −0.86.

[27] Chadwick Alger, "Non-Resolutional Consequences of the United Nations and Their Effect on International Conflict," *Journal of Conflict Resolution*, Vol. 5, No. 2 (June, 1961), pp. 128–47.

[28] Early Soviet support of Security Council resolutions on the Congo is sometimes overlooked. See Alexander Dallin, *The Soviet Union at the United Nations* (New York, 1962), ch. 10.

shaped as they are by domestic, regional, political, economic and ethnic considerations, are more causally determinative of U.N. policy positions than caucusing-group pressures at the U.N. There is, for instance, a considerable degree of overlap between geographic regions and active groups at the United Nations in the case of Africans, Latin Americans, West Europeans and the Soviet bloc. The Commonwealth and Casablanca groups are those with the least geographical basis. The analysis below is directed toward testing just how well caucusing-group memberships and national political variables, the "environment" of the U.N. system, correlate with voting positions there. Hovet, for example, in *Bloc Politics in the United Nations*, has suggested that environmentally based "common interest groups" operate in the U.N. in addition to the more formalized caucuses. Among these groups he includes "underdeveloped countries," "colonial powers," "anti-colonial states" and "Moslem states." [29] In another context, Ernst Haas has suggested that the nature of a state's political system (democracy, oligarchy or totalitarianism), its region, its state of economic development and its Cold War allegiance might be helpful foci for studying international voting and ratification behavior.[30] Bruce Russett has found that military cooperation (alliances and the stationing of troops), economic interdependence (as measured by shares of export and import trade) and foreign aid are partial determinants of conflict in international relations.[31]

Turning to Table III, we see that group memberships do correlate quite highly with factor scores on all but the Cold War membership controversy in the General Assembly. The table brings out quite clearly the regional identification of the protagonists in all conflicts but that one. We can thus confirm, from the higher entries in the table, our earlier interpretations that the East–West controversy is most clearly a contest between Old Europeans and the Soviet bloc; that the North–South conflict pits Africans, Arabs and Asians against the Soviet bloc and, to a lesser extent, against Old Europeans; but these Africans, particularly the Casablanca states, oppose Old Europeans on self-determination issues. Casablanca, Arabs and Brazzaville states took very different positions on Moslem questions (Palestine and West Irian); while on the supranationalist alignment the Soviet bloc and to a lesser extent Old Europeans opposed an Afro-Asian majority.[32]

[29] The chart on page 126 summarizes membership in both kinds of groupings in 1959.
[30] Ernst Haas, "System and Process in the International Labor Organization: A Statistical Afterthought," *loc. cit.*
[31] Bruce M. Russett, "The Calculus of Deterrence," *The Journal of Conflict Resolution*, Vol. 7, No. 2 (June, 1963), pp. 97–109, and *Community and Contention: Britain and America in the Twentieth Century* (Cambridge, 1963), ch. IV.
[32] Arend Lijphart, *op. cit.*, has correctly pointed out the limitations of arbitrarily chosen groups in the study of Assembly politics. The groupings of states used in Table III represent combinations of regular and *ad hoc* caucusing units and regional interest

Table III

CORRELATIONS BETWEEN GROUP MEMBERSHIPS AND FACTOR
SCORES ON THE MAIN CONFLICTS IN THE
16TH GENERAL ASSEMBLY†

Group Memberships	Unrotated Factor Scores			Rotated Factor Scores		
	East vs. West	North vs. South	Self determi- nation	Cold War	Moslem ques- tions	UN Supra- nation- alism
1. Old Europeans	−.58*	−.43	−.74*	.10	−.25	−.08
2. Latin caucus	−.38	.07	−.21	−.36	.00	.06
3. Soviet Bloc	.50*	−.63*	.20	.27	.13	−.79*
4. Arab caucus	.36	.17	.19	.05	.55*	.12
5. Casablanca group	.05	.37	.53*	−.22	−.56*	.09
6. Brazzaville group	.32	.18	.18	.24	.33	.20
7. Africans	.22	.49	.62*	−.02	−.45	.26
8. Asians	.10	.23	.03	.01	.20	.27

†Point biserial correlations over 0.50 in magnitude have been asterisked for
convenience. The rotated factor scores referred to in this table and elsewhere in
this paper are slightly intercorrelated (below 0.10) because Russian abstentions on
Chinese membership have been considered affirmative votes and because self-determination scores have been revised to take into account the positions of extreme colonial powers on two nearly unanimous roll calls not included in the factor
analysis.

The search for a more adequate explanation of the "reasons for" or
the "environmental determinants of" Cold War voting brings us to Table
IV. The large number of asterisked entries suggest immediately that,
except for Moslem questions, we can explain each of the major conflicts
in the United Nations with "environmental variables" at least as accurately
and probably more cogently than with caucusing group variables. Thus
on East–West voting a military alliance with the United States is an extremely good predictor of voting behavior (the correlation is o.77). Describing this conflict (but not the Cold War and Chinese membership
issue) as "democracies versus totalitarians" also has some truth to it. An
ex-colonial past is also relevant, particularly regarding the self-determination aspects of the East–West alignment. Soviet aid and trade and to a
lesser extent similar variables for the Western Big Three are also correlated

groups. They serve as a convenient compromise between inductively found groupings
(as in Figure 1) and Hovet's list of regular caucusing groups (*Africa in the United
Nations*, p. 74.). Old Europeans are a frequently united group of West Europeans, Old
Commonwealth members, the United States and South Africa; Mongolia is considered
only a member of the Soviet bloc; Turkey and Cyprus are considered Asian states. Arabs,
Africans and Asians have been exclusively defined with respect to each other, Old
Europeans and the Soviet bloc. Yugoslavia, Israel and Nationalist China have not been
listed with any group.

Table IV

CORRELATIONS BETWEEN ENVIRONMENTAL VARIABLES AND VOTING POSITIONS ON THE MAIN CONFLICTS IN THE 16TH GENERAL ASSEMBLY†

Environmental Variables	Unrotated Factor Scores		Rotated Factor Scores			
	East vs. West	North vs. South	Self-determination	Cold War	Moslem questions	UN Supra-nation-alism
Economic Variables						
9. Recent U. S. aid	−.18	.17	−.13	−.26	.16	.19
10. Postwar U. S. aid	−.44	−.13	−.48	.05	−.12	.05
11. % trade with U. S.	−.49	.18	−.29	−.45	.00	.20
12. % trade with U. S., U. K., France	−.28	.63*	.22	−.39	−.33	.53*
13. Recent Soviet aid	.50	−.05	.18	.46	.21	−.09
14. Postwar Soviet aid	.54*	−.03	.19	.47	.28	−.03
15. % trade with Soviet Bloc	.57*	−.63*	.19	.38	.20	−.76*
16. Per capita G.N.P. (1955)	−.43	−.46	−.59*	.09	−.19	−.20
17. G.N.P. (1955)	−.01	−.34	−.11	.03	.02	−.25
Political Variables						
18. U. S. military ally	−.77*	.13	−.68*	−.35	−.17	.08
19. Communist state	.59*	−.56*	.24	.38	.20	−.68*
20. Democracy	−.52*	.04	−.47	−.09	−.17	.27
21. Totalitarian regime	.45	−.44	.22	.29	.11	−.53*
22. Colonial Power (since 1917)	−.43	−.46	−.50*	−.11	−.05	−.16
23. Ex-colony (since 1917)	.51*	.58*	.67*	.11	.06	.37
Sociological Variables						
24. % European descent	−.28	−.65*	−.57*	.20	−.12	−.42
25. % Negro	.15	.41	.52*	−.04	−.45	.19
26. % Moslem	.41	.29	.34	.04	.41	.19

†Aid figures are in per capita U. S. dollars; recent aid is from 1957 to 1961 or 1962 (in the Soviet case); trade figures are based on 1961 data. The numbering of variables is continued from Table III. Sources, definitions of variables, data, and estimates of inaccuracies are available from the Yale Political Data Program. N for this table and the previous one is 101, except for correlations with variables, 9, 10, 11, 13, 14 where *a priori* missing data reduced it to 100 or 91. Throughout this and previous tables, Honduras, Gabon and Tanganyika have been omitted because of their high voting absenteeism.

with East–West voting. A significant finding is that in each of the two main geopolitical conflicts, *trade, not aid,* is the better predictor of voting behavior. As we shall see below, the "environmental" approach to U.N. voting using such key variables in world politics as trade, aid and military alliances will predict East–West voting positions with just as much accuracy as caucusing group memberships more immediate to the actual voting.

Trade, colonial past, per capita Gross National Product (an indicator of economic development) and the percentage of a nation's population that is of European descent, probably with similar sympathies, are suggestive correlates of North–South voting, but they raise the important question of their relative explanatory importance when the remaining variables are controlled for, a question regression analysis can be used to answer.

Turning to the substantive conflicts in the Assembly, racial variables, economic development, colonial history and American military alliances all influence policy positions (factor scores) on self-determination. Trade and aid, as indicators of what might be best described as a two-way process of interdependence rather than just "buying votes," help improve our understanding of the reasons for Cold War membership alignments. Even from the simple correlations in Table IV it is evident that *Soviet* (not American) aid either in years since 1957 or in the entire post-World War II period is a good predictor of voting for Communist Chinese membership in the United Nations. Whether the Soviets should be regarded as influential in "buying votes" or as only "rewarding" their friends is a more difficult question which will not be discussed here. On Moslem questions, racial and religious variables do seem to underlie the voting pattern, but these have also been modified by caucusing group policy decisions, as we saw in Table III. As an indicator of economic interdependence, trade with the Big Three (but not Western military alliances this time) correlates highly with supranationalism. Even though data for within-Bloc trade seem to underestimate Bloc solidarity, trade with the Soviet Bloc is as high a correlate of the anti-supranationalist position as was Soviet Bloc membership. From Table IV it also appears that both democracies and ex-colonial states have contributed to the growth of the United Nations in the present era.

Correlations cannot be considered causal explanations until the observer has controlled for the effects of other possibly relevant variables. Multiple regression analysis takes an important step in that direction: it provides a linear model for explaining a "dependent" variable, such as East–West voting positions, as the sum of distinctive contributions from several "independent" variables, such as foreign aid and military alliances. For individual nations, residual differences between actual and predicted values of the dependent variable can be calculated and subjected to further analysis; for the entire U.N. membership, squared multiple correlation coefficients indicate the percentage of voting variation explained by the model.[33]

In a regression equation each coefficient of an independent variable tells the direction and the amount of the average change in the dependent variable associated with a unit change in only that one independent variable. The units of the independent variables may be either *concrete*, in policy terms such as dollars of aid or membership in the Latin American caucusing group, or *standardized* to reflect what on a worldwide scale appear as equi-probable changes.[34] When several logically prior variables are each distinctively related to Assembly voting positions on a particular conflict, a linear regression equation provides a simple but attractive theoretical statement of a multivariate explanatory relationship.

In regression equations (1) through (4), abbreviated alphabetic labels taken from Table IV denote both the independent and the dependent variables. The dependent variables, standardized voting ranks, can be interpreted as distances (roughly, inches) along either axis of Figure 1 or of a similar picture for rotated Cold War and supranationalism alignments. Taken from among the most promising explanatory variables in Table IV, the combinations of independent variables are not exhaustive, but only intended to test several explanations of U.N. voting reviewed earlier in this paper.[35]

Equation (1) tells us, for instance, that either a Western military alliance or one hundred dollars of postwar Soviet Bloc per capita aid

[33] The R^2s for equations (1)–(4) below are exceptionally high ones in social research. The multiple correlation coefficient of the East–West model is 0.88. The equation explains 78% of the major voting alignment in the General Assembly. Similarly, the North–South Model explains 70%, the Cold War and supranationalism models 48% and 44% respectively. Even for factor scores in their present largely uncorrelated form (see note to Table III), high correlations with the rotated self-determination conflict indicate that influences affecting these policy positions differ from those which determine Cold War membership alignments.

Using regional and caucusing-group variables that are much more immediate to the voting (see Table III), the corresponding R^2s are roughly similar: 0.79, 0.78, 0.30 and 0.72. Cold War membership alignments can be explained better by more distant environmental variables, like aid and trade, than by caucusing-group memberships. Supranationalism and self-determination (with group membership regressions explaining 72% and 85% respectively) definitely reflect a good deal of group cohesion. Group cohesion by itself, however, is a poor predictor of what a group has agreed on, for which additional explanations, like equations (1)–(4), are required.

[34] In the case of a standardized dependent variable, standardized β-coefficients are obtained by multiplying a concrete b-coefficient times the standard deviation of its independent variable. β-coefficients are comparable; b-weights are not.

[35] In these equations b-coefficients are given with the independent variables, β-weights are given below them in parentheses. The concrete units for dichotomous variables (*e.g.*, alliances) are 1 or 0; for aid figures they are $100 per capita; for per capita G.N.P. $1,000; and for all percentage figures, 100%. It should be noted that the communist "independent" variables are highly intercorrelated, enough so that further analysis using a single index of communist ties might be desirable.

$$EW = -.29\underset{(-0.31)}{PUSA} + .74\underset{(0.02)}{RUSA} + .23\underset{(0.05)}{TWUUF} - .96\underset{(-0.47)}{USALY} + 2.00\underset{(0.24)}{PSBA} - .23\underset{(-0.02)}{RSBA} + 1.35\underset{(0.28)}{TWSB} + .58\underset{(0.20)}{COMM} \quad (1)$$

$$CWM = .50\underset{(0.54)}{PUSA} - 1.44\underset{(-0.04)}{RUSA} - .15\underset{(-0.03)}{TWUUF} - .63\underset{(-0.31)}{USALY} + 1.85\underset{(0.22)}{PSBA} + 1.46\underset{(0.14)}{RSBA} + 1.01\underset{(0.21)}{TWSB} + .20\underset{(0.07)}{COMM} \quad (2)$$

$$NS = .71\underset{(0.15)}{TWUUF} + .50\underset{(0.25)}{EXECY} - 1.50\underset{(-0.31)}{TWSB} - .38\underset{(-0.13)}{COMM} - .40\underset{(-0.18)}{EURDS} - .39\underset{(-0.16)}{PCGNP} \quad (3)$$

$$UNSUP = .57\underset{(0.28)}{EXECY} + .44\underset{(0.22)}{DEM} - .96\underset{(-0.41)}{TOT} - .11\underset{(-0.04)}{COLP} - .49\underset{(-0.19)}{PCGNP} \quad (4)$$

(Syria, Guinea and Ghana have received about half this amount) would polarize U.N. voting patterns on the East–West controversy. Since 1957, however, both Soviet and American aid have moved toward the uncommitted, away from their own camps. The effect of an increase in trade with the Big Three is roughly one-fifth as large as for a similar Soviet-bloc trade increase. Although the standardized coefficients are similar, dollar for dollar, Soviet aid has been much more strongly related to East–West voting alignments in the United Nations. An "alliance" of communist political–economic systems in Cuba, Guinea, Mali and the Soviet Bloc also had a considerable Eastern influence in 1961 and 1962. Looking specifically at the Cold War membership aspects of the East–West alignment, equation (2) states the opposite tendencies of long-term and short-term American aid, the anti-communist pull of an American military alliance, and consistent relationships between long term *and* recent Soviet aid and voting on Chinese representation in the Assembly.

The third equation tells us that being 100 percent of European descent makes for only about a fourth as much Northern voting as would total trade with the Soviet Bloc. Being a communist state creates about as much Northern voting as a per capita G.N.P. of a thousand dollars. Being an ex-European colony and trading about 70 percent of the time with the Western Big Three would together move a state about an "inch" (on Figure 1) in the Southern direction. On the related supranationalism conflict, ex-colonial status and political democracy are both about equally strong "causes" of supranationalist voting, while totalitarian and developed states tend to demur. An analysis of residuals shows that even equation (4) underestimates the supranationalist tendencies of the Casablanca and Brazzaville groups, as well as the anti-supranationalist tendencies of the Soviet bloc.

Deterministic as the coefficients in the factor matrix and the regression equations just given may seem, they represent opportunities for domestic politicians and foreign service diplomats to reshape international politics by changing these relationships. In the last two decades "issues" on the world scene have been perceived differently (loaded on different factors in succeeding years) with dramatically different consequences; and environmental variables (like military alliances) have become increasingly or decreasingly "influential" in determining policy positions. American foreign aid has increased in its relevance to the Cold War struggle in the U.N., but still remains fairly uncorrelated on a world-wide basis with this conflict. If it were to become highly correlated in this manner, an effective neutral and supranationalist role for the anti-colonial countries would be increasingly difficult. South African racial policies have become increasingly East–West and self-determination issues with foreboding consequences; West Irian remained distinct enough from these contests for some progress to be made. The Soviet Union failed significantly to make the Congo crisis into an anti-European and anti-American self-determination issue, although she and the Casablanca states tried to do so. Many of the elements of such a conflict were certainly there; but fortunately (for us) Russia misperceived Afro-Asian and American supranationalist predispositions. The danger with Cold War issues like Hungary and Tibet is that they will become increasingly perceived as anti-Western self-determination conflicts; the American opportunity—and challenge for our policy-makers —is to persuade others and ourselves of the United Nations' universal supranationalist possibilities.

6

The Use of Aggregate Data

One of the most promising and fastest growing developments in both the fields of international relations and comparative government has been the application of aggregate—usually country-by-country—statistical data and methods to the discipline's inextinguishable store of solutionless problems. Fruitful analyses have been made using this technique of such classical puzzles as these: Does military aid to a country encourage authoritarian tendencies? Does poverty in a country breed violence? Are internally unstable countries more likely than stable ones to be engaged in international turmoil?

Aggregate data for the countries of the world is becoming increasingly available through the diligent efforts of the United Nations, various governmental organizations, and a number of social scientists. An essential starting point for any political scientist interested in this area is the *World Handbook of Political and Social Indicators* put together at Yale by Bruce M. Russett and his associates.[1] The heart of the book consists of a series of tables which rate those countries of the world for which data are available on some 75 political, social, and economic variables, among them: total population, life expectancy, percentage of votes attained by the Communist Party, government expenditures as a percentage of G.N.P.,

[1] Bruce M. Russett, Hayward R. Alker, Jr., Karl W. Deutsch, and Harold D. Lasswell, *World Handbook of Political and Social Indicators* (New Haven: Yale, 1964). See also Karl W. Deutsch, "Toward an Inventory of Basic Trends and Patterns in Comparative and International Politics," *American Political Science Review*, Vol. 54 (March, 1960), pp. 34–57.

and income distribution. Each table is accompanied by a thoughtful discussion of the variable, giving sources, assessing possible error, and noting peculiarities. An introduction acknowledges the previous efforts by social scientists [2] while a series of essays at the end of the book begins an analysis of trends and patterns among the 75 indicators.[3] As a continuing project the Yale Political Data Program intends to work to improve and update the accumulated data.

A related effort, conducted by Arthur Banks and Robert Textor, has been published in a mammoth volume, A Cross-Polity Survey.[4] The authors have gathered information on some of the variables also found in the Russett volume, although the data are presented in categoric groups, rather than as continuous variables. Thus the actual population of a country is never given; rather countries are classified simply as small, medium, large, or very large. But while there is some overlap between the two compendiums, the Banks and Textor volume emphasizes "soft," judgmental variables: countries are rated on such dimensions as "stability of party system," "sectionalism," and "interest aggregation by anomic groups." The ratings are based largely on the thoughtful consideration of one of the authors—finances in this beginning effort were insufficient to set up a panel of expert judges. Some bias and mushiness will of course be inevitable in this procedure, but the advantage is that specific, direct indicators of politically relevant variables become available. The virtues and dangers of using judges to order data are discussed in chapter 8. Each of the 57 variables so derived is then dichotomized in various ways—the size dimension, for example, is made into two variables as "small" countries are compared to larger ones for one new variable while "small" and "medium" countries are compared to larger ones for another—making a total of 194 dichotomous variables.

Dichotomization is a tricky business, of course. Just how tricky can perhaps be judged from the simple, if contrived, example presented in Table 1. The three-by-three cross tabulation at the top is dichotomized both along the A lines and along the B lines giving the two cross-tabulations at the bottom. It is clear that the observed correlation between the two variables depends heavily on which version of the table is chosen.

[2] Most notably perhaps, Raymond B. Cattell, "The Dimensions of Culture Patterns of Factorization of National Characters," *Journal of Abnormal and Social Psychology*, Vol. 44 (1949), pp. 215–53; and Norton Ginsburg, *Atlas of Economic Development* (Chicago: University of Chicago Press, 1961).

[3] For other analyses using these data, see Bruce M. Russett, "Inequality and Instability: The Relation of Land Tenure to Politics," *World Politics*, Vol. 16 (April, 1964), pp. 442–53, *Trends in World Politics* (New York: Macmillan, 1965), chapters 7 and 8, "Measures of Military Effort," *American Behavioral Scientist*, Vol. 7 (February, 1964), pp. 26–28, and *International Regions and the International System* (Chicago: Rand McNally, 1967), especially chapters 2 and 3.

[4] Arthur S. Banks and Robert B. Textor, *A Cross-Polity Survey* (Cambridge, Mass.: M.I.T. Press, 1963).

Table 1

	B	A		
2	15	16	33	← A
2	1	14	17	← B
17	1	2	20	
21	17	32	70	

Dichotomy A

17	16	33
21	16	37
38	32	70

Dichotomy B

4	46	50
17	3	20
21	49	70

Things can get worse when larger tables or cross-plots of continuous variables are reduced to cross-tabulated dichotomies. The suggestion is not necessarily to avoid dichotomization, but at least to hover cautiously over the data when deciding on cutting points. This simple moral applies to any effort to reduce data distributions.

No less than 1,258 pages of *A Cross-Polity Survey* are devoted to reproducing reams of computer output which resulted from a systematic comparison of each of these 194 dichotomous variables with each of the others searching for strong correlations. The result makes for reading which is a bit tedious and unsatisfying. Fortunately the data from both the Russett and the Banks and Textor compilations are available on cards or tape through the Inter-University Consortium for Political Research at the University of Michigan. So armed, the individual researcher can produce his own bales of computer output.[5]

Several studies based on the Banks and Textor data have been published, applying factor analysis and Guttman scaling techniques to the data.[6]

Other contributions in this area have been made by people who have been collecting country-by-country statistics on violence. While Russett and Banks and Textor have been measuring GNP and interest articulation, these analysts have been poring through such sources as *Facts on File*, the *New York Times Index*, and the *Britannia Book of the Year* cheerfully tallying riots, wars, revolutions, and anti-foreign demonstrations. One of the measures so obtained, number of deaths from domestic group violence, is included in the *World Handbook of Political and Social Indicators* while some of the users of the Banks and Textor data have included violence measures in their analyses.[7]

Much of the pioneering work in this area has been accomplished by Rudolph Rummel in his "dimensionality of nations" project which relies heavily on factor analysis as a basic technique.[8] The study reprinted below by Raymond Tanter replicates and elaborates some of Rummel's findings. It is concerned with the much debated question of the relation between internal and international instability. It could be argued that countries which are secure at home, because they have the confidence and ability to wage successful war are more likely to become engaged in wars than

[5] For further review of these two books, see Michael Haas, "Aggregate Analysis," *World Politics*, Vol. 19 (October, 1966), pp. 106–21.
[6] Phillip M. Gregg and Arthur S. Banks, "Dimensions of Political Systems: Factor Analysis of *A Cross-Polity Survey*," *American Political Science Review*, Vol. 59 (September, 1965), pp. 602–14; Arthur S. Banks and Phillip M. Gregg, "Grouping Political Systems: Q-Factor Analysis of *A Cross-Polity Survey*," *American Behavioral Scientist*, Vol. 9 (November, 1965), pp. 3–6; Peter G. Snow, "A Scalogram Analysis of Political Development," *American Behavioral Scientist*, Vol. 9 (March, 1966), pp. 33–36.
[7] Gregg and Banks, *op. cit.*
[8] Rudolph J. Rummel, "Dimensions of Conflict Behavior Within and Between Nations," *General Systems*, Vol. 8 (1963), pp. 1–50, "Testing Some Possible Predictors of Conflict Behavior and Between Nations," *Peace Research Society (International) Papers*, Vol. 1 (1964), pp. 79–111, "Dimensions of Conflict Behavior Within Nations, 1946–59," *Journal of Conflict Resolution*, Vol. 10 (March, 1966), pp. 65–73, "A Social Field Theory of Foreign Conflict Behavior," *Peace Research Society (International) Papers*, Vol. 4 (1966), pp. 131–50, "Some Dimensions in the Foreign Behavior of Nations," *Journal of Peace Research*, (1966), pp. 201–24, "Some Attributes and Behavioral Patterns of Nations," *ibid*, (1967), pp. 196–206, "A Field Theory of Social Action with Application to Conflict Within Nations," *General Systems*, Vol. 10 (1965), pp. 183–211, "A Foreign Conflict Behavior Code Sheet," *World Politics*, Vol. 18 (January, 1966), pp. 283–96, "The Dimensionality of Nations Project," in Richard L. Merritt and Stein Rokkan (eds.), *Comparing Nations: The Use of Quantitative Data in Cross-National Research* (New Haven: Yale, 1966), and "The Relationship Between National Attributes and Foreign Conflict Behavior," in J. David Singer (ed.), *Quantitative International Politics* (New York: Free Press, 1968), pp. 187–214. See also Jack Sawyer, "Dimensions of Nation: Size, Wealth, and Politics," *American Journal of Sociology*, Vol. 73 (September, 1967), pp. 145–72 and Russett, *International Regions*, chapter 12.

are insecure countries which must expend all their energies holding themselves together. Or one could conclude that secure countries are likely to be fat and contented and hence unwarlike, while unstable countries tend to get involved in international conflicts for their cathartic value or in order to divert attention at home from domestic troubles. Neither hypothesis, according to Tanter's analysis, seems to hold: there is little relationship between internal and external instability. This is not the final word on the subject, of course: one might, for example, wish to broaden the historical perspective, test the hypotheses with smaller and more homogeneous sets of countries, or search for intervening variables.[9] But that the approach can make an important contribution to the investigation of this ancient and important question in international relations, seems clear.

Aggregate data can be useful in other problems of interest. Efforts to explain domestic violence, using as a basis a frustration-aggression model, have been made by Ted Gurr and by Ivo and Rosalind Feierabend.[10] J. David Singer and Melvin Small have devised an ingenious method for measuring national status in the international environment through an analysis of diplomatic recognition policies.[11] Charles Wolf has investigated the relationship (he finds little) between military aid and political development.[12] Similar data and approaches have found application in the field of comparative government where, for example, the analysis of the social and economic prerequisites for democratic development have been extensively analyzed—and debated.[13]

Instead of analyzing aggregate data gathered country-by-country one can measure transaction flows *between* countries. Of primary notice in this regard is the work of Karl Deutsch in his important studies of na-

[9] For efforts along this line, see Michael Haas, "Societal Approaches to the Study of War," *Journal of Peace Research*, (1965), pp. 307–23. See also his "Social Change and National Aggressiveness, 1900–1960," in Singer, *op. cit.*, pp. 215–46.
[10] Ted Gurr, "The Conditions of Civil Violence: First Tests of a Casual Model" (Princeton University, Center of International Studies, April, 1967), and "Psychological Factors in Civil Violence," *World Politics*, Vol. 20 (January, 1968), pp. 245–78; Ivo K. and Rosalind L. Feierabend, "Aggressive Behaviors Within Politics, 1948–1962: A Cross-National Study," *Journal of Conflict Resolution*, Vol. 10 (September, 1966), pp. 249–71. See also Raymond Tanter and Manus Midlarsky, "A Theory of Revolution," *ibid.*, Vol. 11 (September, 1967), pp. 264–80.
[11] J. David Singer and Melvin Small, "The Composition and Status Ordering of the International System: 1815–1940," *World Politics*, Vol. 18 (January, 1966), pp. 236–82.
[12] Charles Wolf, Jr., *United States Policy and the Third World* (Boston: Little, Brown, 1967), especially chapter 5. See also Robert D. Putnam, "Toward Explaining Military Intervention in Latin American Politics," *World Politics*, Vol. 20 (October, 1967), pp. 83–110.
[13] James S. Coleman, "The Political Systems of the Developing Areas," Gabriel A. Almond and James S. Coleman (eds.), *The Politics of Developing Areas* (Princeton: Princeton University Press, 1960); Seymour Martin Lipset, *Political Man* (New York: Anchor-Doubleday, 1960), chapter 2; Wolf, *op. cit.*; Phillips Cutright, "National Political Development: Its Measurement and Social Correlates," in Nelson W. Polsby, Robert A. Dentler, and Paul A. Smith (eds.), *Politics and Social Life* (Boston: Houghton Mifflin, 1963). See also Merritt and Rokkan, *op. cit.*

tionalism and internationalism using as vital data international communications flows such as trade, mail, and travel patterns.[14] A related study, carried out by Bruce Russett, attempts to assess trends in the Anglo-American alliance since 1890 by considering a large number of transaction indicators including investment, student exchanges, tourism, international agreements, migration, and diplomatic representation.[15]

Similar indicators have been used for varying purposes by a number of investigators. Steven Brams and Chadwick Alger have extensively analyzed patterns of representation and shared memberships in intergovernmental organizations.[16] Zbigniew Brzezinski uses visits among leaders as well as trade patterns as helpful indicators in assessing the organization of the Soviet bloc.[17] These measures have also been used to assess international alignment,[18] to predict bloc patterns in the United Nations,[19] to test arms race models,[20] to examine patterns of interaction between members of the NATO and Warsaw Pact alliances,[21] to delimit international regions,[22] to assess the role of France in Europe,[23] and to analyze trends in the North Atlantic Area.[24] Within this book, transaction data are found by Alker in the study reprinted in chapter 5 to have relevance to U.N.

[14] Karl W. Deutsch, *Nationalism and Social Communication: An Inquiry into the Foundations of Nationality* (Cambridge: M.I.T. Press, 1953), "Shifts in the Balance of International Communication Flows," *Public Opinion Quarterly*, Vol. 20 (Spring, 1956), pp. 143–60; Karl W. Deutsch, Sidney A. Burrell, Robert A. Kann, Maurice Lee, Jr., Martin Lichterman, Raymond E. Lindgren, Francis L. Loewenheim, and Richard W. Van Wagenen, *Political Community and the North Atlantic Area* (Princeton: Princeton University Press, 1957). See also Philip E. Jacob and James V. Toscano (eds.), *The Integration of Political Communities* (Philadelphia: Lippincott-Preceptor, 1964).
[15] Bruce M. Russett, *Community and Contention: Britain and America in the Twentieth Century* (Cambridge: M.I.T. Press, 1963). For a critique, see R. N. Rosecrance and J. E. Mueller, "Decision-Making and the Qualitative Analysis of International Relations," *Year Book of World Affairs 1967* (London: Stevens, 1967), pp. 12–15.
[16] Steven J. Brams, "Transaction Flows in the International System," *American Political Science Review*, Vol. 60 (December, 1966), pp. 880–98; Chadwick F. Alger and Stephen J. Brams, "Patterns of Representation in National Capitals and Intergovernmental Organizations," *World Politics*, Vol. 19 (July, 1967), pp. 646–63.
[17] Zbigniew K. Brzezinski, *The Soviet Bloc: Unity and Conflict* (New York: Praeger, 1961, revised edition), appendix 1, "The Organization of the Communist Camp."
[18] Henry Teune and Sig Synnestvedt, "Measuring International Alignment," *Orbis*, Vol. 9 (Spring, 1965), pp. 171–89.
[19] William W. Ellis and John Salzberg, "Africa and the U.N.: A Statistical Note," *American Behavioral Scientist*, Vol. 8 (April, 1965), pp. 30–32.
[20] Paul Smoker, "Trade, Defense, and the Richardson Theory of Arms Races: A Seven Nation Study," *Journal of Peace Research*, Vol. 2 (1965), pp. 161–76, "The Arms Race: A Wave Model," *Peace Research Society (International) Papers*, Vol. 4 (1966), pp. 151–92.
[21] Johan Galtung, "East-West Interaction Patterns," *Journal of Peace Research* (1966), pp. 146–77.
[22] Russett, *International Regions*, especially chapters 6–10.
[23] Theodore Caplow and Kurt Finsterbusch, "France and Other Countries: A Study of International Interaction," *Journal of Conflict Resolution*, Vol. 12 (March, 1968), pp. 1–15.
[24] Hayward Alker, Jr. and Donald Puchala, "Trends in Economic Partnership: The North Atlantic Area, 1928–1963," in Singer, *op. cit.*, pp. 287–316.

voting patterns and by Russett in the study reprinted in chapter 2 to be important predictors of the success of the deterrent threat.

The study by Masakatsu Kato, published here for the first time, attempts to develop a rational decision–theoretic model of the American foreign aid allocation process. Like the Tanter study, the model uses multiple regression techniques which are discussed in Appendix A. To test his model, Kato finds both country-by-country and transaction flow indicators to be relevant in his exploratory study.

Questions are raised inevitably and fairly in this sort of analysis about the accuracy of the data. Countries which wish to look "developed," for example, may be inspired to engage in a bit of creative thinking when they report their literacy rate to United Nations' statisticians. Furthermore, the definition of "literacy" can vary; some countries may require a grade school education before considering an individual literate, while others may be inclined to accept a gracefully penned "X" to be proof of literacy. Tanter, in his efforts to assess violence, must rely on the abilities of western newsmen to cut through official efforts in some countries to restrict the outside world's knowledge of violent internal events. He applies certain "error measures" in his analysis, but these are only partly reassuring. Error can never be completely eliminated, of course. One can only seek to minimize its impact by consulting a variety of sources of information, by quizzing impartial area specialists for their estimates of accuracy, and by disclosing possible sources of bias when reporting the results. Sometimes the sources of error are biasing in opposite directions and thus tend to cancel one another out. As the world becomes more technical and as statisticians and statistically-trained political scientists, anthropologists, sociologists, and economists invade its every corner, error and bias in existing estimates is likely to be reduced substantially.

The importance of error is in part a function of the level of analysis. Estimates for the population of Ethiopia, for example, vary considerably. Thus if one is performing a comparative analysis of African countries in which it is vital that the countries involved be accurately scaled for population, it might be best to look for another research project—or else to deal with an Ethiopialess Africa. On the other hand, if the study demands only that one be able to be sure that the population of Ethiopia is significantly smaller than that of India or Pakistan, existing population estimates are quite adequate.

An unpleasantly knotty problem that exists for users of aggregate data concerns the "ecological correlation" phenomena; correlations derived by comparing units such as countries cannot readily be generalized to correlations among individuals.[25] To illustrate, suppose there are three countries, each of which has a population of 10 and suppose the distribu-

[25] On this problem, see especially W. S. Robinson, "Ecological Correlation and the Behavior of Individuals," *American Sociological Review*, Vol. 15 (June, 1950), pp. 351–57.

Table 2

	Country		
	A	B	C
1. Number of Catholics	4	5	6
2. Number of Protestants	6	5	4
	10	10	10
3. Number of Communist votes	4	5	6
4. Number of non-Communist votes	6	5	4
	10	10	10
5. Number of Catholics who voted Communist	0	1	2
6. Number of Protestants who voted Communist	4	4	4
	4	5	6

	Voted Communist	Voted Non-Communist	
Catholics	3	12	15
Protestants	12	3	15
	15	15	30

tions of Catholics and Communist votes within these countries are as given in lines 1–4 of Table 2. As can be seen from lines 1 and 3 of the Table, there is a perfect positive correlation between the number of Catholics a country has and the number of votes received by the Communists. It cannot be inferred, however, that Catholics tend to vote for the Communist Party for it is entirely possible that the party preferences of individuals within the religious groups are as given in lines 5 and 6 of the Table generating the *individual* correlation as shown in the cross-tabulation at the bottom of the Table. Thus while *countries* with more Catholics in the example tend to vote more Communist, as *individuals* Catholics are seen to be devotedly anti-Communist. As long as the unit of analysis is the country, as it is in the two studies reprinted below, one is on safe ground; but glibly to generalize to individual behavior is usually dangerous. It may be found that countries with high illiteracy rates tend to have more domestic violence; it does not necessarily follow, however, that it is the illiterates who are committing the violence. Fortunately, estimation procedures using multiple regression analysis have been developed which, if the circumstances are appropriate, can deal in part with the dilemma.

A final problem in dealing with aggregate data which might be mentioned involves skewness. On some dimensions the countries of the world do not distribute themselves very evenly: on the population dimension, for example, there are many small countries but few large ones; or on Tanter's "riot" dimension, few countries have many riots, while a large number have none. Consequently the distributions of countries on these dimensions are highly "skewed": there are many occupants at the low end of the scale, few at the upper end. When correlated, such dimensions tend to generate lower correlations than might be expected when more equitably distributed variables are correlated.[26] One standard method for dealing in part with this problem is to transform the basic units so that there are finer discriminations at the lower end of the scale than at the top. The logarithmic transformation, used by Tanter on some of his variables, arranges the universe so that there is an equal distance between the numbers 1, 10, 100, 1000, etc. This procedure does not solve the problem, but it often reduces its consequences.

[26] See John B. Carroll, "The Nature of the Data, or How to Choose a Correlation Coefficient," *Psychometrika*, Vol. 26 (December, 1961), pp. 347–62.

DIMENSIONS OF CONFLICT WITHIN
AND BETWEEN NATIONS, 1958-60 [1]

Raymond Tanter

This is a replication of a study by Rudolph J. Rummel (1963). The goals of that study were to determine the dimensions of variation in the domestic and foreign conflict behavior of nations, to locate nations on these dimensions, and to employ these dimensions in order to discover the relationship between both forms of conflict behavior. The goals of the replication are to obtain additional evidence relative to the dimensions of conflict behavior and the relationship between domestic and foreign conflict behavior. Data have been collected across eighty-three nations for 1958, 1959, and 1960 on the same twenty-two measures of conflict behavior used in the previous study. Similarly, these data are to be intercorrelated and factor analyzed, and multiple regression is to be used to examine the relationship between domestic and foreign conflict behavior.

THEORY

Many of the generalizations about international conflict behavior have been discovered through the use of historical analysis. For example, Rich-

Reprinted by permission from *Journal of Conflict Resolution*, Vol. 10 (March, 1966), copyright 1966 by The University of Michigan.
[1] Prepared in connection with research supported by the National Science Foundation, Grant NSF-GS224. The data were collected as part of the Dimensionality of Nations Project supported by that foundation, the Carnegie Seminar supported by the Carnegie Corporation, and the International Development Research Center (IDRC) at Indiana University, supported by the Ford Foundation.
The author wishes to thank Fred Riggs, formerly acting director of the IDRC, and Rudolph Rummel, principal investigator of the Dimensionality of Nations Project, Yale University, for making this study possible. Professor Rummel has aided in the preparation of the research design phase of this study in order to assure continuity from his study (Rummel, 1963) to the present one. I am also quite grateful for his comments on my interpretation of the results, and in reading earlier drafts; any errors, however, are mine. In addition, I am grateful to Milton Hobbs, Harold Guetzkow, J. David Singer, and Dean Pruitt for their comments, and to the Indiana and Northwestern University Research Computing Centers for the generous provision of their facilities.

ard Rosecrance concludes that through time there is a tendency for international instability to be associated with the domestic insecurity of elites (Rosecrance, 1963, p. 304). Two other students of international relations, Ernst Haas and Allen Whiting, suggest an explanation for the relationship between internal and external conflict behavior. They contend that groups seeking self-preservation may be driven to a foreign policy of conflict. The authors reason that the elites become fearful of losing their domestic positions during periods of rapid industrialization and widespread social change; they then try to displace the attention of the disaffected population onto some outside target. But the authors suggest that this form of self-preservation rarely leads to war (Haas and Whiting, 1956, pp. 61–62).

In addition to Rosecrance and Haas and Whiting, Quincy Wright suggests that there is a general relationship between internal and external conflict behavior. Interspersed in his two volumes of A *Study of War* (1942) are propositions such as the following:

> By creating and perpetuating in the community both a fear of invasion and a hope of expansion, obedience to a ruler may be guaranteed. A system of world politics resting upon a balance of power contributes to the integration of each power by maintaining among the peoples the fear of war as well as the hope of dominance [Vol. II, p. 1016]. Rulers have forestalled internal sedition by starting external wars [Vol. I, p. 140]. There is no nation in which war or preparations of war have not to some degree or at some time been used as an instrument of national stability and order [Vol. I, p. 254]. In later stages of the Napoleonic Wars, Napoleon began to appreciate the value of war as an instrument of internal soldarity [Vol. II, p. 725]. Governments have often started war because it appeared to them a necessary or convenient means of establishing, maintaining, or expanding the power of the government, party, or class within the nation [Vol. II, p. 727].

Hopefully, this study will provide a systematic examination of the propositions of such theorists as Rosecrance, Haas and Whiting, and Wright. From a systematic examination and a series of *replications*, it may be possible to construct a general theory of intra- and internation conflict behavior. (See below, pp. 190ff., for a further discussion of such theories.)

REPLICATION

Increasing the number of observations or trials in a particular design is referred to in the literature on the logic of experimentation as increasing the replications. Increasing the replications generally increases the confidence that the findings are not the result of chance factors (Edwards,

1954, p. 273). One frequently comes across references to the need for replication in the literature on research methods. For example, Katz asserts that the history of social psychology shows the significance of the replication of findings in that many of the original propositions have not been confirmed by later studies (Katz, 1953, p. 64). Moreover, Sidman contends that the most appropriate empirical test of the reliability of data is provided by replication (Sidman, 1960, p. 70).

Replication is especially suggested when there is disagreement with a well-established finding, the number of replications warranted being a function of the extent to which the previous findings were firmly established (Sidman, 1960, p. 78). As regards quantitative studies, the finding that there is very little relationship between domestic and foreign conflict behavior (Sorokin, 1937; Rummell, 1963) contrasts with other findings of a negative relationship (Huntington, 1962) and a positive relationship (McKenna, 1962). On the other hand, most of the nonquantitative works support the hypothesis of a positive relationship (Haas and Whiting, 1956; Rosecrance, 1963).[2] The quantitative studies where the generalization was not based on the collected data (such as Wright, 1942) also support the finding of a positive relationship.

The quantitative studies where the generalization was based on the data meet a minimum criterion for replication, e.g., the standardization of the specifications for data. And as Katz points out, "Only when we attain the level of standardizing our specifications for data can we see the extent to which reported findings are true generalizations" (Katz, 1953, p. 64). Moreover, the ability to replicate scientific inquiry depends largely upon an explicit statement of the research design decisions such as data collection and analysis procedures.

POPULATION

To be included in this study, nations had to be sovereign for at least two years and have a population equal to or greater than 800,000 in 1958. As a result of more nations being able to meet these criteria for 1958 than for 1955, the population size increased to eighty-three from the seventy-seven in the 1955–57 study (see Appendix II for the list of nations). Intragroup replication would entail the use of the exact sample employed in the prior study. As with the Rummel study, however, the

[2] The way some of these propositions are stated, however, it is almost possible to interpret them as suggesting a negative relationship. This interpretation, though, does not fit in with the context in which the propositions appear. With the introduction of a time lag between the occurrence of domestic and foreign conflict behavior, the theories of Coser (1956) and Simmel (1955) suggest a negative relationship.

total *population* is being used. Consequently, sampling restrictions of this sort are not applicable.[3]

DATA SOURCES AND CODING RELIABILITY

The New York Times Index, Deadline Data on World Affairs, Brittanica Book of the Year, and *Facts on File* were used as sources of data for the twenty-two conflict behavior measures. The first two sources, however, proved to be far more productive of data than the others. Consequently, most of the data reported in this study were derived from *The New York Times Index* and *Deadline Data,* the others being consulted for an overview.

It may be argued that the cross-reference system of one of the primary data sources, *The New York Times Index,* is such that any reliability tests would have to be conducted over *all* the nations by two or more coders in order to test for the agreement between coders for a subset of nations. That position, however, is valid only as regards foreign conflict behavior measures. That is, when there is conflict between two countries, parts of the conflict behavior are recorded under each country involved as well as in other places. For example, as regards the United States, the bulk of its international activity is recorded under topic headings other than "United States." Although some of these cross-references are given in the *Index,* a large part of them are not. Consequently, only by going through all the nations can one be confident that he is obtaining most of the information on foreign conflict as regards a subset of the countries. For domestic conflict, however, the information is generally contained under the country heading. With these caveats in mind, reliability tests were conducted on the domestic measures. To assure maximum continuity in the codings for the 1955–57 and 1958–60 data, to discover the consistency of the author's codings at different points in time, and to ascertain the extent to which other coders would agree with the author's codings, three partial reliability tests were conducted.

A random sample of five nations from the 1955–57 data reported by Rummel were recoded by the author as regards the nine measures of internal conflict behavior. Agreement ranged from 85 to 100 percent, with purges and major government crises being the variables on which there was least agreement. Since the author did the large portion of the 1958–60 coding, he recoded a random sample of ten nations three months after the initial codings were made. In only two cases were there discrepancies. A third reliability test consists of the author recoding the five nations for

---

[3] See Sidman (1960), p. 73, regarding intragroup and intergroup replication, and pp. 46*ff*., as regards the concept of generality.

1958–60 that were initially coded by two assistants. Perfect agreement was found for these five. Although these partial reliability tests indicate that *some* of the data are reliable, there may be coding errors in the data which might bias the conclusions.

SYSTEMATIC ERROR IN THE DATA SOURCES

Censorship may result in a systematic understatement of the conflict behavior of a given country in the sources. Accordingly, a three point censorship scale for 1958 is derived from the Inter-American Press Survey of 1958 [4] and the Survey of the World's Press by the International Press Institute,[5] and for 1959 [6] and 1960 [7] from Associated Press Surveys of World Press Freedom. Values for each year were then summed across the three years for each nation so that those with high censorship had low scores.

Lack of world interest in a country may also result in an understatement of its conflict behavior. World interest may be operationalized as the number of embassies or legations *in* each country for 1959. The assumption is that this value for each nation reflects world interest in that nation. Although there are obvious exceptions to this assumption, such as the values for East Germany and China, the assumption appears to be valid for most other nations. A second measure of world interest is derived from one of the data sources—*Deadline Data on World Affairs*. It is the number of index cards per country in the card file itself.

These three error measures are included in the correlation and factor analysis. If censorship has no correlation with the conflict behavior measures, then systematic bias as tapped by the censorship measure does not distort the conclusions. Negative correlation of censorship and the conflict behavior measures is not crucial because one can assume the direction of systematic bias to be under- instead of overstatement. Aside from possible exaggeration by the press, one would not expect nations to overstate the number of riots and revolutions it has. So if censorship is negatively correlated with riots, it might be inferred that the correlations between riots and the other conflict behavior measures would undergo little change even if censorship were suppressing knowledge of such incidents. Positive correlations between the censorship and the conflict behavior measures indicate that censorship in a nation could be distorting the results; positive correlation, however, is a necessary but not sufficient condition for such systematic error to distort the results of this study.

A high positive correlation between the world interest measures and

[4] *New York Times*, March 29, 1959.
[5] *New York Times*, April 13, 1959.
[6] *New York Times*, January 3, 1960.
[7] *New York Times*, January 1, 1961.

the conflict behavior measures might mean that lack of world interest in some countries could be causing their conflict behavior to go unreported. Positive correlation, however, is a necessary but not sufficient condition for such systematic error to distort the conclusions. (In the Rummel study [1963] the direction of the correlation between the world interest measure and the conflict behavior measures was inadvertently stated as negative for systematic error to distort the results.)

RESULTS [8]

In order to determine how well the 1958–60 data reflect a longer period, the data were compared and correlated with Rummel's 1955–57 data.[9] Table 1 contains the correlations of the 22 measures of conflict behavior for both 1955–57 and 1958–60. In the upper left hand corner of the matrix the domestic variables are intercorrelated with themselves; the values to the left are the 1958–60 correlations. The fact that all the correlations for each period are positive indicates a remarkable degree of similarity in the direction of the relationships. Out of a total of 36 correlations for each period there are 10 which are greater than or equal to .50. In other words, 28 percent of the domestic correlations for each period are $\geq$ .50.

This stability of the ratio of high correlations to the total for the domestic variables, however, is not found for the foreign variables. (The foreign variables for each period are located in the bottom right hand side of the matrix; the 1955–57 values are to the right of the diagonal while 1958–60 values are to the left). Out of a total of 78 correlations 23, or 29 percent, are $\geq$ .50 for the 1955–57 period, while only nine, or 12 percent, are $\geq$ .50 for the 1958–60 period. The direction of the relationships, however, argues for similarity between the periods. There are only two negatives for 1958–60 and three for 1955–57.

The other portions of the matrix, the correlations of domestic with foreign variables for both periods, are much more similar, although the negative range is greater in the earlier period. (The domestic–foreign

---

[8] Biomedial (BIMD) Computer Program 24 was used to test for outliers, and a visual test of linearity from the cross tabulation of each variable with every other. Outliers greater than three standard scores from the mean were "brought in" through transformation. No curvilinearity was found which might distort the conclusions.

[9] In addition, Richardson's data (1960) for thirty nations on war from 1825–1945 were correlated with 1958–60 data on war, war and military action, and number killed due to all foreign conflict; Harry Eckstein's data (Eckstein, 1962) for 1946–59 on total violence, internal warfare, and a coup are correlated with 1958–60 measures for seventy nations; and Raymond Cattell's correlations (Cattell, 1949) for five measures of conflict behavior were compared with similar correlations from 1958–60. The results indicate that the 1958–60 data are not unique to that period and appear to be moderately general to longer time periods.

Table 1

CORRELATION MATRIX, 1955–57 AND 1958–60 [a]

Measures [b]	1	2	3	4	5	6	7	8	9	10	11	12	13	14	15	16	17	18	19	20	21	22	23	24	25
1. Assass	38	28	45	35	31	45	19	(51)	33	23	28	01	03	16	-09	15	15	19	06	28	20	18	29	08	21
2. Strike	43	28	24	29	46	(56)	(50)	(57)	(51)	20	-01	-01	14	13	07	-04	01	-01	-10	-09	07	04	03	-03	00
3. Gu-War	49	36	24	09	17	13	33	20	(52)	00	00	-23	-08	17	-11	-10	01	-10	-11	05	-09	-04	06	05	-07
4. Gvtcrs	43	42	(55)	09	30	36	38	41	20	21	29	10	28	-01	05	09	26	09	-05	05	13	34	12	05	22
5. Purges	29	04	25	24	30	42	49	36	(57)	24	13	08	32	18	24	26	08	17	24	13	27	19	12	-21	03
6. Riots	(51)	(55)	34	41	25	42	32	(69)	(53)	36	16	19	18	26	08	15	08	12	13	02	21	19	29	05	19
7. Revolu	31	20	(65)	42	(51)	30	19	23	(62)	05	-04	-11	03	12	-11	-04	12	-04	07	-12	04	12	-02	-08	-06
8. Demons	46	(54)	32	44	19	(73)	19	23	45	38	26	29	14	26	28	36	16	20	23	21	35	21	47	-07	30
9. D-Kill	(51)	33	(67)	46	41	47	(69)	39	39	16	-04	00	-03	25	16	05	02	07	14	-06	12	22	18	-22	-01
10. F-Dmst	29	28	27	12	17	38	26	22	31	21	(53)	39	36	14	29	(50)	33	25	39	38	46	35	42	05	18
11. Negsan	23	00	20	14	20	17	10	13	13	21	39	47	33	05	33	(64)	35	24	45	38	48	30	(57)	03	33
12. Protst	04	15	05	-01	07	29	-01	24	04	27	39	02	19	09	47	(66)	39	(51)	15	23	39	31	(60)	-10	29
13. Sevdip	08	19	27	28	05	23	19	21	11	22	20	02	09	-08	12	38	(54)	07	24	15	11	02	04	-15	-08
14. Er-Amb	05	27	08	10	-03	16	-13	18	-08	19	36	(54)	09	-08	10	12	-08	01	43	24	45	32	24	-14	13
15. Er-Les	27	11	10	08	11	17	-01	15	04	16	32	20	13	25	10	(50)	13	33	43	-15	45	32	42	-23	34
16. Threat	10	01	07	-08	06	20	-05	18	07	42	(55)	(59)	05	42	22	07	13	(55)	(68)	(55)	(81)	(63)	(72)	-19	25
17. Milact	05	03	05	06	19	12	06	10	12	17	30	39	08	28	07	47	24	38	45	54	(65)	(72)	19	-09	07
18. War	00	-06	-05	01	03	01	-02	02	07	-06	21	22	22	25	-09	24	42	38	32	37	(56)	(77)	(51)	-10	20
19. Trpmvt	14	01	01	-07	19	40	02	24	14	30	24	49	11	23	22	42	26	22	37	30	(62)	(53)	(74)	-13	33
20. Mobili	00	04	07	00	31	05	04	03	-06	25	30	36	16	38	04	48	43	41	39	44	(46)	41	19	-17	07
21. Accusa	18	-07	17	07	32	19	16	18	12	25	47	(64)	12	40	29	(62)	49	38	39	38	(51)	(70)	(63)	-27	09
22. F-Kill	34	06	30	21	35	24	23	15	27	25	40	30	13	22	05	39	(60)	(52)	46	38	(51)	44	-16	08
23. Cards	03	10	05	-02	12	30	-05	31	09	28	35	(77)	-02	(53)	22	(67)	38	23	(55)	43	33	33		-26	33
24. Censor	-03	19	-09	02	-28	17	-16	13	-13	21	-27	00	14	07	-18	-16	-37	-22	06	-09	-41	-26	00		39
25. D-Emby	01	34	04	06	-08	44	-17	40	-02	22	02	(52)	-02	37	21	21	06	01	34	15	14	-08	28	(57)	

[a] To the right of the principal diagonal of the matrix are the 1955–57 correlations, N = 77; to the left are the 1958–60 coefficients, N = 83. Parenthesis indicates correlations ≥.50. Correlations are rounded off and multiplied by 100. No significance tests are given throughout this study because the entire universe under investigation is being analyzed.

[b] See Appendix I for full names of the variables as well as their definitions.

intercorrelations for 1955–57 are in the upper right hand corner of the matrix, while those for 1958–60 are in the lower left hand corner). An analysis of the percentage of correlations that fall within certain intervals argues for a similarity across both periods. This type of analysis does not tell one *which* variables have similar intercorrelations over both periods. An example of correlations between intra- and international characteristics that are similar across periods is furnished by "riots" and "anti-foreign demonstrations." The 1955–57 correlation is .36, and for 1958–60 it is .38. One of the most similar correlations across both periods, at the international level, is that between accusations and mobilizations, which is .46

Table 2

CORRELATIONS BETWEEN
1955–57 AND 1958- 60 DATA[a]

Measures	Correlations[b]
1. Assass	24
2. Strike	33
3. Gu–War	(65)
4. Gvtcrs	36
5. Purges	05
6. Riots	(69)
7. Revolu	(55)
8. Demons	44
9. D–Kill	(55)
10. F–Dmst	38
11. Negsan	47
12. Protst	(57)
13. Sevdip	08
14. Er–Amb	14
15. Er–Les	38
16. Threat	(66)
17. Milact	43
18. War	41
19. Trpmvt	(58)
20. Mobili	15
21. Accusa	(71)
22. F–Kill	48

[a]Each value for a 1955–57 measure is correlated with the corresponding values for 1958–60; $N = 74$ Parenthesis indicates correlates $\geq$ 50.

[b]Egypt, Syria and Yemen were originally included in the 1955–57 study but were excluded, along with the UAR for 1958–60, in the calculations of these correlations.

for 1955–57 and .44 for 1958–60; one of the least stable is the correlation at the intranational level between purges and general strikes: .46 in 1955–57 and .04 in 1958–60.

The variability in Table 1 in the correlation of purges with general strikes might be partially explained by the very low correlation of 1955–57 purges with 1958–60 purges in Table 2. Out of 22 correlations, eight (36 percent) are ≧.50. The variables which have the most similar intercorrelations generally appear to be those that happen most often, or those in which coding is not much of a problem (e.g., accusations, threats, riots).

• • •

[*The data of Table 1 are then factor analyzed as discussed in Appendix B. The variables are seen to cluster around dimensions as denoted in Tables 11–14.*]

• • •

From the two sets of regressions for the 1955–57 and 1958–60 cross sections, there appears to be only a small relationship between domestic and foreign conflict behavior. This apparent lack of relationship at one point in time may be investigated further by means of time lag regressions.

TIME LAG REGRESSIONS

The 1955–57 foreign predicts 22.3 percent of the variance in the foreign variables for 1958–60 (Table 11). But only half as much variance

Table 11

PREDICTIONS OF 1958–60 FOREIGN CONFLICT BEHAVIOR:
INDEPENDENT VARIABLES—1955–57 NUMBER KILLED
IN FOREIGN CONFLICT BEHAVIOR, EXPULSION OR
RECALL OF AMBASSADORS, AND SEVERANCE
OF DIPLOMATIC RELATIONS[a]

1958–60 Dependent Variable	Standard Deviation	Standard Error	Multiple R	R^2
Protest	.35	.33	.40	.16
War	.68	.52	.66	.43
Severance of diplomatic relations	.16	.15	.28	.08

[a]The independent variables are representative variables from the 1955–57 study (Rummel, 1963, p. 13). $N = 74$.

Table 12

PREDICTIONS OF 1958–60 FOREIGN CONFLICT BEHAVIOR:
INDEPENDENT VARIABLES—1955–57 ANTI-GOVERNMENT
DEMONSTRATIONS, REVOLUTIONS, AND
GUERILLA WARFARE[a]

1958–60 Dependent Variable	Standard Deviation	Standard Error	Multiple R	R^2
Protest	.35	.32	.42	.18
War	.68	.69	.12	.01
Severance of diplomatic relations	.16	.14	.40	.16

[a] These independent variables are representative variables from the 1955–57 study (Rummel, 1963, p. 13). $N = 74$.

(11.7 percent) in the 1958–60 foreign is explained by the 1955–57 domestic (Table 12).

Table 13 contains the results of the prediction of 1958–60 domestic by 1955–57 domestic variables. The domestic conflict behavior of the 1955–57 period explains 27.5 percent of the total variance of the 1958–60 domestic.

The 1955–57 foreign, however, cannot predict the 1958–60 domestic variables. The results in Table 14 show that only 8.5 percent of the variance in the 1958–60 domestic is explained by the 1955–57 foreign variables.

From the time lag regressions one may conclude that there is a *moderate relationship* between domestic conflict behavior at one time and the same behavior at a later point in time. Similarly, there is a *moderate*

Table 13

PREDICTIONS OF 1958–60 DOMESTIC CONFLICT BEHAVIOR:
INDEPENDENT VARIABLES—1955–57 ANTI-GOVERNMENT
DEMONSTRATIONS, REVOLUTIONS, AND GUERRILLA WARFARE[a]

1958–60 Dependent variable	Standard deviation	Standard error	Multiple R	R^2
Anti-government demonstrations	.38	.34	.44	.19
Revolutions	.26	.22	.60	.36

[a] These independent variables are representative variables from the 1955–57 study (Rummel, 1963, p. 12). $N = 74$.

Table 14

PREDICTIONS OF 1958–60 DOMESTIC CONFLICT BEHAVIOR:
INDEPENDENT VARIABLES—1955–57 FOREIGN KILLED, EXPULSION
OR RECALL OF AMBASSADORS, AND SEVERANCE OF DIPLOMATIC
RELATIONS

1958–60 Dependent variable	Standard deviation	Standard error	Multiple R	R^2
Anti-government demonstrations	.38	.38	.16	.03
Revolutions	.26	.25	.37	.14

[a]These independent variables are representative variables from the 1955–57 study (Rummel, 1963, p. 12). $N = 74$.

relationship between foreign conflict behavior at the two points in time. In the absence of the time lag, only seven percent and 4.3 percent of the variance are explained by the 1958–60 foreign and domestic measures respectively. With the introduction of the lag, the explained variance increases to 8.5 and 11.7 percent. Although this is still a very small amount of variance on which to make a generalization, there seems to be some relationship between domestic and foreign conflict behavior with a time lag.[17]

•   •   •

Relations Between Domestic and Foreign Conflict Behavior. The merged factor analysis and the regression of both forms of conflict behavior on one another suggest only a small relationship between the two. A stronger relationship was expected on the basis of the theories of scholars such as Lewis Coser and Georg Simmel:

(1) The unity of a group is frequently lost when it does not have an opponent (Simmel, 1955, p. 97).

(2) Hostilities preclude the group boundaries from disappearing and they are frequently consciously cultivated to guarantee existing conditions (Simmel, 1955, p. 97).

(3) If a group with basic consensus regarding its preservation engages in outside conflict, internal cohesion is likely to be increased (Coser, 1956, pp. 92–93).

(4) Groups may look for enemies to help maintain and/or increase internal cohesion (Coser, 1956, p. 104).

[17] The range of the multiple R is $\geq 0 \leq +1.0$. Thus R cannot be negative. In order to see whether the time lag resulted in any negative relationships between domestic and foreign conflict behavior, reference was made to the zero order correlations. None of the negative correlations was greater than $r = -.08$.

(5) Exaggeration of the danger of an enemy serves to maintain group structure when it is threatened by internal dissension (Coser, 1956, p. 106).

Whereas Simmel and Coser agree as to the tendency for between-group relations to be largely a result of within-group relations, the experimental data of Muzafer Sherif and his colleagues suggest otherwise. Their general thesis is that inter-group attitudes and behavior are determined *primarily* by the nature of relations between groups and *not primarily* by the pattern of relations and attitudes within groups themselves (Sherif *et al.*, 1961, p. 38; italics in original). They conclude, however, that when friendliness already characterizes between-group relations, harmonious in-group relations probably contribute to solutions of mutual problems between groups (Sherif *et al.*, 1961, p. 200).

The theories and findings of Coser, Simmel and Sherif are based upon small groups. Thus, expectations at the national and international levels on the basis of their propositions should be qualified. The finding in this study of a small relationship between domestic and foreign conflict behavior, especially with a time lag, can be viewed more clearly in the perspective of other empirical studies at the national and international levels.

Another theorist, Samuel Huntington, contends that a decrease in the frequency of interstate conflict is likely to increase the frequency of domestic violence.[18] He thus admits that some relationship exists between the internal and external conflict behavior of nations, but he asserts that it does not follow that external peace stimulates internal conflict or that there is any *necessary* relationship between the two. Furthermore, he admits that in this century the data appear to suggest a general relation between the inhibition of external war and the prevalence of internal war (Huntington, 1962, pp. 40–41). This agrees with Rummel's cross-sectional finding of a small inverse relationship between subversion and foreign conflict behavior (Rummel, 1964, p. 47); but little evidence is provided for Huntington's hypothesis in the present study.

Rummel also found a consistently positive relationship between domestic conflict behavior other than subversion and the *diplomatic* and *belligerency* dimensions. In the cross sectional correlations of Table 1 the highest correlations between domestic and foreign variables are between riots and troop movements (.40), and riots and anti-foreign demonstrations (.38). Since anti-foreign demonstrations help to define the *belligerency* dimension, and the riots variable does not appear on the *internal war*

---

[18] Although Huntington's hypotheses deal with the relationship between internal and external conflict behavior, he appears to have the international system as the unit of focus rather than the individual nations. In order for the propositions from the 1955–57 and 1958–60 studies to be comparable to Huntington's, one would have to sum each variable across all the nations and then examine the relationship between domestic and foreign conflict behavior at the *system* level. The design of this study, however, uses the *nation* as the unit, and examines the internal and external relationship across each nation.

dimension, this study provides evidence in favor of a small positive relationship between domestic conflict behavior other than *subversion* and one of the variables which helps to define the *belligerency* dimension.

Another facet of the relationship between the *diplomatic* dimension and domestic conflict behavior is suggested by Joseph McKenna (1962). McKenna suggests some internal effects of diplomatic behavior. He contends that diplomatic protests may function to assure domestic interests that the government is active on their problems and to provide propaganda for home consumption so that the general public may become aroused in support of the official policy toward the state to whom the protest is directed. More generally, he contends that the purpose of foreign policy is to influence external events so that domestic values are maintained and furthered (McKenna, 1962, p. 20; p. 26). Three of his findings bear directly on the theme of this study. He finds that the nations to whom United States protests were directed most frequently were characterized by revolution and other forms of domestic turmoil. Secondly, protest to major powers was less likely than to minor powers because the internal stability of the former probably minimized the number of offensive incidents directed at United States citizens. Thirdly, resistance to American demands was motivated by the domestic politics of the recipient (McKenna, 1962, p. 20; pp. 38–40; p. 201). The first two propositions suggest a positive relationship between domestic and foreign conflict behavior. Thus, he suggests a positive relationship between protests, on the *diplomatic* dimension, and revolution and/or turmoil. But, in the present study, the highest correlation between protests and a domestic variable is that with riots (.29), and in the oblique biquartimin matrix of the merged factor analysis, riots and revolutions appear on factors different from protests (cf. Tables 1 and 6). [Table 6 not reprinted.—Ed.]

The studies of Sorokin (1937) and Richardson (1960) may also be relevant to interpreting the findings in the present study. Sorokin visually examines data through seventeen centuries, 525 A.D. to 1925, and finds a small association between unsuccessful external wars and internal disturbances. As with the present study, he concludes that the presence or absence of general war and internal disturbances are fairly independent of one another (Sorokin, 1937, p. 487; p. 492).

From 1820 to 1945, Richardson finds 112 mainly internal as compared with 137 mainly external fatal quarrels (Richardson, 1960, p. 186).[19] Even though he is primarily interested in the relationship between deadly quarrels and such variables as the rate of armaments increase, trade, language differences, contiguity, and other nonconflict variables, he does allude to

[19] A fatal quarrel is a war in which a nation was involved which resulted in more than 3,163 death, e.g., more than $\log_{10}$ (deaths) $= 3.5$. Richardson contends that there is ambiguity as regards the classification of some forms of fatal quarrels; consequently, he categorizes them in three groups: mainly internal, mixed, and mainly external (1960, ch. 2; pp. 186–87).

the possible relationship between intranation solidarity and external threats (Richardson, 1960, p. 156). But a proposition about such a relationship does not emerge from his data, nor does he subject one to systematic test.

Implications of Findings for Theory Construction. The principal finding of a small relationship between domestic and foreign conflict behavior may have implications for theory-building. There may be no "simple" relationship between domestic and foreign conflict behavior, but there may be a causal relationship which is being obscured by other phenomena. That is, the relationship may be mediated by a third variable such as the personality characteristics of the national decision-makers as is suggested by Haas and Whiting (1956, pp. 61–62).

Evidence against the "third variable" interpretation for *aggregate* data, however, is provided by the Dimensionality of Nations Project of which the present work is a substudy. The 22 domestic and foreign conflict behavior measures were included in a factor analysis of 236 national and international characteristics across 82 nations. A domestic and a foreign conflict behavior dimension came out *separate* from one another as well as from economic development, political orientation, and Catholic culture dimensions. The fact that domestic and foreign conflict behavior dimensions remain separate within the larger context adds evidence that they are unrelated to other aggregate data at one point in time. Thus, having *controlled* for such things as the level of development, political orientation, and Catholic culture, the domestic and foreign conflict behavior dimensions remain separated. (Cf. Rummel, Guetzkow, Sawyer, and Tanter, *Dimensions of Nations*, forthcoming, 1966).

The "third variable" interpretation, however, may be valid for individual level characteristics as distinct from aggregate data. It may prove theoretically useful to inquire into the nature of the decision-maker's characteristics in order to see whether the relationship between domestic and foreign conflict behavior would increase. For example, the decision-making scheme presented by Richard Snyder and Glenn Paige (1958) might be relevant for suggesting third variables that mediate between the domestic and foreign conflict behavior relationship.

•   •   •

Appendix I

DEFINITIONS OF CONFLICT BEHAVIOR MEASURES

The criteria by which the conflict behavior measures were chosen and brief definitions of the measures themselves are the same as those used in the 1955–57 study.

Measures of Conflict Behavior. With respect to the methods and goals of this study, any act or occurrence chosen to index conflict behavior must: (1) be capable of empirical delimitation; (2) be an act or occurrence of sufficient interest to be generally reported—that is, data must be available; (3) be applicable to all countries (e.g., "colonial violence," if made a measure, would not be applicable to those countries without colonies) if spurious factors are not to result; (4) be as diverse as possible to cover the greatest possible range of conflict behavior; and (5) be an act of or within, or an occurrence with respect to, seven or more countries (this is to prevent the correlations from being dependent on too few such happenings and, therefore, to reduce the role of aberrations on what are meant to be general conclusions).

On the basis of these criteria, nine measures of domestic and thirteen measures of foreign conflict were chosen for this study. The domestic conflict measures and a brief definition of the conflict act or occurrence are as follows:

1. *Number of assassinations*: any politically motivated murder or attempted murder of a high government official or politician.

2. *Number of general strikes*: any strike of 1,000 or more industrial or service workers that involves more than one employer and that is aimed at national government policies or authority.

3. *Presence or absence of guerrilla warfare*: any armed activity, sabotage, or bombings carried on by independent bands of citizens or irregular forces and aimed at the overthrow of the present regime.

4. *Number of major government crises*: any rapidly developing situation that threatens to bring the downfall of the present regime—excluding situations of revolt aimed at such an overthrow.

5. *Number of purges*: any systematic elimination by jailing or execution of political opposition within the ranks of the regime or the opposition.

6. *Number of riots*: any violent demonstration or clash of more than 100 citizens involving the use of physical force.

7. *Number of revolutions*: any illegal or forced change in the top government elite, any attempt at such a change, or any successful or unsuccessful armed rebellion whose aim is independence from the central government.

8. *Number of anti-government demonstrations*: any peaceful public gathering of at least 100 people for the primary purpose of displaying or voicing their opposition to government policies or authority, excluding those demonstrations of a distinctly anti-foreign nature.

9. *Number of people killed in all forms of domestic violence*: any deaths resulting directly from violence of an intergroup nature, thus excluding deaths by murder and execution.

The measures of foreign conflict definitions are as follows:

1. *Number of anti-foreign demonstrations:* any demonstration or riot by more than 100 people directed at a particular foreign country (or group of countries) or its policies.

2. *Number of negative sanctions:* any nonviolent act against another country—such as boycott, withdrawal of aid—the purpose of which is to punish or threaten that country.

3. *Number of protests:* any official diplomatic communication or governmental statement, the purpose of which is to complain about or object to the policies of another country.

4. *Number of countries with which diplomatic relations severed:* the complete withdrawal from all official contact with a particular country.

5. *Number of ambassadors expelled or recalled:* any expelling of an ambassador from, or recalling for other than administrative reasons an ambassador to, a particular country—this does not involve expulsion or recall resulting from the severance of diplomatic relations.

6. *Number of diplomatic officials of less than ambassador's rank expelled or recalled:* replace "ambassador" by "officials of lesser . . . rank" in above definition.

7. *Number of threats:* any official diplomatic communication or governmental statement asserting that if a particular country does or does not do a particular thing it will incur negative sanctions.

8. *Presence or absence of military action:* any military clash of a particular country with another and involving gunfire, but short of war as defined below.

9. *Number of wars:* any military clash for a particular country with another and in which more than .02 percent of its population are militarily involved in the clash.

10. *Number of troop movements:* any rapid movement of large bodies of troops, naval units, or air squadrons to a particular area for the purpose of deterring the military action of another country, gaining concessions, or as a show of strength.

11. *Number of mobilizations:* any rapid increase in military strength through the calling up of reserves, activation of additional military units, or the de-mothballing of military equipment.

12. *Number of accusations:* any official diplomatic or governmental statement involving charges and allegations of a derogatory nature against another country.

13. *Number of people killed in all forms of foreign conflict behavior:* the total number of deaths resulting directly from any violent interchange between countries.

See Appendix I in the 1955–57 study (Rummel, 1963) for more extensive definitions.

Appendix II

LIST OF NATIONS

Afghanistan	Germany (Fed. Rep.)	Panama
Albania	Greece	Paraguay
Argentina	Guatemala	Peru
Australia	Haiti	Philippines
Austria	Honduras	Poland
Belgium	Hungary	Portugal
Bolivia	India	Rumania
Brazil	Indonesia	Saudi Arabia
Bulgaria	Iran	Spain
Burma	Iraq	Sweden
Cambodia	Irish Republic	Switzerland
Canada	Israel	Thailand
Ceylon	Italy	Turkey
Chile	Japan	Union of South Africa
China	Jordan	USSR
Republic of China	Korea (Dem. Rep.)	UK
Colombia	Korea (Rep. of)	USA
Costa Rica	Lebanon	Uruguay
Cuba	Liberia	Venezuela
Czechoslovakia	Libya	Yugoslavia
Denmark	Mexico	Laos
Dominican Republic	Nepal	N. Vietnam
Ecuador	Netherlands	S. Vietnam
El Salvador	New Zealand	Morocco
Ethiopia	Nicaragua	Sudan
Finland	Norway	Tunisia
France	Outer Mongolia	UAR
Germany (DDR)	Pakistan	

REFERENCES

CATTELL, R. "The Dimensions of Culture Patterns of Factorization of National Characters," *Journal of Abnormal and Social Psychology*, 44 (1949), 443–69.
COSER, LEWIS A. *The Functions of Social Conflict*. Glencoe, Ill.: Free Press, 1956.

ECKSTEIN, H. "The Incidence of Internal Wars, 1946–59." Appendix I of *Internal War: The Problem of Anticipation*, report submitted to Research Group in Psychology and the Social Sciences, Smithsonian Institution, January 15, 1962.

EDWARDS, A. L. "Experiments: Their Planning and Execution." In G. LINDZEY (ed.), *Handbook of Social Psychology*. Cambridge, Mass.: Addison Wesley, 1954, 259–88.

HAAS, E. R., AND A. S. WHITING. *Dynamics of International Relations*. New York: McGraw-Hill, 1956.

HUNTINGTON, S. P. "Patterns of Violence in World Politics." In S. P. HUNTINGTON (ed.), *Changing Patterns of Military Politics*. New York: Free Press, 1962, 17–50.

KATZ, D. "Field Studies." In H. FESTINGER and D. KATZ (eds.), *Research Methods in the Behavioral Sciences*. New York: Dryden Press, 1953, 56–97.

McKENNA, JOSEPH C. *Diplomatic Protest in Foreign Policy*. Chicago: Loyola University Press, 1962.

RICHARDSON, LEWIS F. *Statistics of Deadly Quarrels*. Pittsburgh, Pa.: Boxwood Press, 1960.

ROSECRANCE, RICHARD N. *Action and Reaction in World Politics*. Boston: Little, Brown, 1963.

RUMMEL, R. J. "The Dimensions of Conflict Behavior Within and Between Nations," *General Systems Yearbook*, 8 (1963), 1–50.

————. "Testing Some Possible Predictors of Conflict Behavior Within and Between Nations," Proceedings of the Peace Research Conference, Nov. 18–19, 1963. [1964]

————, HAROLD GUETZKOW, JACK SAWYER, AND RAYMOND TANTER. *Dimensions of Nations*. Forthcoming, 1966.

SHERIF, M., et al. *Intergroup Conflict and Cooperation: The Robbers Cave Experiment*. Norman: University of Oklahoma Institute of Group Relations, 1961.

SIDMAN, M. *Tactics of Scientific Research*. New York: Basic Books, 1960.

SIMMEL, GEORG. *Conflict and the Web of Intergroup Affiliations*. Glencoe, Ill.: Free Press, 1955.

SNYDER, R., and G. PAICE. "The United States Decision to Resist Aggression in Korea: The Application of an Analytical Scheme," *Administrative Science Quarterly*, 3 (1958), 341–78.

SOROKIN, P. *Social and Cultural Dynamics*, Vol. III. New York: American Book, 1937.

WRIGHT, QUINCY. *A Study of War*. Chicago: University of Chicago Press, 1942.

A MODEL OF U.S. FOREIGN AID ALLOCATION:
AN APPLICATION OF A RATIONAL
DECISION-MAKING SCHEME

Masakatsu Kato

The following is a preliminary analysis of American foreign aid allocation by means of a multiple regression model. In the background of this
particular quantitative approach lies the belief of the author that it is
beneficial to approach the topics of international relations with some systematic conceptual scheme. One such analytical scheme is the rational
decision concept. It conceptualizes and relates behavior of various kinds
in terms of goal-orientation by postulating the goals and the available
means of the decision-maker. It seems that this decision framework provides us with a powerful means to conceive and interpret behavior in a
rigorous and coherent way.

In the initial part of this paper, I shall present a set of assumptions
about the decision-maker and his tasks. Then, some logical predictions
about allocation behavior are developed from the assumptions. Finally
these predictions are tested by inference from the data analysis.

I. INTRODUCTION

The major theme of American foreign policy during the two postwar
decades can be summed up as containment of the Soviet bloc. This goal
is a corollary of further goals: in a world where two blocs of nations are
competing with each other in a zero-sum game fashion, the deterrence
of communist expansion has been the immediate task in order to encourage diversity and national independence in the world.[1] Thus U.S. military
strategy has been designed to offer a protective shield from communist
military and subversive threats throughout the world.

The foreign aid program has been regarded as an integral part of this

This article is published here for the first time.
[1] Kenneth Waltz, *Foreign Policy and Democratic Politics* (Boston: Little, Brown, 1967),
p. 191.

global strategy. Its specific rule has been to provide the opportunity for military, economic, and political viability of countries vulnerable to communist manipulation. Although the priorities of immediate aid goals differ according to the nature of the problems in a particular country, the generalization is valid: the foreign aid program is designed to lessen the probability of a communist takeover in a nation.[2]

Bilateral U.S. aid may be divided into two groups, military and economic aid. Military aid provides military hardware and advisers together with supporting assistance to lessen the economic burden on the recipient countries for their military undertaking. Economic aid consists of loans and grants, technical assistance, and the delivery of agricultural surplus commodities in order to promote economic and social welfare.

II. THE CONCEPTUAL SCHEME

The allocation of foreign aid occurs each year. The specific amount of allocation is an index of U.S. commitment to a country for the fiscal year. By allocating aid, the decision-makers expect some kind of return which contributes to the increment of their values. To the extent that the annual fund for aid is limited and that there are many nations in need of aid, allocation of aid is analogous to the allocation of scarce resources among several alternatives. In order to apply this decision task approach, the following assumptions are made concerning the aid allocation.

First, it is assumed that there is one identifiable decision-making unit which is responsible for the entire process of allocating foreign aid. This simply means that this decision-making unit is assumed to think and act as if it were an individual decision-maker. This is indeed an oversimplification of reality, but it may be improved by attributing some known behavioral characteristics of actual process to the hypothetical decision unit.

The second assumption is that the decision unit has a set of goals which are hierarchically ordered in terms of preference: [3]

   (1) military containment of communist aggression and subversion (strategic goal),
   (2) political and economic isolation of communist bloc (cold war goal),
   (3) promotion of trade and commercial interests of the U.S. (trade goal),

---

[2] Charles Wolf, Jr., *United States Policy and the Third World* (Boston: Little, Brown, 1967), pp. 21–22.
[3] I am not very sure about the validity of the following particular ordering of these goals (values), and it is largely based on my *a priori*, intuitive feelings about the nature of "national interest." Wolf has an interesting discussion of U.S. values in foreign policy, *op. cit.*, ch. 1.

(4) promotion of economic development of underdeveloped nations (economic development goal), and

(5) economy in programming and administering the aid program (domestic economy goal).

It is further assumed that among these goal preference orderings, the transitivity relationship holds, other things being equal. This is a very strong assumption but for heuristic purposes, it is included.

Thirdly, it is assumed that the decision-making unit is a maximizer in the sense that it attempts to maximize the expected increment of the value payoffs. This means that in allocating foreign aid to countries, the decision unit is willing to allocate more, other things being equal, to the countries whose use of aid adds a greater increment of values to the decision-maker. In this analysis, for example, this assumption leads us to expect that those values which are more salient to the purpose of aid tend to have greater impact on the amount of aid actually allocated.

The fourth assumption is that the information of the state of the world (both domestic and foreign) available to the decision-maker is limited to that of the previous year at the time of the current allocation process. This means that only the previous year's events affect the information relevant to the allocation process of aid. This assumption is adequate to cover the crucial phase of budgetary process in the Bureau of Budget and the Congress. But according to Wildavsky, the whole budgetary process takes some 18 months, so that theoretically an assumption of two years of information lag (events occurring during two previous years influence the decision-making of the aid program) seems to be more desirable.[4] So an alternative model is also assumed, and its workability will be tested later. Two alternative models of decision environment are

Type I: events in year $(t - 1)$ → allocation in year (t) for
year $(t + 1)$

Type II: events in years $(t - 2, t - 1)$ → allocation in year (t) for
year $(t + 1)$

On the basis of these assumptions, the following hypotheses are advanced with respect to three categories of aid allocation: general aid, military aid, and economic aid. Admittedly the derivation of these hunches is not rigorous in logic, but I believe the following set of predictions is fairly reasonable and does possess some logical connection with the assumptions presented above. (This problem is further explored elsewhere.)

Hypothesis (1). In general aid allocation, where military and economic aid are combined, the order of saliency of goals (values) is the same

[4] Aaron Wildavsky, The Politics of the Budgetary Process (Boston: Little, Brown, 1958), pp. 194–199.

as assumed above, i.e., strategic goal, cold war goal, trade goal, economic development goal, and domestic economy goal.

Hypothesis (2). In military aid allocation, the strategic goal is most important and the cold war goal is next most important. The rest are secondary in importance.

Hypothesis (3). In economic aid allocation, the strategic goal is not as important as in military allocation. Instead, the trade and cold war goals are most salient. Both the economic development and the domestic economy goals are more salient than in military allocation.

Hypothesis (4). Since the geographical location of a recipient country is relevant to the objectives of U.S. foreign policy, it is expected that there will be two patterns of allocations depending on whether the country lies on the communist bloc border. Those countries that border on the communist bloc are called strategic countries and those that don't are called nonstrategic.

Hypothesis (4–a). In military allocation to strategic areas, the strategic goal and loyalty in the cold war are the most important.

Hypothesis (4–b). In economic allocation to strategic areas, the strategic goal, the trade goal, and cold war competition are most salient.

Hypothesis (4–c). In military aid to nonstrategic countries, the strategic and trade goals are most salient.

Hypothesis (4–d). In economic aid to nonstrategic areas, the trade and economic development goals are most important.

Hypothesis (4–e). The domestic economy goal is, relatively speaking, most salient in nonstrategic economic aid allocation, then in strategic economic aid and nonstrategic military aid, and is least salient in strategic military aid allocation.

III. METHOD

The five goals in the assumption may be operationalized into specific empirical indicators. This specification of empirical indicators of these goals enables us to make the above set of predictions more specific and allows quantification of these indicators.[5] The following indicators are chosen for the five goals (the numbers associated with variables are later used to identify B weights in the regression equations):

Strategic goal: (7) the presence or absence of communist (-backed) subversion or aggression, (10) proximity to communist border, and (6) military alliance with the U.S.

Cold war goal: (8) amount of trade with the Soviet Union, (12) the political support given to U.S. foreign policy stands in the U.N., and (9) the presence or absence of communist bloc aid to the country.

Trade goal: (11) a country's contribution to U.S. trade.

Economic development goal: (5) the level of G.N.P. per capita (assumed to express the need for development aid).

[5] For the specific processes used in deriving these indices, consult Appendix I.

Domestic economy goal: (13) the level of deficit in balance of payment of the U.S., and (4) the proportion of aid program in G.N.P. of the U.S.[6]

In addition, we measure the previous year's allocation: (1) of general aid, (2) of military aid, and (3) of economic aid.

The aid figures considered here are the final congressional appropriations. The appropriation figures are used partly because they are generated yearly rather than bi- or tri-yearly as authorization figures are, thus being easier to handle in the model, and partly because they show more concrete commitment of the entire aid-decision process than authorization figures do. The period covered is from fiscal year 1961 to fiscal year 1964. The number of aid-recipient countries included is sixty underdeveloped nations.[7] So each sample consists of the amount of aid allocated for a fiscal year and for a preceding fiscal year and the events related to the indices.

As mentioned above, the method of investigation used here is multiple-regression analysis.[8] It is important to note here that, when we use multiple-regression analysis, we are assuming (1) the variables in the explanatory set are mutually independent of each other, (2) distribution of each variable is normal, and (3) the relationship between the dependent and independent variables is linear. The validity of these assumptions may or may not be tenable depending on the actual distribution of each sample variable and on the workability of the particular regression model.

The regression coefficients may be standardized so that some kind of comparison may be made among the estimators.[9] These standardized regression coefficient estimators, called B weights, are used here for the purpose of comparison. Then we can tell, by examining the value of B weights, the extent to which the aid allocation is influenced by the changes in the events related to the goals of the decision-maker. The stronger the relation between an independent variable and the dependent variable, the greater the value of B of the independent variable. The statistical significance of B's will be tested in order to know the level of reliability on which we are making inferences. Also the statistical significance of a regression equation will be tested by the F-ratio test. To have an idea of

[6] Another plausible index would be some kind of self-help measure by the recipient so that the efficiency with which aid is used may be expressed. This is not included in this paper due to the lack of a proper indicator.

[7] These countries are non-European except Spain and Greece. Specific selection criteria include: (a) independent status as of the fiscal year, (b) the availability of a set of reasonable data for the indices, and (c) the existence of U.S. aid in one form or another during the period.

[8] Those who have some knowledge of statistics may be interested to consult, for further details, Alexander M. Mood and Franklin A. Graybill, *Introduction to the Theory of Statistics* (New York: McGraw-Hill, 1963), pp. 331–334.

[9] The B weights of X on Y is expressed as:

$$B_{yx} = b_{yx} \frac{\sigma_x}{\sigma_y} \text{ where } b_{yx} \text{ is the } b \text{ weight and } \sigma\text{'s are estimates of variance.}$$

the efficiency or the fitness of a regression model, we will look into the multiple R^2, which indicates the proportion of changes in the dependent variable accounted for by the changes in the independent variable by making the linearity assumption.

The set of predictions introduced above may now be expressed more precisely in terms of specific B's. The predictive classification of B's shown in Table I by no means rigorous, but hopefully it will serve its purpose. No attempt is made here to further determine the rank ordering within the cells (the numbers associated with B weights are the same as for the variables).

Table II shows only those variables that are predicted to be salient in aid to strategic and nonstrategic countries (see H 4–a, H 4–b, H 4–c, and H 4–d).

Table I

PREDICTION OF SALIENT VARIABLES IN MILITARY AND ECONOMIC
AID ALLOCATION IN TERMS OF B's

	High Saliency	Medium Saliency	Low Saliency
Military aid (H2)	B_6 (alliance) B_7 (threat) B_{10} (geography)	B_9 (communist aid) B_8 (Soviet trade) B_{12} (U.N. voting) B_{11} (U.S. trade)	B_4 (economy) B_5 (economic need) B_{13} (balance of payments)
Economic aid (H3)	B_{10} (geography) B_{11} (trade) B_9 (communist aid)	B_{12} (U.N. voting) B_6 (alliance) B_7 (threat) B_5 (economic need)	B_8 (Soviet trade) B_{13} (balance of payments) B_4 (economy)

Table II

PREDICTION OF MOST SALIENT VARIABLES IN
FOUR CATEGORIES OF AID ALLOCATION

	Military Aid	Economic Aid
Aid to strategic countries	B_6 (alliance) B_{12} (U.N. voting) B_9 (communist aid) B_7 (threat)	B_9 (communist aid) B_{11} (U.S. trade) B_6 (alliance) B_7 (threat)
Aid to nonstrategic countries	B_6 (alliance) B_7 (threat) B_{11} (U.S. trade)	B_{11} (U.S. trade) B_5 (economic need)

IV. RESULTS

Before testing specific predictions, the two alternative models on the information lag, type I and type II (see page 200) are tested to see their fitness. The two models were tested for general aid, military aid and economic aid. When the previous year's allocations are included in the equation as independent variables, the following result is obtained in terms of R^2. In terms of prediction, they both do well, accounting for nearly 50 per cent to 85 per cent of variances in aid allocation. We note in Table III that there is a marked difference in the size of R^2 between the two models in military allocation.

Earlier it was pointed out that institutional decision-making in reality was incremental. This proposition can be tested by examining the share of variance explained by the variable of previous allocation. Table IV shows the R^2 of the previous year's allocation in models I and II. The contrast between economic and military decision-making is striking: over 80 per cent of allocation is determined by the previous year's allocation in economic aid, while a much smaller percentage of aid is determined by previous allocation in military aid. Although we noted above that there is a considerable gap in R^2 for military aid between the two models, now it seems both models agree that around 40 per cent to 50 per cent of the

Table III

COMPARISON OF TYPE I AND TYPE II MODELS WITH
REGARD TO THEIR FITNESS AS EXPRESSED BY R^2.
BOTH EQUATIONS WERE SIGNIFICANT AT 0.05 LEVEL.
N STANDS FOR SAMPLE SIZE.

	General	Military	Economic	N
Model I	78%	49%	77%	230
Model II	67%	85%	71%	111

Table IV

COMPARISON OF TYPE I AND TYPE II MODELS WITH
REGARD TO THE SIZE OF VARIANCE EXPLAINED
BY THE PREVIOUS ALLOCATION

	Total	Military	Economic
Model I	51.3%	0.02%	84%
Model II	34.3%	34.7%	85%

variance is explained by substantive events $(49 - 0.02 = 48.98, 85 - 34.7 = 50.3)$. So there is no serious disagreement between the two models. The reason for the greater value of R^2 of military aid in Model II in the Table seems to be that in administering aid to countries since the early sixties, military aid has been more selectively committed to these countries around the Sino-Soviet border, thus becoming more stable in allocation (Model II includes fewer newly developed nations due to the time length of the model).

There are several reasons for the above-mentioned discrepancy between the two kinds of aid. Economic aid, development loans, and alliance for progress loans in particular are authorized on long term bases, thus making them relatively stable commitments. Also since economic aid is often appropriated for specific projects, its allocation tends to be stable. In contrast, the need of military aid is always estimated by the changing overall defense requirements, and particularly by crisis needs.

In testing the specific predictions, we note that since the primary interest of this paper is the substance of decision-making, it is more relevant to consider the models without the variable of previous allocation. Besides, the removal of that variable gives an important statistical advantage: often it is highly correlated with other variables, thus contributing to the problem of multicolinearity.

A test of hypothesis 1 gives the result shown in Table V. Both models are significant beyond the 0.05 level. In both models B_{10} (geography), B_5 (economic need) B_6 (alliance), B_7 (threat), and B_{11} (U.S. trade) are all significant at the 0.05 level or above, and thus we can be sure of much of the result. The strategic goal variables—B_{10} (geography), B_6 (alliance), and B_7 (threat)—are largest, followed by the trade variable (B_{11}). So thus far our prediction is confirmed. But the variable of economic need (B_5) has the second largest B, contrary to the prediction. The rank order between cold war variables (B_9, B_{12}, B_8) and domestic economy variables (B_4, B_{16}) does not conform to our prediction. The positive and large B_5 (economic need) indicates that other things being equal, aid tends to be allocated to countries of higher standards of living. Thus our first prediction is partially supported, indicating that strategic values are the key considerations in foreign aid.

The testing of hypotheses 2 and 3 would be more meaningful since we are more sure of the logical connection between the purposes of aid and the goals of the decision-makers. The result is shown in Table VI.[10]

The military aid model has eight of its ten B's significant at the 0.05

[10] From this test on, the testing is conducted with model I. Model II has sample sizes too small for further breakdown of data to test these predictions. Besides it suffers from the effects of multicolinearity.

Table V

RANK ORDERING OF B's FOR MODELS I AND II
(STAR MARKS SIGNIFICANT B's)

Rank Order	Model I	Model II
1	B_{10}* geography	B_{10}* geography
2	B_5* economic need	B_5* economic need
3	B_6* alliance	B_6* alliance
4	B_7* threat	B_7* threat
5	B_{11}* trade	B_{11}* trade
6	B_9 communist aid	B_{12} U.N. voting
7	B_{13} balance of payments	B_4 domestic economy
8	B_4 domestic economy	B_9 communist aid
9	B_{12} U.N. voting	B_{13} balance of payments
10	B_8 Soviet trade	B_8 Soviet trade
R^2	.3835	.4419

level and the regression model itself is significant at the 0.05 level. Our prediction of strategic (B_6, B_7, B_{10}) and trade variables (B_{11}) is well supported. The variable of economic need for development (B_5) does not come out as expected, having greater saliency than expected. Again cold war variables (B_8, B_{12}, B_9) do not have much impact on aid. Interestingly, the rank order of B's between the cold war variables and domestic economy variables (B_4, B_{13}) suggests that the latter are more salient.

Table VI

COMPARISON OF MILITARY AND ECONOMIC AID IN
TERMS OF SALIENCY OF B's
(STAR MARKS SIGNIFICANT B's)

	High Saliency	Medium Saliency	Low Saliency	R^2
Military	B_6* (alliance) B_{10}* (geography) B_7* (threat)	B_{11}* (trade) B_5* (economic need) B_9* (communist aid) B_4* (domestic economy)	B_{13}* (balance of payment) B_8 (Soviet trade) B_{12} (U.N. voting)	.4904
Economic	B_{10}* (geography) B_{11}* (trade) B_{13} (balance of payments)	B_5 (economic need) B_9 (communist aid) B_4 (domestic economy) B_{12} (U.N. voting)	B_7 (threat) B_6 (alliance) B_8 (Soviet trade)	.1206

The economic aid model does not do so well as the military aid model, and it has only two significant B's: geography (B_{10}) and U.S. trade (B_{11}). Our expectation as to the relative high saliency of geography, trade, and economic need (B_5) in economic aid is confirmed. The surprise is that domestic economy goal variables (B_4, B_{13}) have greater impact on aid than strategic (B_6, B_7) or cold war (B_{12}, B_8, B_9) variables.

Comparison of these two results shows a sharp contrast in the relative saliency of variables in military and economic aid allocation. First, we note that the saliency of alliance and threat variables shifts from a high to a low level as we move from military aid to economic aid. Secondly, the trade variable is more important in economic aid, i.e., higher rank order of saliency. Thirdly, domestic economy variables have a greater impact on economic aid than on military aid. The opposing direction of the impact of the trade variable (negative in military and positive in economic aid) on these two kinds of aid makes further contrast. This suggests that in military aid the trade goal of the U.S. is not so important (since it sacrifices its interests in trade) while it is highly salient for economic aid. Also we note, lastly, that the sign of the deficit in the balance of payments variable is positive in military and negative in economic aid. This suggests that allocation of economic aid is cut back as the deficit in balance of payments increases, while military aid allocation slightly tends to be increased as the deficit increases (remember that the impact of this variable on aid is greater in economic aid). Thus the contrast between military aid allocation and economic aid allocation is quite clear: military aid is more directly goal-oriented, while economic aid is subject to the restriction imposed from the consideration of trade or state of domestic economy.

Another important finding so far is: (1) that the economic need variable is much more salient than predicted in all three cases we have examined, and (2) that the saliency rank between the cold war and domestic economy variables is the reverse of our prediction. This consistent pattern of findings seems to suggest that perhaps our assumed ordering of goals of the decision-makers must be revised. In this respect it is interesting to note that despite the annual controversy on banning aid to certain countries because of their stand in cold war issues, in actual allocation of aid, that kind of consideration does seem to have less impact on aid than the consideration of need of the country for economic development and considerations about the U.S. economy.

Table VII

COMPARISON OF SALIENT B's IN FOUR CATEGORIES OF AID
(STAR MEANS THE B IS SIGNIFICANT AT 0.05 LEVEL)

	Military	Economic
Strategic	B_9* (communist aid) B_{11}* (trade) B_7* (threat) B_6* (alliance)	B_9 (communist aid) B_6 (alliance) B_{13} (balance of payment) B_5* (economic need)
Non-strategic	B_6* (alliance) B_4* (domestic economy) B_{13}* (balance of payment) B_{11}* (trade)	B_{11}* (trade) B_5 (economic need) B_7 (threat) B_8 (Soviet trade)

The testing of hypothesis 4 with the control variable of geography produced the results shown in Table VII.[11] Prediction 4–a about strategic military aid is rather well supported. Although strategic variables (B_7, B_6) are not the largest in terms of B's, they are most salient. The impact of communist aid (B_9) is negative, suggesting that military aid to the countries bordering the communist bloc is reduced by the intrusion of communist aid. Again, as in general military aid, the trade variable (B_{11}) has a negative influence on this category of aid. Prediction 4–c about non-strategic military aid is not well supported. Only alliance and trade variables are as salient as expected, and domestic economy variables are much more salient than expected.

[11] For the complete regression equation, see Appendix II.

When we compare military aid to strategic and nonstrategic countries, military aid to nonstrategic countries is more constrained by domestic economy factors. It is also striking to note that trade influences military aid to these two categories of nations in opposed directions: it has a negative impact on military aid to strategic countries and a positive impact on nonstrategic aid.[12] The aid competition from the communist bloc (B_9) is strongly negative in the strategic areas while it is positive in nonstrategic areas. Thus this indicates that military aid tends to compete against communist aid in nonstrategic areas while it would be reduced in strategic areas. Though in military aid to both areas the variable of alliance is salient, it seems that strong signs of loyalty and reliability are at stake in strategic areas. A similar pattern emerges with respect to the threat variable (B_7), which is positive in strategic areas and negative in nonstrategic areas.[13] This suggests that the occurrence of military threat in strategic areas is reacted to by pouring in additional military aid while under a similar situation in nonstrategic areas (largely Africa and Latin America) military aid is reduced.

We now turn to testing the results of economic aid. The strategic economic aid model is not significant at the 0.05 level. But we proceed with the interpretation in the hope that it would provide us with some clues about the pattern of decision-making. Hypothesis 4–b on strategic economic aid is partially supported. Cold war (communist aid, B_9) and alliance (B_7) are as predicted, while the domestic economy variable (B_{13}) contradicts the prediction. The major deviations from the expectation include: (1) the relatively high saliency of the domestic economy variable, and (2) the relatively low saliency of the trade variable.

Hypothesis 4–d about nonstrategic economic allocation is fairly well supported. The trade variable (B_{11}) is predominant as expected (the only significant B value in the equation). So is the economic need variable (B_5) with a negative sign, as expected. One of the strategic variables has a large B, but since its sign is negative the result supports the expectation: if communist threat occurs in this region, economic aid is reduced.

In comparing economic aid to strategic and nonstrategic areas, we note that economic aid to the former tend to compete against communist aid more vigorously than in the latter area.[14] Also in contrast are the rank positions and signs of strategic variables (B_6, B_7): both are positive in strategic

---

[12] The interpretation here is as follows: to the extent the U.S. government provides aid without much trade benefits from the recipient country, it is making some kind of sacrifice—trade in exchange for the value of military contribution of the recipient.

[13] It should be noted that B_7 in non-strategic areas is not significant, though the regression model is. Thus I am not sure of the extent to which the following inference can be made with this B.

[14] In fact, B_9 in nonstrategic aid has a slight negative sign. The confidence I have for these inferences, however, is rather low since in both cases, B_9 is not statistically significant.

areas and negative in nonstrategic areas. These two sets of findings tend to support our basic consideration that strategic and cold war factors tend to have greater saliency in allocation of economic aid to strategic areas.

Another contrast is the variable of economic development (B_5). It is positive in strategic areas, indicating that the aid tends to go to nations with a higher standard of living, while the contrary is true in nonstrategic areas. The trade variable (B_{11}) is obviously more salient in nonstrategic economic allocation than in its strategic counterpart. Then we see that with respect to the variables of communist aid (B_9), threat (B_7), alliance (B_6), trade (B_{11}) and economic need (B_5), the differences between strategic and nonstrategic allocation are in the same pattern for both military and economic aid.

Hypothesis 4–e predicts that the domestic economy variable would be least salient in strategic military aid and then in nonstrategic military and in strategic economic aid, and most salient in nonstrategic economic allocation. This indicator suggests the extent to which the considerations of domestic economy influence foreign aid. The findings do not support this particular ordering. The prediction is supported in that it is less significant in strategic military aid than in strategic economic and nonstrategic military aid as predicted, but it deviates from the prediction in that it is least salient in nonstrategic economic aid. So that in the order of saliency of domestic economy, the order is: nonstrategic military aid and strategic economic aid, strategic military aid, and lastly nonstrategic economic aid.

V. CONCLUSION

The major findings through data analysis are summarized in Table VIII. It shows the relative saliency order of variables and of the deviations from the predictions.

In comparing strategic and nonstrategic aid allocation, strategic variables (particularly "alliance") and communist aid variables are most salient. In contrast, the trade variable is more salient in nonstrategic aid allocation. The economic development need variable works in two opposing directions, negative in strategic and positive in nonstrategic areas. The pattern of military and economic aid allocation found in the table is approximated in strategic aid allocation while there is no such pattern in nonstrategic aid allocation. The major deviations from the predictions include: (a) high saliency of domestic economy in nonstrategic military aid allocation and the lack of saliency in nonstrategic economic aid, and (b) the low saliency of trade in strategic economic allocation.

Then none of the hypotheses are perfectly supported by the data, although some of them are better supported than others. Predictions (1), (2), (4–a) and (4–c) are relatively well supported, while predictions (3),

Table VIII

Aid Type	Order of Saliency			Deviations from Prediction
General	strategic > trade >	domestic economy		(a) strong saliency of economic need
				(b) greater saliency of trade over cold war
	economic need	the cold war		(c) low saliency of cold war in general
Military	strategic	> trade >	economic domestic need > economy the cold war	(a) greater saliency of economic need over the cold war
				(b) low saliency of cold war
Economic	strategic (geography)	> trade >	economic need > the cold domestic war economy strategic (alliance, threat)	(a) greater saliency of domestic economy and economic need over the cold war and strategic

(4–b), (4–d) and (4–e) are not supported too well. Implications of this finding are discussed below.

Despite the inconclusive results of testing the predictions, we have noted above that there emerge distinct patterns of variable saliency according to various types of aid allocation. A comparison of saliency variables in, first, military and economic aid with respect to strategic, trade, and domestic economy variables, and, secondly, in strategic and nonstrategic area allocation with respect to strategic, communist aid, economic development need, and trade variables, discloses several striking contrasts as shown above. If the assumptions of this decision model are tenable, our findings may support the interpretation that there are in fact considerable rational elements in foreign aid allocation—attempts are made toward maximizing values relevant to the specific goals of different aid.[15]

On the other hand, there are some consistent deviations from the prediction. Most notable is the saliency ordering among trade, economic development need, and cold war variables. In fact the saliency of cold war factor is so low with the exception of communist aid in strategic aid that the original assumption of the preference order of values must be altered. The logical alteration would place the preference order as follows: (1) strategic goal, (2) trade goal, (3) economic development goal, (4) domestic economy goal, and (5) cold war goal. This new preference ordering would give us, in retrospect, a consistent basis on which optimization of aid allocation can be interpreted. The implication of the new preference ordering of goals of decision-makers is that they are chiefly concerned with strengthening and maintaining the (strategic) containment of communism and with promoting U.S. trade interests, and that they are also concerned with developing backward nations as well as keeping the domestic economy in a healthy status. It also implies that cold war maneuvering, i.e., support of U.S. policies in U.N. voting, trading with the Soviet Union, and, to a degree, receiving aid from the communist bloc, does not seriously affect the objectives for foreign aid. Although this is not a very exhaustive elaboration of goals of decision-makers, a somewhat similar argument is presented by Charles Wolf.[16]

There are some questions and doubts to be raised about several choices of indices of goals. Most seriously questionable is the variable of economic development need (B_5), which is indexed by G.N.P. per capita. It seems this alone is an inadequate indicator of the need of economic development vis-à-vis allocation of aid since it does not account for the country's ability to make an efficient use of aid. The findings here (the importance of this variable in strategic aid allocation) seem to allow another interpretation

[15] There is another set of data which support this belief. When we compare the average sum of aid from two dimensions (types of aid vs. strategic or nonstrategic) the result is as follows. There are systematic differences between strategic and nonstrategic aid amounts. More interesting is the fact that the ratio of nonstrategic and strategic military aid is smaller than the ratio of nonstrategic and strategic economic aid, thus indicating greater relative emphasis on economic aid in nonstrategic areas.

	Total (millions of dollars)	Military	Economic
Nonstrategic	22.24	5.58	16.36
Strategic	121.90	71.75	54.56

[16] Op. cit., pp. 3–20.

of this index: relative economic strength of a recipient nation. This interpretation of the index is quite sensible, obviously economically stronger nations would be more attractive partners in building a minimum winning coalition against the communist bloc.[17] Also it appears necessary to make indicators more concise; indices of cold war and strategic variables would be more precisely separated.

Methodologically speaking, it is obvious that greater logical vigor must be applied in order to clarify relationships between the values or goals, and the means or the types of aid allocation. An introduction of tighter definitions of means–ends reaction would allow more rigorous statistical testing methods. Also it may be pointed out, it may very well be the case that the relation between the aid and the independent variables are not well approximated by the linearity assumption.

Appendix 1

The following are some of the definitions and measurements of concepts used in the regression model. Some variables are not mentioned on the assumption that they are already explicit enough as presented in the text.

The index of Gross National Product Per Capita is expressed in terms of dollars. Because there was no available consistent data on this, the following formula was used to calculate G.N.P.P.C.:

$$\text{G.N.P.P.C.} = \frac{\text{G.N.P.}}{\text{population} \times \text{exchange rate}}$$

Since many of the figures were estimates among underdeveloped nations, this method of obtaining G.N.P.P.C. is not very reliable. This really brings up many sticky problems about measurement. Also there is much controversy as to what exactly G.N.P.P.C. measures. We admit the existence of these delicate problems of measurement, but we proceed here to use it as an indicator of economic needs of a country.

The index of alliance is the presence of a U.S. military base. It seems to be a very credible form of commitment on the part of recipient to let U.S. military forces operate from it. This includes presence or commitment of U.S. combat troops also.

The indicator of communist threat includes the two forms "threat"; outright military invasion of a country, or more indirect subversive operations. As sources of information, the *New York Times* and two yearbooks

[17] See William H. Riker, *The Theory of Political Coalitions* (New Haven: Yale University Press, 1962).

were used (see the bibliography). There must be agreement of at least two of these sources before a guerrilla can be branded communistic.

The Soviet trade index is the percentage of a country's Russian trade in its total international trade, showing the degree of dependency on Russia for trade.

Another indicator of level of association with the communist camp is represented by the presence or absence of communist aid. There was no discrimination made between economic or military aid. The source of information is also the *Times* and the yearbooks.

U.N. voting is the indicator of the measure of political support of a recipient to the U.S. policy. Its index is the number of issues (out of three) on which the country voted *against* the U.S. on cold war issues at the U.N. General Assembly. For each year, three salient cold issues were chosen, roll-call votes on which were used to get the index. These issues included the problems of the U.N. Congo operation, Tibet, Korea, Hungary, Cuba (1961–62), the U.N. peace-keeping force, the position of the secretary general, and disarmament.

Appendix II

1. Total aid. (all coefficients with * are significant at 0.05 level or above). Model I.

$$Y = 0.0181X_4 + 0.2434\overset{*}{X_5} + 0.2371\overset{*}{X_6} + 0.1703\overset{*}{X_7} + 0.0004X_8$$
$$- 0.0605X_9 + 0.3295\overset{*}{X_{10}} - 0.1172X_{11} - 0.0025X_{12} - 0.0298X_{13}$$
$$R^2 = .3835 \qquad F = 13.630 \qquad n = 230$$

Model II.
$$Y = 0.1058X_4 + 0.2911X_5 + 0.2652X_6 + 0.1522X_7 - 0.0326X_8$$
$$- 0.0713X_9 + 0.3242X_{10} - 0.1406X_{11} - 0.1284X_{12} - 0.0466X_{13}$$
$$R^2 = 0.4419 \qquad F = 7.92 \qquad n = 111$$

2. Military aid:
$$Y = -0.1019\overset{*}{X_4} + 0.1893\overset{*}{X_5} + 0.3386\overset{*}{X_6} + 0.2471\overset{*}{X_7} - 0.0199X_8$$
$$- 0.1711\overset{*}{X_9} + 0.2786\overset{*}{X_{10}} - 0.2471X_{11} - 0.0502X_{12} + 0.0999\overset{*}{X_{13}}$$
$$R^2 = 0.4904 \qquad F = 19.07 \qquad n = 230$$

3. Economic aid:
$$Y = 0.0762X_4 + 0.1197X_5 - 0.0189X_6 + 0.0615X_7 - 0.0106X_8$$
$$+ 0.1009X_9 + 0.2157\overset{*}{X_{10}} + 0.1197\overset{*}{X_{11}} + 0.0441X_{12} - 0.1204X_{13}$$
$$R^2 = .1206 \qquad F = 3.00 \qquad n = 230$$

4. Strategic allocation: (a) Military aid

$$Y = -0.1199X_4 + 0.2239X_5^* + 0.3020X_6^* + 0.3097X_7^* + 0.0528X_8$$
$$- 0.3485X_9^* - 0.3341X_{11}^* - 0.0446X_{12} + 0.0917X_{13}$$
$$R^2 = 0.5233 \qquad F = 6.95 \qquad n = 57$$

(b) Economic aid

$$Y = 0.1328X_4 + 0.1718X_5 + 0.2773X_6 + 0.1532X_7 - 0.0042X_8$$
$$+ 0.3039X_9 + 0.1145X_{11} + 0.0682X_{12} - 0.2524X_{13}$$
$$R^2 = 0.1356 \qquad F = 0.99 \qquad n = 57$$

5. Non-strategic allocation: (a) Military aid

$$Y = -0.3119X_4^* + 0.0427X_5 + 0.3896X_6^* + 0.3896X_7 + 0.0173X_8$$
$$+ 0.0505X_9 + 0.2024X_{11}^* - 0.0601X_{12} + 0.2182X_{13}$$
$$R^2 = 0.2553 \qquad F = 5.79 \qquad n = 152$$

(b) Economic aid

$$Y = -0.0004X_4 - 0.1049X_5 - 0.0584X_6 - 0.1206X_7 + 0.0990X_8$$
$$- 0.0031X_9 + 0.3397X_{11}^* - 0.0755X_{12} + 0.0461X_{13}$$
$$R^2 = .1312 \qquad F = 2.55 \qquad n = 152$$

DATA SOURCES

Britannica Book of the Year, Encyclopaedia Britannica, Inc., Chicago. 1960–1964.

Statistical Abstract of the U.S., U.S. Department of Commerce, Bureau of the Census, Vol. 78–81.

Statistical Year Book, The United Nations, New York: 1960–1964.

The International Year Book, New York: Funk & Wagnalls Company, 1960–1964.

The New York Times Index, New York: New York Times Company, Vol. 42–48.

Foreign Assistance Act of 1963, 1964, Hearings, Committee on Foreign Affairs, U.S. House of Representatives, Eighty-eighth Congress, 1st and 2nd Sessions (Washington: U.S. Government Printing Office, 1963, 1964).

Foreign Assistance Act of 1963, 1964, Hearings, Committee on Foreign Relations, U.S. Senate, Eighty-eighth Congress, 1st and 2nd Sessions (Washington: U.S. Government Printing Office, 1963, 1964).

7

Content Analysis

On returning from a trip to Latin America, Senator Robert Kennedy observed that of the dozens of questions he had been asked on his tour by bureaucrats, students, political activists, and ordinary citizens, only two concerned Cuba or Fidel Castro. From this bit of data he concluded that Castroism was of less than overwhelming concern to Latin Americans. Mr. Kennedy's observation was an expression of quantitative content analysis, and one which seems to be quite meaningful.[1] Although a bit more self-conscious about it, political scientists also dabble in content analysis and are making increasing use of it to advance their propositions about the political order.[2]

When properly performed, content analysis has an important advantage over more impressionistic modes of investigation: it is systematic. In non-

[1] Survey evidence seems to corroborate the Senator's observation. Polls conducted throughout Latin America in 1960 and 1961 by the United States Information Agency show, even discounting substantially for respondent reticence, prevailing disinterest and negativism toward Castro. In rural Brazil, 86 percent said they never heard of Castro. USIA Special Memorandum, "The Impact of Castro upon Latin American Public Opinion," February, 1961. For similar evidence from the Dominican Republic, see Hadley Cantril, *The Human Dimension* (Princeton: Princeton University Press, 1967), pp. 13–14.

[2] For standard treatments of the subject, see Bernard Berelson, *Content Analysis in Communications Research* (Glencoe, Ill.: The Free Press, 1952), Ithiel de Sola Pool (ed.), *Trends in Content Analysis* (Urbana, Ill.: University of Illinois Press, 1959); Harold D. Lasswell, Nathan Leites, and associates, *Language of Politics: Studies in Quantitative Semantics* (South Norwalk, Conn.: Stewart, 1949); Robert C. North, Ole R. Holsti, M. George Zaninovich, and Dina A. Zinnes, *Content Analysis: A Handbook with Applications for the Study of International Crisis* (Evanston, Ill.: Northwestern University Press, 1963); Ole R. Holsti, "Content Analysis," in Gardner Lindzey and Elliott Aronson (eds.), *The Handbook of Social Psychology*, 2nd ed. (Reading, Mass.: Addison-Wesley, 1968); and Philip J. Stone, Dexter C. Dunphy, Marshall L. Smith, Daniel M. Ogilvie, and associates, *The General Inquirer: A Computer Approach to Content Analysis* (Cambridge, Mass.: MIT Press, 1966), ch. 1 and 2.

systematic research, a single utterance, editorial, or anecdote may be glibly seized to represent an entire personality, political movement, or historical era. If Bismarck said once that he expected the next war to start with some damn foolishness in the Balkans, the content analyst argues, how many times did he say it would start with some damn foolishness in Scandinavia, or in the Baltic; and how many times did' he refuse to speculate? The answer to this quite proper question can only be ascertained when one tediously examines *all* of Bismarck's sage pronouncements about the next war. To be sure, since Bismark was accompanied constantly neither by a Boswell nor a tape-recorder, all his utterances on the subject are not preserved; nevertheless, one who wishes to comment on Bismarck's prescience must at least make a systematic effort to examine all the records that are available, something a horror of drudgery frequently precludes.

Content analysts however are committed to drudgery. At times they can for certain purposes reduce the burden by appropriate sampling procedures and there have been some zealous efforts to develop computer techniques in an effort to automate the ritual somewhat.[3] So far even this latter process usually requires a tedious preliminary translation of the text into fragmentary sentences which are simple enough for the computer to comprehend. Thus content analysis, when carried out on an extensive scale, remains a costly undertaking, a consideration which must be borne in mind when assessing the value of the results.

In international relations, content analysis has been applied in a number of areas. Propaganda analysts, including today's breed of Kremlinologists and Pekinologists, have for decades ruminated upon the doings of mysterious foreign politicians from their pronouncements and often the ruminations are basically quantitative: intensities are gauged, frequencies are noted, and alterations of emphasis are observed.[4] In addition, newspapers, favored grist for generations of content analysts, have frequently been used to study international political phenomena.[5]

---

[3] See Stone et al., *op. cit.*; Ole R. Holsti, "An Adaptation of the 'General Inquirer' for the Systematic Analysis of Political Documents," *Behavioral Science*, Vol. 9 (October, 1964), pp. 382–88; and B. Douglass Jansen, "A System for Content Analysis by Computer of International Communications for Selected Categories of Action," *American Behavioral Scientist*, Vol. 9 (March, 1966), pp. 28–32.

[4] See especially Alexander George, *Propaganda Analysis: A Study of Inferences Made from Nazi Propaganda in World War II* (Evanston, Ill.; Row, Peterson, 1959); also essays in Lasswell and Leites, *op. cit.*

[5] Among the studies which might be mentioned in this regard are Robert C. Angell, Vera S. Dunham, and J. David Singer, "Social Values and Foreign Policy Attitudes of Soviet and American Elites," *Journal of Conflict Resolution*, Vol. 8 (December, 1964), pp. 329–491; Alan Coddington, "Policies Advocated in Conflict Situations by British Newspapers," *Journal of Peace Research* (1965), pp. 398–404; Johan Galtung and Mari Holmboe Ruge, "The Structure of Foreign News: The Presentation of the Congo, Cuba and Cyprus Crisis in Four Norwegian Newspapers," *Journal of Peace Research* (1965), pp. 64–91; Bo Ohlström, "Information and Propaganda: A Content Analysis of Editorials in Four Swedish Daily Newspapers," *Journal of Peace Research* (1966), pp. 75–88;

Diplomatic documents represent a rich source, and content analytic procedures have been increasingly applied to them with the most notable developments being carried out at Stanford University under the general direction of Professor Robert C. North. Ole Hosti's article, which is reprinted below, is one of numerous publications from Stanford based on the documents from the crisis period of 1914 which led to World War I.[6] Documentation from that crisis is especially voluminous, available, and complete and thus is highly enticing. In one study, Dina Zinnes has attempted to compare the 1914 crisis documents with those generated in the Brody experiment (see Chapter 4) and finds substantial similarities in perception and behavior between the diplomats of Europe and the high school students of Evanston.[7]

The Stanford group has also cast its analytic eye on the available documents from the Cuban missile crisis of 1962,[8] the acrimonious verbiage of the Sino-Soviet debate,[9] and the public pronouncements of John Foster

---

J. Zvi Namenwirth and Thomas L. Brewer, "Elite Editorial Comment on the European and Atlantic Comunities in Four Continents," in Stone et al., *op. cit.*, pp. 401–27; H. S. Foster, "How America Became Belligerent: A Quantitative Study of War News," *American Journal of Sociology*, Vol. 40 (1935), pp. 464–75; E. J. Rosi, "How 50 Periodicals and the *Times* interpreted the Test Ban Controversy," *Journalism Quarterly*, Vol. 41 (1964), pp. 545–56; Quincy Wright and C. J. Nelson, "American Attitudes Toward Japan and China," *Public Opinion Quarterly*, Vol. 3 (1939), pp. 46–62.

[6] Others include Dina A. Zinnes, Robert C. North, and Howard E. Koch, Jr., "Capability, Threat, and the Outbreak of War," in James N. Rosenau (ed.), *International Politics and Foreign Policy* (New York: Free Press, 1961), pp. 469–82; Ole R. Holsti and Robert C. North, "The History of Human Conflict," in Elton B. McNeil (ed.), *The Nature of Human Conflict* (Englewood Cliffs, N.J.: Prentice-Hall, 1965), pp. 155–171 and "Comparative Data from Content Analysis: Perceptions of Hostility and Economic Variables in the 1914 Crisis," in Richard L. Merritt and Stein Rokkan (eds.), *Comparing Nations: The Use of Quantitative Data in Cross-National Research* (New Haven, Conn.: Yale, 1966), pp. 169–90; Dina A. Zinnes, "Hostility in International Decision-Making," *Journal of Conflict Resolution*, Vol. 9 (September, 1962), pp. 236–43 and "The Expression and Perception of Hostility in Prewar Crisis: 1914," in J. David Singer (ed.), *Quantitative International Politics* (New York: Free Press, 1968), pp. 85–119; Ole R. Holsti, Robert C. North, and Richard A. Brody, "Perception and Action in the 1914 Crisis," *ibid.*, pp. 123–58; Robert C. North, "Perception and Action in the 1914 Crisis," *Journal of International Affairs*, Vol. 21 (1967), pp. 103–22; and Robert C. North, Richard A. Brody, and Ole R. Holsti, "Some Empirical Data on the Conflict Spiral," *Peace Research Society (International) Papers*, Vol. 1 (1964), pp. 1–14.

[7] Dina A. Zinnes, "A Comparison of Hostile Behavior of Decision-Makers in Simulate and Historical Data," *World Politics*, Vol. 18 (April, 1966), pp. 474–502. See also Charles F. Hermann and Margaret G. Hermann, "An Attempt To Stimulate the Outbreak of World War I," *American Political Science Review*, Vol. 61 (June, 1967), pp. 400–16.

[8] Ole R. Holsti, Richard A. Brody, and Robert C. North, "Measuring Affect and Action in International Reaction Models: Empirical Materials from the 1962 Cuban Crisis," *Journal of Peace Research*, (1964), pp. 170–90.

[9] Ole R. Holsti, "East–West Conflict and Sino-Soviet Relations," *Journal of Applied Behavioral Science*, Vol. 1 (1965), pp. 115–30 and "External Conflict and Internal Consensus," in Stone et al., *op. cit.*, pp. 343–58; and M. George Zaninovich, "Pattern Analysis Within the International System: The Sino-Soviet Example," *Journal of Conflict Resolution*, Vol. 6 (September, 1962), pp. 253–68.

Dulles.[10] Other content analysts have examined international treaties [11] and documents generated by cold war disarmament negotiations.[12] Content analysis needn't be used entirely by itself, of course. Brody, for example, used the method to quantify the messages generated by his teenage subjects in the experiment reported in chapter 4.

For the purposes of Holsti's study the 5269 documents from 1914 were carefully analyzed and some 4883 "perceptions" were unearthed. These perceptions, divided and counted in various ways, furnish the evidence for testing most of his hypotheses. The crisis period itself is divided into two subperiods—one encompasses the first month and is found to be a time of relatively lower stress, and the second embraces the last week leading up to the outbreak of war and is regarded as a time of relatively higher stress. The Mann–Whitney U-test is then applied in a comparison of these two periods to determine whether the differences found between the periods could have occurred by chance.

It should be said that the problems of dichotimization, lamented in chapter 6, are present here too; the statistical support for several of Holsti's hypotheses would be somewhat less convincing if the documents from July 28—the day Austria declared war—were put in the later period rather than the earlier.[13] It might also be mentioned that Holsti's hypotheses 2 and 3 are somewhat improperly operationalized. He never really measures the *range* of alternatives, but instead counts, for example, the number of times a country sees that it has more than one course of action. The content of the perceived alternatives and therefore the range they take is never really assessed by this measure.

This proclivity in some content analyses to stress how many times a certain class of material appears rather than the precise content of the perception itself has been criticized by propaganda analysts.[14] They argue that whether the material appears at all is often far more important than how many times it, or something like it, is repeated. For example, in ana-

[10] Ole R. Holsti, "The Belief System and National Images: A Case Study," *Journal of Conflict Resolution*, Vol. 6 (September, 1962), pp. 244–52 and "Cognitive Dynamics and Images of the Enemy," *Journal of International Affairs*, Vol. 21 (1967), pp. 16–39.
[11] Jan. R. Triska, "Soviet Treaty Law: A Quantitative Analysis," *Law and Contemporary Problems*, Vol. 29 (Autumn, 1964), pp. 896–909; Peter H. Rohn, "Institutionalism in the Law of Treaties," *Proceedings of the American Society of International Law*, (April, 1965), pp. 93–98.
[12] Lloyd Jensen, "Soviet-American Bargaining Behavior in the Postwar Disarmament Negotiations," *Journal of Conflict Resolution*, Vol. 7 (September, 1963), pp. 522–41 and "Military Capabilities and Bargaining Behavior," *Journal of Conflict Resolution*, Vol. 9 (June, 1965), pp. 155–63.
[13] The data on which calculations in Holsti's article are based are given in fuller form in his "Perceptions of Time, Perceptions of Alternatives, and Patterns of Communication as Factors in Crisis Decision-Making," *Peace Research Society (International) Papers*, Vol. 3 (1965), pp. 79–120.
[14] See especially Alexander George, "Quantitative and Qualitative Approaches to Content Analysis," in Pool, *op. cit.*, pp. 7–32.

lyzing Soviet statements about the Arab–Israeli war of 1967, one is interested in determining whether the Russians did or did not support the Arab charge that the United States furnished air cover for the Israeli attack. Had the Soviets made the charge they doubtless would have repeated it interminably, but a tedious tallying of the instances of redundancy would add little to our knowledge.

If frequency does not *always* measure importance, however, often it does. Much of the relevance of the observation of Senator Kennedy noted at the outset of this chapter is due to his presumably precise count of a kind of statement.

Students of international relations, whether they apply content analytic techniques or the more traditional historical ones to the situation, must deal almost exclusively with communications in written form. Occasionally the participants are available for interviews afterward or have their oral communications transcribed at the time, but even in these cases, they are aware that what they are saying is for the record and may come back to haunt them at a later date. Thus there are the inevitable problems, especially in this increasingly telephonic age, connected with the erratic and selective availability of relevant documents. As noted above, the 1914 crisis period is extraordinarily attractive because events conspired to cause the early and rather thorough publication of great volumes of diplomatic documents from this period. Even in this case, however, there are signs that there has been a tendentious selectivity in the release of the French documents while important Serbian documents are still unavailable. Additionally, even private documents are not always honest reflections of the author's state of mind; as one former State Department official has recently noted, "statesmen today are so terribly conscious that historians will soon be along to pore over their documents and judge their actions that they are tempted to write the documents with this fact in mind." [15]

Furthermore, a great deal of human communication is simply not transmitted in verbal—much less written—form. Actions, whether the raised eyebrow or the atomic explosion, can speak both louder and softer than words.[16] They can also speak differently: the word, "hypocrisy," finds frequent application in the language. When actions are gross enough—mobilization, the withdrawal of ambassadors, or armed attack—they can readily be taken into account by the analyst, and documentary and action data can be used to reinforce each other in a broader theory of conduct, a route chosen by some investigators.[17]

More important, perhaps, it is frequently the case that what is being

[15] Roger Hilsman, *To Move a Nation* (Garden City, N.Y.: Doubleday, 1967), p. xvi.
[16] Tacit communication is extensively analyzed by Thomas Schelling. See his *The Strategy of Conflict* (New York: Oxford University Press, 1963) and *Arms and Insecurity* (New Haven, Conn.: Yale University Press, 1966).
[17] North, Brody, and Holsti, *op. cit.*

communicated is not being *said*—especially in diplomacy where this knack has been raised to high art. Euphemism, tone, analogy, and Aesopian language with its more sophisticated developments are used to cloud the issue.[18] Sometimes the subject that is being talked about is so well understood by the communicators that it need never be directly mentioned: in the records of the Japanese cabinet debates about surrender in August, 1945, the atomic bomb is barely mentioned, yet commentators are reluctant to conclude that its existence had no bearing on the final decision.

Another concern involves the difference between written and unwritten verbal communication. The very fact that a communication is put in writing rather than being transmitted orally is a meaningful step, one fully appreciated by diplomatic analysts. A written communication tends to be more formal, more serious, and less remediable than a verbal one; and its author expects to be held more fully accountable for what he has said.[19] The fact that a series of messages have appeared in print may be far more important than any variations of intensity noticeable among the written communications. Thus analysts of documents generated by the disputants in the Sino-Soviet debate may find that the polemical shrillness varies from time to time, but the major increase of hostility was registered when the dispute broke out in print. Documentary analysis in this case taps only a truncated portion of the hostility scale.

Content analysis in international relations, then, can only give part of the picture. As with the analysis of roll calls in legislatures, the material analyzed reflects only partially and imperfectly the stuff of the political arena. And theory based on the method, therefore, can only be partial.

Unlike the typical experimenter or survey researcher, the content analyst of diplomatic documents deals with data generated under comparatively "natural" circumstances. On the other hand, he is unable to control the context in which the communication analyzed is generated.[20] Nevertheless, the content of the communication is determined in great measure by the circumstances under which it is uttered.

Communications intended for private ears can be expected to differ from those intended for public ones, although some analyses of the 1914 documents reportedly suggest that the difference may not always be great.[21] Private documents may vary among themselves according to their intended receiver, diaries, for example, presumably being more intimate than letters to acquaintances. General MacArthur's privately expressed

---

[18] See George's *Propaganda Analysis.*
[19] Consider for example the import of the query, "Will you put that in writing?"
[20] For a similar comparison, see Robert E. Mitchell, "The Use of Content Analysis for Explanatory Studies," *Public Opinion Quarterly,* Vol. 31 (Summer, 1967), pp. 230–41.
[21] There is also impressionistic evidence that former Secretary of State John Foster Dulles' "public assessments of various characteristics of the Soviet regime were identical with his private beliefs." (Holsti, "The Belief System . . .," *op. cit.,* note 3.)

estimate of the probability of success of the Inchon landing in 1950 varied
—depending on the audience—from near certainty to 5,000 to 1 against
him.[22] There may be important differences even among public documents
depending on the context. It has often been noted that speeches by statesmen to congregations of their own countrymen tend to differ from those
delivered to foreigners, just as the views of American politicians on civil
rights tend to be different when they are voiced in Mississippi rather than
in Michigan. Even when the audience is constant, communications can
differ if the contextual format alters slightly: observers have noted that
formal prepared statements by the precise and purposeful Robert S.
McNamara show considerable discrepancies from his informal, extem-
poraneous statements uttered before the same Senate committees.[23]

The contextual conditions can demand a certain patterning of communications behavior, forcing the speakers into roles.[24] Generals defending
budget requests can be expected to stress the unpreparedness of the present
military force while the traditional Japanese method for conducting committee meetings apparently called for frequent statements of positions
which bore little relation to the resolutions finally taken.[25]

The actual stimulus which serves to generate the response to be analyzed is of major importance. Survey analysts and experimenters characteristically are able to control the stimulus while content analysts in this area
can only compare reactions to stimuli which happen to be similar. The
danger in part is that the stimulus will differ significantly from instance to
instance.

At one point in the political dialogue on American policy in Viet
Nam Secretary of State Rusk frequently looked like a relative hawk within
the administration while Secretary McNamara tended to look like a relative
dove. This difference seems to stem in part from the fact that Rusk's
public pronouncements were stimulated by the questions of the doves on
the Senate Foreign Relations Committee, while McNamara's were stimulated by the queries of the hawks on the House Armed Services Committee: Rusk thus often seemed to be urging a tougher policy while Mc-
Namara seemed to opt for a softer one when in fact the two men might
not differ much under constant stimuli. Even seasoned political speech-
makers like General de Gaulle seem to have been stimulated at times by

[22] See Trumbull Higgins, *Korea and the Fall of MacArthur: A Precis in Limited War*
(New York: Oxford University Press, 1960), pp. 45ff.
[23] Bernard Brodie, *Escalation and the Nuclear Option* (Princeton: Princeton University
Press, 1966), p. 11 *n.*
[24] Sometimes the patterning of communication behavior demanded by the context can
render communication impossible. There seems to be no way the passenger in the rear
seat of an automobile can get a front seat passenger to roll an open window half way up.
The front seat passenger invariably seems to assume that the request is simply a polite
way of asking that the window be closed all the way.
[25] Roberta Wohlstetter, *Pearl Harbor: Warning and Decision* (Stanford: Stanford University Press, 1962), p. 345.

enthusiastic audiences into making pronouncements that, in more sober moments, might be considered inopportune.

It is also possible that the subject will be inspired to disclose his feelings only when the stimulus is appropriate. Suppose, for example, one compares documents generated in a crisis with those generated in a noncrisis situation and finds a great deal of hatred expressed in the crisis. It may be concluded that crisis stimulates hate, but another possible conclusion is that crisis simply stimulates one to express the hatred felt constantly at all times. Either conclusion is interesting, of course, but the implications are substantially different. The stimulation to express one's feelings seems to vary even among noncrisis situations. In one study it is found that Soviet official expressions of affect for the United States were strongly positive during Soviet–American negotiations at Camp David, while during the period in which the test ban treaty was signed the Soviets were not stimulated to express very much affect—either positive or negative—toward the United States.[26]

A basic assumption in both content analysis and survey research is that the subject, under certain circumstances, will say what he thinks. The problem here is partly that some people never say what they think, but also that people, even under the same conditions, differ considerably in the manner in which they divulge what is on their minds. The style of some is articulate and sophisticated, while others prefer to substitute redundancy for eloquence. Some are direct and sincere, while others, especially in the diplomatic corps, speak with forked tongues. The talk of some is filled with florid irrelevancies, while that of others is clipped and to the point. Some, like the Chinese Communists, continually pitch their remarks at a shrill scream while others are characteristically restrained—and because of it more effective when they have something shrill to say. Some let themselves go in their communications, while others, like good Bolsheviks (and Yankees), live under a code which stresses that personal feelings must be controlled.[27] Furthermore, the style of speech for an individual can vary greatly depending on the context.[28]

The problems stressed in this discussion bear most heavily on the dilemma of aggregation. When each of these considerations are controlled —in a comparison of newspapers' editorial reactions to a single event, for example—one is presumably relatively safe. But to gain statistical power, aggregation and its inevitable blurring of distinctions often must be resorted to. Can Kaiser Wilhelm's paranoic concern about the abstract British threat to Germany as expressed in his private marginalia be justly aggregated as a perception of hostility with an Austrian prime minister's

[26] Holsti, "External Conflict . . .," op. cit., p. 351.
[27] See Brodie, op. cit., p. 143.
[28] See Northrup Frye, The Well-Tempered Critic (Bloomington, Ind.: Indiana University Press, 1963).

formal denunciation of Serbian terror? Only a continual process of breaking down and restructuring aggregates can indicate whether more has been gained than lost in the aggregation.

Whatever the problems of dealing with diplomatic documents, Holsti's examination of the extensive 1914 materials is suggestive of what can be accomplished with content analysis. The study contains numerous direct quotes from the documents themselves which helps to put the numbers in verbal context. A determination of how readily his results may be generalized to other crisis situations awaits, as he notes, further research.

Often it is the quantitative, rather than the qualitative, nature of Holsti's findings which is of interest. Few historians would be surprised to learn that the decision-makers of 1914 more frequently saw only one course of action open to them while seeing their opponents to have several courses of action available; it is the extreme numerical imbalance of these perceptions which is striking.

Too often, it seems, the laboriously gained quantitative power of the data is submerged in homogenizing indexes or factor analyses with the results being reported blandly in terms of tendency statements or dichotomous proclamations that statistical significance has or has not been obtained. Historians and propaganda analysts have already pored over the documents using a form of content analysis of their own and usually have a reasonable idea of what is going on. The contribution of quantitative content analysis in this area is likely less to be the emergence of astonishing new interpretations of historical events than the refinement of earlier qualitative speculations by adding a quantitative tone to them. To pin a number on an "obvious" qualitative finding is no small achievement.

THE 1914 CASE *

Ole R. Holsti

This paper will employ techniques of content analysis to examine some features of top-level communications between national policy makers during a momentous period of stress. It is concerned with the effects of stress upon: (1) the manner in which decision-makers perceive time as a factor in their formulation of policy; (2) the contrasting ways in which they view policy alternatives for their own nations, for their allies, and for their adversaries; and (3) the flow of communications among them.

I. HYPOTHESES AND DATA

Specifically, the following hypotheses will be tested with data from the 1914 crisis leading up ot the Great War in Europe:

Hypothesis 1. As stress increases in a crisis situation:
  (a) time will be perceived as an increasingly salient factor in decision-making.
  (b) decision-makers will become increasingly concerned with the immediate rather than the distant future.
Hypothesis 2. In a crisis situation, decision-makers will perceive:
  (a) their own range of alternatives to be more restricted than those of their adversaries.
  (b) their allies' range of alternatives to be more restricted than those of their adversaries.
Hypothesis 3. As stress increases, decision-makers will perceive:
  (a) the range of alternatives open to themselves to become narrower.
  (b) the range of alternatives open to adversaries to expand.

Reprinted by permission from *The American Political Science Review*, Vol. 59 (June, 1965), pp. 365–378.
* An earlier version of this paper was read at the International Peace Research Conference, Chicago, November 16–17, 1964. This study was supported in part by the United States Naval Ordnance Test Station, China Lake, California, under Contract N60530–9666. The author very gratefully acknowledges the research assistance of Mrs. Jean Heflin and Mrs. Elizabeth Hart; the criticisms and suggestions of Richard Brody, Richard Fagen, Todd LaPorte and Lois Swirsky of the Department of Political Science, Stanford University; and the help of Mrs. Arlee Ellis and Mrs. Violet Lofgren in typing the various drafts of this manuscript.

Hypothesis 4. The higher the stress in a crisis situation:

(a) the heavier the overload upon the channels of communication.
(b) the more stereotyped will be the information content of messages.
(c) the greater the tendency to rely upon extraordinary or improvised channels of communication.
(d) the higher the proportion of intracoalition—as compared with inter-coalition—communication.

These hypotheses have been developed in large part from recent decision-making literature and from the voluminous experimental literature of psychology. The advantages of precise measurement, easy replication, and tight control over the experimental variables have permitted psychologists to probe into many aspects of human performance under varying situational conditions. Results obtained primarily from observations of undergraduate students may at first blush be suspect when generalized to foreign policy leaders. The strong support of these hypotheses in the experimental literature, however, at least suggests that they warrant testing in historical crisis situations.[1]

The 1914 crisis provides a particularly suitable case for a test of the hypotheses. The available documentation relating to the outbreak of the Great War surpasses that of any crisis of similar magnitude. Among the nations directly involved, only the Serbian archives have remained relatively inaccessible to the investigator. A generation of careful scholarship produced document collections of unquestioned authenticity, including those of Austria-Hungary, France, Great Britain, Germany and Russia.[2] Finally, the crisis is a classic example of war through escalation. The minor war between Austria-Hungary and Serbia, which crisis-hardened European dip-

[1] This literature is reviewed in my "Perception of Time, Perceptions of Alternatives, and Patterns of Communication as Factors in Crisis Decision-Making," as the earlier version of this paper, noted above, was entitled. See also F. E. Horvath, "Psychological Stress: A Review of Definitions and Experimental Research," in L. von Bertalanffy and Anatol Rapoport, eds., *General Systems Yearbook*, IV (Ann Arbor, Society for General Systems Research, 1959).
[2] Austro-Hungarian Monarchy, Ministerium des k. and k. Hauses und des Äusseren, *Österreich-Ungarns Aussenpolitik von der bosnischen Krise 1908 bis zum Kriegsausbruch 1914; Diplomatische Aktenstücke des Österreich-ungarischen Ministeriums des Aussern*, Ludwig Bittner and Alfred Pribram, Heinrich Srbik and Hans Uebersberger, eds., vol. VIII (Vienna and Leipzig, 1930.)
France, Commission for the Publication of Documents Relative to the War of 1914, *Documents Diplomatiques Francais* (1871–1914), 3d series, vols. X and XI (Paris, 1936).
Great Britain, Foreign Office, *British Documents on the Origins of the War*, 1898–1914, vol. XI, G. P. Gooch and Harold Temperley, eds. (London, 1926).
Max Monteglas and Walther Schücking, eds., *Outbreak of the World War*, *German Documents Collected by Karl Kautsky* (New York, Oxford University Press, 1924).
Russia, Komissiia po izdaiiu dokumentov spokhi imperializma: *Mezhdunarodnye otnosheniia v ipokhu imperializma; dokumenty iz arkhivov tsarkogi i vremennogo pravitel'stv 1878–1915 gg.*, seriia III, toma IV and V (Moskva-Leningrad, 1931 and 1934).
In this paper references to these collections are made by *document number*, rather than page number.

lomats expected to remain localized,[3] engulfed nearly the entire continent within ten days. The existing international system—still commonly referred to as the archetype of a functioning "balance of power" system—was unable to cope with the situation as it had previously in the recurring Balkan crises. While extensive war plans had been drawn up by the various general staffs, there is little evidence that any European decision-maker wanted or expected a general war—at least in 1914.

The data for this paper were derived in whole from documents signed and sent by designated British, French, Russian, German, and Austro-Hungarian decision-makers; that is, those persons filling the roles of: head of state; head of government; foreign minister; under-secretary of foreign affairs; minister of war; chief of the general staff. The data in the present paper are derived from the *complete verbatim text* of published documents meeting the criteria of authorship and date (June 27–August 4). While these documents do not record all messages initiated by the designated leaders—notably lacking are face-to-face or telephone conversations—they do embody a substantial portion of all their communications.

The initial step in the content analysis of these documents was to develop a coding unit—*the perception*—defined in terms of the following elements: the *perceiver*; the perceived, or *agent*; the *action* or *attitude*; and the *target*. For example, the assertion by a Russian decision-maker that "The Austrian, as well as German, hope is the ultimate annihilation of Serbia," was coded as two separate perceptions, in each case the *perceiver* being the author of the document.[4]

Perceiver	Agent	Action or Attitude	Target
Sazonov	Austrian	hope is the ultimate annihilation of	Serbia
Sazonov	German	hope is the ultimate annihilation of	Serbia

The 1914 documents yielded 4883 such perceptions.

The independent variable in each hypothesis—the level of *stress*—can be defined as resulting from a perceived threat to high priority values. Eight of the ten hypotheses postulate changes deriving from *increased*

[3] The reaction of Sir Arthur Nicholson, British Undersecretary of State for Foreign Affairs, was typical: "I have my doubts as to whether Austria will take any action of a serious character and I expect the storm will blow over" (Great Britain, *op. cit.*, #40). At about the same time Winston Churchill, First Lord of the Admiralty, wrote, "I went to bed with a feeling things might blow over . . . we were still a long way, as it seemed, from any danger of war." Winston S. Churchill, *The World Crisis, 1911–1914* (New York, 1928), p. 208. As late as July 28 the Kaiser wrote of the crisis in the Balkans, "A great moral victory for Vienna; but with it every reason for war drops away" (Montgelas and Schücking, *op. cit.*, #271).
[4] For a full description of the coding operations, see Robert C. North *et al.*, *Content Analysis: A Handbook with Applications for the Study of International Crisis* (Evanston, Northwestern University Press, 1963). Some problems of sampling in the use of historical documents are discussed in Holsti, *op. cit.*, pp. 21–22.

stress. The outbreak of war between Serbia and Austria-Hungary will be used as the dividing point between the period of *lower* (June 27–July 28) and *higher* (July 29–August 4) stress. Intuitively one would expect that European decision-makers—except perhaps the Serbs and Austrians, by then already committed—were under greater stress during the latter period. This premise is supported by measures of both attitude and action. The documents yielded 882 *perceptions of hostility* directed against the perceivers' nations, which were scaled by the Q-Sort method. [In this method judges are required to rate the perceptions along the hostility continuum according to certain proportions—much like grading on a curve—such that designated shares of the perceptions are rated high, medium, low, etc.—Ed.] The results indicate significantly higher intensity during the July 29–August 4 period for each alliance ($Z = 10.81$ and 3.88; both are significant at the .0001 level). A scaling of the *actions* taken by members of each alliance also reveals a significantly higher level of *violence* or *potential violence* during the last week prior to the outbreak of general war ($Z = 2.24$ and 5.58, significant at the .025 and .0001 levels respectively).[4a] Thus the two periods meet the requirements necessary to test the hypotheses.

II. PERCEPTIONS OF TIME

To test the first two hypotheses, the entire set of nearly five thousand perceptions derived from the decision-makers' documents was recoded; every statement making reference to time as a factor in decision-making was extracted. The 160 time perceptions were initially classified according to date[5] and stated reason for the relevance of time (Table I).

Time perceptions in these data fall into four major categories which correspond to the development of events within the crisis. During the earliest period—through July 20—some 68.1 per cent of the references to time focus on the prospects of early Austro-Hungarian actions against

[4a] For a more detailed discussion of the data and scaling methods see, *ibid.*, pp. 19–20.
[5] In earlier studies of the 1914 crisis using content analysis data, the data were divided into twelve periods of approximately equal volume of documentation as in Table I; thus time periods early in the crisis are longer than those in the days immediately preceding the outbreak of war. See Ole R. Holsti and Robert C. North, "History as a 'Laboratory' of Conflict," in Elton B. McNeil, ed., *The Nature of Human Conflict* (Englewood Cliffs, 1965); Holsti and North, "Perceptions of Hostility and Economic Variables," in Richard Merritt, ed., *Comparing Nations* (New Haven, Yale University Press, 1965); North *et al.*, "Perception and Action in the Study of International Relations: The 1914 Crisis," in J. David Singer, ed., *The International Yearbook of Political Behavior Research: Empirical Studies in International Relations* (1965, in press); Holsti *et al.*, "Violence and Hostility: The Path to World War," paper read at American Psychiatric Association meeting, Los Angeles, Calif. (May, 1964).
    The statistical tests of hypotheses 1a, 3a, 3b, 4a and 4b are based on these twelve periods.

Table I

FREQUENCY AND TYPE OF PERCEPTIONS OF TIME AS A FACTOR IN
DECISION-MAKING: COMBINED TOTALS FOR AUSTRIA-HUNGARY,
GERMANY, FRANCE, RUSSIA AND GREAT BRITAIN

Period	Total Perceptions	Time Perceptions					Total
		A	B	C	D	E	
June 27–July 2	306	3	0	0	0	0	3
July 3–16	349	11	1	0	1	3	16
July 12–20	211	1	0	0	1	1	3
July 21–25	634	11	17	9	0	1	38
July 26	300	0	3	0	0	0	3
July 27	287	0	7	1	2	2	12
July 28	407	0	1	0	0	0	1
July 29	456	0	5	1	1	0	7
July 30	342	1	1	5	2	0	9
July 31	529	0	0	10	5	2	17
August 1–2	583	0	2	11	8	7	28
August 3–4	479	0	0	2	18	3	23
Total	4883	27	37	39	38	19	160

Code of relevance of time:

    A—Factor in Austro-Hungarian action toward Serbia.
    B—Factor in localizing conflict.
    C—Factor in mobilization.
    D—Factor in political commitments.
    E—Others.

Serbia. Count Alexander Hoyos, for example, wrote on July 7 that "From a military standpoint . . . it would be much more favorable to start the war now than later since the balance of power would weigh against us in the future." [6] Hoyos's fear that "through a policy of delay and weakness, we at a later moment, endanger this unflinching support of the German Empire." [7] was not wholly without foundation. Germany was exerting considerable pressure on its ally not to postpone a showdown until a less clearly defined future. Gottlieb von Jagow, German Foreign

[6] Hoyos's assessment that time was working against the Dual Monarchy was supported by General Conrad, Austro-Hungarian Chief-of-Staff: "In the years 1908–1909 it would have been a game with open cards," he said. "In 1912–1913 the chances were in our favour. Now it is a sheer gamble [ein va-banque spiel]." Quoted in Edmund Taylor, The Fall of the Dynasties (Garden City, 1963), p. 206.
[7] Austria-Hungary, op. cit., #10118.

Minister, wrote on July 15: "We are concerned at present with the pre-eminent political question, perhaps the last opportunity of giving the Greater-Serbia menace its death blow under comparatively favorable circumstances." [8]

Once the content of the Austrian ultimatum became known, the 48-hour deadline given the Serbian government to reply became an immediate subject of concern. The time perceptions from July 21 through 29 focus predominantly (54.0 per cent) on the necessity of delaying the course of events in the Balkans in the hope of averting war, or at least containing it within a local area.

By July 30 it was apparent that war between Austria-Hungary and Serbia could not be prevented. At the same time, it was increasingly evident that such a war was likely to spread. As late as August 1 many European decision-makers asserted that if time permitted a reconvening of the concert powers, general war might be avoided. The British Foreign Minister wrote: "I still believe that if only a little respite in time can be gained before any Great Power begins war it might be possible to secure peace." [9] By this time, however, the pressure of time had taken a different meaning for many of them. A major concern (48.1 per cent of all time perceptions from July 30 to August 2) was that one's nation not be caught militarily unprepared in case of war.

The dilemma was obvious. Time was required to avert a general European war; above all, a moratorium on military operations was necessary. So on August 1 King George V wrote of his efforts "to find some solution which permits in any case the adjournment of active military operations and the granting of time to the powers to discuss among themselves calmly." [10] But increasingly this consideration was overshadowed by the fear that a potential adversary might gain a head start in mobilizing its military power. Although no *official* mobilization orders except those of Austria-Hungary and Serbia were issued until July 29, there were increasing rumors and suspicions of secret preparations—some of them well founded, as it turned out.[11]

In the early hours of the morning of July 30, the Kaiser wrote on the margin of a message from the Czar,

[8] Montgelas and Schücking, *op. cit.*, #48.
[9] Great Britain, *op. cit.*, #411.
[10] France, *op. cit.*, #550.
[11] Winston Churchill mobilized the British Navy contrary to a decision of the Cabinet. "At the Cabinet [meeting of August 1] I demanded the immediate calling out of the Fleet Reserves and the completion of our naval preparations. . . . However, I did not succeed in procuring their assent. . . . I went back to the Admiralty and gave forthwith the order to mobilise. We had no legal authority for calling up the Naval Reserves, as no proclamation had been submitted to his Majesty in view of the Cabinet decision, but we were quite sure that the Fleet men would unquestioningly obey the summons." Churchill, *op. cit.*, pp. 230–231.

. . . the Czar—as is openly admitted by him here—instituted "mil. measures which have *now come into force*" against Austria and us and as a matter of fact five days ago. Thus it is almost *a week ahead* of us. And these measures are for a *defense* against *Austria*, which is *in no way* attacking him!!! I can not agree to any more mediation, since the Czar who requested it has at the same time secretly mobilized behind my back. It is only a maneuver, in order to hold us back and to increase the start they have already got. My work is at an end! [12]

Later the Kaiser added, "In view of the colossal war preparations of Russia now discovered, this is all too late, I fear. Begin! Now!" [13]

The previous day Russia had ordered—and then cancelled—a general mobilization. Later it was decided in St. Petersburg that the mobilization of the four southern military districts would deter an Austro-Hungarian attack on Serbia without alarming Berlin. But technical difficulties caused the Russians to reverse their decision once again on July 30 in favor of general mobilization—German warnings notwithstanding.

In response to what was perceived as a mounting threat against its eastern frontiers, the German Empire proclaimed a "state of threatening danger of war" on July 31 and dispatched a twelve-hour ultimatum to Russia demanding a cessation of military preparations. Berlin then ordered mobilization on August 1. A general mobilization was simultaneously ordered in Paris. Although official British mobilization was delayed until August 2, many had advocated such action considerably earlier. On July 31 Arthur Nicolson had urged immediate military preparations: "It seems to me most essential, whatever our future course may be in regard to intervention, that we should at once give orders for mobilization of the army." [14]

So, ten days after the small scale mobilizations by Serbia and Austria-Hungary on July 25, each of the major European nations had ordered a general mobilization; the armies totalling less than 400,000 men called to fight a limited war had grown to nearly twelve million men. As each mobilization was ordered it was described as a necessary defensive reaction—made more urgent by the pressure of time—to a previous decision within the other alliance, although such an act was commonly regarded in 1914 as tantamount to a declaration of war. Thus, each mobilization acted as a stimulus that elicited an almost reflex-like response.[15]

[12] Montgelas and Schücking, *op. cit.*, #390.
[13] *Ibid.*, #433.
[14] Great Britain, *op. cit.*, #368.
[15] In some cases, the escalation of measures and counter-measures was sustained almost by accident, or by the failure to perceive the effects of one's actions. The mobilization of the Russian Baltic fleet is a good example: "On 25 July, when the Tsar looked over the minutes and resolutions of the Council of Ministers of the 24th, he not only approved them by adding 'agreed,' but, where it was the question of mobilizing the districts of Kiev, Moscow, Odessa and Kazan and the Black Sea fleet, he inserted in his own hand 'and Baltic' without any of his ministers drawing his attention to the fact that the mobilization of the Baltic fleet constituted an act of hostility toward Germany." Luigi

In the final hours of the crisis leaders in both coalitions became increasingly concerned (78.2 per cent of all time perceptions August 3–4) that other nations make their intentions known immediately. Allied states, members of the opposing coalition, and even neutral states were subjected to demands for immediate commitment to one side or the other.

The first hypothesis (1a, above) relating the stress of crisis to perceptions of time states that:

> As stress increases in a crisis situation, time will be perceived as an increasingly salient factor in decision-making.

In order to perform a valid test of the hypothesis, the frequency of time references for each of the twelve periods (Table I) was adjusted as follows:

$$\frac{\text{Time Perceptions} \times 100}{\text{Total Perceptions}}$$

The resulting scores were then divided into two periods, June 27–July 28, and July 29–August 4.

A Mann–Whitney U-Test of the direction and magnitude of differences between the two periods was applied to the data for each coalition.[16] The hypothesis is strongly supported by the data for the Triple Entente (France, Russia and England), whose leaders perceived time as a factor in decision-making significantly more frequently during the culminating stages (July 29–August 4) of the crisis than during the earlier period (June 27–July 28) ($U = 3, p = .009$). The data for the Dual Alliance (Germany, Austria-Hungary) reveal that differences between the early and later periods of the crisis are in the predicted direction, but that the difference is not statistically significant ($U = 11.5, p = .19$).

Albertini, *The Origins of the War of 1914*, 3 vols. (New York, Oxford University Press, 1953), II, p. 558.

Although the Russian Baltic Fleet was no match for the German Navy, the Kaiser apparently felt genuinely threatened. In response to Bethmann-Hollweg's plea that the German Fleet be left in Norway, he wrote, "there is a Russian Fleet! In the Baltic there are now five Russian torpedo boat flotillas engaged in practice cruises, which as a whole or in part can be at the Belts within sixteen hours and close them. Port Arthur should be a lesson! My Fleet has orders to sail for Kiel, and to Kiel it is going to sail!" Montgelas and Schücking, *op. cit.*, #221.

[16] This test is used to determine if there is a systematic difference between scores in two samples or populations. Each item is given a rank order score; in the case of hypothesis 1a, each time period receives a rank score based on the adjusted frequency with which time is perceived as a salient factor in decision-making. The value of U (the statistic in this test) is given by the number of times that a score in one group (July 29–August 4) precedes a score in the other group (June 27–July 28). Thus, the lower the value of U, the more significant is the difference. Sidney Siegel, *Nonparametric Statistics for the Behavioral Sciences* (New York, 1956), pp. 116–127.

According to the second hypothesis (1b) concerning perceptions of time:

> As stress increases in a crisis situation, decision-makers will become increasingly concerned with the immediate rather than the distant future.

Of the total of 160 statements in which time is perceived to be a factor in decision-making, only eight reveal a concern for the more distant future. When the data are divided into the early and later periods of the crisis, all perceptions of the distant future occur during the June 27–July 28 period, and one are found in the last week of the crisis, a distribution which is statistically significant (Fisher exact $p = .002$).

These data confirm again the relevance of the "Thomas Theorem": "If men define situations as real, they are real in their consequences." An analysis of European military technology and doctrines reveals that "objectively" time was of incalculably less importance than in the 1960s. Estimates of the time required for Austria-Hungary to field a full army ranged from three to four weeks. The necessities of harvesting the summer's crops were an important factor in military timetables. Russia's inability to mount a rapid offensive against Germany could be discounted; this assumption in fact was the basis of the Schlieffen plan.

Yet in the situation of high stress the decision-makers *perceived* that time was crucial—and they *acted* on that assumption. In the culminating phases of the crisis, leaders in the various capitals of Europe increasingly perceived potential enemies as able to deliver a sudden punishing blow. As a result, the penalties for delaying immediate military action were perceived to be increasingly high. Or, to use the language of modern deterrence theory, the nations of each coalition perceived those of the other alliance as able and willing to launch a massive, crippling first-strike, and thus hastened their own preparations.[17] Hence the entire European concert system—which was assumed to act as an equilibrating mechanism—became instead a "runaway system."

---

[17] A question of possible interest to deterrence theorists is: Would the "capacity to delay response" have materially altered the outcome in 1914? Although we can only speculate, one point does seem clear. The ability of the weapons system to delay response successfully may be a necessary, but is not a sufficient, factor. None of the states in 1914 had the ability to unleash a rapid destructive blow, crippling the retaliatory capabilities of the adversary. But during the final week prior to the outbreak of general war, decision-makers in the capitals of Europe increasingly attributed this ability and intent to potential enemies. Thus the capacity to delay response is not likely to be effective unless decision-makers: (a) perceive the net rewards of delay to be higher than those of immediate action; and (b) are willing to attribute the same preferences to the adversary's decision-makers.

III. PERCEPTIONS OF ALTERNATIVES

The entire original set of 4883 perceptions was recoded to test the hypotheses relating to perceived alternatives. This process yielded 508 statements classified as perceptions of "choice," "necessity," or "closed alternatives." [18]

The "choice" category includes all statements in which more than one course of action is perceived.

The "necessity" category includes all statements indicating that the author sees only one possible course of action.

The "closed" classification includes all statements indicating that some course of action is not possible.

The initial hypothesis (2a) to be tested with these data is that:

> In a crisis situation, decision-makers will tend to perceive their own range of alternatives to be more restricted than those of their adversaries; that is, they will perceive their own decision-making to be characterized by *necessity* and *closed* options, whereas those of the adversary are characterized by *open* choices.

Table II reveals that British, French, Russian and German decision-makers perceived significantly fewer options open to themselves than to their adversaries.[19] In one respect the data for Austria-Hungary are similar to those of the other nations—the decision-makers in Vienna perceived themselves to be acting out of necessity and closed options rather than open choice. There are only three Austro-Hungarian statements regarding the options of the enemies and none are perceptions of choice. This finding is not surprising. After the earliest phase of the crisis, the policy of punishing Serbia was pursued in Vienna with a single-mindedness not evident in the British policy of seeking a mediated solution; nor in the German policy of trying to preserve the "dignity and honor" of her ally, while averting a general war which many Germans perceived would end

---

[18] The inter-coder reliability was 0.87.

[19] There may, of course, be political and strategic reasons for such assertions, quite aside from the way in which the situation is actually perceived. This is particularly likely in documents which are intended for wide public circulation. On the other hand, the most "private" documents—intended only for circulation within the various decision groups—do not differ materially from the entire set of documents in respect to the findings reported here. See, for example, the Kaiser's marginal annotations, or the various minutes of Sir Eyre Crowe, Assistant Under-Secretary of State in the British Foreign Office.

Table II

PERCEPTIONS OF ALTERNATIVES: FREQUENCY OF "CHOICE,"
"NECESSITY," AND "CLOSED" ALTERNATIVES FOR
OWN NATION AND ENEMIES

GERMANY

	Choice	Necessity		Choice	Closed
Self	10	109	Self	10	19
Enemies	21	3	Enemies	21	0

$\chi^2 = 73.6$ $p < .001$ $\chi^2 = 22.2$ $p < .001$

AUSTRIA-HUNGARY

	Choice	Necessity		Choice	Closed
Self	13	80	Self	13	7
Enemies	0	3	Enemies	0	0

Fisher exact $p = .65$ Fisher exact $p = 1.00$

RUSSIA

	Choice	Necessity		Choice	Closed
Self	7	20	Self	7	7
Enemies	6	2	Enemies	6	0

Fisher exact $p = .02$ Fisher exact $p = .04$

FRANCE

	Choice	Necessity		Choice	Closed
Self	1	13	Self	1	6
Enemies	12	2	Enemies	12	3

$\chi^2 = 17.8$ $p < .001$ Fisher exact $p = .006$

GREAT BRITAIN

	Choice	Necessity		Choice	Closed
Self	7	20	Self	7	23
Enemies	21	2	Enemies	21	0

$\chi^2 = 21.6$ $p < .001$ $\chi^2 = 29.3$ $p < .001$

disastrously;[20] nor in the Russian policy which, like that of Germany, sought to support the prestige of a weak ally without a world war.

Leaders of the Triple Entente nations perceived few acceptable alter-

[20] An earlier study of the 1914 crisis revealed, for example, that German decision-makers were fully aware of Germany's inability to wage a successful two-front war in 1914. Dina A. Zinnes, Robert C. North, and Howard Koch, Jr., "Capability, Threat and the

natives open to themselves in regard to the Balkan crisis. Sir Edward Grey wrote on July 24 that "We can do nothing for moderation unless Germany is prepared *pari passu* to do the same." [21] Almost to the end leaders in Berlin opposed mediation. According to Bethmann-Hollweg, "We cannot mediate in the conflict between Austria and Serbia but possibly later between Austria and Russia." [22] Nor were the Russians inclined to mediation because, in the words of Sazonov, "We have assumed from the beginning a posture which we cannot change." [23] Yet the same leaders tended to perceive more freedom of action for members of the other alliance.[24]

The tendency to perceive one's own alternatives to be more restricted than those of the adversary is also evident in the reaction to the events leading up to general war. On July 28 Nicholas II had warned that "I foresee that I will succumb very soon to the pressure put upon me and will be compelled to take extreme measures which will lead to war." [25] Three days later—in the course of his desperate last minute correspondence with the Kaiser, the Tsar asserted, "It is technically impossible to stop our military preparations which were obligatory owing to Austria's mobilization." [26]

The reaction of German decision-makers to the series of events leading up to mobilization and war was almost identical to that of the Tsar. On the one hand they repeatedly asserted that they had no choice but to take vigorous military measures against the threat to the east.[27] These were, on the other hand, interspersed with statements that only Russia was free to act in order to prevent war.[28] And Wilhelm, like the Tsar, finally

---

Outbreak of War," in James N. Rosenau, ed., *International Politics and Foreign Policy* (New York, 1961). Admiral Tirpitz wrote, "It [the German Government] was convinced from the very beginning that we should not win . . . that government itself was most deeply convinced of its hopelessness." Alfred von Tirpitz, *My Memoirs* (London, Hurst & Blackett, Ltd., 1919).

[21] Great Britain, *op. cit.*, #103.

[22] Montgelas and Schücking, *op. cit.*, #247.

[23] Russia, *op. cit.*, #118.

[24] After the outbreak of war between Serbia and Austria-Hungary, Grey wrote: "The whole idea of mediation or mediating influence was ready to be put into operation by any method that Germany could suggest if mine was not acceptable. In fact, mediation was ready to come into operation by any method that Germany thought possible if only Germany would 'press the button' in the interests of peace" (Great Britain, *op. cit.*, #263).

[25] Russia, *op. cit.*, #170.

[26] Montgelas and Schücking, *op. cit.*, #487.

[27] "Then I must mobilize too! . . . He [Nicholas] expressly stated in his first telegram that he would be presumably forced to take measures that would lead to a European war. Thus he takes the responsibility upon himself." *Ibid.*, #399.

[28] "The responsibility for the disaster which is now threatening the whole civilized world will not be laid at my door. In this moment it still lies in your [Nicholas] power to avert it." *Ibid.*, #480.

asserted that he had lost control of his own military and that only the actions of the adversary could stop further escalation.[29]

> On technical grounds my mobilization which had already been proclaimed this afternoon must proceed against two fronts, east and west as prepared. This cannot be countermanded because I am sorry your [George V] telegram came so late.[30]

The same theme of a single option open to one's self, coupled with perceptions that the initiative for peace rested with the enemy, are evident in the French and Austrian statements regarding their own mobilizations.[31] During the last week only the British consistently stated that they were able to act with some degree of freedom. Owing in part to a badly divided Cabinet, to estimates of public apathy, and to pressure from the business community for neutrality, Grey asserted that British "hands were free." [32]

---

[29] To students of strategy the assertions of the Kaiser and the Tsar may appear to be a "real life" application of the tactics of "commitment: a device to leave the last clear chance to decide the outcome with the other party, in a manner that he fully appreciates; it is to relinquish further initiative, having rigged the incentives so that the other party must choose in one's favor." Thomas C. Schelling, *The Strategy of Conflict* (New York, Oxford University Press, 1960), p. 37.

The behavior of military leaders in St. Petersburg and Berlin proved, however, that neither monarch was merely bluffing. After Sazonov and General Tatischev had browbeaten the vacillating Nicholas into ordering general mobilization, the former called General Ianuschkevitch and said: "Now you can smash the telephone. Give your orders, General, and then—disappear for the rest of the day."

In Berlin Moltke effectively undermined belated German efforts to restrain Austria-Hungary by wiring: "Stand firm to Russian mobilization. Austria-Hungary must be preserved. Mobilize at once against Russia. Germany will mobilize."

In Vienna Conrad von Hotzendorf insured himself against any second thoughts Francis Joseph might have had by ordering mobilization one day ahead of schedule.

One factor which contributed to the perceptions of a single alternative was the rigidity of the various mobilization plans. The Russian attempt to mobilize against only Austria was anathema to the Russian generals because no such plan had been drawn up. According to General Dobrorolski, "The whole plan of mobilization is worked out ahead to its final conclusion and in all its detail. . . . Once the moment is chosen, everything is settled; there is no going back; it determines mechanically the beginning of war." Virginia Cowles, *The Kaiser* (New York, 1964), pp. 343–46.

Similarly the Kaiser's last minute attempt to reverse the Schlieffen plan—to attack only in the east—shattered Moltke, who replied: "That is impossible, Your Majesty. An army of a million cannot be improvised. It would be nothing but a rabble of undisciplined armed men, without a commissariat. . . . It is utterly impossible to advance except according to plan; strong in the west, weak in the east." Moltke, *Erinnerungen*, quoted *ibid.*, pp. 348–9.

[30] Montgelas and Schücking, *op. cit.*, #575.

[31] Austria-Hungary, *op. cit.*, #11203; France, *op. cit.*, #532, #725.

[32] Great Britain, *op. cit.*, #447. These statements explain, in part, the Kaiser's violent reaction to Grey's telegram of July 29 that, "There would be no question of our intervening if Germany was not involved, or even if France was not involved. But we know very well that if the issue did become such that we thought British interests required us to intervene, we must intervene at once, and the decision would have to be very rapid." *Ibid.*, #286. Upon reading this, Wilhelm wrote, "The net has been suddenly thrown

According to the second hypothesis (2b) relating stress to perceptions of alternatives:

> In a crisis situation, decision-makers will tend to perceive their allies' range of alternatives to be more restricted than those of their adversaries.

European leaders perceived fewer alternatives open to themselves than to their adversaries; they regarded their allies to be in a similar position. On the one hand German documents are replete with explanations that Austria was pursuing the *only* policy open to her, thus preventing Germany from playing a moderating role in Vienna.[33] On the other hand the Kaiser was apparently convinced that England could perform the very function which he felt was impossible for Germany—the restraining of the most belligerent member of the coalition.[34] The assumption of British freedom, coupled with restrictions on German policy, is nowhere as clear as in one of the Kaiser's marginal notes:

> He [Grey] knows perfectly well, that if he were to say one single serious sharp and warning word at Paris and Petersburg, and were to warn them to remain neutral, both would become quiet at once. But he takes care not to speak the word, and threatens us instead! Common cur! England *alone* bears the responsibility for peace and war, and not we any longer! [35]

This approach to the problems of allies was not confined to Berlin. Nicolson wrote on July 29: "I do not think that Berlin quite understands that Russia cannot and will not stand quietly by while Austria administers a severe chastisement to Serbia."[36] Grey assessed the requirements of his French ally in similar terms.[37] At the same time, however, he believed that Germany could constrain her southern ally.[38]

---

over our head, and England sneeringly reaps the most brilliant success of her persistently prosecuted purely anti-German world policy . . ." Montgelas and Schücking, *op. cit.*, #401.

[33] "Thus, there remains nothing for the Austro-Hungarian Government to do unless it is willing to make the final sacrifice of its status as a Great Power, but to enforce its demands by the use of heavy pressure, or, if need be, by taking military measures." *Ibid.*, #423.

[34] "Instead of mediation, a serious word to Petersburg and Paris, to the effect that England would not help them would quiet the situation at once." *Ibid.*, #368.

"If Grey wanted really to preserve peace he need only as Prince Henry suggested on 20th July intimate to the two allies France and Russia—not to mobilize but to wait, until the pour-parlers which I was directing had succeeded or otherwise between Vienna and Russia." *Ibid.*, #720.

[35] *Ibid.*, #368.

[36] Great Britain, *op. cit.*, #264.

[37] "France did not wish to join in the war that seemed about to break out, but she was obliged to join in it, because of her alliance," *Ibid.*, #447.

[38] "But none of us could influence Austria in this direction unless Germany would propose and participate in such action in Vienna." *Ibid.*, #99.

Only when mobilizations and other actions had gone too far to be stopped, were some futile attempts made to restrain the militant members of each alliance. For example, at the last minute Bethmann-Hollweg tried to hold Austria in check, but he was effectively countermanded by Moltke's wire to Vienna urging immediate general mobilization.[39]

Because there are relatively few perceptions of allies' alternatives, the data for the second hypothesis have been aggregated by alliance rather than by nation (Table III). For both the Triple Entente and the Dual Alliance there is a significant ($p \leq .02$) difference between the choice and necessity perceptions for allies and enemies. The difference between perceptions of choice and those of closed alternatives is in the predicted direction, but in the region of doubt.

Hypothesis 3a states that:

> As stress increases, decision-makers will perceive the range of alternatives open to themselves to become narrower.

A valid test of the hypothesis, free from the effects of message volume, required a prior adjustment of frequency of "necessity" and "closed" perceptions similar to that performed on the time data. The resulting figures were again divided into two periods: June 27–July 28 and July 29–August 4. A Mann–Whitney U-Test reveals that the difference for each coalition is in the predicted direction and is statistically significant ($U = 7$, $p = .05$).

According to the final hypothesis (3b) relating crisis-induced tension to perceived alternatives,

> As stress increases, decision-makers will perceive the range of alternatives open to adversaries or potential adversaries to expand.

To test the hypothesis, frequency of perception was again adjusted for message volume and the data are divided into the periods of lower (June 27–July 28) and higher (July 29–August 4) stress. A Mann–Whitney U-Test lends only partial support to the hypothesis. For both alliances, differences between the early and later periods are in the predicted direction—the "choice" alternatives open to members of the opposing coalition were perceived to be increasing as the crisis deepened. In the case of the Dual Alliance, the increase in perceptions of the open alternatives for adversaries is significant ($U = 5$, $p = .02$); for the Triple Entente, however, the difference is not sufficient to support the hypothesis ($U = 10, p = .13$).

[39] On July 30, Bethmann-Hollweg concluded a telegram to Vienna: "Under these circumstances we must urgently and impressively suggest to the consideration of the Vienna Cabinet the acceptance of mediation on the above mentioned honorable conditions. The responsibility for the consequences that would otherwise follow would be an uncommonly heavy one both for Austria and for us." Montgelas and Schücking, op. cit., #395.

Table III

PERCEPTIONS OF ALTERNATIVES: FREQUENCY OF "CHOICE," "NECESSITY," AND "CLOSED" ALTERNATIVES FOR ALLIES AND ENEMIES

	DUAL ALLIANCE			TRIPLE ENTENTE	
	Choice	*Necessity*		*Choice*	*Necessity*
Allies	13	20	Allies	30	17
Enemies	21	6	Enemies	39	6
	$\chi^2 = 8.9 \; p = .005$			$\chi^2 = 6.4 \; p = .02$	

	Choice	*Closed*		*Choice*	*Closed*
Allies	13	3	Allies	30	7
Enemies	21	0	Enemies	39	3
	Fisher exact $p = .07$			$\chi^2 = 2.5 \; .20 > p > .10$	

IV. PATTERNS OF COMMUNICATION

The data used to test hypotheses relating to communication in crisis differ from those in earlier sections of this paper in one important respect: all 5269 documents in the Austro-Hungarian, British, French, German and Russian collections, rather than those authored by selected decision-makers, were counted and classified into four categories:

(1) Documents from officials abroad (ambassadors, ministers, attachés, consuls, etc.) to their central decision-makers.
(2) Documents from central decision-makers to their officials abroad.
(3) Documents from the central decision-makers of one nation to those of another nation.
(4) Documents circulated within a central decision-making unit.

Two units of measurement are used to describe message volume—the document and the word. An index of the average number of words per line in each volume was determined by an exact count of every fiftieth page. The number of lines in each document was then counted and multiplied by the index figure. No attempt was made to adjust message volume for linguistic style, which may affect word counts.[40]

The initial communication hypothesis (4a) to be tested is that:

The higher the stress in a crisis situation, the heavier the overload of channels of communication.[41]

[40] For an attempt to adjust for linguistic differences—that is, the necessity to use a different number of words in various languages to express the same idea—see Dina A. Zinnes, "Expression and Perception of Hostility in International Relations," Ph.D. Dissertation, Stanford University, 1963, pp. 137–43.
[41] Hypothesis 4a clearly presupposes the existence of a quantitative definition of "overload." This problem is discussed, but not resolved, below.

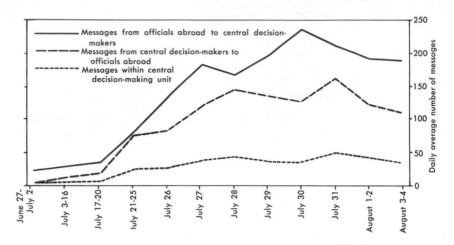

Fig. 1. Daily average message volume by type and date. Figures for Austria-Hungary, Germany, France, Russia and Great Britain combined.

Figure 1—in which message volumes for all five nations have been aggregated by type—reveals sharp increases in daily average message volume during the latter stages of the crisis. During late June and early July, for example, the average frequency of messages from a nation's diplomats abroad was approximately four per day. By July 30, this figure had risen over tenfold.

For purposes of testing the hypothesis, the data have again been divided into two periods: June 27–July 28, and July 29–August 4. A Mann–Whitney U-Test for the direction and magnitude of differences between the two periods was applied to the message volume—measured both in documents and words—of each nation and for each type of communication (Table IV).

The increase in message volume appears to depend on three factors: the degree of involvement in the early stages of crisis, the channel of communication, and the unit of measurement.

Austria-Hungary was most deeply involved in the crisis during the early period, and increases in Austro-Hungarian message volume from the early to the later period of the crisis are generally lower than for Germany. Similarly, among members of the Triple Entente, Russia was the first to be involved in the Balkan crisis, and the increase in Russian message volume is less significant than that for either France or England. Thus, the less dramatic increase in message volume for Austria and Russia during the most intense period of crisis may be interpreted as adding support to the hypothesis.

The change in message volume also appears to depend on the source

Table IV

DIFFERENCES IN MESSAGE VOLUME BETWEEN EARLY
(JUNE 27–JULY 28) AND LATE (JULY 29–AUGUST 4) PERIODS
OF THE 1914 CRISIS: MANN–WHITNEY U–TEST

	Messages from Officials Abroad to Central Decision-Makers		Messages from Central Decision-Makers to Officials Abroad		Messages within Central Decision-Making Unit	
Daily Average Volume—No. of Documents	U	$p*$	U	$p*$	U	$p*$
Austria-Hungary	0	.008	5	.133	15	n.s.
Germany	2	.005	3	.009	3	.009
England	1	.003	5	.024	8	.074
France	3	.009	5	.024	7	.035
Russia	2	.005	9	.101	14	n.s.
Daily Average Volume—No. of Words						
Austria-Hungary	2	.033	11	n.s.	12	n.s.
Germany	6	.037	4	.015	6	.037
England	5	.024	10	.134	14	n.s.
France	7	.053	12	n.s.	6	.037
Russia	11	n.s.	11	n.s.	15	n.s.

$*n_1 = 7$ $n_2 = 5$, except for Austria-Hungary, $n_1 = 7$, $n_2 = 3$.

and destination of the documents. The rate of increase was highest for messages from ambassadors and other officials abroad to the various capitals of Europe. This finding is generally consistent with Taylor's thesis that the decision-makers in 1914 were "snowed under by the blizzard of information" [information input] and that "decisions" [information output] tended to lag behind events." [42] The differences in message volume within the central decision-making unit between the early and late period of the crisis are in the predicted direction, but rather marginal. This is probably the result, in large part, of increased reliance upon oral communication during the final days prior to war.

Finally, when the rate of communications is measured by the number

[42] Taylor, *op. cit.*, pp. 220–21.

of documents, the change from the early to the later period of the crisis is more significant than when a word count is used.

The second communication hypothesis (4b) states that: [43]

> The higher the stress in a crisis situation, the more stereotyped will be the information content of messages.

The average length of messages has been taken as a measure of stereotypy, on the premise that richness of information concerning the course of events, possible alternatives, and completeness of detail are more characteristic of longer documents. The data lend strong support to the hypothesis. The average length of messages decreased systematically as war approached. Each document written immediately following the assassination averaged 326 words in length. During the two days immediately prior to England's entry into the war the average message was only 97 words long. A Mann–Whitney U-Test reveals that documents were significantly ($U = 2$, $p. = .005$) shorter during the period of highest stress (July 29–August 4).

Prior to World War I, the normal and most important channel of communications between two nations was the diplomatic corps. When leaders in London wished to communicate with their counterparts in Berlin, the message was sent to the British Ambassador to Germany, who would then convey its contents to the proper German decision-makers.[44] Direct communication between top level leaders was clearly the exception to normal procedures. According to the third hypothesis (4c) relating stress to communications:

> The higher the stress in a crisis situation, the greater the tendency to rely upon extraordinary or improvised channels of communication.

Of the 2780 inter-state messages, 1530 occurred from June 27 to July 28; of this total, only 74 (4.8 per cent) were direct communications between central decision-makers. During the last seven days of the crisis, on the other hand, 116 out of 1250 (9.3 per cent) messages were sent directly to another state's decision-makers, bypassing the ambassadors. The difference between the two periods is statistically significant ($X^2 = 21.3$; $p < .001$).

As crisis deepens, the need for clear and unimpeded communication between potential adversaries is likely to become both more urgent and more difficult. It is unlikely that similar difficulties in communication

---

[43] This hypothesis is not dissimilar to Lasswell's prediction that "style grows terse . . . when the crisis is recognized as serious." Harold D. Lasswell *et al.*, *The Language of Politics* (New York, George Stewart, 1949), p. 28.

[44] A more comprehensive description of the normal patterns of communication in 1914 may be found in Zinnes, *op. cit.*, pp. 20–24.

will arise between members of the same coalition. Hence the hypothesis (4d) that:

> The higher the stress in a crisis situation, the higher the proportion of intra-coalition—as against inter-coalition—communication.

When inter-nation messages are classified according to date and divided into inter-coalition and intra-coalition communications, the results support the hypothesis. During the first month after the assassination, 830 out of 1530 (54.3 per cent) inter-nation messages were exchanged between members of opposing coalitions. During the week prior to the outbreak of general war, on the other hand, inter-coalition messages account for only 580 out of 1250 (46.4 per cent) messages. The difference between the two periods in regard to communications within and between alliances is significant ($X^2 = 17.3; p < .001$).

The four communication hypotheses have generally been supported by the 1914 data, but some interesting questions remain unanswered. For example, the assumption that information input overload is as dysfunctional as lack of information, is supported by evidence on at least five levels—the cell, the organ, the individual, the group, and the organization.[45] Although there is strong evidence that channel capacity is inversely related to the size of the system, we know comparatively little about *what magnitude of input constitutes overload* at complex levels such as foreign policy decision-making units.

A second problem is that the communication hypotheses have been concerned solely with the volume of messages without regard to their content. While these two factors are not independent of each other, further research on information input overload must consider such factors as the ratio of signal to redundancy and noise.

/The most difficult aspect of studying communications in historical situations is the assessment of its impact on policy. For example, how is the behavior of decision-makers changed by communication overload? In his survey of the experimental literature, Miller has identified a number of coping mechanisms: omissions, error, queuing, filtering, cutting, categories of discrimination, employing multiple channels, and escape.[46] Some insights can be derived from the 1914 data; the employment of multiple channels during the latter stages of the crisis—through more frequent direct communication between decision-makers—has already been noted. But data regarding such consequences as selective filtering of incoming information is at best fragmentary. Thus, even with the relatively complete documentation available for the 1914 crisis, the findings on some important questions are only suggestive.

[45] James G. Miller, "Information Input Overload and Psychopathology," *The American Journal of Psychiatry*, Vol. 116 (1960), pp. 695–704.
[46] Miller, "Information Input Overload," *Self Organizing Systems*—1962, n. p.

V. CONCLUSION

In conclusion it may be useful to consider some questions of more general concern. First, do the concepts and findings in this paper have any relevance beyond the historical one of illuminating a series of unique events?

The factors of perceived time, perceived alternatives, and patterns of communication are usually treated as generic concepts in the decision-making literature. The experimental evidence from psychology supports the assumption that they are among the key factors which affect the performance of individuals and groups, particularly those engaged in complex tasks. Further support for the findings in this paper appears to be forthcoming from laboratory simulation studies.[47] Their ultimate importance for the student of international politics must, however, be established in case studies of actual foreign policy decision. In this connection, a study of the Cuban missile crisis of 1962 assessed the importance of the factors discussed in this paper; it was shown that the crucial factors in the settlement of the crisis without recourse to war included the ability of President Kennedy and his advisers: (1) to maintain multiple options for both the United States *and* the Soviet Union; (2) to lengthen decision time, again for *both* the U.S. and the U.S.S.R.; and (3) to use effectively multiple channels of communication.[48]

A second question concerns research strategy. Are these hypotheses merely a matter of "common sense," and if so, do they warrant the extensive research effort which is entailed in the use of content analysis? A major drawback to the type of data used in this study is found in the very nature of content analysis, which requires considerable expenditure of scarce research resources. Recent developments in programming computers —such as the IBM 7090—for content analysis have gone a long way toward solving the problem.[49] An adaptation of the "General Inquirer" system of automated content analysis permits studies such as that of the 1914 crisis

[47] A full report of the findings from this simulation will be found in a doctoral dissertation by Charles F. Hermann, Northwestern University.
[48] Holsti, *et al.*, "The Management of International Crisis: Affect and Action in American–Soviet Relations, October 1962," to appear in a reader edited by Richard C. Snyder and Dean Pruitt, in press. The theoretical and practical implications of such future studies may be somewhat different. For example, should one find that 1914-like results appear only in every tenth case, the social scientist might reject the hypotheses. The criteria of practical relevance might be less rigid. Given twentieth century military technology, such findings should give little rise to complacency. As Brodie, *op. cit.*, p. 175, has pointed out, today a *single case* of deterrent failure is too many.
[49] Philip J. Stone *et al.*, "The General Inquirer: A Computer System for Content Analysis and Retrieval Based on the Sentence as a Unit of Information," *Behavioral Science*, Vol. 7 (1962), pp. 484–494.

with substantial reduction of manual effort while materially increasing speed, reliability, and flexibility.[50]

The more fundamental question of research strategy relates to the choice of "common sense" hypotheses for extensive research. Yet as Robinson [51] has shown, in his study of some propositions similar to those in this paper, decision-makers generally characterize their *own* activities in terms of classical economic models of decision-making (reviewing all alternatives for the optimum one). They often apply the same model to the decision processes of *other states*. Moreover, it is not difficult in almost every case to develop precisely the reverse proposition. For example, it is wholly consistent with the concept of crisis as a situation of potentially high penalties, *as well as with common sense*, to hypothesize that: [52]

> As stress increases, decision-makers will be motivated to search for, and to consider an increasing number of alternative policies.

While the last two decades have seen a great deal of theorizing about international relations, as well as the development of numerous promising techniques of generating and analyzing data, a basic theory—solidly grounded in empirical evidence—remains a distant goal. Given the rudimentary state of international relations as a discipline, it may be that research directed toward illuminating and rendering more precise our nations, even of "common sense," is not wholly misdirected, either from the standpoint of developing a viable theory of international relations or of contributing to a more stable world.

[50] Holsti, "An Adaptation of the 'General Inquirer' for the Systematic Analysis of Political Documents," *Behavioral Science*, Vol. 9 (1964), pp. 382–88.

[51] Robinson, *op. cit.*, pp. 7–8.

[52] A series of assertions which tend to contradict the hypotheses in this paper may be found in Theodore Abel, "The Elements of Decision in the Pattern of War," *American Sociological Review*, Vol. 6 (1941), pp. 853–59, in which the author writes:

"1. The decision to fight, unless the opponent abandons resistance without a struggle, is not reached on the spur of the moment. In every case the decision is based upon a careful weighing of chances and of anticipating consequences. . . . In no case is the decision precipitated by emotional tensions, sentimentality, crowd-behavior, or other irrational motivations.

"2. The rational, calculating decision is reached far in advance of the actual outbreak of hostilities."

8

The Use of Judges to Generate Quantitative Data

It was stated—proclaimed, in fact—in the introductory chapter of this book that any variable which can be meaningfully conceived can be measured. Of course a counter-proclamation flourishes in the literature which insists that, in the field of international relations, what's important can't be measured and what can be measured isn't important.

This chapter is concerned with a very simple and obvious method for measuring the seemingly unmeasurable: consultation with a panel of expert judges. One assembles a group of people who are supposed to understand what the dimension under discussion is all about and asks them to order cases on the dimension. For example one might wish to determine, as one pair of researchers have, which countries are most closely aligned to the United States. Instead of simply trusting one's own judgment or relying on "objective" indicators of the variable, "alignment" (such as U.N. voting or alliance membership), one could put the question directly to a group of experts and take their rankings as a measure.

The advantages of the method are considerable. Some of the difficulties of dealing with "objective" indicators have been noted in chapter 6. Where objective indicators generally only reflect the variable of interest (as the number of telephones per capita is taken to indicate economic development), experts can be asked relatively direct questions about the basic dimension. Furthermore they can be asked to render a judgment for a precise point in time—or for a general period—while objective data often are available only for the wrong place at the wrong time. And the data from the judges can be gathered under controlled circumstances, while objective data too often are gathered idiosyncratically.

There is a fringe benefit. In formulating his inquiry so that sensible questions about it can be asked of the judges, the researcher is forced to define carefully the problem in his own mind—something he may otherwise be tempted to put off.

Of course the method has its difficulties too. Experts remain, despite their exalted status, people. By aggregating judgments, individual peculiarities may tend to be cancelled out; but much human bias and short-sightedness will inevitably remain [1] although experts presumably have fewer biases—or less capricious ones—than more ordinary people. Methods of standardization such as ranking, percentaging, and the use of standard units can help to make differing perspectives more comparable and additive.

Psychologists, of course, have been using the procedure for decades. Most of their methods of scaling depend at one point or another on controlled assessment by one or more judges.[2]

The approach is used in other areas too—at times so unquestioningly that it is scarcely a matter of debate or notice. Take boxing, for instance. Unless one boxer is knocked out by the other (an objective indicator) the determination of the championship and more importantly the recipient of the prize money is usually at the whim of three subjective judges. Gymnastics, except that it has no counterpart to the knockout, is scored similarly. To determine which is the nation's best college basketball team, Associated Press sportswriters are polled. To find what a good movie is we rely on the New York film critics or—in moments of desperation—on the membership of the Academy of Motion Picture Arts and Sciences. To select the great physicists we consult the Nobel prize committee's list. The world is filled with panels of judges soberly and largely without objection scaling wines for bouquet, TV commercials for "creativity," automobiles for endurance, poems for elegance, perfumes for fragrance, and young women in bathing suits for a quality which is euphemistically known as "beauty." Even the venerable and tediously objective United States census uses variables which are based on the judgment of its field staff such as "soundness of plumbing" and "condition of housing" (sound, deteriorating, dilapidated).

The method is constantly being used unconsciously in social science research. Forced to rate an entity on a dimension, researchers often feel free to make definitive pronouncements ("the scientific approach has contributed very little to the theory of international relations," "Uruguay

[1] Some psychologists in fact are building an entire theory on the idea that individual differences in judgment reflect differences in attitude and involvement. See Carolyn W. Sherif, Muzafer Sherif, and Robert E. Nebergall, *Attitude and Attitude Change: The Social Judgment–Involvement Approach* (Philadelphia: Saunders, 1965).
[2] For a highly readable introduction, see Allen L. Edwards, *Techniques of Attitude Scale Construction* (New York: Appleton-Century-Crofts, 1957).

is the most democratic country in Latin America") after consulting a panel of experts with only one member—themselves.

The *conscious* use of panels of judges has been comparatively rare in political science. Once in a while a great game is played of ranking the presidents, usually with witty and self-conscious disclaimers that anything serious is meant.[3] And members of a Senate committee a few years ago, charged with the responsibility of designating the Great Senators of all time, found, after consulting their own consciences as well as a number of political scientists and historians, that exactly one Great Senator came from each of the states of each of the committee members.[4]

Perhaps the earliest conscious application of the method in political science was Frank Klingberg's effort, in connection with Quincy Wright's study of war project in the 1930's, to measure the relations among states and to predict the likelihood that specific pairs of states would soon be at war.[5] A number of scaling approaches are experimented with and several different panels are consulted (one including undergraduates, appallingly enough) and the predictions that emerge seem reassuringly accurate. Klingberg also makes an effort to compare his results with "headline happenings" in the *New York Times* and finds substantial correspondence.

Since Klingberg's study a number of investigations have made use of expert panels in an effort to predict political, social, and technological events, and also to assess the biases of different sorts of judges.[6] To improve predictions and other judgments the promising "Delphi method" has been developed. In this approach experts undergo successive rounds of questioning by interview or questionnaire and are given opportunity to reconsider and improve their previous estimates.[7]

---

[3] For a critique of the exercise, see Curtis A. Amlund, "President-Ranking: A Criticism," *Midwest Journal of Political Science*, Vol. 8 (August, 1964), pp. 309–15. Modern president-rankers may be appalled to learn that James Bryce placed Grant in the front rank of American presidents. *The American Commonwealth*, Vol. I (New York: Macmillan, 1924), p. 83.

[4] Ranking is done in other areas too. The French magazine, *Connaissance des Arts*, regularly polls connoisseurs to determine the most preferred living painters, and panels of musicologists have been regularly asked to rank composers in order of eminence. See Paul R. Farnsworth, *The Social Psychology of Music* (New York: Dryden, 1958), chapter 6 and appendix. Panelists rate ballets in *Ballet Review*.

[5] Frank L. Klingberg, "Studies in Measurement of the Relations Among Sovereign States," *Psychometrika*, Vol. 6 (1941), pp. 335–52. Also in James N. Rosenau, *International Politics and Foreign Policy: A Reader in Research and Theory* (New York: Free Press, 1961), pp. 483–91. See also Quincy Wright, *A Study of War* (Chicago: University of Chicago Press, 1942), volume II, chapter 36 and appendixes 41 and 43.

[6] See Lloyd Jensen, "American Foreign Policy Elites and the Prediction of International Events," *Peace Research Society (International) Papers*, Vol. 5 (1966), pp. 199–209; A. Kaplan, A. L. Skogstad, and M. A. Girshick, "The Prediction of Social and Technological Events," *Public Opinion Quarterly*, Vol. 14 (Spring, 1950), pp. 93–110; and T. W. Milburn and J. F. Milburn, "Predictions of Threats and Beliefs About How to Meet Them," *American Behavioral Scientist*, Vol. 9 (March, 1966), pp. 3–7.

[7] See Norman Dalkey and Olaf Helmer, "An Experimental Application of the Delphi

In a study mentioned earlier, Henry Tuene and Sig Synnestvedt measured cold war alignment by consulting a panel of area specialists and international relations generalists chosen from the *American Political Science Association Directory*. They find a high amount of agreement among the judges and between the judges' pronouncements and certain "objective" indicators of alignment.[8]

There have been a few other uses of the expert panel in studies relevant to international relations. William Kotsch has used judges to rate the "degree of Soviet success" in international events; the study is notable more for the high degree of agreement attained by the judges than for its basic mathematical structure.[9] Peter Rohn consulted a group of experts to validate a power index for international governmental organizations[10] while Raymond Nixon has used judges to measure freedom of the press.[11] Content analysts and experimenters constantly rely on judges to scale messages on various dimensions; the method can be seen in action in Holsti's paper reprinted in chapter 7. And Richardson, in his analysis of "deadly quarrels," has trusted the judgment of historians to determine the causes of specific wars.[12]

The paper reprinted here by Russell Fitzgibbon is the latest in a series of articles in which he has attempted to assess the state of democracy in Latin America by polling an expert panel of Latin American specialists. Many of the strengths and weaknesses of this kind of data can be seen in his discussion. For example, while the general patterning of the results makes a good deal of sense and while some of his evidence suggests that judgmental data may sometimes be more accurate than "objective" indicators, the level of agreement among the judges indicates that expert consensus in this area has not exactly been achieved.[13]

Method to the Use of Experts," *Management Science*, Vol. 9 (April, 1963), pp. 458–67, and Bertrand de Jouvenel, "A Letter on Predicting," *American Behavioral Scientist*, Vol. 9 (June, 1966), p. 51. See also Barry M. Blechman, "The Quantitative Evaluation of Foreign Policy Alternatives: Sinai, 1956," *Journal of Conflict Resolution*, Vol. 10 (December, 1966), pp. 408–26.

[8] Henry Tuene and Sig Synnestvedt, "Measuring International Alignment," *Orbis*, Vol. 9 (Spring, 1965), pp. 171–89.

[9] William J. Kotsch, "An Arithmetic Approach to International Relations," *American Behavioral Scientist*, Vol. 9 (October, 1965), pp. 23–24.

[10] Peter H. Rohn, "A Legal Theory of International Organization," *The Turkish Yearbook of International Relations 1964*, pp. 19–52.

[11] Raymond Nixon, "Freedom in the World's Press: A Fresh Appraisal with New Data," *Journalism Quarterly*, Vol. 42 (Winter, 1965), pp. 3–14, 118–119.

[12] Lewis F. Richardson, *Statistics of Deadly Quarrels* (Pittsburgh, Penn.: Boxwood Press, 1960).

[13] The disagreement, however, does not appear to be nearly as great as it is among political scientists when they consider the state of the discipline. See Albert Somit and Joseph Tanenhaus, *American Political Science: A Profile of a Discipline* (New York: Atherton, 1964), chapter 2.

MEASURING DEMOCRATIC CHANGE
IN LATIN AMERICA

Russell H. Fitzgibbon

The continuing struggle between democracy and various forms of totalitarianism for control of men's minds and actions does not, as time passes, lose either intensity or interest. The conflict is focused and dramatized by the nature of international politics in what we earlier referred to as a bipolarized world. The sharpness of the competition makes it important, even impressive, that we study, as carefully and thoroughly as may be, not only the form and philosophy of one or another system of political control but also the component elements of different types, how and why they change, and what trends may be deduced from as penetrating analysis as is possible.

• • •

. . . not only the nature of the change but also the measurement of it assumes increasing importance as time passes. The present author became interested in the problem—and the measurement—more than twenty years ago and in consequence undertook surveys among Latin Americanists knowledgeable about the politics of the area. The surveys began in 1945 and have been repeated at five-year intervals. They now provide a study in depth of the course and rapidity of change of various compenents of democracy in the Latin American scene. It should be stressed that this is change and achievement as seen by a group of specialists who have long observed and weighed Latin American political phenomena. Their evaluations are informed but, of course, subjective. It should also be underlined that the surveying techniques used were not those of a "Gallup poll" in which carefully selected random groups of laymen participating in a social process are asked for opinions; the progressively larger number of respondents taking part in the five surveys have been chosen as highly qualified experts who are observers of, not participants in, the process of change.

Analyses of earlier surveys have previously been published in article

Reprinted by permission from *The Journal of Politics*, Vol. 29 (February, 1967), pp. 129–166.

form.[2] They have attracted widespread attention and interest, mostly favorable. It is true that in a critical review of Howard Cline's *Mexico: Revolution to Evolution, 1940–1960*, Lesley B. Simpson referred to Russell Fitzgibbon's astonishing attempt to measure (by IBM computer) the progress of democracy in Latin America."[3] It must be concluded, alas, that the adjective in the quotation was meant to be pejorative rather than complimentary. This author stands in awe of Professor Simpson's erudition; his staccato, impressionistic, and eminently readable *Many Mexicos* has deservedly become a classic. At the same time, it is respectfully submitted that he just may have missed the point of the successive surveys. On the other hand, several authors have commented in recent volumes on the methods and problems involved in the surveys, and Professors John D. Martz and Robert D. Tomasek reprinted the 1961 article, cited above, in collections of readings.[4] At least three professional papers were tied directly to the 1960 analysis[5] and in 1963 the RAND Corporation organized a seminar, participated in by about a dozen staff members and the present writer, to discuss problems and techniques involved in the surveys.

It was necessary initially to decide whether to rely for measurement on objective data derived from census-type or other statistical materials or, on the other hand, to tap the expertise of experienced students of the Latin American scene. The decision was made for the latter alternative. Both approaches have their respective advantages. Reliance on statistical data as a base would seem to assure elimination of all subjective or emotional considerations and to presume mechanical efficiency and accuracy; it would ostensibly mean use of quantifiable or "hard" data rather

---

[2] "Measurement of Latin-American Political Phenomena; A Statistical Experiment," *American Political Science Review*, Vol. 45 (1951), pp. 517–23; "How Democratic is Latin America?", *Inter-American Economic Affairs*, Vol. 9 (Spring, 1956), pp. 65–77; "A Statistical Evaluation of Latin-American Democracy," *Western Political Quarterly*, Vol. 9 (1956), pp. 607–19; (with Kenneth F. Johnson), "Measurement of Latin American Political Change," *American Political Science Review*, Vol. 54 (1961), pp. 515–26.
[3] *Hispanic American Historical Review*, Vol. 43 (1963), p. 296.
[4] Harold E. Davis (ed.), *Government and Politics in Latin America* (New York: Ronald Press, 1958), pp. 91–92, 237, 294–95; Rosendo A. Gomez, *Government and Politics in Latin America* (New York: Random House, 1960), pp. 92–93; Edwin Lieuwen, *Arms and Politics in Latin America* (New York: Praeger, 1961), p. 57; Robert E. Scott, *Mexican Government in Transition* (Urbana: U. of Ill. Press, 1959), pp. 301–02; William S. Stokes, *Latin American Politics* (New York: Crowell, 1959), pp. 511–13; John D. Martz (ed.), *The Dynamics of Change in Latin American Politics* (Englewood Cliffs: Prentice-Hall, 1965), pp. 113–29; Robert D. Tomasek (ed.), *Latin American Politics: Studies of the Contemporary Scene* (Garden City: Doubleday, 1966), pp. 4–22.
[5] Charles Wolf, Jr., "The Political Effects of Military Programs: Some Indications from Latin America," *Orbis*, Vol. 8 (1965), pp. 871–93; (same author), "The Political Effects of Economic Programs: Some Indications from Latin America," *Economic Development and Cultural Change*, Vol. 14 (1965), pp. 1–20; Dwaine Marvick, "A Memorandum on Fitzgibbon's Survey of Latin American Specialists," paper (processed, 19 pp.) read before the American Sociological Association, Washington, August, 1962.

than judgmental or "soft" variables. But there are difficulties: for one thing, applicability of the data to the problem must first be determined, often a subordinate problem of considerable complexity in itself. Furthermore, there is seemingly firm evidence that in at least one or two Latin American states the governmentally published "census-type" information has at times been "doctored" to present a more favorable national picture of one or another aspect. Use of the area specialists as a source of evaluations does open the door to subjective applications of the various criteria. Furthermore, the breadth, depth, and recency of the information on which respondents base their subjective and perhaps unconscious reactions will vary greatly. A considerable panel of respondents will run the gamut from very "liberal" to quite "conservative" points of view. But, granting such handicaps, the overall assessments made by specialists are likely to introduce desirable nuances and balances which are impossible in the use of cold statistical information, even of the most accurate sort.[6]

It is interesting, of course, to set one approach off against the other, and that is attempted in part later in the present paper.

The surveying method itself was relatively simple. In the first place, fifteen criteria contributing, directly or indirectly, to the state of democracy in a given Latin American country were devised (see Figure 1). Some of them, it is obvious, are preconditions of democracy, others are contemporary manifestations of it, still others are products of it; some can be characterized as political in nature, others as administrative, economic, social, or cultural. An admixture of the kind might initially seem open to criticism, especially inasmuch as the criteria were not arranged as the characterizations in the preceding sentence suggest. The main reason for the choice of criteria was that these particular measurements appeared to the writer to include the important conditioning and reflective components of the total picture of viable democracy in the Latin American context. The arrangement seemed to be a logical one, progressing from the very elemental factor of basic education and seminal socioeconomic conditions, through conditions directly contributory to a democratic process, such as freedom of speech, press, etc. (necessary for meaningful campaigning), honest elections, and free party organization and activity, to more refined products of such a development, such as scientifically evolved public administration and intelligently organized local government.

It seemed important to devise such criteria in the light of the total Latin American culture. To apply the standards and critiques of mature

---

[6] The advantages and risks of the two approaches are well summarized in Marvick *op. cit.*, p. 5. Cf. also Seymour M. Lipset, "Some Social Requisites of Democracy: Economic Development and Political Legitimacy," *American Political Science Review*, Vol. 53 (1959), pp. 69–105, *passim*; and Gabriel Almond and James S. Coleman (eds.), *The Politics of the Developing Areas* (Princeton: Princeton Univ. Press, 1960), pp. 532–76, *passim*.

Your familiarity level	Argentina	Bolivia	Brazil	Chile	Colombia	Costa Rica	Cuba	Dominican Rep.	Ecuador	El Salvador	Guatemala	Haiti	Honduras	Mexico	Nicaragua	Panama	Paraguay	Peru	Uruguay	Venezuela	(Leave blank)	
1. Educational level	232	99	161	211	173	228	192	122	115	138	111	57	111	183	119	156	97	131	235	173		1
2. Standard of living	217	85	156	177	156	201	144	121	109	139	118	58	114	177	122	148	105	130	213	177		2
3. Internal unity	177	113	175	217	161	235	178	137	117	150	122	86	129	214	138	156	128	136	229	184		3
4. Political maturity	200	112	184	238	184	243	151	115	115	140	117	58	115	214	122	139	96	146	230	183		4
5. Freedom from foreign domination	230	149	215	219	216	223	85	157	184	176	162	174	164	236	163	128	152	193	229	189		5
6. Freedom of press, etc.	225	130	194	244	218	245	59	146	165	169	143	60	137	206	134	184	86	200	246	212		6
7. Free elections	193	121	157	243	204	247	56	116	131	158	130	57	122	190	107	181	71	182	246	230		7
8. Party organization	187	121	172	238	200	234	70	119	133	154	131	61	123	175	113	177	82	188	237	218		8
9. Judiciary	199	116	181	225	201	230	63	123	145	145	129	61	125	187	117	156	89	169	227	187		9
10. Governmental funds	182	105	152	204	179	217	131	123	135	150	130	59	125	178	125	136	108	157	205	185		10
11. Social legislation	187	148	164	206	168	215	178	126	128	153	128	65	119	209	119	146	102	156	226	196		11
12. Civilian supremacy	145	106	131	241	198	247	115	111	110	128	105	84	108	235	108	172	70	152	245	189		12
13. Ecclesiastical freedom	211	195	223	228	157	229	186	170	150	174	174	156	171	219	175	199	162	168	243	217		13
14. Government administration	183	101	161	205	169	209	127	115	127	142	123	64	117	188	128	147	108	157	207	180		14
15. Local government	177	102	159	190	167	212	86	111	118	140	130	60	113	171	114	141	91	149	201	174		15
(Leave blank)																						
	A	Bo	Br	Ch	Co	CR	Cu	DR	Ec	ES	G	Ha	Ho	M	N	Pn	Pr	Pe	U	V		

Comments:

Your name _____

Date mailed back _____

Continue on reverse if necessary*

Fig. 1.

Western political societies to the developing states of Latin America would be roughly analogous to using a skilled machinist's fine precision tools for construction of a garage workbench. To use uncritically the definitions, approaches, and measurements that would be useful in studying conditions in, say Canada, the Netherlands, Norway, or in the United States, would, as applied to Latin America (or various other parts of the world) suggest only a pathological or distorted situation.[7] This is not a matter of drawing invidious contrasts but simply one of trying to fit norms of measurement to the thing to be measured.

Once the criteria were phrased, it appeared desirable to weight them, inasmuch as they would obviously have differing degrees of impact in conditioning the resultant total evaluations. Freedom and honesty of elections in a given country would surely be of greater significance than, say, the influence (now largely historical) of ecclesiastical pressures on politics. As they finally evolved, the criteria used, with the weighting for each criterion given in parentheses, were as follows:

      1. An educational level sufficient to give the political processes some substance and vitality (weighting of 1).

      2. A fairly adequate standard of living (1).

[7] Cf. Gabriel A. Almond, "Comparative Political Systems," *Journal of Politics*, Vol. 18 (1956), pp. 391–409, *passim*. The dramatically different nature of the Latin American milieu from that in the United States is vividly analyzed in Victor Alba, *Alliance without Allies: The Mythology of Progress in Latin America* (New York: Praeger, 1965).

3. A sense of internal unity and national cohesion (1).

4. Belief by the people in their individual political dignity and maturity (1).

5. Absence of foreign domination (1).

6. Freedom of the press, speech, assembly, radio, etc. (1½).

7. Free and competitive elections—honestly counted votes (2).

8. Freedom of party organization; genuine and effective party opposition in the legislature; legislative scrutiny of the executive branch (1½).

9. An independent judiciary—respect for its decisions (1).

10. Public awareness of accountability for the collection and expenditure of public funds (1).

11. Intelligent attitude toward social legislation—the vitality of such legislation as applied (1).

12. Civilian supremacy over the military (1½).

13. Reasonable freedom of political life from the impact of ecclesiastical controls (½).

14. Attitude toward and development of technical, scientific, and honest governmental administration (1).

15. Intelligent and sympathetic administration of whatever local self-government prevails (1).

Were the surveys being started *de novo*, it is quite possible that the author would select, organize, phrase, or arrange the criteria somewhat differently. (Friends have suggested, probably entirely correctly, that others might have been included, different weightings given, etc.). But, for the sake of comparability of successive analyses, it has seemed desirable to retain the criteria in their original form with the same weightings.

Brief explanatory paragraphs amplified each of the criteria as circulated among the respondents and attempted to establish a reasonable uniformity of approach to evaluations. Respondents were asked to express their evaluations for each state on each criterion in letter terms, A through E, signifying respectively a judgment of excellent, good, average, poor, or insignificant (virtually no) democratic achievement in respect to the particular state and criterion. Respondents were also asked to provide self-ratings of their presumed "familiarity level" with respect to each state and each criterion in terms of "great" (familiarity), "moderate," or "little." Evaluation sheets (see Figure 1) were distributed among the respondents [8]

[8] In the first two surveys ten persons participated each time; in the third survey, twenty, in the fourth, forty; and in the last one fifty. The list below indentifies by superscript numbers the respective surveys participated in by each person: Robert J. Alexander [4-5] (Rutgers), Marvin Alisky [4-5] (Arizona State), Samuel F. Bemis [1-2] (Yale), George I. Blanksten [2-5] (Northwestern), Spruille Braden [4-5] (former Assistant Secretary of State), Frank R. Brandenburg [4-5] (Committee for Economic Development), Ben Burnett [5] (Whittier), James L. Busey [4-5] (Colorado), Ronald H. Chilcote [5] (California, Riverside), Howard Cline [4-5] (Director, Hispanic Foundation, Library of Congress), George G. Daniels [5] (*Time*), Harold E. Davis [3-5] (American), John C. Dreier [5] (Hopkins), Jules Dubois [3-5] (*Chicago Tribune*), Alex T. Edelmann [5] (Nebraska), Charles G. Fenwick [5]

with this presumptuous request for 335 judgments: on fifteen criteria for each of twenty states and on familiarity levels for fifteen criteria and twenty states. Respondents cooperated most generously.

Once the evaluation sheets were all in hand, analysis proceeded with the aid of an electronic computer at almost all points.[9] Evaluations, as well as criteria, were assigned numerical values. A judgment of A in a given cell was given a value of five points, one of B a value of four points, and so on to one point for an E. Considering the varying weights of the criteria ($\frac{1}{2}$ to 2) it was thus possible for a respondent to give a state a maximum evaluation of eighty-five points (all A's) or a minimum rating of seventeen (all E's). A necessary first step was compilation of original or "raw" scores for the several states, determined simply by adding cell evaluations, with proper regard for weightings of criteria. Raw scores for the several states in the five surveys, 1945 to 1965, inclusive, are shown in Table I. In Figure 1, raw-score totals, by state and criterion for the 1965 survey, have been added to the reproduction of the evaluation form.

Use of the raw scores permits a crude determination of how the respondents collectively view the course of Latin American democracy over twenty years. Total raw scores (with appropriate division for the latest three surveys to account for the larger numbers of participants) were: 1945: 9,763½; 1950: 9,943; 1955: 9,760; 1960: 10,827½; 1965: 10,656½.

(former Director, Department of International Law and Organization, Pan American Union), Russell H. Fitzgibbon [1-5] (University of California, Santa Barbara), William Forbis [4] (*Time*), Jesús de Galíndez [3] (Columbia), Federico G. Gil [4-5] (North Carolina), Rosendo Gomez [4-5] (Arizona), Stephen S. Goodspeed [3-5] (California, Santa Barbara), Frances R. Grant [5] (Secretary General, Inter-American Association for Democracy and Freedom), Paul E. Hadley [4-5] (Southern California), Robert M. Hallett [3] (*Christian Science Monitor*), Simon G. Hanson [5] (*Inter-American Economic Affairs*), Clarence H. Haring [1] (Harvard), Robert D. Hayton [5] (Hunter), Hubert C. Herring [1-5] (Claremont Graduate School), Henry F. Holland [4] (former Assistant Secretary of State), Preston E. James [4-5] (Syracuse), Bertram B. Johansson [4-5] (*Christian Science Monitor*), Kenneth F. Johnson [5] (Colorado State), Miguel Jorrín [3-5] (New Mexico), Harry Kantor [3-5] (Florida), Merle Kling [4-5] (Washington, St. Louis), Leo B. Lott [4-5] (Ohio State), Austin F. Macdonald [1-4] (California, Berkeley), William Manger [4-5] (former Assistant Secretary General, Organization of American States), John D. Martz [5] (North Carolina), Herbert L. Matthews [4-5] (*New York Times*), J. Lloyd Mecham [1-5] (Texas), Edward G. Miller, Jr.[4-5] (former Assistant Secretary of State), Dana G. Munro [1-5] (Princeton), Harry B. Murkland [3-4] (*Newsweek*), Martin C. Needler [5] (Michigan), L. Vincent Padgett [4-5] (San Diego State), C. Neale Ronning [5] (Tulane), William L. Schurz [3-4] (American Institute of Foreign Trade), Robert E. Scott [3-5] (Illinois), K. H. Silvert [4-5] (Dartmouth), James H. Stebbins [4] (former Executive Vice President, W. R. Grace and Company), William S. Stokes [1-5] (Claremont Men's), Graham H. Stuart [1-2] (Stanford), Tad Szulc [5] (*New York Times*), Philip B. Taylor, Jr. [3-5] (Hopkins), Edward Tomlinson [5] (*Reader's Digest*), Martin B. Travis, Jr.[3-5] (State University of New York), Henry Wells [5] (Pennsylvania), Arthur P. Whitaker [1-5] (Pennsylvania), A. Curtis Wilgus [4-5] (Florida).

[9] In a moment of whimsy, Mr. Royer programmed the computer to conclude its print-outs of occasional data with a neatly typed "sir." In view of the increasing respect which he and the writer developed for the computer's abilities, it was perhaps only appropriate that the machine, too, should be somewhat respectful.

Table I

RAW SCORES BY STATES

	1945		1950		1955		1960		1965	
	Points	Rank	Points	Rank	Points	Rank	Points	Rank	Points	Rank
Argentina	628	5	536	8	499½	8	704½	4	662	6
Bolivia	308	18	334	17	374½	15	439	16	401	17
Brazil	481½	11	605	5	633	5	648½	7	574½	8
Chile	712½	3	732½	2	713	3	741.5	3	755	3
Colombia	683½	4	597½	6	507	6	651.5	6	638½	7
Costa Rica	730	2	702½	3	746	2	768	2	781.½*	1½*
Cuba	590½	6	659	4	504	7	452	15	381	18
Domin. Rep.	301	19	320½	19	307	19	315	18	426	14
Ecuador	379½	14	474	9	487	10	556½	10	448	12
El Salvador	411½	13	424	14	461½	11	508½	12	510½	11
Guatemala	416	12	472½	10	393½	14	483½	13	437	13
Haiti	330½	16	329	18	367	17	309½	19	248	20
Honduras	328	17	379	15	418½	12	452½	14	423½	15
Mexico	545½	7	569½	7	639½	4	664	5	674	4
Nicaragua	345½	15	354	16	329½	18	370½	17	420	16
Panama	528	8	471	11	498	9	519½	11	542.5	10
Paraguay	289	20	293½	20	291½	20	284	20	331	19
Peru	494	10	428	13	369½	16	562½	9	556	9
Uruguay	772	1	788½	1	820	1	785	1	781.5	1.5*
Venezuela	504	9	451	12	397	13	611½	8	665	5

*Tie

The fluctuations are a rough indication of shifts in the democratic weather-vane over the years. The considerable jump in 1960 is probably to be accounted for by what Tad Szulc aptly used as a book title, "the twilight of the tyrants" (Perón, Somoza, Rojas Pinilla, Pérez Jiménez, for example), during the preceding half decade. The consensus appeared to be that by 1965 the state of democracy had slightly worsened from its 1960 condition.

Certain statistical difficulties are inherent, however, in the use of raw scores. Scores ranged through several hundred points and minima and maxima were widely separated.[10] One respondent is inclined to view the foibles and failures of the Latin American political process leniently, another will see them harshly; their respective evaluations, in consequence, will be high and low. Conveniently, the raw-score totals in each survey straddled 1,000 points. It seemed desirable, therefore, to adjust or "normalize" evaluations by allotting each respondent 1,000 points for all states and recalculating individual state scores on the basis of that uniform total. Such a statistical adjustment resulted in a change of totals for each state but, except possibly in cases of very close evaluations, relative rankings would remain the same.[11] Later parts of the present analysis are based on adjusted scores. Omitting fractions (which are statistically insignificant), adjusted scores are shown in Table II and, graphically, in Figure 2.

In addition to recording the adjusted-point score and the rank order for each state in the first two columns of each survey's data, as shown in Table II, the third column indicates the percentage position of each state in each survey. Utility of this calculation flows from the fact that, although the rank-order indicates an even distribution from first-ranked to last, this is not really the case, as is seen from distributions in the first column for each survey. In the 1965 results, for example, "1" and "2" are as far removed from each other as "3" and "4," but in points Uruguay and Costa Rica are separated by one though Chile and Mexico are distant from each other by seventy-eight points. Percentages are those of the spread between lowest and highest possible scores in each survey. If raw scores were to be used, the variation would be that between 170 and 850, but, in view

---

[10] Minima and maxima in raw scores given by a single respondent in the five surveys were: 1945: 750 and 1,229½, a range of 479½; 1950: 798 and 1,184, a range of 386; 1955: 741½ and 1,186, a range of 444½; 1960: 911½ and 1,334½, a range of 423; 1965: 903½ and 1,386½, a range of 483.

[11] Alteration of rankings as between raw and adjusted scores occurred in only one instance in the five surveys. Table I indicates that Costa Rica and Uruguay are tied in 1965 for first rank with 781½ points each. Actually, Costa Rica led by an infinitesimal margin. Total raw scores accumulated by Costa Rica and Uruguay were, respectively, 3,908½ and 3,907½. Inasmuch as the third, fourth, and fifth surveys involved larger numbers of respondents, it was necessary to divide their raw and adjusted scores by, respectively, two, four, and five to make them comparable with results in the first two surveys. In the rounding necessary, this meant that the two states appeared to have identical raw scores in 1965. After adjustments were calculated, as indicated above, Uruguay took first rank with 738 points to 737 for Costa Rica.

Table II

ADJUSTED SCORES BY STATES

	1945			1950			1955			1960			1965		
	Points	Rank	%	Points	Rank	%	Points	Rank	%	Points	Rank	%	Points	Rank	%
Argentina	634	5	63.9	542	8	53.3	513*	7½*	47.8*	652	4	78.0	622	6	71.7
Bolivia	315	18	19.2	335	17	23.4	384	15	29.5	406	16	39.2	377	17	33.6
Brazil	495	11	44.4	612	5	63.4	651	5	67.4	600	7	69.2	539	8	58.8
Chile	745	3	79.4	740	2	81.9	735	3	79.3	688	3	83.7	713	3	85.8
Colombia	718	4	75.6	602	6	62.0	524	6	49.4	602	6	70.1	599	7	68.1
Costa Rica	765	2	82.2	713	3	78.0	773	2	84.7	713	2	90.8	737	2	89.6
Cuba	619	6	61.8	667	4	71.4	513*	7½*	47.8*	422	14	41.7	361	18	31.1
Domin. Rep.	310	19	18.5	318	19	20.9	312	19	19.3	290	18	20.9	396	14	36.6
Ecuador	387	14	29.3	479	9	44.2	498	10	45.7	514	10	56.2	419	12	40.1
El Salvador	417	13	33.5	422	14	36.0	469	11	41.6	468	12	49.0	476	11	49.0
Guatemala	426	12	34.7	478	10	44.1	398	14	31.5	445	13	45.3	408	13	38.4
Haiti	336	16	22.1	331	18	22.8	375	17	28.2	283	19	19.7	233	20	11.2
Honduras	331	17	21.4	378	15	29.6	426	12	35.5	414	15	40.4	395	15	36.4
Mexico	562	7	53.8	570	7	57.4	657	4	68.2	613	5	71.9	635	4	73.7
Nicaragua	349	15	23.9	351	16	25.7	336	18	22.7	341	17	28.9	392	16	35.9
Panama	537	8	50.3	468	11	42.6	505	9	46.7	478	11	50.6	508	10	54.0
Paraguay	304	20	17.6	293	20	17.3	297	20	17.1	261	20	16.3	308	19	22.9
Peru	505	10	45.8	425	13	36.4	378	16	28.7	518	9	56.9	520	9	55.8
Uruguay	804	1	87.7	804	1	91.2	850	1	95.6	767	1	96.2	738	1	89.7
Venezuela	518	9	47.6	448	12	39.7	404	13	32.3	564	8	64.1	625	5	72.1

*Tie

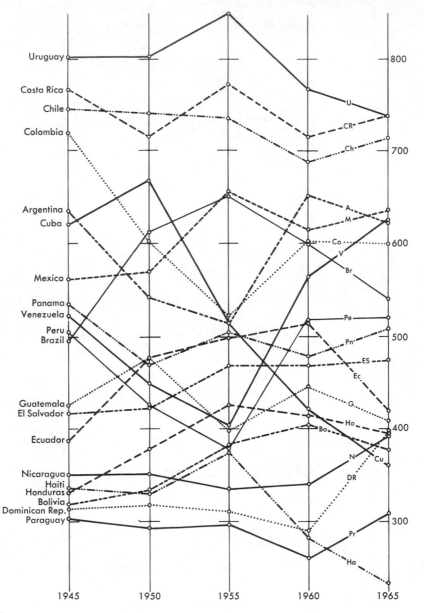

Fig. 2.

of the adjustment of state scores, minima and maxima also need to be adjusted.[12] Using the minimum possible score in each survey as o per cent

[12] Adjusted minima and maxima for the successive surveys were: 1945: 178 and 892; 1950: 173 and 865, 1955: 176 and 881; 1960: 158 and 792; 1965: 161 and 804.

Table III

PERCENTAGE AND POINT CHANGES BY STATES, 1945–1965

	% Change 1945–50	% Change 1950–55	% Change 1955–60	% Change 1960–65	% Change 1945–65	Maximum Point Shift	Net Point Shift 1945–65
Argentina	−10.6	− 5.5	+30.2	− 6.3	+ 7.8	139	− 12
Bolivia	+ 4.2	+ 6.1	+ 9.7	− 5.6	+14.4	91	+ 62
Brazil	+19.0	+ 4.0	+ 1.8	−10.4	+14.4	156	+ 44
Chile	+ 2.5	− 2.6	+ 4.4	+ 2.1	+ 6.4	57	− 32
Colombia	−13.6	−12.6	+20.7	− 2.0	− 7.5	194	−119
Costa Rica	− 4.2	+ 6.7	+ 6.1	− 1.2	+ 7.4	60	− 28
Cuba	+ 9.6	−23.6	− 6.1	−10.6	−30.7	306	−258
Domin. Rep.	+ 2.4	− 1.6	+ 1.6	+15.7	+18.1	106	+ 86
Ecuador	+14.9	+ 1.5	+10.5	−16.1	+10.8	127	+ 32
El Salvador	+ 2.5	+ 5.6	+ 7.4	0.0	+15.5	59	+ 59
Guatemala	+ 9.4	−12.6	+13.8	− 6.9	+ 3.7	80	− 18
Haiti	+ .7	+ 5.4	− 8.5	− 8.5	−10.9	142	−103
Honduras	+ 8.2	+ 5.9	+ 4.9	− 4.0	+15.0	95	+ 64
Mexico	+ 3.6	+10.8	+ 3.7	+ 1.8	+19.9	95	+ 73
Nicaragua	+ 1.8	− 3.0	+ 6.2	+ 7.0	+12.0	56	+ 43
Panama	− 7.7	+ 4.1	+ 3.9	+ 3.4	+ 3.7	69	− 29
Paraguay	− .3	− .2	− .8	+ 6.6	+ 6.3	47	+ 4
Peru	− 9.4	− 7.7	+28.2	− 1.1	+10.0	142	+ 15
Uruguay	+ 3.5	+ 4.4	+ .6	− 6.5	+ 2.0	112	− 66
Venezuela	− 7.9	− 7.4	+31.8	+ 8.0	+24.5	221	+107

and the maximum as 100 per cent, appropriate distribution of adjusted point scores can be calculated, as shown in the third column for each survey. Especially for the 1960 survey but in a few instances in earlier surveys, a seeming anomaly can be noted by comparing the second and third columns. In the case of six states in the 1960 survey, the rank position declined from that of 1955 but the percentage increased. The explanation lies in the considerably higher total scores allotted by respondents in 1960 over those assigned in 1955.

The first four columns of Table III (derived from Table II) indicate percentage changes by states for successive quinquennia of the surveys. The fifth column combines these and shows the net percentage change over twenty years. The sixth column reflects maximum point shifts by states through the five surveys, and the last column indicates the net point change between first and fifth surveys, i.e., between 1945 and 1965.

Even a cursory examination of Table II reveals the tendency of certain states to remain in relatively the same ranking in successive surveys. This is illustrated in a different way by determination of the respective numbers of evaluations of excellent, good, average, poor, and insignificant (A

Table IV

DISTRIBUTION OF EVALUATIONS BY STATES

	Excellent	Good	Average	Poor	Insignificant
Argentina	558 (216)	767 (302)	407 (193)	130 (39)	88 (0)
Bolivia	46 (17)	202 (75)	538 (220)	772 (320)	392 (118)
Brazil	310 (97)	713 (249)	723 (303)	177 (91)	27 (10)
Chile	874 (380)	805 (279)	250 (88)	20 (3)	1 (0)
Colombia	328 (123)	773 (315)	680 (263)	142 (48)	27 (1)
Costa Rica	1009 (446)	783 (272)	152 (32)	6 (0)	0 (0)
Cuba	208 (81)	450 (114)	514 (131)	363 (143)	415 (281)
Domin. Rep.	48 (17)	178 (78)	517 (283)	595 (294)	612 (78)
Ecuador	75 (20)	337 (81)	825 (316)	580 (277)	133 (56)
El Salvador	92 (43)	347 (131)	881 (381)	526 (179)	104 (16)
Guatemala	58 (18)	218 (73)	769 (293)	761 (326)	144 (40)
Haiti	34 (20)	107 (35)	276 (50)	578 (125)	955 (520)
Honduras	49 (11)	164 (67)	718 (291)	790 (320)	229 (61)
Mexico	463 (215)	837 (326)	525 (186)	99 (22)	26 (1)
Nicaragua	41 (22)	145 (70)	594 (268)	799 (320)	371 (70)
Panama	129 (53)	449 (185)	861 (354)	425 (141)	86 (17)
Paraguay	22 (14)	90 (45)	305 (150)	769 (306)	764 (235)
Peru	135 (71)	386 (178)	865 (354)	444 (138)	120 (9)
Uruguay	1272 (473)	586 (226)	85 (48)	7 (3)	0 (0)
Venezuela	267 (156)	667 (357)	692 (212)	221 (25)	103 (0)

through E) allotted the several states in total on the five surveys. The sixty-one respondents participating in from one to five surveys gave each state a total of 1,950 evaluations (in chronological order for the five surveys, they were 150, 150, 300, 600, and 750). If a given state had received from every respondent in each survey an evaluation of B, it then would have had 1,950 B's and no other evaluations. The actual distribution is reflected in Table IV. Figures in parentheses indicate distribution for the 1965 survey alone.

Nearly as large a number of possibilities—1,500—was presented by the five surveys for total concentration of evaluations or partial or complete distribution by the respondents. In other words, all respondents could evaluate a given criterion as applied to a particular state as poor, or, on the other hand, their evaluations could wholly or partially cover the range from excellent to insignificant. The calculation is a test of how like-minded the respondents are; the answer is: they are not. Table V indicates the nature of the spread or concentration of evaluations in the respective surveys (with statistics for 1965 alone given in parentheses). In 197 instances, a considerable majority of them in 1960 and 1965 because of the larger numbers of respondents, evaluations represented the whole gamut from A to E inclusive (Column 5). In only seven instances in the five surveys were all respondents agreed on their evaluations for a specific criterion applied to a given state (Column 1). All respondents were in accord in 1950 that civilian supremacy over the military in Cuba should be rated as good and that progress toward free elections in the Dominican Republic was insignificant; in 1955, all concurred in adjudging that freedom of party organization and operation in the Dominican Republic was insignificant and that Uruguay's position in regard to freedom of expression, freedom of elections, nature of party organization, and civilian supremacy should be rated excellent. No unanimity in evaluations was shown in 1945, 1960, or 1965.

Spread of evaluations over two, three, or four ratings, not necessarily contiguous (i.e., A and B; B and C; B, C, and D; etc.) reflected all the variation shown in Table V. Like-mindedness was least with respect to (1) Panama, in which case twenty-two of the seventy-five evaluations reflected the complete range of ratings and thirty-seven more represented a spread over four possibilities, and (2) El Salvador, which showed a complete distribution of evaluations in seventeen instances and a spread over four ratings in forty-six other cases. Concurrence of viewpoint was most in evidence with regard to Uruguay, Costa Rica, and Chile; it was doubtless not coincidence that those three were uniformly regarded as the most democratic of the Latin American states.

Analysis of the data is possible also with respect to the criteria used as well as the state involved. Any consensus revealed may give clues to the direction and tempo of shifts occurring among the various components

Table V

CONCENTRATION OR SPREAD IN EVALUATION, BY STATES

	1	2	3	4	5
Argentina	0 (0)	11 (0)	28 (7)	30 (8)	6 (0)
Bolivia	0 (0)	6 (0)	29 (4)	29 (7)	11 (4)
Brazil	0 (0)	6 (0)	33 (3)	28 (7)	8 (5)
Chile	0 (0)	15 (0)	47 (12)	12 (3)	1 (0)
Colombia	0 (0)	10 (0)	29 (4)	30 (10)	6 (1)
Costa Rica	0 (0)	27 (7)	45 (8)	3 (0)	0 (0)
Cuba	1 (0)	8 (0)	23 (4)	24 (4)	19 (7)
Dominican Republic	2 (0)	12 (0)	19 (0)	25 (8)	17 (7)
Ecuador	0 (0)	1 (0)	24 (1)	39 (11)	11 (3)
El Salvador	0 (0)	0 (0)	12 (1)	46 (9)	17 (5)
Guatemala	0 (0)	3 (0)	26 (0)	31 (11)	15 (4)
Haiti	0 (0)	12 (3)	33 (6)	21 (2)	9 (4)
Honduras	0 (0)	0 (0)	24 (1)	38 (13)	13 (1)
Mexico	0 (0)	3 (0)	33 (9)	29 (5)	10 (1)
Nicaragua	0 (0)	3 (0)	25 (0)	36 (9)	11 (6)
Panama	0 (0)	0 (0)	16 (1)	37 (6)	22 (8)
Paraguay	0 (0)	9 (0)	38 (1)	19 (9)	9 (5)
Peru	0 (0)	4 (0)	25 (1)	40 (11)	6 (3)
Uruguay	4 (0)	36 (1)	29 (12)	6 (2)	0 (0)
Venezuela	0 (0)	1 (0)	24 (5)	44 (10)	6 (0)

of Latin American democracy. Table VI reflects the points attained by each criterion in successive surveys, the corresponding ranks, and point changes for appropriate periods. The same data are shown graphically in Figure 3. Scrutiny of the shifts as seen by successive panels of specialists shows interesting trends that can now be backed up by measurable methods, although perhaps only gross deductions are justifiable at this stage.

Insofar as the cumulation of evaluations of excellent, good, etc., is concerned, it presumably stands to reason that such distribution, as it affects the criteria, would show less divergence than as applied to the states. The distribution for the five surveys is indicated in Table VII, with that for the fifth survey alone being shown in parentheses in each case. Concentration or spread of evaluations, as applied to criteria, is presented in Table VIII, analogous to Table V affecting the states; 1965 survey results are indicated in parentheses. Implications of Table VIII are that respondents found disagreement easiest with respect to the state of internal unity and the absence or presence of foreign domination; the two criteria represented, respectively, complete spreads in twenty-eight and twenty-seven instances.

CHANGES IN EVALUATIONS, BY CRITERIA, 1945–1965

Criteria	1945		1950			1955			1960					Change in Points 1960–65	Change in Points 1945–65	% Gain 1945–65
	Points	Rank	Points	Rank	Change in Points, 1945–50	Points	Rank	Change in Points, 1950–55	Points	Rank	Change in Points, 1955–60	Points	Rank			
Educational level	521	15	586	6	+65	562	8	−24	590	13	+28	609	10	+19	+88	16.9
Standard of living	525	13	563	11	+38	559	9	− 4	571	15	+12	573	14	+ 2	+48	9.1
Internal unity	623	4	639	3	+16	627	3	−12	666	4	+39	636	4	−30	+13	2.1
Political maturity	561	8	576	8	+15	582	6	+ 6	617	10	+35	621	8	+ 4	+60	10.7
Lack of foreign domination	659	2	669	2	+10	686	2	+17	724	2	+38	729	2	+ 5	+70	10.6
Freedom of speech, etc.	650	3	609	5	−41	605	5	− 4	689	3	+84	680	3	− 9	+30	4.6
Free elections	552	9	538	15	−14	541	12	+ 3	659	5	+118	628*	5½*	−31	+76	13.8
Free party organization	546	10	548	14	+ 2	533	14	−15	630	7	+97	627	7	− 3	+81	14.8
Judicial independence	574	5	581	7	+ 7	547	10	−34	620	9	+73	615	9	− 5	+41	7.1
Government funds	523	14	552	12	+29	544	11	− 8	602	12	+58	597	12	− 5	+74	14.1
Social legislation	562	7	622	4	+60	609	4	−13	629	8	+20	628*	5½*	− 1	+66	11.7
Civilian supremacy	567	6	568	10	+ 1	521	15	−47	632	6	+111	600	11	−32	+33	5.8
Lack of ecclesiastical control	732	1	717	1	−15	722	1	+ 5	739	1	+17	761	1	+22	+29	4.0
Government administration	539	12	569	9	+30	565	7	− 4	612	11	+47	594	13	−18	+55	10.2
Local government	542	11	551	13	+ 9	540	13	−11	583	14	+43	562	15	−22	+19	3.5

*Tie

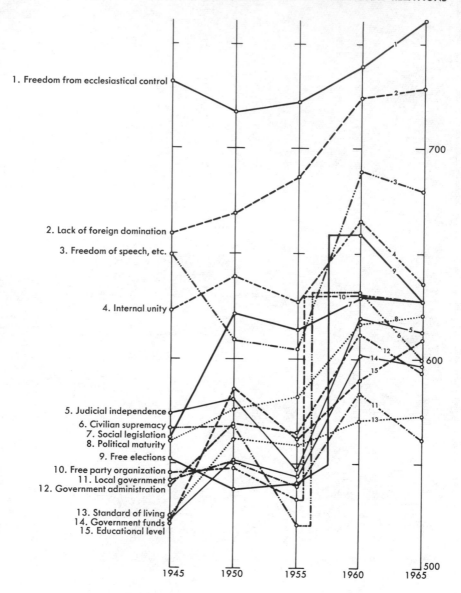

Fig. 3.

Development of a stereotypic point of view is apparently easier with regard to the states than it is respecting the criteria. As Tables VII and IV indicate, only one of the criteria, that on the lack of ecclesiastical influence, shows a disparity between the largest and smallest numbers of evaluations of more than 10:1. In the case of the states, such a ratio is

Table VII

DISTRIBUTION OF EVALUATIONS, BY CRITERIA

	Excellent	Good	Average	Poor	Insignificant
Educational level	342 (139)	496 (198)	742 (319)	692 (256)	328 (88)
Standard of living	136 (56)	548 (214)	918 (367)	734 (267)	264 (96)
Internal unity	391 (144)	668 (243)	824 (323)	547 (231)	170 (59)
Political maturity	377 (169)	548 (197)	737 (293)	651 (253)	287 (88)
Lack of foreign domination	652 (264)	756 (318)	695 (255)	384 (124)	113 (39)
Freedom of speech, etc.	688 (276)	560 (221)	589 (241)	415 (151)	348 (111)
Free elections	556 (234)	510 (186)	551 (228)	494 (191)	489 (161)
Free party organization	446 (182)	574 (245)	602 (241)	500 (188)	478 (144)
Judicial independence	367 (157)	610 (233)	675 (280)	556 (188)	392 (142)
Government funds	243 (94)	553 (224)	858 (357)	602 (224)	344 (101)
Social legislation	295 (117)	669 (269)	850 (331)	563 (202)	223 (81)
Civilian supremacy	481 (212)	474 (153)	589 (217)	583 (259)	473 (159)
Lack of ecclesiastical control	715 (320)	830 (296)	737 (275)	251 (89)	67 (20)
Government administration	175 (67)	672 (259)	893 (350)	577 (223)	283 (101)
Local government	154 (62)	538 (202)	917 (339)	655 (274)	336 (123)

Table VIII

CONCENTRATION OR SPREAD IN EVALUATIONS, BY CRITERIA

	1	2	3	4	5
Educational level	0 (0)	20 (1)	52 (8)	28 (11)	0 (0)
Standard of living	0 (0)	21 (1)	50 (8)	29 (11)	0 (0)
Internal unity	0 (0)	6 (1)	25 (5)	41 (7)	28 (7)
Political maturity	0 (0)	18 (2)	30 (3)	42 (12)	10 (3)
Lack of foreign domination	0 (0)	5 (0)	29 (6)	39 (8)	27 (6)
Freedom of speech, etc.	1 (0)	17 (1)	38 (8)	34 (9)	10 (2)
Free elections	2 (0)	18 (1)	33 (6)	35 (8)	12 (5)
Free party organization	2 (0)	11 (2)	35 (1)	39 (13)	13 (4)
Judicial independence	0 (0)	6 (0)	40 (6)	40 (7)	14 (7)
Government funds	0 (0)	5 (0)	27 (3)	47 (7)	21 (10)
Social legislation	0 (0)	8 (0)	51 (5)	35 (12)	6 (3)
Civilian supremacy	2 (0)	16 (1)	31 (3)	36 (11)	15 (5)
Lack of ecclesiastical control	0 (0)	7 (1)	35 (6)	37 (8)	21 (5)
Government administration	0 (0)	6 (0)	40 (8)	45 (8)	9 (4)
Local government	0 (0)	3 (0)	45 (4)	41 (13)	11 (3)

exceeded in fifteen instances. It would seem a reasonable deduction that "images" generally held in common, whether favorable or unfavorable, are more easily formed with regard to the states than the criteria.

The question is also raised: how are the criteria interrelated, what is their correlation, what impact does one have on others? Intuitive answers are possible in some degree, but they are often unsatisfactory, even to the person who gives them: they leave the frustration of lack of proof of the "hunch." With only fifteen criteria involved in the present analysis, correlations could not be made with the impressiveness of those reached in the comprehensive Yale Political Data Program, for example, an operation that involved many scores of kinds of data. And yet, with the use of a chi-square formula, supplemented with determination of correlations, as given by the coefficient of contingency, a satisfactory measure of the interrelationship of the various criteria as seen by the respondents can be ascertained.[13] Values of the correlations are indicated in Table IX. The upper right diagonal half of the table gives the chi-square values for each pair of criteria; the lower left half gives corresponding values of the coefficient of contingency correlation. Criterion numbers, at top and side for columns and rows, are those identifying the criteria as given on p. 256.

High values in the lower half of the table indicate a high degree of

[13] A more complete description of the process of determining correlations, as used in the 1960 survey, is given in Fitzgibbon and Johnson, op. cit., pp. 522–25.

Table IX

CORRELATIONS AMONG CRITERIA

Criteria	1	2	3	4	5	6	7	8	9	10	11	12	13	14	15
1		1362.3	926.8	1185.3	282.1	849.1	720.2	683.3	794.6	770.1	892.9	611.8	318.5	857.8	737.6
2	.759		875.7	1033.1	271.5	641.9	570.7	542.5	748.9	764.9	777.5	483.5	309.5	834.6	754.3
3	.694	.683		1330.2	280.2	550.4	533.0	572.3	531.0	627.4	685.2	614.0	407.7	715.2	598.3
4	.736	.713	.756		382.9	979.4	936.2	858.4	885.8	882.5	980.2	797.4	375.3	990.6	561.3
5	.469	.462	.468	.526		587.8	410.5	337.0	502.8	414.0	265.4	302.5	371.6	376.2	361.8
6	.678	.625	.596	.703	.608		1532.1	1351.3	1254.0	880.7	739.4	764.1	460.7	795.7	948.8
7	.647	.603	.590	.695	.539	.778		1650.9	1273.4	888.8	779.8	1055.6	403.9	867.2	888.7
8	.637	.593	.603	.680	.502	.758	.789		1159.6	835.0	709.2	854.5	325.5	794.6	849.0
9	.665	.654	.589	.685	.578	.746	.748	.733		1145.3	990.0	710.6	471.3	1130.3	1192.1
10	.660	.658	.621	.685	.541	.684	.686	.675	.731		1045.7	645.6	387.5	1214.0	1033.4
11	.687	.661	.638	.704	.458	.652	.662	.644	.705	.715		577.7	356.2	996.0	821.9
12	.616	.571	.617	.666	.482	.658	.717	.679	.645	.626	.605		293.8	703.2	619.4
13	.491	.486	.538	.522	.520	.562	.536	.496	.566	.528	.512	.477		332.3	351.5
14	.680	.674	.646	.705	.523	.666	.681	.665	.728	.740	.706	.643	.499		1426.7
15	.652	.656	.612	.700	.515	.693	.686	.678	.737	.713	.672	.618	.510	.767	
C averages	.648	.628	.618	.677	.513	.672	.668	.652	.679	.662	.640	.616	.517	.666	.658

correlation. Greatest correlation shown is that between freedom of elections and freedom of party organization and expression; the result is not
unexpected, but the table reveals just how high the respondents feel the
correlation is. Lowest degree of correlation is that between freedom from
foreign domination and the nature of social legislation; these two criteria,
the respondents believe, have little interaction on each other.

Averages for correlation values (C) are shown at the bottom of Table
IX. Again, a high average indicates high correlation. Somewhat surpris-
ingly, the greatest overall correlation is that of judicial independence with
the other criteria. In order following it are: political maturity, freedom of
expression, freedom of elections, governmental administration, attitude
toward public funds, nature of local government, party organization, educational level, social legislation, standard of living, internal unity, civilian
supremacy, freedom from ecclesiastical influence, and freedom from foreign
domination. It should be stressed, however, that these are *averages* of
correlations. Highest individual instances of correlation were between
freedom of election and both freedom of party organization and of expression and between governmental administration and local government.

Continued caution about blind reliance on statistical determination
of correlations is important. As was suggested in the published analysis
of 1960 survey results, "the size of the scores obtained in the chi-square
analysis is no absolute basis for judgment. Rather, the scores act as a guide
to further inquiry. The scores themselves are not nearly so important as
the reason for their occurrence. If intuitive 'hunches' about the analytical
categories can be confirmed statistically, there is every reason to suggest
their continued use. If the statistical procedures tend to contradict well
based intuition then an additional analysis into latent structures and
operative sub-variables may remove the contradiction or reveal errors in
method."

Evaluation sheets sent to respondents for the 1960 and 1965 surveys
included provision for indicating self-assessment as to the respondent's
familiarity with both states and criteria (see Figure 1). From the beginning
of the surveys, many respondents have protested that they were not qualified to pass judgment on certain criteria applied to particular states (the
author, as a participant, it may be added, shares the feeling as it relates
to himself). It was only the author's insistence, on the ground that statistical analysis required complete filling of the sheets, that ultimately
elicited loyal, though reluctant, cooperation in some instances. Unfortunately, no analysis of the "familiarity level" assessments could be undertaken in 1960, but it has been done this time. The computer was
programmed to make a relatively intricate digest of the influence of
familiarity levels on evaluations, but it turned out that a simpler analysis
was in reality more revealing.

As a general conclusion, it may be asserted that those who tend to be

Table X

INFLUENCE OF FAMILIARITY LEVELS ON EVALUATIONS

States	Little		Great	
	A + B	D + E	A + B	D + E
Argentina	15	0	247	15
Bolivia	25	131	21	81
Brazil	34	9	167	38
Chile	15	0	302	2
Colombia	35	18	182	24
Costa Rica	97	0	244	0
Cuba	36	122	57	145
Dominican Republic	15	130	24	80
Ecuador	27	117	23	46
El Salvador	71	93	49	31
Guatemala	16	102	55	81
Haiti	20	275	5	53
Honduras	24	166	17	65
Mexico	0	0	348	17
Nicaragua	26	164	25	56
Panama	32	45	56	33
Paraguay	21	281	11	61
Peru	21	24	93	36
Uruguay	60	0	243	0
Venezuela	33	4	187	2
Totals	623	1,681	2,356	866

Criteria				
1	14	17	115	125
2	0	0	105	163
3	0	0	115	113
4	8	8	178	170
5	0	0	348	79
6	0	0	279	153
7	0	0	289	257
8	0	0	237	178
9	150	154	65	37
10	90	112	45	39
11	45	42	100	61
12	0	0	132	238
13	48	13	162	28
14	69	88	37	40
15	115	242	19	40
Totals	539	676	2,226	1,721

less self-confident in their evaluations, i.e., the respondents who indicate "little" familiarity with a given state or criterion, are harsher or more unfavorable in their evaluations. Ones who are more confident of their acquaintance with particular states or criteria (who recorded "great" familiarity) look more favorably on achievement in the appropriate categories. Results, for 1965, are shown in Table X. The first two columns of figures indicate the numbers of instances in which those who expressed *little* familiarity with the states or the criteria evaluated the one or the other as either excellent or good $(A + B)$ or, on the other hand, poor or insignificant $(D + E)$. The third and fourth columns show the same results on the part of respondents who expressed *great* familiarity with particular states or criteria. It will be noted that in all pairs of additions, for both states and criteria, the totals of unfavorable evaluations are substantially greater than the favorable ones from those who felt little familiarity, but that the reverse is true in all cases for those who consider themselves quite familiar with the states or criteria.

A related area of analysis involved determination, from the 1965 survey, of which states and which criteria appeared to be most familiar to the respondents. This, as shown in Table XI, required only a simple calculation. The first three columns of figures show, for both states and criteria, the numbers of respondents indicating, respectively, little, moderate, or great familiarity. These self-ratings are assigned, respectively, values of one, two, and three points per unit and totals are indicated in the fourth column; ranking then follows in the last column. As might be expected, neighboring Mexico is the state with which most respondents consider themselves familiar, then the ABC countries of South America, and least of all, Paraguay, Haiti, and Honduras. Similarly, respondents collectively regard themselves as most familiar with the criterion of freedom of elections, least so with the nature of local government.

It also seemed worthwhile to attempt to determine the relationship of respondents' professions or approach to Latin America as a factor in the sorts of evaluations they gave. With a sample of no more than fifty (respondents), it would be possible to use only relatively broad categories in order to have subgroups sufficiently large to be statistically significant. The only categories thus possible were (a) those engaged in academic pursuits and (b) all others. The "academics" and "non-academics" numbered, respectively, thirty-six and fourteen. Identifications had to be somewhat arbitrary, inasmuch as in a few cases individuals straddled a professional fence or had had both kinds of careers at one time or another. The panel includes a small group engaged in journalism, several who formerly were in government service, and a very small number who, because of the diversity of their professional interests, would have to be labeled "miscellaneous;" in no case are these subgroups large enough to treat separately from a statistical standpoint. Had circumstances permitted,

Table XI

FAMILIARITY WITH STATES AND CRITERIA

States	Little	Moderate	Great	Points	Rank
Argentina	1	27	22	121	2½
Bolivia	14	27	9	95	13
Brazil	4	25	21	117	4
Chile	2	25	23	121	2½
Colombia	6	23	21	115	5
Costa Rica	7	26	17	110	8½
Cuba	13	21	16	103	10
Dominican Republic	17	23	10	93	14
Ecuador	17	24	9	92	15
El Salvador	22	19	9	87	17
Guatemala	13	23	14	101	11
Haiti	21	25	4	83	19
Honduras	23	18	9	86	18
Mexico	0	17	33	133	1
Nicaragua	20	22	8	88	16
Panama	10	31	9	99	12
Paraguay	25	19	6	81	20
Peru	5	30	15	110	8½
Uruguay	4	29	17	113	6
Venezuela	4	30	16	112	7

Criteria					
1	2	30	18	116	8½
2	0	29	21	121	7
3	0	34	16	116	8½
4	1	25	24	123	6
5	0	22	28	128	3
6	0	22	28	128	3
7	0	15	35	135	1
8	0	23	27	127	5
9	21	23	6	85	14
10	14	30	6	92	13
11	6	32	12	106	11
12	0	22	28	128	3
13	4	34	12	108	10
14	12	32	6	94	12
15	27	19	4	77	15

it would have been interesting and probably desirable to include a selection of Latin Americans among the respondents, though a few are included who (though United States citizens) are of Latin birth or ancestry.

The author would have guessed that those who dwelt in groves of academe would have been more lenient in judgment of Latin American political achievement and that the "hard-boiled" and "practical" men of affairs, in direct professional contact with Latin America, would have viewed the several countries with more jaundiced eyes. That turned out decidedly not to be the case. The approach of the "eggheads" (to label them irreverently) was definitely the more rigorous. To determine the differentials at all accurately, it was necessary to calculate what, for want of a better term, can be called a "respondent index" for each survey participant. This was based on the total letter evaluations made by each respondent. They varied from a high of 1.10680 (most critical or rigorous) to a low of .72124 (most lenient or favorable).

Of the fourteen non-academic participants, two came above the median point, twelve below it. Twenty-three of the academic respondents were above the median, thirteen below that point. . . . Perhaps there are deductions to be made from such distribution but the author shies away in timidity from making them.

The problem of comparing objective and subjective measurements, i.e., those making use of census-type data and, on the other hand, the evaluations of specialists, is complex and, at this stage of development of analyses, not entirely satisfactory or reliable. The Lipset and Almond-Coleman studies, cited above, employed a limited number of indices of development. The precise relevance of those, or a larger number, to the aspects whose measurement is sought, is difficult to be assured of.

It seemed desirable, at any rate, to select as large a number of indices as could be found which presumptively contributed to improvement of the human situation in Latin America, on the assumption that that in turn would be conducive to democratic development. The relationship here is indirect and tenuous, but perhaps as good as can be devised, granted the reliance on objective data only. As a source of information, the *Statistical Abstract of Latin America* for 1963 was used.[14] The writer selected from it thirty-three indices over which human endeavor has some ability to control the results, and each with statistics for at least half of the Latin American states. They divided broadly into five categories: demographic, economic, social, cultural, and political. In some instances, indicated below by the characterization "reversed," a low figure reflects high achievement, e.g., for infant death rate or illiteracy.

---

[14] The *Statistical Abstract of Latin America* for 1964 (copyright, 1965) was available but in some ways was less satisfactory than that for the preceding year. Many of the data are carried over unchanged from the 1963 issue and certain indices used in the 1963 issue are omitted from that for 1964.

Table XII

	No. of Indices Applicable	Total of Percentages	Average of Percentages	Objective Rank	Subjective Rank 1960	Subjective Rank 1965
Argentina	32	2,347	73	2	4	6
Bolivia	29	1,308	45	14	16	17
Brazil	30	1,437	48	10	7	8
Chile	31	1,954	63	5	3	3
Colombia	31	1,627	52	9	6	7
Costa Rica	30	1,695	56.5	7	2	2
Cuba	23	1,656	72.0	4	14	18
Domin. Rep.	24	948	40	18	18	14
Ecuador	30	1,232	41.1	16	10	12
El Salvador	28	1,320	47.1	12	12	11
Guatemala	32	1,311	41	17	13	13
Haiti	26	693	27	20	19	20
Honduras	28	989	35	19	15	15
Mexico	31	1,681	54	8	5	4
Nicaragua	23	1,056	46	13	17	16
Panama	28	1,585	56.6	6	11	10
Paraguay	23	1,021	44	15	20	19
Peru	29	1,372	47.3	11	9	9
Uruguay	17	1,253	74	1	1	1
Venezuela	31	2,240	72.3	3	8	5

The indices used were: *demographic:* (1) crude death rate (reversed); (2) infant death rate (reversed); (3) annual percentage increase in population (reversed); (4) life expectancy of males at birth; (5) urban population as a percentage of the total; *economic:* (6) percentage of economically active population in manufacturing; (7) per capita energy consumption; (8) motor vehicles per 1,000 persons; (9) miles of road per 1,000 square miles of area; (10) miles of railway per 1,000 square miles of area; (11) percentage of government receipts from direct taxes; (12) percentage of government receipts from customs (reversed); (13) annual per capita growth rate of GDP; (14) per capita share of national income in U.S. dollars; (15) per capita currency circulation in U.S. dollars; *social:* (16) number of persons per physician (reversed); (17) number of persons per hospital bed (reversed); (18) number of persons per dentist (reversed); (19) per capita daily caloric intake; (20) per capita production of quality meats; (21) per capita production of milk; (22) percentage of dwellings with electricity; (23) telephones per 1,000 persons; (24) percentage of government budget used for public health and welfare; *cultural:* (25) illiteracy (reversed); (26) school enrollment as percentage of school-age population; (27) per capita expenditures for education in U.S. dollars; (28) percentage of national income used for education; (29) percentage of central government budget used for education; (30) daily newspaper circulation per 1,000 persons; (31) per capita frequency of cinema attendance; (32) radio receivers per 1,000 persons; *political:* (33) percentage of population voting.

The best performance, either direct or reversed, was treated as 100 per cent and other percentages calculated therefrom. Totals of percentages for each state, for all indices for which information was available, were then determined and an average worked out (taking into account the varying number of indices applicable to each state). The detailed analyses were much too comprehensive to be reproduced here, although a summary is shown in Table XII. For comparison's sake, the specialists' state rankings in 1960 and 1965 (from Table II) are included. Inasmuch as the time lag of reproduction of data in the *Statistical Abstract* is probably at least a year or two "after the fact," comparison of objective rankings with subjective rankings for 1960 is likely to be more valid than with those for 1965.

These views, however, purport to give total pictures of Latin America, either objective or subjective. And the pictures, assuming them to be photographs, are not, as it were, taken from the same angle. It would consequently be better, if possible, to get a more accurate comparison of objective and subjective measurements. Of the fifteen criteria used in these surveys, the first two—the educational level and the standard of living—are the ones which lend themselves best to comparison with the census-type data. For a more accurate comparison, then, the data included

Table XIII

	Educational Level						Standard of Living					
	Objective		Subjective				Objective		Subjective			
			1960		1965				1960		1965	
	%	Rank	%	Rank	%	Rank	%	Rank	%	Rank	%	Rank
Argentina	62	7	99	3	99	2	91	2	100	1	100	1
Bolivia	48	12	42	18	42	18	23	20	41	18	39	19
Brazil	67	5	67	8	69	9	36	10	75	9	72	7.5
Chile	72	4	90	4	89	4	55.8	4	79	5	81	6
Colombia	54	10	74.9	7	74	7	46	6	76	8	72	7.5
Costa Rica	77.6	3	100	1.5	97	3	56.2	5	93	3	93	3
Cuba	65	6	75.1	6	82	5	61	3	77	7	66	10
Dominican Republic	47	14	52	13	52	13	24	19	68.2	10	55.7	14
Ecuador	47.2	13	51	14	49	15	29	15	58	14	50	17
El Salvador	41	17	59	11	59	11	32.4	11	63	12	64	11
Guatemala	35	18	48	16	47	16.5	28.7	16	53.5	16	54	15
Haiti	22	20	29	20	24	20	30	13	31	20	26	20
Honduras	41.6	16	44	17	47	16.5	31.7	12	43	17	52	16
Mexico	52	11	80	5	78	6	40	9	81	4	82	4.5
Nicaragua	34	19	49	15	51	14	28	17	54.1	15	56.3	13
Panama	79	1	63	9	66	10	41	8	67.6	11	68	9
Paraguay	58	8	34	19	41.5	19	29.5	14	41	19	48	18
Peru	42.5	15	56	12	56	12	26	18	62	13	60	12
Uruguay	55	9	100	1.5	100	1	94	1	95	2	98	2
Venezuela	78.4	2	62	10	73	8	45	7	78	6	82	4.5

in Indices 25–29, as listed above, were compared with 1960 and 1965 evaluations on Criterion 1 (educational level) and the data in Indices 19–23 above with respective evaluations on Criterion 2 (standard of living). Results are shown in Table XIII. It is not possible to compare objective and subjective percentages in the table, inasmuch as they were calculated differently; percentages do serve the purpose, however, of indicating relative differentials among states by either the objective or subjective measurement. Comparison of rank orders is possible and it indicates, especially insofar as the educational level is concerned, that little correlation exists between the objective and subjective approaches; correlation is somewhat better in respect to measurement of the standard of living, although considerable discrepancies are in evidence, particularly with regard to the Dominican Republic, Haiti, and one or two other states. The author trusts it is not merely rationalization which leads him to believe that the subjective measurements may be more accurate than the objective. It is, of course, very possible that the objective indices available did not give an accurate or complete profile of a given aspect of a state, but it is difficult to believe, for example, that Argentina would have no better than seventh or Uruguay ninth rank among Latin American states in respect to the educational level.

Overall conclusions to be drawn from surveys of this kind are, and perhaps will always have to be, tentative. As has been stressed repeatedly, it is not democratic achievement per se that is being measured, but rather attitudes regarding democratic achievement. This may be a distinction without a difference, but the distinction needs to be made. With that caveat, a number of deductions may be indicated. Three Latin American states, Uruguay, Costa Rica, and Chile, have uniformly occupied the first three rankings over a twenty-year period. Paraguay, Haiti, Nicaragua, and Bolivia have regularly been included among the lowest six states throughout five surveys; the Dominican Republic and Honduras were in that unenviable bottom half dozen four times each. No state has yet "cracked" the monopoly of the top three; Peru and Cuba have, once each, been in the lowest bracket, for which blame is probably due, respectively, to Odría and Castro. As is revealed by percentage measurements in Table II, states show a tendency to "bunch" in the successive surveys. Such grouping is indicated in Table XIV. Gaps between groups are in no case less than 5 per cent.

Greatest change in democratic ranking naturally takes place among the states that are consistently neither at the top nor the bottom. The plummeting of Cuba from fourth rank in 1950 to eighteenth in 1965 is most spectacular. Venezuela's improvement from twelfth rank in 1950 to fifth in 1965 is also significant.

With regard to conclusions to be drawn from scrutiny of the data involving the criteria, the immediate postwar half decade appeared to

Table XIV

		Bunching		
1945	1950	1955	1960	1965
Uruguay	Uruguay	Uruguay	Uruguay	Uruguay
Costa Rica			Costa Rica	Costa Rica
Chile	Chile	Costa Rica		Chile
Colombia	Costa Rica	Chile	Chile	
	Cuba		Argentina	Mexico
Argentina		Mexico		Venezuela
Cuba	Brazil	Brazil	Mexico	Argentina
	Colombia		Colombia	Colombia
Mexico	Mexico	Colombia	Brazil	
Panama	Argentina	Argentina	Venezuela	Brazil
Venezuela		Cuba		Peru
Peru	Ecuador	Panama	Peru	Panama
Brazil	Guatemala	Ecuador	Ecuador	El Salvador
	Panama	El Salvador	Panama	
Guatemala	Venezuela		El Salvador	Ecuador
El Salvador	Peru	Honduras	Guatemala	Guatemala
Ecuador	El Salvador	Venezuela	Cuba	Dom. Rep.
		Guatemala	Honduras	Honduras
Nicaragua	Honduras	Bolivia	Bolivia	Nicaragua
Haiti	Nicaragua	Peru		Bolivia
Honduras	Bolivia	Haiti		Cuba
Bolivia	Haiti		Nicaragua	
Dom. Rep.	Dom. Rep.	Nicaragua	Dom. Rep.	Paraguay
Paraguay	Paraguay	Dom. Rep.	Haiti	
		Paraguay	Paraguay	Haiti

reflect improvement in the overall situation, especially with regard to such matters as the educational level, social legislation, and the standard of living. Conditions in the first half ow the 1950's deteriorated, as one after another dictator consolidated a hold on power. The last half of the same decade witnessed a remarkable improvement, as one by one the *caudillos* fell from power, almost always violently. The quinquennium just past has written a balance sheet with both red- and black-ink entries. For the period of two decades, however, the respondents are of the opinion that progress has been general and in some ways remarkable. More than half of the criteria employed showed better than 10 per cent improvement during the twenty years.

The nature of the political process in Latin America is subtle and fluid, as, indeed, it is everywhere. Latin America possesses enough of a common denominator to make analysis of changes in that whole community of states useful and perhaps significant. No one realizes better than the present writer that the approach and methodology used in the current series of surveys are subject to improvement. They do, however, provide an in-depth attitudinal and judgmental consensus by a panel of specialists whose expertise cannot be challenged.[15] Presumably the technique could be extended to other areas, perhaps Africa and Asia, although the common denominator would doubtless be less substantial in both of those continents.

[15] Cf. Charles Wolf, Jr., "The Political Effects of Economic Programs," *op. cit.*, p. 20.

9

Mathematical and Statistical Models

Because they do not necessarily involve quantification, mathematical models might more appropriately be discussed in a book concerned with theory-building. However, since numbers frequently find themselves being attached to even the most austere and impractical of models and since many writers treat—and attack—mathematics and quantification in the same breath,[1] it seems that a discussion of the matter in the present context will serve some purpose.

Most theorizing in international relations is expressed in verbal terms and the principles and insights of a theory are linked therefore (if at all) by the rules followed in verbal logic: if A is more important than B and B is more important than C, then logic insists that A must be more important than C—a relationship which was there all the time, of course, but one which may only have been clearly seen after logical rules were applied. Other internally consistent sets of rules exist in mathematics and statistics which, if appropriately imposed on a problem, can be rewarding. For example, Kato, in the article reprinted in chapter 6, finds that certain verbal notions he has about foreign aid can be expressed in terms of the multiple regression model of statistics. When translated into this form, the logic of the model gives him a method for testing the validity of his ideas.

As noted in the Russett article reprinted in chapter 2, some of the

---

[1] For example, Stanley H. Hoffmann, "International Relations: The Long Road to Theory," *World Politics*, Vol. 11 (April, 1959), p. 359; and Hedley Bull, "International Theory: The Case for a Classical Approach," *ibid.*, Vol. 18 (April, 1966), pp. 372–73.

basic concepts in the proliferating literature on deterrence can be expressed simply but fruitfully in a version of the economists' expected utility model. A useful verbal description of the deterrence notion is Kenneth Waltz's: "A state will use force to attain its goals if, after assessing the prospects for success, it values those goals more than it values the pleasures of peace." [2]

Translated into expected utility terms, this deterrence calculation states that a would-be attacker will be deterred from starting a war when the following holds:

$$V_v \cdot p_v + V_d (1 - p_v) < V_{sq}$$

where V_v = the value to him if he is victorious in the war
V_d = the value to him (negative?) if he is defeated in the war
V_{sq} = the value of the status quo (the value to him if there is no war)
p_v = the probability that he will be victorious in the war.

The symbol "<" means "is less than" and the quantity $(1 - p_v)$ is the probability of defeat. The expected utility model says then: to find which of two alternatives (starting a war or not starting a war) is the most preferable, determine the value to the decision-maker of each of the outcomes under each alternative (V_v and V_d for the war alternative, V_{sq} for the non-war alternative), multiply each value by the probability that it will be attained (p_v for victory, $[1 - p_v]$ for defeat; the probability of "attaining" the status quo value if there is no war is of course unity), add up the products, and compare the aggregate results for the two alternatives.[3]

To assure that there will be no war, the quantity to the left of the inequality should be kept smaller than the value to the right. To deter a would-be attacker, then, one must seek (a) to make the value of victory as low as possible (e.g., by threatening to use a scorched earth policy), (b) to make the value of defeat as low as possible (e.g., by threatening to pursue a Carthaginian peace), (c) to make the probability of victory as low as possible (e.g., by having a very good military force), and (d) to make the value of the status quo as high as possible (e.g., by giving economic aid—sometimes known as "deterrence by reward").

That last sentence may seem to make sense, despite all its parentheses, but in fact the mathematics of the inequality says that it is not quite true. Any decrease in p_v means an increase in $(1 - p_v)$. Suppose then that the attacker is a masochist who prefers defeat to victory, that is, that V_d is greater than V_v for him. Then to deter, one wishes to make the probability

[2] *Man, the State and War* (New York: Columbia, 1954), p. 160.
[3] For an elaborate and provocative effort to apply—and quantify—a similar approach to the Israeli decision to go to war in 1956 (the conclusion is that it was a good idea), see Barry M. Blechman, "The Quantitative Evaluation of Foreign Policy Alternatives: Sinai, 1956," *Journal of Conflict Resolution*, Vol. 10 (December, 1966), pp. 408–26.

of victory as *high* as possible. That case may seem rather bizarre and the relation—after it is pointed out—rather obvious and trivial, but the point is that such unexpected findings, ones that can escape the analyst when a problem with numerous variables is kept only in verbal form, frequently emerge when a mathematical model is applied.

The deterrence notion has also been expressed this way: "a confrontation of superior force, if accurately perceived by the responsible decision-makers, will deter the weaker state from waging an avoidable war."[4] A glance at the mathematical expression discloses that this verbal pronouncement stresses only the p_v term. Clearly, even if this term were very low in the calculations of the decision-makers, they might still rationally opt for war under a number of circumstances. They might conclude, for example, that the war is worth the risk because the status quo has become intolerable, because they have little to lose, or because they have a great deal to gain.

A similar analysis could be applied to the deterrence of crime where V_v would stand for the value to the criminal if his crime is successful, V_d for the value to him if he is caught and convicted, and p_v for the probability that he will be successful. Proponents of capital punishment stress the necessity of making V_d as negative as possible to deter crime. But one would also be able generally to reduce crime by decreasing the gain the criminal can expect from a successful crime, by increasing the chances that he will be caught, or by making it worth his while to go straight by getting him a lucrative job or simply by giving him money.[5]

As in any exercise devoted to generalization or theory-building, the use of mathematical models involves simplification and abstraction. It is always hoped that restricting assumptions can be relaxed and that more complexity can be introduced into the model so that it more closely approximates reality. In this respect, mathematical theories have an advantage over verbal ones because mathematics becomes complex more gracefully. Verbal theories, as layers of complexity are added, tend to become vague and incoherent; their meaning gets lost and the relationship among concepts becomes blurred and entangled.

The mathematical expression of the simple deterrence calculation, described above, is already richer than the verbal expression in that the relevant variables are more specifically identified and their interrelationships are more precisely delimited. Complexity is readily increased. The

---

[4] Dina A. Zinnes, Robert C. North, and Howard E. Koch, Jr., "Capability, Threat, and the Outbreak of War," in James N. Rosenau (ed.), *International Politics and Foreign Policy* (New York: Free Press, 1961), p. 470.
[5] Even such a devoted underworld figure as Captain Macheath can be expected to become solidly middle class when, in Brecht's "Three-Penny Opera," he is released from jail and "raised, together with his heirs to the rank of peer and presented Castle Marmarel and a yearly income of 10,000 pounds till the day of his death."

problem of deterring, say, the Soviets from attacking Western Europe is only partly bound up with their calculations about victory or defeat in a war there. A more important element in their calculation must be whether there *will be* a war if they attack, that is, whether the United States will actually risk its own cities in a nuclear war to defend Europe. Thus two other variables enter the calculation: p_w, the probability that there will be war with the United States, and V_{nw}, the value to the Soviets if they attack Europe and the United States decides not to defend it. The calculation then becomes

$$V_{nw} (1 - p_w) + [V_v \cdot p_v + V_d (1 - p_v)] \cdot p_w < V_{sq}$$

That may not *look* graceful, but a verbal expression would likely be hopelessly cluttered.

The element, p_w, can be further elaborated to include two subconsiderations: the probability the United States will *want* to wage war (a psychological estimate of morale and determination) and the probability the United States will be *able* to wage war (an estimate of how crippling a surprise strike against American retaliatory power could be). Also, each value is a function both of gain and cost and these elements can be separated out.

The reprinted article by Daniel Ellsberg approaches the problem of deterrence from a different angle. Ellsberg is concerned with the interrelated calculation made by the great powers about whether they should wait with their nuclear weapons thus risking a strike by the other side, or whether they should lash out before the opposition has a chance to strike. In part, his analysis is an elaboration of the V_{sq} term. The whole problem is similar in many respects to the dilemma of 1914, discussed in Holsti's article reprinted in chapter 7, when waiting seemed too costly to be tolerated. Other work in the area of deterrence applying modeling procedures has been done by Douglas Hunter who has elaborated Ellsberg's ideas and applied some of them to the problem of deterrence of the Japanese in 1941,[6] and by Glenn Snyder, who has found game theoretic formulation a useful aid to thinking in this area.[7]

Modeling of a similar sort has found application, mostly by economists, in several areas of interest in international relations. Among these

[6] Douglas E. Hunter, "Application of Deterrence Theory to the 1941 Japanese Decision for War," Security Studies Project, UCLA, 1964. See also Bruce M. Russett, "Pearl Harbor: Deterrence Theory and Decision Theory," *Journal of Peace Research*, (1967), pp. 89–106.
[7] Glenn H. Snyder, *Deterrence and Defense* (Princton: Princeton University Press, 1961), especially Chapters 1 and 6. See also John R. Raser, "Deterrence Research," *Journal of Peace Research*, (1966), pp. 297–327. For other applications of game theory, see Morton A. Kaplan, *System and Process in International Politics* (New York: Wiley, 1957) and William H. Riker, *The Theory of Political Coalitions* (New Haven: Yale, 1962).

have been arms reduction,[8] patterns of conflict,[9] nuclear power dynamics,[10] nuclear war,[11] alliance patterns,[12] the duration and magnitude of wars,[13] and the cold war itself.[14]

A number of efforts have been made to express the dynamics of the arms race in mathematical form. Lewis Richardson began the discussion with his application of simultaneous differential equations to the problem [15] while more recent developments have often relied on basically equivalent graphical approaches.[16] Paul Smoker has attempted to approach reality more adequately by applying a wave model to the arms race phenomenon [17] while Martin McGuire has applied economic modeling procedures to the problem of secrecy in a two-nation nuclear arms race.[18]

Michael Intriligator, in the essay below, reviews the Richardson approach, observes inadequacies and oversimplifications, and suggests refinements. It may be useful to compare the approach here with that adopted in Huntington's study of arms races in chapter 2.

[8] Walter Isard and Tony E. Smith, "A Practical Application of Game Theoretical Approaches to Arms Reduction (and to Goal Determination among Regional Planning Authorities," *Peace Research Society (International) Papers*, Vol. 4 (1966), pp. 85–98.

[9] Kenneth E. Boulding, *Conflict and Defense* (New York: Harper, 1962).

[10] Erland Brun Hansen and Jorgen Wilian Ulrich, "Some Problems of Nuclear Power Dynamics," *Journal of Peace Research* (1964), pp. 137–49.

[11] Norman C. Dalkey, "Solvable Nuclear War Models," *Management Science*, Vol. 11, (July, 1965), pp. 783–91.

[12] Mancur Olson, Jr., and Richard Zeckhauser, "An Economic Theory of Alliances," *Review of Economics and Statistics*, Vol. 48 (August, 1966), pp. 266–79.

[13] Herbert K. Weiss, "Stochastic Models for the Duration and Magnitude of a 'Deadly Quarrel,'" *Operations Research*, Vol. 11 (January–February, 1963), pp. 101–21; William J. Horvath, "A Statistical Model of the Duration of Wars and Strikes," *Behavioral Science*, Vol. 13 (January, 1968), pp. 18–28.

[14] Murray Wolfson, "A Mathematical Model of the Cold War," Department of Economics, Oregon State University, mimeo.

[15] Lewis F. Richardson, *Arms and Insecurity* (Pittsburgh: Boxwood Press, 1960). See also Anatol Rapoport, "Lewis F. Richardson's Mathematical Theory of War," *Journal of Conflict Resolution*, Vol. 1 (September, 1957), pp. 249–99.

[16] Boulding, *op. cit.*, and Arthur L. Burns, "A Graphical Approach to Some Problems of the Arms Race," *Journal of Conflict Resolution*, Vol. 3 (December, 1959), pp. 326–42. See also William A. Caspary, "Richardson's Model of Arms Races: Description, Critique, and an Alternative Model," *International Studies Quarterly*, Vol. 11 (March, 1967), pp. 63–88.

[17] Paul Smoker, "The Arms Race: A Wave Model," *Peace Research Society (International) Papers*, Vol. 4 (1966), pp. 151–92. See also his "The Arms Race as an Open and Closed System," *ibid.*, Vol. 7 (1967), pp. 41–62.

[18] Martin C. McGuire, *Secrecy and the Arms Race: A Theory of the Accumulation of Strategic Weapons and How Secrecy Affects It* (Cambridge: Harvard University Press, 1965).

THE CRUDE ANALYSIS OF STRATEGIC CHOICES

Daniel Ellsberg

Many of the significant implications for U.S. military objectives of specific military choices—such as the introduction of a new weapons system, a change in basing or deployment, new operational procedures or protective measures—depend upon their impact on the limited set of U.S. and Soviet "decision elements" shown in the following diagram:

U.S.	Soviet Union	
	Wait	Strike (p)
Wait	u_{11}, v_{11}	u_{12}, v_{21}
Strike (q)	u_{21}, v_{12}	—

We shall not try to define a "game" corresponding to this schema, though the format might suggest that interpretation; rather, it depicts some major, interrelated elements in two concurrent U.S. and Soviet "decision problems": whether or not to launch an all-out nuclear attack upon the opponent. "Strike" denotes such an attack; the "Wait" strategy may be interpreted either as a "representative" or as a "best" *alternative* to Strike. The inclusion of a U.S. Strike strategy does not imply active consideration of such an alternative at any given moment; as a possibility, it is relevant particularly to *Soviet* calculations, for reasons indicated below.

The u's and v's are, respectively, U.S. and Soviet "von Neumann–Morgenstern utilities"[1] for certain (highly aggregated) consequences of

Originally published as RAND P-2183, The RAND Corporation, December 15, 1960. Reprinted by permission of The RAND Corporation.
[1] I.e., they indicate not merely order of preference among these outcomes but the decision-maker's preferences among "gambles": strategies which offer a set of possible outcomes with given subjective probabilities. It is assumed here that utility numbers can be assigned to outcomes so that the decision-maker's actual choices among strategies can be described as maximizing the "mathematical expectation of utility," the average of these utilities weighted by their respective subjective probabilities.

their actions; "p" and "q" are, respectively, the U.S. and Soviet subjective probabilities (expectations, estimates of likelihood) that a choice of Wait will encounter an opponent's choice of Strike during a certain time period. Though all of these are "subjective" variables, they clearly depend upon estimates of objective outcomes under specified circumstances, based upon some form of explicit or tacit "systems analysis." For purposes of this discussion, the v's may be regarded as U.S. estimates of Soviet utilities, estimates which are not held with perfect confidence.

U_{21} and v_{21} are thus, respectively, U.S. and Soviet utility payoffs for "strike first" outcomes: the consequences of a surprise nuclear attack upon the opponent. U_{12} and v_{12} are "strike second" payoffs, reflecting the consequences of being struck first by the opponent. U_{11} and v_{11} are "no all-out war" payoffs, corresponding to situations in which neither opponent chooses Strike.[2]

The precise effects of a change in military "posture," hardware, policy or plans upon these eight variables (including p and q) are, of course, hard to determine, uncertain, and subject to controversy; nevertheless, rough estimates are often made, and these are, in fact, the basis for most policy recommendations as to choices among military alternatives. Indeed, many such recommendations reflect estimates of effects only upon some subset (e.g., one) of these eight factors. The above schema has the advantage of directing attention *at least* to these eight, gross consequences of a military change. A typical, major military innovation will affect *all* of these variables, and in what may be opposing directions for a given or for different military objectives. Within a given set of strategic policy alternatives, "conflicts" may be inescapable; an improvement in terms of one dimension of choice (one military sub-goal) may be unavoidably associated with losses with respect to another. Analyses which ignore several of these dimensions are thus likely to be inadequate. Isolated sub-optimizing processes which overlook "conflicts" and "spill-over effects" among related sub-goals may end by lowering overall military security rather than raising it.

While the above highly simplified and abstract schema can by no means be regarded as an *adequate* model for the comparison of U.S. military alternatives, it may represent a minimum framework which is an advance over that implicit in much current discussion. Assuming that it is possible to estimate the gross effects of a major military innovation (e.g., an airborne alert, the introduction of IRBMs in Europe, a fallout shelter program) upon the factors in this schema,[3] the question arises: what

---

[2] The utility subscripts have been chosen to show corresponding elements in the concurrent, related but separate U.S. and Soviet decision problems; if a "game" formulation were being followed, the subscripts for the v's would be transposed.

[3] However these estimates are derived, and whether or not they are "reliable," the schema can be helpful in deriving their policy implications, in order to test the "consistency" of given policy recommendations with coresponding estimates and objectives.

effects, or complexes of effects, are "good"? For practical purposes the overall goal of enhancing military security—reducing the likelihood of major losses from the threat or use of enemy military force—must be broken down into military sub-goals, a list of specified strategic objectives. Some of these correspond directly to elements in our schema. Thus, it is a major U.S. objective to *lower* p: roughly, to "improve the reliability of deterrence." Likewise, there is the goal of *raising* u_{12}: improving the strike-second outcome if deterrence should fail. Possible conflicts between these two sub-goals are well known. However, by guaranteeing retaliation (lowering v_{21}) it may be possible to lower p greatly, more than compensating for the lower u_{12} which is associated with the low v_{21}. But what is the effect upon p of improving u_{12}, by planning counterforce tactics, or introducing civil defense? To answer this sort of question we must look at the impact not only upon u_{12} but upon all the elements in this framework, for p depends upon the whole configuration of factors in rather a complex way.

To the extent that a Soviet Strike represents a deliberate decision, it must reflect the fact that in Soviet calculations of payoffs and likelihoods at some moment Strike appeared preferable to its best alternative. The goal of the U.S. "deterrence" policy is to ensure that this never arises: that at all times Strike appears inferior in Soviet calculations to some alternative ("Wait"). In our schema this condition appears equivalently as:

(1) $V(\text{Wait}) > V(\text{Strike})$, where V is the Soviet utility function; or

(2) $(1 - q)v_{11} + q \cdot v_{12} - v_{21} > 0$; or

(3) $(v_{11} - v_{21}) - q(v_{11} - v_{12}) > 0$.

Even though U.S. estimates may indicate that this condition holds at a given moment, p may not be 0; some U.S. uncertainty ($p > 0$) may remain, reflecting:

(a) the possibility that U.S. estimates are critically mistaken;

(b) the possibility that factors affecting Soviet calculations may *change* critically within the relevant period;

(c) the possibility that Soviet behavior may be non-calculated, impulsive or erratic, imperfectly coordinated, or subject to "unauthorized actions" by subordinates.

Each of these likelihoods is likely to be smaller, the *larger* the interval, $V(\text{Wait}) - V(\text{Strike})$.[4] Other things being equal, the "worse" Strike appears relative to its best alternative, then the more likely that the Soviets *are* "deterred," the more likely that they will *stay* deterred as payoffs undergo exogenous shifts, and the more care that Soviet decision-makers will take to avoid accidents, false alarms, hasty decisions, unauthorized actions, or uncoordinated, unmonitored policies. The size of this interval, then, provides a sub-criterion among military choices on the path

---

[4] A unit interval having been established by the arbitrary assignment, say, of values 0 and 100 to two specified outcomes.

towards lower p. It is, in effect, an index of the sensitivity of the Soviet decision to "counter-deterrent" shifts in payoffs (if q is given), such as: (a) a drop in the "no all-out war" outcome v_{11} (due to Soviet losses or expectation of losses in a limited war, shifts in prestige, influence or alliances, "cold war" failures, domestic set-backs or uprisings, political rivalries with third parties); (b) a drop in the Soviet "strike second" outcome v_{12} (due to increased U.S. force size or ability to exploit weaknesses in Soviet warning systems or defenses, or prospect of U.S. "annihilation tactics" in a U.S. first strike); a rise in the Soviet "strike first" outcome v_{21} (a reduction in U.S. "strike second" or retaliatory capability, due to changes either in U.S. or in Soviet posture procedures, tactics). The larger the interval, $V(\text{Wait}) - V(\text{Strike})$, the larger (in utility terms) the payoff "disturbances" required to make Strike appear preferable to Wait. This might be regarded as one index of the "reliability of deterrence."

Another important index of this reliability is the sensitivity of the Soviet decision to shifts in q, the Soviet expectation of a U.S. first strike.

To understand why q is relevant at all to the Soviet choice, let us recall the earlier condition of deterrence:

$$V(\text{Wait}) - V(\text{Strike}) = (v_{11} - v_{21}) - q(v_{11} - v_{12}) > 0.$$

Since typically $v_{11} > v_{12}$, it follows that a *necessary* condition for deterrence is:

$$(v_{11} - v_{21}) > 0, \text{ or } v_{11} > v_{21}.$$

It cannot be taken for granted that this condition will hold; it does not follow automatically from the existence on both sides of nuclear weapons.[5] But in any case, this condition is not *sufficient*. Perhaps the most significant aspect of the current strategic balance is that, under typical conditions of technology and posture: [6]

$$v_{21} > v_{12}.$$

It follows that deterrence can fail $[(v_{11} - v_{21}) - q(v_{11} - v_{12}) < 0]$, even though $(v_{11} - v_{21})$ is positive and large: if q, the Soviet expectation of a U.S. Strike, is sufficiently great.

An important question is: How high would q have to be to make Strike appear preferable to the Soviets? A threshold value $\tilde{q}$, below which the Soviets would be deterred and above which they would prefer Strike, is given by:

$$(v_{11} - v_{21}) - q(v_{11} - v_{12}) = 0, \text{ or } \tilde{q} = \frac{v_{11} - v_{21}}{v_{11} - v_{12}}.$$

We will refer to $\tilde{q}$, that probability of a U.S. Strike which would, with given Soviet payoffs, make the Soviets indifferent between Strike and Wait, as the "critical risk" of a U.S. Strike. This threshold expectation, defined as a function of Soviet payoffs, seems a highly significant property of the payoff structure. Among the most important consequences of military choices is their impact upon this parameter, which serves as an index of the sensitivity of the Soviet decision to their expectation of being struck.

Extreme vulnerability of the U.S. retaliatory force can imply a *low* Soviet critical risk. It leads to an extreme advantage of the "strike first" over the "strike second" outcome, with $(v_{11} - v_{12})$ much greater than $(v_{11} - v_{21})$. With the resulting low $\tilde{q}$, the Soviets would find Strike preferable if they attached even moderate likelihood to a future U.S. Strike. This is clearly an undesirable state of affairs; a Soviet Strike could appear a rational response even to highly ambiguous indications of a U.S. attack, of the sort generated periodically by any warning system. Under the general objective of improving the "reliability of deterrence" it seems desirable to reduce the sensitivity of the Soviet decision to fluctuations in q; thus, it becomes a sub-goal to increase the critical risk of $\tilde{q}$.

The principal method of achieving high q—implying that the Soviets will not prefer Strike to Wait unless they are *very sure* of a U.S. Strike—is to reduce the vulnerability of the U.S. retaliatory force by measures which do not improve markedly the U.S. "strike first" capability: e.g., the *replacing* of highly vulnerable weapons by Polaris submarines, airborne alert, hardened or land mobile missiles. As v_{21} is lowered relative to v_{12}, a situation is approached in which the Soviets would prefer Wait even if they were *certain* that the United States would attack ($\tilde{q} = 1$, corresponding to $v_{21} = v_{12}$).[7]

A further sub-goal, towards improving the reliability of deterrence and lowering p, is to lower q, the Soviet expectation of a U.S. Strike. Most military choices operate directly upon payoffs, U.S. and Soviet, with indirect effects on expectations. Changes in U.S. payoffs will influence q by affecting the Soviet image of the U.S. rational incentives to Strike. Just as p corresponds to the U.S. estimate of the reliability of U.S. deterrence, q is essentially the Soviet estimate of the reliability of Soviet deterrence. To lower q, then, is to increase, in Soviet eyes, indices of the reliability of Soviet deterrence which are analogous to indices of U.S. deterrence: to increase $U(\text{Wait}) - U(\text{Strike})$ in U.S. calculations; to increase $\tilde{p} =$

---

[7] Conceivably, this result might be nailed home by making v_{21} appear *worse* than v_{12}; suppose that the Soviets were led to fear U.S. "annihilation tactics" with a large retaliatory force in case of a Soviet first strike, but were also made aware that the United States was preparing for a strictly countermilitary campaign, avoiding cities and aiming at quick cessation, if war should arise under any other circumstances. See Herman Kahn, *On Thermonuclear War* (Princeton, 1960), pp. 162–89.

$\dfrac{u_{11} - u_{21}}{u_{11} - u_{12}}$, the U.S. "critical risk"; to lower p.[8] This adds two new criteria of choice (lowering p being already included) to our list of military sub-goals.

Having presented some apparatus of analysis at this length, there is little space in which to apply it here. Let us consider one example, by now rather familiar. Suppose that, as is frequently done, lowering the Soviet "strike first" outcome v_{21} were taken as the only significant sub-goal under the objective of improving the reliability of deterrence; and suppose it were proposed to achieve this by emplacing "soft," fixed, slow-reaction IRBM's in Europe. Like any increase in our inventory of offensive weapons, this move *would* tend to decrease v_{21}. But only a little; fixed IRBM's are subject to no-warning attack by large numbers of accurate, high-yield Soviet medium-range missiles and bombers, and their existence would have a small or negligible effect on the expected outcome of a well-planned Soviet Strike. Even so, if other effects were ignored, as they often are, the move could seem desirable on the basis of this one criterion.

However, if we ask the impact of this move upon the other factors in our schema, conflicts with other criteria are likely to emerge. The most marked effects of the innovation would probably be: (a) a sharp decrease in v_{12}, the Soviet "strike second" outcome; (b) a sharp increase in u_{21}, the U.S. "strike first" outcome. Neither of these effects, at first glance, might seem undesirable in themselves, to count as "costs." Yet the drop in v_{12} relative to v_{21} would imply a lower Soviet critical risk $\bar{q}$; it would take less assurance than before of a U.S. Strike to make a Soviet Strike seem preferable. And meanwhile, the actual Soviet expectation q might be *increased*; for the rise in u_{21} relative to u_{12} (which would change negligibly) would mean lower U.S. critical risk $\bar{p}$, and for given p a reduced interval $U(\text{Wait}) - U(\text{Strike})$, so that Soviet deterrence would appear less reliable than before.[9] Thus, the several criteria we have considered for the reliability of U.S. deterrence would indicate that this move might be associated with *higher* p than before.[10] Furthermore, Soviet recognitions of this effect could lead, via Schelling's "reciprocal fear of surprise attack," to higher q and a further upward pressure on p.

[8] An interdependence between p and $\bar{q}$ emerges here; it has been ably explored under the heading, "The Reciprocal Fear of Suprise Attack," by Thomas Schelling, in *The Strategy of Conflict* (Harvard, 1960), pp. 207–229. I would suggest, without developing the point here, that this interaction is most significant when $\bar{p}$ and $\bar{q}$, the U.S. and Soviet critical risks, are both low.

[9] Herman Kahn has emphasized that such an improvement in u_{21} may significantly improve u_{11}, by deterring the Soviets from such acts short of all-out Strike as might "provoke" a U.S. first strike if the U.S. first strike outcome were sufficiently high. See Kahn, *op. cit.*, pp. 136–144 and *passim*. The objections, which I share, to such a policy of "Type II Deterrence" are too lengthy to discuss here. At any rate, note that this sub-goal, if accepted, would in this case conflict with the various criteria of the deterrence of a Soviet Strike (Kahn's "Type I Deterrence").

[10] This argument follows Wohlstetter, *op. cit.*, pp. 222–230, particularly p. 229.

These results are to be contrasted to those of the measures mentioned earlier for reducing the vulnerability of the retaliatory force (raising q by reducing v_{21} relative to v_{12}); moreover, a complex of such measures may be designed to raise u_{12} much more sharply than u_{21}, thus providing "second strike insurance" against the failure of deterrence while at the same time raising $\tilde{p}$, increasing the reliability of Soviet deterrence and lowering Soviet fears of attack.

Other specific arms control, civil defense and active defense measures may be examined in terms of our schema; their implications for the various criteria will depend upon their differential effects upon all of the factors discussed. The discovery, in a particular case, that the implications in terms of several of the criteria (sub-goals) conflict is not a failure of the approach; on the contrary, it is a signal of the need for closer analysis in that case, for the weighing of criteria, or for the invention of new alternatives which avoid or alleviate the conflict.

It is clear that this simple framework cannot capture all the complexities of strategic choices. It is in no sense a machine for providing answers; at most, it is a machine for asking useful questions, and for preliminary testing of alleged answers. As such, it can be helpful; simple as it is, it is far more flexible and complex than single-variable models implicit in much "literary" discussion. Unfortunately, there has been an historical tendency on the part of policy-makers to reject the aid of abstract frameworks of the present sort on the grounds that they are "too simplistic," and then to make practical decisions on the basis of much cruder, implicit models.

SOME SIMPLE MODELS OF ARMS RACES

Michael D. Intriligator

I. INTRODUCTION

Some aspects of arms races have a structure similar to that of economic models of competition. This Memorandum explores this similarity by using reaction curves to analyze and advance previous theoretical studies of arms races. In particular the classical ratio goal and Richardson models are extended by explicit consideration of alternative strategic assumptions and constraints on weapons holdings.

The limitations of reaction curve analysis must, however, be constantly borne in mind. The greatest shortcoming is undoubtedly the use of a single policy variable, namely aggregate stocks of weapons. The use of weapons stocks as a policy variable ignores certain factors that are crucially important in arms races: the diversification of weapons as a response to uncertainty and the possibilities of weapons developments and improvements. Other shortcomings of reaction curve analysis are the limitation to two contending nations and the assumption that the only influence on weapons stocks are the opponent's weapons stocks. Because of these shortcomings and other limitations the analysis and conclusions are presented not for direct application but rather as indicative of a path of analysis for, and conclusions that might be applicable to, the much more complicated actual situation. The analysis simplifies the situation without entirely losing its meaning; the conclusions hopefully will provoke further study.

II. CLASSICAL MODELS

The ratio goal and Richardson models are classical models of arms races. Both models make the simplifying assumption of two contenders, each having a choice of a single policy variable, levels of weapons stocks. These models and their extensions can therefore be analyzed by reaction curves.

Originally published as RAND RM-3903-PR, The RAND Corporation, April, 1964. Reprinted by permission of The RAND Corporation.

Reaction curves in the theory of duopoly (two sellers of a good) indicate the optimum choice of output of one seller given the output of his competitor. The reaction curves used here to analyze arms races similarly indicate the optimum choice of weapons stocks given the weapons stocks of the opponent. Such reaction curves are similar to the lines of constant power of Ash[1] and the lines of objective security of Burns.[2]

The classical examples of arms races, battleship building and army mobilization, were often studied by means of ratio goals.[3] To the extent that the outcome of an encounter of fleets or armies depended on size ratios it was reasonable to assume that arms races were based on ratios of battleship tonnage or numbers of divisions. The attempt to obtain some ratio goal more favorable than parity (equality of weapons) on both sides, together with the assumption of some protective weapons, that is, a nonzero optimal weapons stock at zero opponent's weapons, are shown in Fig. 1 where W_A is the stock of weapons held by A and W_B is the stock of weapons held by B. AA' is the reaction curve for A, showing the weapons A desires to hold (W_A) as a function of the weapons held by B (W_B). This reaction curve shows that if B holds no weapons ($W_B = 0$) there is a positive stock of weapons that A desires and that if B increases its holdings, A also increases its holdings. The ratio goal is shown as the dotted line through the origin. In attempting to meet the ratio goal, the reaction curve AA' comes closer and closer to this dotted line. The reaction curve shows how much A *would like* to hold (as a function of weapons hold by B), not the actual combination of weapon stocks (W_A, W_B). If, however, the actual combination differs from the desired combination, A will attempt to move the actual combination to the reaction curve. A succeeds in moving the combination by increasing or decreasing W_A, hence the arrows show direction of movement.

The reaction curve AA' for A is combined with a similar reaction curve BB' for B in Fig. 2. It is assumed that A and B both want protective weapons and have ratio goals. In addition to the dotted ratio goal for B there is shown a dotted parity line, along which holdings of weapons are equal ($W_A = W_B$). The left and right arrows of Fig.1, which show how A varies its actual weapons levels to attempt to reach the reaction curve, are supplemented in Fig. 2 by up and down arrows which show how B similarly varies its actual weapons levels. The result of combining these reaction curves is clearly an endless arms race spiralling to higher and higher weapons stocks, since A and B together will move an actual point

[1] M. A. Ash, "An Analysis of Power with Special Reference to International Politics," *World Politics*, Vol. III, No. 2, January 1951, pp. 218–237.
[2] A. L. Burns, "A Graphical Approach to Some Problems of the Arms Races," *Journal of Conflict Resolution*, Vol. III, No. 4, December 1959, pp. 326–342.
[3] Samuel P. Huntington, "Arms Races: Prerequisites and Results," *Public Policy: Yearbook of the Graduate School of Public Administration*, Harvard University Press, Cambridge, Massachusetts, 1958.

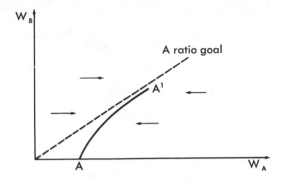

Fig. 1. Reaction curve: ratio goal.

above BB' or to the right of AA' into the central area in which weapons stocks on both sides increase.

The classical battleship building arms race would, however, yield a finite equilibrium configuration if the A ratio goal were above the B ratio goal, as shown in Fig. 3. At the equilibrium point D both A and B are simultaneously satisfied with their holdings of weapons. By the direction of the arrows shown it is clear that D is a stable equilibrium in that small movements away from D will give rise to forces restoring D. The condition necessary to ensure an equilibrium such as D is that the product of the ratio goals be less than one. Assuming both sides have the same ratio goal the necessary condition is that each ratio goal be less than one, implying counter-intuitively a ratio goal for both sides that gives weapons superiority to the opponent.

The Richardson model [4] represents an arms race by a set of differential equations, indicating for each country the effect of stocks of weapons in both countries on weapons production. Letting $W_A = d\,W_A/dt$ and $W_B = d\,W_B/dt$ represent the production of weapons in countries A and B respectively, the Richardson model is:

$$\dot{W}_A = a_1\,W_B - a_2\,W_A + a_3$$
$$\dot{W}_B = b_1\,W_A - b_2\,W_B + b_3$$

Each of the coefficients has an interpretation: a_1 (and b_1) are "defense coefficients," indicating the influence of the opponent's weapon stocks on weapons production; a_2 is a "fatigue and expense coefficient," indicating the burden of supporting weapons, and a_3 is a "grievance term," including all factors other than weapons stocks responsible for weapons production.

[4] Lewis F. Richardson, *Arms and Insecurity,* Boxwood Press, Pittsburgh, 1960; and Anatol Rapaport, "Lewis F. Richardson's Mathematical Theory of War," *Journal of Conflict Resolution,* Vol. I, No. 3, September 1957, pp. 249–299.

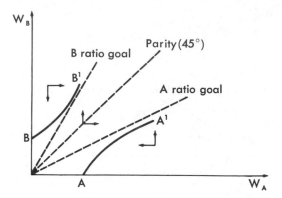

Fig. 2.   Arms race with no equilibrium: ratio goals.

The first coefficient then represents military, the second economic, and the third political–social bases for arms races. All coefficients are assumed positive.

The Richardson model can be represented by means of reaction curves given by the combinations of weapons stocks (W_A, W_B) yielding no change in weapon stocks:

$$\dot{W}_A = a_1\, W_B - a_2\, W_A + a_3 = 0$$

$$\dot{W}_B = b_1\, W_A - b_2\, W_B + b_3 = 0$$

These lines of no change in weapons stocks are shown in Fig. 4. The line $\dot{W}_A = 0$ corresponds to the reaction curve AA' and the line $\dot{W}_B = 0$ corresponds to the reaction curve BB'. The interpretation of these lines as reaction curves is clear from the arrows indicating direction of movement. An equilibrium point like that shown in Fig. 4 is reached if the

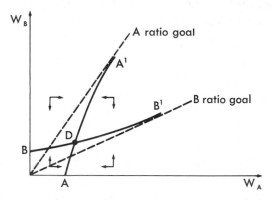

Fig. 3.   Arms race with equilibrium: ratio goals.

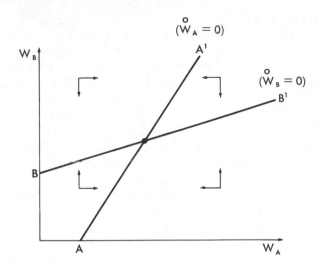

Fig. 4.   Arms race with equilibrium: Richardson model.

slope of AA' exceeds the slope of BB', that is, if $a_1/a_2 \cdot b_1/b_2 < 1$. If such an equilibrium point exists it is stable, as is seen from the direction of the arrows. An unstable equilibrium might exist, however, if the grievance terms are negative. This situation of good will leads reasonably to a downward spiral of weapons for slight movements below equilibrium but ironically to an upward spiral of weapons for slight movements above equilibrium.

The Richardson model with equilibrium is similar to the ratio goal model with equilibrium, as seen by a comparison of Figs. 3 and 4. Both models require that the product of ratios be less than unity. If symmetry is assumed in that the ratio goals or coefficients for both sides are the same, the ratio goal model requires for equilibrium that the ratio goal be less than one, whereas the Richardson model requires for equilibrium that the defense coefficient be smaller than the fatigue and expense coefficient. Similarly the Richardson model without an equilibrium ($a_1/a_2 \cdot b_1/b_2 < 1$) is similar to the ratio goal model without equilibrium (Fig. 2).

III. STRATEGY

Classical models of arms races have many shortcomings, including the use of a single policy variable and neglect of strategic uses of weapons and constraints on weapons stocks. The extension to several policy variables will not be undertaken here, but the implications of alternative strategies and constraints on weapons stocks will be considered.

Strategy must be considered explicitly for nuclear weapons. The naval encounters or military maneuvers of the past, in which ratios of weapons stocks were a major determinant of the outcome, have no counterpart in nuclear warfare. Nuclear warfare and hence nuclear arms races depend fundamentally on the assumed uses of nuclear weapons. In a deterrent strategy, for example, nuclear weapons could be used to deter the opponent from striking by threatening to inflict upon him unacceptable damage. In an arms depriving strategy, on the other hand, nuclear weapons could be used to disarm the opponent by threatening to destroy his nuclear weapons.[5] These alternative strategies lead to reaction curves that differ from those above because of scale effects of weapons according to which increasing the numbers of weapons proportionately for both sides aids a deterrer and harms an arms depriver. According to Schelling:

> For anything like equal numbers on both sides, the likelihood of successfully wiping out the other side's missiles ["weapons"] becomes less and less as the missiles on both sides increase. And the *tolerance* of the system increases too. For small numbers on both sides, a ratio of 2 or 3 to 1 may provide dominance to the larger side, a chance of striking first and leaving the other side a small absolute number for striking back. But, if the initial numbers on both sides are higher, it may take a ratio of 10 to 1 rather than 2 or 3 to 1 to have a good chance of striking with impunity; neither side needs to panic if it falls behind a little bit, and neither has any great hope that it could draw far enough ahead to have the kind of dominance it would need.[6]

Scale effects therefore imply that the reaction curve of a deterrer will rise less than proportionately to the increase in opponent's weapons, and the reaction curve of an arms depriver will rise more than proportionately to the increase in opponent's weapons. Reaction curves for A and B acting as either deterrer or arms depriver are shown in Fig. 5. It is assumed that both a deterrer and an arms depriver would like to hold protective weapons when the opponent holds no weapons.

Strategy and scale effects lead to several conclusions. First, reaction curves *cannot* be analyzed by ratio goals or Richardson models because of scale effects. Second, if both countries are arms deprivers there is no equilibrium point as in the case of the ratio goal or Richardson models with no equilibrium point, which results in an endlessly spiralling arms

---

[5] Arms depriving is a counterforce strategy.
[6] Thomas C. Schelling, 'Surprise Attack and Disarmament," Klaus Knorr (ed.), NATO *and American Security*, Princton University Press, Princeton, 1959, p. 185. Also see the asymptotic relations of deterrence effect to number of weapons in Bernard Brodie, "Anatomy of Deterrence," *World Politics*, Vol. II, No. 2, January 1959, pp. 173–191.

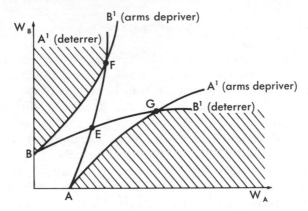

Fig. 5. Reaction curves for arms deprivers and deterrers.

race. Third, if both countries are deterrers there is an equilibrium point (E) of mutual deterrence similar to the ratio goal or Richardson models with equilibrium point. This equilibrium point is stable in that any deviations about the point establish self-correcting forces restoring the equilibrium. Fourth, the situation of an arms depriver facing a deterrer can lead to stable equilibrium points (F or G). Fifth, the most explosive situations are those indicated by shading in Fig. 5, in which one side has sufficient weapons to disarm its opponent, and the opponent has insufficient weapons to deter. Richardson's conclusion that increasing weapons stocks tends to increase the probability of war is qualified, if not reversed, by the fact that weapons serve as a deterrent. If both sides hold sufficiently large amounts of weapons neither side need fear that the other will initiate war with a disarming strike.

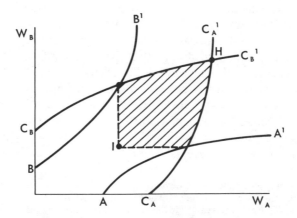

Fig. 6. Arms race: arms deprivers with constraints.

IV. CONSTRAINTS

Classical models of arms races neglected constraints on weapons stocks as well as strategy. Reaction curves indicate the tastes of policy-makers but do not take into consideration the scarcity of resources and the existence of institutions that act as constraints on the policy-maker (budgets for example). To tastes, embodied in reaction curves, must be added resources and institutions, embodied in constraint curves. If the constraints are based on resources they are probably independent of the opponent's weapons stocks. If the constraints are based on institutions, however, they probably increase with the opponent's weapons stocks. For example, if the opponent adds more weapons, budgets are increased, pushing out the constraint curve.[7]

Constraints are important only to the extent that they actually constrain. The stable equilibrium of mutual deterrence at E in Fig. 5 would be reached if E were within the constraints of both sides, in which case the constraints are not binding and tastes alone generate an equilibrium. Constraints will, however, become binding in the case of no equilibrium point, for example, in the case of two arms deprivers in Fig. 5. This case is shown in Fig. 6 in which A and B both act as arms deprivers with reaction curves of AA' and BB' respectively. The constraint curves $C_A C'_A$ and $C_B C'_B$ have been added to the reaction curves for A and B respectively.

Several results emerge from Fig. 6. First, constraints have done what the tastes of two arms deprivers could not do: establish an equilibrium point. To the extent that each side attempts an arms depriving policy they inevitably push weapons stocks to the maximum permitted by the constraints, point H. H is a stable equilibrium to the extent that it is reached via the process of interacting weapons acquisitions and would be returned to if there were any deviation from H. It is not an equilibrium in the sense that both sides are satisfied; neither side has been able to obtain sufficient weapons to disarm the opponent. Second, H is desirable in that neither side need fear being disarmed by the opponent. Third, this property is true not only of H but also of all points above and to the right of I (the shaded area). Any point in the shaded area has the property that, given the constraints, the opponent could never attain adequate weapons for an arms depriving strategy. To this extent it appears plausible that after the contenders have reached H and realized that neither side could

---

[7] Kenneth Boulding in *Conflict and Defense*, Harper, New York, 1962, refers to these constraint curves as "maximum home strength boundaries" based on "resources, will-to-strength, and so on" (pp. 234–241). However, he inexplicably considered only the cases in which constraints are either independent of or decrease with opponent's weapons stocks.

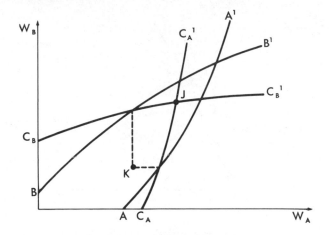

Fig. 7.   Arms race: deterrers with constraints.

attain adequate weapons to disarm the opponent, in their mutual self-interest they would each disarm voluntarily down to I. I and H are alike in that they ensure that one side will not be the victim of an arms de-priving strategy of the opponent, but I is a point at which both sides hold less weapons than H and hence the costs of holding weapons, the prob-ability of accidentally firing a weapon, and so on, are reduced.[8] Of course both sides would be reluctant to let weapons stocks fall below I. If A chose a W_A to the left of I then B could, within the limits of its constraints, attain the reaction curve and thus have sufficient weapons to disarm A. Similarly B would never choose a W_B below I. In particular, the point of general and complete disarmament, the origin, is dangerous in that either country could easily attain enough weapons to use an arms depriving strategy successfully.

The case of two deterrers with binding constraints is illustrated in Fig. 7. The attempt to build up weapons to deter the opponent leads to an arms race that terminates at J at which there is a stable but uneasy equilibrium. The equilibrium is uneasy because it indicates that neither side has enough weapons to deter the opponent so that J is a point of fears, anxiety, threats, and bluffs. Again there is little to recommend J over K: both indicate that neither side has enough weapons to deter the opponent and that the opponent cannot attain deterrent capability within the confines of the constraints. The entire area between J and K is, how-ever, one of mutual fears and distrust.

[8] The shift from H to I based on effective communication to each side of the constraints relevant to the opponent is similar to the shift in non-zero-sum games, such as the Prisoner's Dilemma, from certain payoff configurations to other strictly dominating (for both) configurations. See R. D. Luce and H. Raiffa, *Games and Decisions*, John Wiley & Sons, New York, 1957.

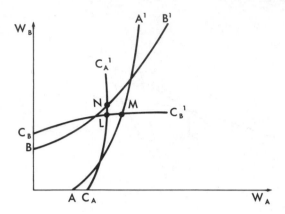

Fig. 8.   Arms race: arms depriver and deterrer with constraints.

The case of a deterrer (A) and arms depriver (B) is illustrated in Fig. 8. If both constraints are operative, L is reached at which A cannot deter B and B cannot disarm A. If the constraint on A is nonoperative (for example, shifted out beyond A's reaction curve) then M is reached at which A deters B but B doesn't disarm A. Similarly if the constraint on B is nonoperative, then N is reached at which A doesn't deter B and B disarms A.

V. CONCLUSION

Some of the limitations of the classical treatments of arms races, the ratio goal and Richardson models, have been overcome by rephrasing the models by means of reaction curves and extending the models to allow for strategy and constraints. Allowing for deterring and arms depriving strategies leads to a point of stable mutual deterrence and to a delineation of explosive situations. Allowing for constraints on weapons stocks leads to nonexplosive stable equilibria. There are still, however, many severe limitations to this type of analysis. The diversity of weapons, and, further, the many dimensions of policy, have been ignored here. Their treatment will have to await a further analysis of arms races.

Appendix A—Multiple Correlation and Regression Analysis

Suppose there exists a roomful of American men and the problem is to guess, with no further knowledge, the height of any given man in the room. The best guess would be to opt for the average height of American men, which, someone who is five feet eight once told me, is five feet, eight inches tall. It would be a bad idea, for example, to guess five foot two because while one would be accurate for the short men in the group, one would be wildly wrong on those who are taller than average. The best tactic then is to guess the average.

Of course, the guess will be wrong to varying degrees—men of average height will be accurately guessed, but the height of tall men will be underestimated and that of short men overestimated. One can measure the amount of variation of true heights from guessed heights simply by measuring how bad each guess is (guesses for men five foot six and five foot ten would each be off by two inches, for example), and calculating the average misestimate. One such measure, the average squared misestimate, is known as the *variance*.

One purpose of multiple correlation analysis is to add variables to consideration which improve the guesses and thus reduce the variance. Suppose further information about the men in the room now becomes available: suppose for example each men's weight is known. There is a positive correlation between height and weight—while tall skinny men

305

and short fat ones exist, by and large tall men tend to be heavier than short ones. Therefore, by taking the new information about weight into account one can improve the guess over the monotonous five foot eight estimate relied on previously.

How improved the guesses are will depend on the strength of the correlation between height and weight. If the correlation is perfect, the guesses will be perfectly accurate. Suppose, to simplify slightly, men come in only three heights: 5′6″, 5′8″, and 5′10″; and that each height is invariably associated with a weight of 140, 160, and 180 pounds respectively. Then one cleverly guesses a height of 5′6″ for each 140-pound man, a height of 5′8″ for each 160-pound man, and a height of 5′10″ for each 180-pound man. Now, when an attempt is made to measure the variance of the true heights from the guessed height, it is found that such variance is zero. It can be proclaimed, then, that, by taking weight into account in our estimates of height for the men in the room, it is possible to "explain" (as it is called) 100 per cent of the variance in the guesses when the average was used as the only guideline of estimate.

Perfect correlation is a rather rare thing, of course, and in real life, while it would be possible to improve guesses of height by knowing weight, there would still be variance from the new guesses left to be explained. The percentage of variance explained by a variable is known as r^2 and the square root of this quantity is known as r, otherwise, the correlation coefficient or the percentage of "variation" explained. Both are written to range from 1.00 for perfect correlation (100 per cent of the variance is explained) to 0.00 (none of the variance is explained.) Additionally, r is given a plus or minus sign to indicate the direction of correlation—height and weight are positively correlated, for example, while health and smoking frequency are negatively correlated.

A matrix of correlations is given in the Tanter article, reprinted on page 186. Looking at the upper left hand corner of that table one sees, for example, that those countries which have strikes are also likely to have assassinations: there is a positive correlation of .38, for the 1958–60 data, between strikes and riots. Squared, this number is .1444. If one were trying to guess how many strikes a country had by guessing for each country the average number of strikes for all countries, one could reduce the variance of such estimates by about 14 per cent if one took into account the number of assassinations. (Or, if one has a greater sense of fulfillment by dealing with larger numbers, it could be said that the information explains 38 per cent of the *variation*.)

To further improve the estimate, one can add yet more variables. Height is probably positively correlated with shoe length—taller men have longer shoes. Therefore, if one knows *both* each man's weight and his shoe length one can presumably predict his height with better accuracy than by using either alone. One then has a multiple r^2 (usually capitalized) and multiple r.

With this much information, other tables in Tanter's article become readily readable. In his Table 12, for instance, he has measured some 74 countries in 1958–60 on three complex variables, all having to do with foreign conflict. They are called "protest," "war," and "severance of diplomatic relations." He is interested in finding out how well he can predict the scores of each of these three dimensions by knowing certain things about the *domestic* violence of the countries for an earlier period, 1955–57. Are, in other words, countries with domestic turmoil at one period of time likely to be engaged in foreign conflict at a later date, or is there no particular relation? He has in this table measured for the 1955–57 period three indicators of domestic violence: number of anti-government demonstrations, number of revolutions, and amount of guerrilla warfare. How much of the variance on the three foreign conflict indices for 1958–60 can be explained by knowledge of these three domestic variables for the earlier period?

Taking the "protest" dimension, the table shows that the total amount of variance to be explained (the standard deviation, .35, squared) is .1225. The amount of variance still unexplained after all three of the domestic violence measures have been taken into account (the standard error, .32, squared) is .1024. The explained variance, thus, is .1225 − .1024 = .0201. This, expressed as a fraction of the variance to be explained and allowing for minor computational peculiarities, comes out to be .18, which is, magically enough, the R^2. (The multiple R is, as noted above, the square root of this.) Thus 18 per cent of the variance on the protest dimension can be explained by knowledge of the three domestic variables. The ability of the three domestic measures to predict scores on the "severance of diplomatic relations" dimension is worse and on the "war" dimension they are of no help at all—just as, for example, knowing a man's shirt color is presumably of no help in guessing his height. When three measures of a nation's *foreign* conflict behavior for 1955–57 are used, however, as in Table 11, one's ability to predict its score on the war dimension increases dramatically.

This is multiple correlation analysis. Multiple regression analysis characticistically puts its emphasis on "b-coefficients" and "beta-weights" in regression equations of the sort used at the end of Alker's article (p. 167). The effort here is to gauge how much change in the dependent variable (e.g. height, or the East–West dimension in Alker's first equation) is produced by a change of one unit in each independent variable (e.g., weight, or the variables at the right of the equation). In a sense then these coefficients give an indication of the relative importance of each independent variable in producing change in the dependent variable. The beta-weights are the b-coefficients standardized—placed on a more or less comparable scale in terms of the distribution on the variable. Beta-weights, used both in the Alker and the Kato articles, are on the same scale and can be more readily compared—a unit in one beta-weight is comparable to a unit in another—than are the b-coefficients which are based on differing scales.

Significance tests are usually used in correlation and regression analysis, although there is debate as to their meaning when no sampling is involved. At any rate, they relate, under assumptions of random sampling, the probability that a certain statistical value (beta-weight, r, R^2, etc.) could have been obtained by bad luck in sampling. If the probability is appropriately small, the result is accepted as "significant."

Appendix B—Factor Analysis: A Cautionary Note

The use of factor analysis, a statistical method first developed by psychologists thirty years ago, is becoming increasingly fashionable in quantitative treatises in political science. Because it seems to promise to make order of disorder and sense of nonsense, factor analysis might appear to be invaluable to the practitioners of a primitive science who have the use of elegant new computing machinery to apply to an increasingly abundant supply of data, but have precious little theory to guide them in such an application.

Crudely put, factor analysis examines the intercorrelations among a group of variables and can be made to suggest a number of "underlying" statistical factors or dimensions each of which seems to explain the behavior of a different subset of the original variables. Thus by grinding into the machinery fifty seemingly diverse variables, one might find at the end that the procedure has declared that twenty of the original variables seem more or less to fit together on one factor, another ten on a second, five more on a third, with the rest remaining puzzlingly independent. The gain clearly is that the magnitude of the problem has been reduced; rather than having to deal with fifty individual variables, one can argue that several clusters of them seem to be interrelated enough so that each cluster can be treated as a single variable.

An illustration of a factor matrix can be seen in Alker's Table I on pp. 146*ff.* The computer has labored and, using mathematically-specified criteria, has brought forth a factor solution. The numbers in the matrix indicate how well each variable correlates with each of the factors: the variables numbered 8022–8025, for example, correlate ("load") rather heavily with the first factor, but relate rather poorly to the other factors; the variables numbered 8009 and 8037 on the other hand are seen to load mostly on the second factor; and so forth.

If elegant in conception, factor analysis can often be exasperating in practice. For while it is true that the method is "objective" in the sense that the decision as to which variables are to "load" on which factors is made entirely by the impartial machinery, the criteria which the machinery applies in making this decision are manipulated by the operator—and depending on these criteria the outcome can vary widely. Thus factor analysis can generate not one, but a number—in fact an infinite number—of solutions to the same problem. Alker's Tables I and II illustrate two different factor solutions based on the same correlation matrix. The criteria used to derive the first solution demand that the first factor be determined in the manner such that it explains the maximum amount of variance among all the variables; the second factor is to explain the maximum amount of the remaining variance; and so forth. (The concepts of correlation and variance are discussed in Appendix A.) The other solution instead seeks to generate factors which have many high and low loadings and few of the middle-range loadings which are difficult to interpret. This latter set of criteria is known as "simple structure." In a similar manner innumerable other sets of criteria could be dreamed up and applied. The solutions used by Alker are "orthogonal" solutions; that is, the factors are not correlated with each other. Another whole set of solutions, known as "oblique" solutions, exist which do permit the factors to be correlated.

Claims that factor analysis is an "economical" procedure, therefore, should best be cautiously weighed. While it is helpful to have the mass of information contained in the intercorrelations of dozens of variables reduced to one or two factor matrixes, one must really tediously sort through many exasperatingly different factor matrixes to determine which are most appropriate to the concerns under investigation. To seize upon the first factor solution that pops out of the machine is profoundly arbitrary.

In choosing among these solutions the one most likely to represent Truth in some fashion or other, one is commonly urged to select the one that makes the most "sense"—in other words to embrace the "objective" solution which is most subjectively appealing. In an argument a few years ago over such central psychological concerns as agreement response set, anal expression, social desirability, and (of course) the Minnesota Multiphasic Personality Inventory, two teams of psychologists factor analyzed the same sort of data, selected different solutions, and came to precisely the opposite conclusions.

There is, despite Juliet's protestations, a great deal in a name and the ultimate agony in factor analysis comes in the labeling of the factors. It is the hour for creativity and one does the best one can. Each factor is examined in turn with special emphasis placed on the variables which load most heavily on it to see if, as a cluster, they could be said to point to some underlying "dimension." Alker, for example, finds that his first factor reflects what could be called an "East–West" dimension.

Factor analysis probably seems "objective" because this naming ritual, a most subjective element, comes at the end of the process. It would be possible to reverse the procedure by setting up a panel of expert judges to determine for example which issues in the U.N. best reflect the East–West conflict and then to rate countries by their alignment on such a scale. This method is obviously not without pitfall, but the point is that it is not clearly less "objective" than the factor analytic method.

It should also be noted in this cautionary overview, that, in almost all factor analytic solutions, variables found to correlate reasonably well with a given factor do not necessarily correlate well *with each other*. Two variables, for example, each of which correlates at the .70 level with a given factor may correlate perfectly with each other, may correlate not at all with each other, or may correlate at any level in between.

In applying factor analysis it is generally considered wise to avoid using two or more variables which measure the same thing; for psychologists this usually means checking over the wording of questions on personality questionnaires to make sure that no two are too much alike. If variables which measure essentially the same thing are allowed to remain in the analysis, these multiple measures will be of course highly intercorrelated and will tend to pull off a factor to themselves, perhaps masking in the process interesting relationships with other variables. Therefore, one should perform some analyses with only one variable left to represent each of these clusters of like-minded variables to see if one can ferret out meaningful, but previously obscured, patterns.

Once a factor matrix has been selected, it is possible to generate "factor scores" for each individual—a device which can be fruitful, as Alker's article shows. To do this, each individual's vote on each variable is weighted according to the variable's loading on the factor under question. In Alker's Table I, for example, the "East–West" factor score for an individual country would rest heavily on how it voted on such issues as 8006 and 1010, but very little on such issues as 8009.